THE

ECONOMY

OF

THE AGES.

NEW YORK:
UNITED STATES PUBLISHING COMPANY,
411 BROOME STREET.
1869.

PREFACE.

Christ is the miracle of the ages, and therefore demonstrates His own divinity. He who *works* a miracle proves that God is with him. But he who is himself the grandest miracle, needs no other attestation from heaven, having the demonstration complete within himself that he is not of this world, nor produced by its forces. No one, then, understanding who and what Christ is, can have a moment's doubt as to His true character, and whence He is. He stands forth in such sublime grandeur, so immeasurably beyond all that human thought ever conceived, or can ever comprehend, that He is His own witness forever.

The Bible is the history of this great miracle of God in the work of creation and redemption, and therefore is its own best attestation, even as is Christ himself. There is no demonstration to the truth of the Bible, like the Bible itself. If a man will understand what this book is and what it contains—if he will comprehend in any proper measure what that magnificent economy is which it develops, sweeping through the vast ages, and fulfilling all the grandest designs of Infinite wisdom and love, he can have no more doubt of its inspiration, than he can question whose hands reared these heavens. If any man, therefore, doubts as to the truth and divinity of the Scriptures, it is a demonstration that he has not begun to understand them or know what they contain. He is arguing about a matter of which he is profoundly ignorant; and the first thing he needs to do is to study the Bible, and find out what it is, and what it reveals. A skeptical lawyer once applied to a Christian friend for some able treatise on the evidences of Christianity, stating that he was determined to investigate the matter thoroughly. His friend handed him a copy of the Bible. "Oh," said the infidel, "I do not want this. I want some able argument to prove the truth of the Bible." Said his friend, "Take this book and study it. The Bible itself is the best argument you can find." The lawyer doubtingly took it, and began at the beginning, reading on until he came to the Ten Commandments. He there paused to consider that wondrous compendium of duty, embracing every obligation that man could owe to God or his fellow-man; and the question came, Where did Moses get that law? As a lawyer he saw its amazing comprehensiveness, its beauty, its perfection, and that nothing comparable to it could be found in all the records of human history. Where then did Moses get it? The question was settled in the mind of the lawyer. He did not need to read any further. The system that could furnish such a law was not of man, but of God. And if the *law* proves the divinity of the Scriptures, what shall we say of the magnificent scheme of redemption, even of Him, who is "the end of the law for righteousness to every one that believeth?"

Men are ignorant of the Bible. Its own friends are but very imperfectly acquainted with it, being painfully deficient. Its enemies are profoundly ignorant. If they could know what the Bible is, their skepticism would cease in a moment. We have great doubt whether there is an infidel to be found, who could give a clear and intelligible statement of the plan of salvation, which the Scriptures undertake to reveal. For such a man, then, to argue against the Bible is folly. He

needs first to inform himself about the matter upon which he is passing judgment, and which he says he does not believe. He never can believe until he begins to comprehend the subject, knowing what it is his faith must accept.

Is it not also a deep dishonor to the church that she knows so little about her own sacred Scriptures, and is divided into so many sects, contending for different explanations of the same? Is it impossible to understand what they do mean, and what the grand features of the system of truth which they reveal? We speak now, of course, of its friends, who love the Bible and accept its method of salvation. Did not God give a revelation for the purpose of instructing men in the knowledge of His will and ways? And was it a failure on His part? Did He not make it intelligible? Did He fail of adapting it most eminently to its end? Certainly there was no failure here. God gave a revelation preëminently fitted to the grand purpose of acquainting mankind with His plan of saving the world. It might, of course, be perverted by ignorance, wickedness, or unbelief. But we must also concede that it might be understood by faith. Yet how extensively does the impression prevail that Christians cannot come to any common understanding of the Scriptures—that that blessed consummation must be left to the future state, and that here they must continue divided, and dispute their different systems and interpretations to the end! Some will contend that God has so constituted minds that they cannot see truth alike, some being born Calvinists, and others Arminian, so that they must differ, and God himself could not reveal a system which they could both alike accept. We do not believe this. We think it dishonorable to God. Neither do we believe that there is a necessity for the present divided state of doctrine respecting the Word of

God, any more than for the ignorance of the same which is found in our churches. Unbelief and ignorance are the source and cause of the divisions found among them, and not any thing that is wanting in God's mode of revealing truth. There was nothing wanting in God's revelations to His ancient Israel. They were passingly wonderful. But the people were stiff-necked and rebellious, refusing to walk in His ways. We, too, are unbelieving, as well as ignorant. We have failed to study the Scriptures, and failed to comprehend the Divine methods of instruction. We have not understood properly the elements of God's grand system of grace, nor the means which He adopted from the beginning for unfolding it. We need, therefore, to go back to first principles, submitting our minds to God's own system and plan of unfolding His work of salvation; and when we become wise enough to begin at the beginning of a science, to learn its elements, we may come to a better and more harmonious view of what the Bible teaches.

The demand of our times is for an exhibition of Bible truth and doctrine that will witness for itself, bearing its own credentials, so that men, when they read, will say, That is God's word undeniably—that is the gospel of Christ, which cannot be controverted.

Such a development of divine truth is demanded for our church-members of all denominations, to make them intelligent, Bible Christians, as they ought to be, rooted and grounded in the faith. It is a painful fact that the great body of them know very little about the Bible, or its doctrines—have never studied them, and are liable to be led astray by any plausible error or system of infidelity. The pulpit fails in its high task of indoctrinating the people, while few have a disposition to study theology, if they had the means so to do, which perhaps they have not. To most, also, it would be an uninviting theme—a field of metaphysical controversy from which they instinctively draw back. The ordinary conception of the doctrines of the Bible is that of a valley of dry bones, to which, perhaps, the manner and matter of theological discussion have given no little occasion. The Bible, however, does not necessarily present a field for metaphysical speculation. Its great truths are *facts*—facts which can be substantiated beyond cavil or denial, as any other in the history of the world. The Bible deals with facts. It can be proved also what those facts and truths are which it undertakes to set forth, and for which it is responsible. If it cannot, then the Bible is a failure to man, as a revelation from heaven, and we need another by which the facts will be brought within our reach. When, moreover, theological discussion is brought out of the domain of metaphysics into the field of fact, where the system may be made clear and intelligible, and clothed with living power, then may the masses in our churches be instructed and established therein. Then, too, may the skepticism of our times stand rebuked and condemned. That infidelity now has the advantage of assailing a revelation which is not understood, in regard to the meaning of which its own friends are not agreed; and it is a great advantage. The skepticism of our age is bold and rampant, as well as deeply insidious. It cannot be met as of old by proving the inspired truth of the Bible and Christianity. Infidelity admits all this itself. It is the strongest friend of the Bible and its teachings, according to its own claim. Jesus Christ himself is its great Apostle. What is demanded now, therefore, is to set forth this inspired system in such a light as to confound infidelity itself, so that when these enemies of the faith attempt to call over the name of the Lord Jesus, it will be as of old, when certain vagabond Jews, exorcists, undertook to call over them that had evil spirits; "the spirit answered, Jesus I know, and Paul I know; but who are ye? And the man in whom the evil spirit was, leaped on them, and overcame them, and prevailed against them, so that they fled out of that house, naked and wounded." In our day infidels are calling over the name of the Lord Jesus. Every system of error is running to shelter itself under the Word of God, and claiming the inspiration of heaven. And is it so that there is not power enough in the church of God to confound, and drive them out from this house naked and wounded. Cannot this very revelation which they have impiously invoked fill them with confusion, and cause them to flee in terror? Truly, indeed, the church needs to take shame unto herself, and sit in sackcloth and ashes before the Lord, if she has so lost her hold upon these divine and living oracles, and so doubtfully established their meaning, that infidelity can enter into her precious inheritance and sit with her in these heavenly places, appropriating all to its own behoof, intrenching itself in this very citadel of her strength, and scornfully disputing her claims. Let the church see in this her own deep shame, and how she has been shorn of her strength, even as Sampson, when robbed of his locks in the lap of the treacherous Delilah, so that he was betrayed and delivered into the hands of the Philistines, to become sport for them, and be "made to grind in their prison-house." From the very dust let her cry unto God that He will take away her reproach. Let her seek unto her Saviour, that He will clothe her with salvation; and unto the Holy Spirit, that He will reveal the truth unto her apprehension, so that she shall appreciate and rejoice in it. Then shall the watchmen on Zion's walls see eye to eye, and our blessed Christianity be no more the glory and boast of infidelity.

It is not out of place here to call attention to the fact, that in the following pages we have gone over the entire field of revelation and the work of redemption, and yet have not touched upon any controverted points dividing evangelical denominations. We have not sought to avoid the questions at issue, but they have not come in our way. This fact has deeply impressed our mind, and made us to realize more than ever what an excrescence and fungus growth upon our Christianity those metaphysical systems are, which have occupied so large a field in our theology. They have not this prominent position in the Bible. Why should they have in our statements of Bible truth? They are parts of human philosophy rather than of divine revelation. Is it not time that the church had laid aside philosophy to accept the simple facts of God's revealed Word, upon which all may unite, and in the love of which all may walk together in sweet harmony? These facts are plain and undeniable, and need not be in controversy among such as love the Bible and accept the salvation which it reveals for sinners. It can be demonstrated that they are the facts of the Bible; and when the friends of Christ will stand united firmly in their maintenance, then will the hosts of infidelity and error be driven from their strongest entrenchments, compelled to fight under their own banner, and in their own uniform.

It might perhaps be imagined that a treatise, which confined itself to the obvious facts of revealed truth, upon which all true Christians could unite, would be devoid of interest and spirit, and of necessity contain nothing fresh or new. Whether this be so, those who read the following pages can determine. We know, however, for ourselves, that it has been a rich field of exploration, where we have gathered hid treasures, of which we had no previous knowledge or suspicion even that such were to be found. We know that many of them are hidden from the mass of our most intelligent Christians, to say nothing of our theologians, but that they at once commend themselves as facts which cannot be questioned, as soon as they are stated.

We commend this attempt, therefore, to set forth the fundamental truths of redemption to all who love the Bible, and desire to know more of its divine teachings; and we commend it also to those who have no faith in the Bible as a revelation from God, since it may serve to show them what the Bible is, and to demonstrate that such a scheme as is there developed, so harmonious in all its relations, and involving such a boundless range, could never, by any possibility, have originated with human counsels. The Bible is its own best witness that it is of God, which none but a Divine hand could have written, which none but a Divine mind could have conceived.

CONTENTS.

CHAPTER I.

METHOD OF STUDY.

CHAPTER II.

CREATION.

CHAPTER III.

CREATION OF MAN.

CHAPTER IV.

THE CONSTITUTION OF HUMANITY.

CHAPTER V.

THE CONSTITUTION OF HUMANITY.

CHAPTER VI.

THE TEMPTATION AND FALL.

CHAPTER VII.

A REMEDIAL SYSTEM.

CHAPTER VIII.

A REMEDIAL SYSTEM.

CHAPTER IX.

THE GODHEAD REVEALED.

CHAPTER X.

THE GODHEAD REVEALED.

CHAPTER XI.

THE GODHEAD REVEALED.

CHAPTER XII.

THE TRINITY.

CHAPTER XIII.

PERSONALITY OF THE HOLY SPIRIT.

CHAPTER XIV.

PERSONALITY OF THE WORD.

CHAPTER XV.

HUMAN DEPRAVITY.

CHAPTER XVI.

BONDAGE OF SIN.

CHAPTER XVII.

A SIN OFFERING.

CHAPTER XVIII.

FAITH.

CHAPTER XIX.

TYPES.

CHAPTER XX.

THE TREE OF LIFE.

CHAPTER XXI.

THE CHERUBIM.

CHAPTER XXII.

THE CHERUBIM.

CHAPTER XXIII.

THE DOCTRINE OF A REMNANT.

CHAPTER XXIV.

THE DOCTRINE OF A REMNANT.

CHAPTER XXV.

THE DOCTRINE OF A REMNANT.

CHAPTER XXVI.

THE DAY OF THE LORD.

CHAPTER XXVII.

THE PRIESTHOOD.

CHAPTER XXVIII.

PRIESTHOOD OF CHRIST.

CHAPTER XXIX.

CHRIST A SIN-OFFERING.

CHAPTER XXXV.

THE FIRST RESURRECTION.

CHAPTER XXXVI.

THE REIGN OF CHRIST.

CHAPTER XXXVII.

THE JUDGMENT.

CHAPTER XXXVIII,

HEAVEN.

THE ECONOMY OF THE AGES;

OR

THE HISTORY OF REDEMPTION UNFOLDED.

CHAPTER I.

THE METHOD OF STUDY.

The Bible is God's text-book of redemption, in which He has undertaken to unfold His plan of salvation for the human race; and if this be so, we cannot question that the book itself is wisely adapted to its appointed end in the instruction of mankind; as perfect as the work whose nature and history it develops. Divine wisdom, of necessity, must be displayed in the arrangement and plan of the text-book, so as to develop, in the clearest and most perfect manner, the grand scheme of which it treats, and bring it most easily within the apprehension of those who were to be instructed thereby. God would not fail in a matter of such importance as this. He would not furnish an ill-arranged treatise on His grandest work of redemption. His six days' work of creation was complete in every part; and, when finished, He saw that it was very good. There had been no failure at any point. So likewise His greater work of redemption was perfect also, as well as the revelation which developed its plan and history. We cannot question, therefore, that God began the development of this system at the right point, so as to make it most intelligible to the human race, and bring it most easily within the reach of their thoughts. To accomplish this, he began with the elements, laying down first principles. The whole scheme was new—beyond the range of human thought, and to be communicated by a revelation from heaven. God, therefore, must of necessity begin at the beginning, and through a period of four thousand years did He continue the work of revelation, until the book of prophecy was closed by John. The system of truth was developed gradually from age to age during this long period—developed, too, in its order, as fast as the Divine plans matured, and as the race was prepared for its reception. God began this work of instruction in the infancy of the race, and wisely adapted Himself to its feebleness and necessities, revealing truth in its simplest form, and such truth as the years of its childhood required. Redemption was a stupendous work, to be carried forward through a series of dispensations, and, from its own nature, could be developed only gradually and more fully as the end drew on. The Bible, now, is the history of that divine working, its continuous development from the germ to its perfected state. Must there not be wisdom, then, in our studying this system in the natural order, following closely upon the track of the divine revelations? Is there not a very necessity here laid upon us, if we would comprehend the elements of this subject, and go on unto perfection? Are we wiser than God, that we can improve upon His method of instruction, or afford to lose the benefit of His plan of revelation?

Yet how signally have we failed of this most simple idea in our systems of theology, which have an artificial arrangement of their own, without any reference to the

Bible as a proper text-book, whose lessons were to be followed in their order. We begin at the end with the last developed truths of the New Testament, assuming that these are the most simple and easily comprehended, while the earliest are exceedingly obscure, and sometimes hardly worthy of our attention.

While there may be a partial truth in this, it being an undoubted fact that the light of divine truth has greatly accumulated, yet does not this theory do injustice to God's work of redemption, and His plan of educating the race into its profound mysteries? That redemption is a history—a history of stupendous facts, developed through the ages. It has been a *growth*, the present point having been reached only after centuries of patient toil and instruction: the race having been carried forward slowly step by step, led on to higher and higher truth as the way was prepared for its reception. This was the divine plan, in which there was the deepest wisdom, and of which we cannot afford to lose the benefit. God has been training our humanity from feeble childhood up towards manhood, to which it has not even yet attained; and He has most wisely and successfully dealt with it in its education, by beginning with the rudiments, and leading on to more enlarged truths and deeper mysteries as they could be comprehended, and the world was prepared to receive them.

Should we not now follow this divine method of instruction in our study of the system, beginning at the point where God began, and following upon the track of His working and revelations from age to age? This we have not done. On the contrary, we have begun where God ended His revelations, and studied backward upon His track, failing too, in many cases, to reach the starting-point, or understand what the rudiments of the system were. We do not teach other sciences after this method, nor permit our children thus to study backwards to the elements of knowledge; and why should we deal thus with the deeper science of theology? Had God's more simple method been followed, and the facts studied in the order of their development, some of the controversies which have been waged for centuries in the church might, we doubt not, have been avoided. We could hardly have been led astray. But, adopting a method of our own, we have put first what should have been last, and become bewildered amid the confusion which we ourselves have made. It is not always because truths are difficult or profound that we do not comprehend them—for God has made plain that which is necessary for us to understand—but because we have overlooked some plain instruction that lay directly before our eyes, as a boy may work long and fruitlessly at a problem, only because he has made some obvious mistake, or given no heed to some simple fact, which, as soon as noticed, makes all plain. We have undervalued the Old Testament, and the system of instruction there contained. Some are ready even to cast aside the volume, except as a mere historical record. For its theology they have little respect, regarding it as standing in need, not only of great additions, but of no little correction also; while it is a mystery to them that so large a portion of what purports to be a revelation from heaven, should contain mere matters of history. Such persons understand but little of those grand elementary lessons with which God began the education of the race, and through which He has brought it to its present standing. There is a mine of wealth in that Old Testament revelation, which is utterly hidden from their eyes.

We assume, then, that the divine method of instructing our world was the wisest and best possible; and in the succeeding pages shall make it our guide, beginning with the rudiments, and following God's successive revelations in their natural order, as He saw fit to develop them. The peculiar nature and wisdom of this system will be better understood as we proceed with our task. We shall aim to follow the Scriptures as our text-book, seeking to unfold the facts as they are here presented; for the great truths of revelation and redemption are facts, not dogmas—facts which may be substantiated as such. These we shall aim to develop in their order, as brought to view successively from the opening to the closing page of this book of God. And the result will show how much wisdom there is in this plan of study.

CHAPTER II.

CREATION.

Creation is the starting point of all divine revelation, where the eternal Infinite begins to make known His being and perfections, coming out from His own eternity and the hiding-place of His power. The history of creation, then, must begin the lessons in theology. Man must be conscious of, and learn his own existence, as well as that of the creation to which he belongs, as the necessary means of knowing God. The Scriptures therefore begin with the history of this creation, than which nothing could have been more philosophical.

What then is the Bible doctrine of Creation?

This is clearly stated by the Apostle in Heb. xi. 3. By faith we understand the worlds were framed by the word of God, so that things which are seen are not made of things which do appear. Two facts are here laid down. First, that the worlds are of God's creation. Second, that this is a revealed truth, which we receive by faith, not being discovered by reason,

That grand passage with which the volume of revelation opens, "In the beginning God created the heavens and the earth," has settled forever a thousand doubts and controversies, solving that deep and difficult problem of the origin of the universe. We have never been troubled to know whence this universe came. We can scarcely realize that there need to have been any difficulty respecting it. But little do we understand what a debt of gratitude we owe to that simple, but sublime revelation, which puts all doubt at rest, In the beginning God created the heavens and the earth. If we would learn the priceless value of these words, we must go where this divine record has never reached, and there propound the question, Whence came this mighty frame-work of worlds? It was a problem which the acutest heathen philosophers could not solve. The most rational conclusion they could reach was, that they had always been in existence—that matter was eternal; nor has this idea even yet vanished from the world under all the light of revelation.

The conception of an act of absolute creation is a very difficult one for the human mind to reach. We conceive readily of material already in existence fashioned into new forms, a thing to a certain extent within our own power. And we can conceive of a God who, by a system of chemistry and assimilation which we cannot trace out or imitate, can build up these magnificent forms of vegetable and animal life around us, which, however, are but a new arrangement of existing atoms. The process of decay and dissolution is continually going on; and the material thus liberated, enters into new forms of life and beauty. This thought we readily reach; and this is the process which the wisdom of this world will argue has been going on in an endless series without a beginning. It is another and different conception to come to the end of that series, beyond which there is an absolute void, except one infinite mind, which puts forth its omnipotent fiat, and every atom of matter springs into being. He speaks, and it is done. The conception of a Being possessed of such power is well nigh too lofty for the mind to grasp; and the unaided human mind never does attain the thought. In this province we are beyond the range of all experience—beyond all the powers of created intelligence; for no such intelligence is adequate to the work of creation, even to the calling of an atom into existence. Reason, therefore, alone will not lead us to attribute such power to another. Thus heathenism has never reached the conception of one infinite, eternal mind possessed of omnipotence and all perfection, and adequate to the government of the universe. Its deities have always been limited and local, and therefore multiplied in number. An infinite God is the subject of revelation alone, and consequently an object of faith. The multiplication of deities is necessitated the moment that the mind falls below the conception of one supreme, eternal Being: and the universal prevalence of polytheism in all ages, aside from revelation, shows how difficult the conception is. It was well nigh impossible, even with the aid of revelation, to preserve the Jewish nation from the controlling power of this polytheism. That people felt themselves poor, defenceless, and contemptible in the eyes of the nations, with only one Being to care for them: nor could they be contented in such a forlorn condition. They demanded other gods beside Jehovah; and simply because they could not rise to the conception of Him as an almighty, infinite One. The moment that conception of God enters and takes possession of the mind, all temptation to polytheism ceases by necessity.

Creation being the highest conception of omnipotence, is beyond the reach of all these finite deities, and consequently was never attributed to them. The universe was a power above the gods, to which they themselves were subject, as to the control of fate. It is by revelation, and so by faith, that we have come to the knowledge of one infinite, eternal Being, who is God over all: and the means by which the conception of such infinitude is reached, is by presenting Him as the author of creation. There was consequently the profoundest wisdom in first revealing Jehovah as the Creator of all things: carrying us back to the point when the foundations of the earth were laid, and giving us the history of the stupendous work. It is a truth revealed to *faith*, that God thus spake and it was done, making the universe to hang upon His omnipotent word as the grand centre of its whole being and revolution.

It has been thought easy, by means of the argument from design, to reach to the great Designer. This argument may be simple, after revelation has first made plain the existence of an infinite mind, whose power was adequate even to the act of creation out of the empty void. But blot out all knowledge of such a Being, and then give this problem of the universe to be solved, to tell whence it is, and how it came; and it is matter for question, whether the mind, unaided by light from above, would ever arrive at that vast conception of an original Creator, to whom all finite existence was due, from whom it all began. Does the argument from design establish more than the fact of a simple manufacturer, who puts materials together and fashions them? Does it prove also an original Creator of the materials? A watch proves a watch-maker. But does it prove that he made the materials of which the watch is constructed? A tree proves a mind which formed it thus to grow. But does it prove that that mind created of nothing the matter which enters into its composition? The argument from design does not go back of the thing constructed. There it stops of necessity. Whence then originated the atoms of which this universe is composed? How came they into being? For by the supposition they are not arranged, or put together in construction. They are simple elements. Will the unaided human mind from this point reach over the mighty chasm and grasp that stupendous thought of an absolute creation and an omnipotence which is adequate thereto? We have no evidence of it. The deep problem never was thus solved. It is by revelation, not by reason, that we have reached that glorious truth. It is by faith, not philosophy, that it has been made plain and simple to our apprehension. Our children accept it as a matter of faith, a thing taught them. They do not reason it out. We received it in the same manner. So did our fathers; and thus we trace back the history until we come to the divine record, "In the beginning God created the heavens and the earth." By faith, therefore, we understand the worlds were framed by the word of God, so that things which are seen were not made of things which do appear.

When and to whom was this revelation first made?

It was put in the form of a *written record* for our instruction in the time of Moses. But this fact does not imply that the revelation was originally made to him. Moses puts on record what was known long before, which is as true of the facts of creation contained in the first chapter of Genesis, as of the matters of history following. There is no reason to doubt that God communicated to Adam in the beginning this sublime history of creation. He was not left to search out this matter by his unaided powers, or grope in darkness respecting it; while there was the same necessity that it should be revealed to Adam and the first generations, as to Moses and the generations coming after him.

We learn also from the divine record that God was on terms of familiar intercourse with our first parents, the communications doubtless being more full than we have specific account of. The history in the Book of Genesis is exceedingly brief, covering a period of twenty-three centuries, the writer not undertaking to relate all the events transpiring, not even all the important ones; but those only which Divine wisdom deemed it essential that future ages should understand. Among these the fact of God's familiar intercourse with our first parents is made clear from the narrative, furnishing ground for the presumption that there were communications made that are not recorded. The fact also that this account of the creation was given to Moses to be placed on record, presupposes rather that the revelation had already been made to our first parents for their instruction. It was committed to Moses for preservation, *because* it was one of the revelations already made in the beginning, designed for the entire race, and therefore too valuable to be left any longer exposed to loss by accident, or the uncertainties of tradition. It must now be made permanent and secure for all time to come.

We are authorized, then, to conclude that God gave to Adam, and through him to the race, that magnificent panorama of creation recorded in the Book of Genesis. The natural and necessary interpretation also of this history, according to the laws of Exegesis, aside from any teachings of geology, as ably shown by a recent writer,* is, that ages were employed in the preparation of this earth, as a fitting abode for our race. The Bible itself teaches that the ages or dispensations of God have been running far back into the past, and that man's appearance upon the eventful stage was in the midst of those ages,

* "The Six Days of Creation," by Tayler Lewis.

and not at their beginning—that he was the crowning work of the Deity in a series of creations, the joy and wonder of the whole, and destined to act his noble part through ages to come, in which the earth was to be the theatre for the sublimest wonders of our God. One of the terms employed in the Scriptures to designate worlds, inwoven with the whole structure of its thought, and so made familiar to its ancient readers, is *ages* or dispensations: as if God had been working and measuring by these rather than by the building of material structures. The Apostle uses this term when he says, Through faith we understand the *worlds* were framed by the word of God, so that things which are seen were not made of things which do appear, Heb. xi. 3. The language itself shows that the idea prominent to the mind of God in revealing creation as His work, is not worlds as material structures, but series or ages of duration, through which he carries forward His designs to their final completion. These ages He is framing still. We are in the midst of the grandest of all, where not molluscs, or fishes, or quadrupeds, or giant vegetation find chief development; but where man, made in the likeness of God himself, and to whom the dominion here has been given, is the sublime actor. If ages, too, of possession were given to the more insignificant brute and vegetable creation—if this earth was their inheritance through such revolving cycles, what shall be the length of those ages during which God shall administer here the vast affairs of His moral universe, and work out all the deep problems of His providence and grace? If unknown ages were required to lay the foundations of earth, and prepare it for its great Lord, surely His occupancy of the same can be for no brief and limited period.

If God, then, communicated to Adam the history of creation, as we have reason to believe that He did, the revelation was undoubtedly conveyed in intelligible terms and understood. A revelation is made to be understood; and the language employed is the best adapted to this end. Adam thus was made acquainted with that work of creation, which had been progressing through long dispensations preceding, and of which be stood forth the crown and glory. The knowledge of this was necessarily involved in that dominion which was conferred upon him as the universal head. He was constituted the lord of all, and so understood it; not that he was a superior animal among the other tribes, as the lion is the king of the forest, or the eagle of the feathered fowl; but that when God arrived at the creation of man, He passed out of, and beyond the brute realm, to form a being of a nobler nature, allied to himself, made in His own image, to whom the supremacy and dominion could be entrusted. Adam was made to know his high destination and pre-eminence as a Son of God, in whom Heaven took chief delight—the lord of all this inferior creation, over whom the morning stars sang for joy, and for whom the earth had long been wailing in earnest expectation as her rightful lord to own him willing subjection and reverence. "God blessed them; and God said unto them, Be fruitful and multiply, and replenish the earth, and *subdue it:* and have dominion over the fish of the sea, and over the fowl of the air, and over every living thing that moveth upon the earth." In the creation of man God had reached the climax, the end of His long series, where he rested from his work, and rejoiced in it all as very good. He had finished by forming a race fitted for dominion, whom the whole creation beside might own as its rightful lord, not knowing any superior; for the brute creation could rise to no conception of God. They could recognize man and bow to his authority, but to none above him. To them, therefore, and to their knowledge, he was absolutely lord.

Adam was given plainly to understand that this was the place of distinction and preëminence that he occupied in the creation, bearing the very image of his Maker. Therefore was he made to comprehend that wondrous history going before; how God through long cycles had been working to the era of his advent, and what an hour of joy it was, when at last He said, "Let us make man in our image, after our likeness; and let them have dominion over the fish of the sea, and over the fowl of the air, and over the cattle, and over all the earth, and over every creeping thing that creepeth upon the earth."

CHAPTER III.

CREATION OF MAN.

If we would read aright the history of man and the dealings of Divine Providence toward him, we must understand the peculiar and distinguished position which he holds in the universe. In the preceding chapter we have shown that one principal source of knowledge on this point, furnished to this very end, is the work of creation. As we trace back this magnificent history of the animal and vegetable worlds now entombed in the rocks, we are filled with profoundest wonder. What is the object, what the explanation, we are ready to ask, of this mighty series of creations, rising one above another, and carried forward age after age? The vastness of this work fills us with amazement; and still more is our wonder excited, as we trace out its perfect order, marking how God began with the lowest forms of animal life, and rose in a continually ascending series to new and more perfected forms of beauty, giving to each new creation a wider range of existence. As we contemplate this boundless extent of life from the minutest animalcule, which the microscope alone can reveal, to the gigantic Megatherion, we are ready to say, It was not for these that God created and fitted up this earth. These are not the end of His designs, but only the preparatory steps to some other object—the scaffolding to some glorious temple yet to be reared. If, too, the great Builder was at such expense, and employed revolving cycles to erect this vast scaffolding, what must be the glory of that nobler temple, which shall stand to His eternal praise?

God intended that we should know, and that the universe should know what an estimate He put upon our humanity, and for what a place of honor He designed it. We have often studied this in the light of redemption and the wonders there displayed. But not here alone has God given expression to His thoughts on this subject. He has engraved this truth also in the everlasting rocks and mountains. The bottoms of the fathomless oceans are written over with its grand memorial. This earth was made for *man*. It tells of him from its first foundations. Its rocks are a vast mausoleum of the dead, each prophesying of his advent, owning him their lord, and waiting for his coming. The fragment of chalk which you hold in your hand, is composed of the minute shells of animalculæ, which the unaided vision cannot distinguish; and those wide extended cliffs have been the slow accumulation of these sepultured dead. Could the Almighty afford to work upon this scale in laying the foundations of earth, waiting the hour in the distant future when it would be ready for the entrance and possession of its lord? The mind is overwhelmed at the thought. Yet by this very process God designed to teach the grandeur and worth of that being, for whom this earth was made, and to whom it was to be given as his possession forever.

We can comprehend the thoughts and feelings of God only so far as He gives them expression. He must reveal himself. How then shall He tell us what His estimate of our race is, and what the place of honor for which it is designed in His counsels? It must be acted out. We must read it in His wondrous workings for our race. It is not enough for God to declare in words that He loves us truly and well. We cannot know by these what the height and depth of that love is, having no line or plummet by which to measure the thoughts of the Infinite. But when we see God so loving the world as to give His only begotten Son—when we behold Him so honoring our race, as to work through cycles of duration in fitting up this earth as their dwelling place, and in every new creation forming a higher type of his perfected manhood, then do we begin to catch a glimpse of those thoughts of eternal love, which God had toward us. We begin to see what meaning is contained in those words, loving us "from the foundation of the world." The very foundations of the earth—its mighty layers of rock do tell us in unmistakable language that God was thinking of and planning for us. Our memorial is written there to abide while time shall last. There lie the types of that glorious manhood, toward which the Divine mind was reaching from the outset. He loved us literally from the foundations of the earth, choosing us to be His sons, and from the beginning prepared for us these beautiful mansions.

But let us pass to another and more specific point: THE PECULIAR CONSTITUTION OF OUR HUMANITY IN THE UNION OF MIND WITH A MATERIAL BODY.

In most discussions setting forth the greatness of man, and his exaltation in the scale of being, we have been wont to resort to the soul, to dwell upon its capacities—its immortality and destiny. We have done this, too, so exclusively, as to show that we had little to say for the body, and that we considered man as deriving his glory almost entirely from his spiritual nature. The world is not yet redeemed from that heathen philosophy which so long held empire, that the body is a clog to the soul, a prison-house, and the origin of its misery, from which we are to look for deliverance. Ancient philosophy taught men to look forward to redemption as consisting in a release from their prison-house of clay. Then only could the emancipated spirit soar to regions of light and blessedness. Accordingly, the teachings of Christianity concerning a resurrection were regarded with abhorrence. Athens' brilliant philosophers turned away in disgust from Paul, when he started the idea of a restoration of the body from the grave, and would hear no more. The world is not rid of the influence of this long-controlling heathen philosophy. It clings to us still, and corrupts even our Christianity. We little esteem the body, and undervalue it as a constituent part of our godlike humanity. We speak of the immortality of the soul, as if it were only a part of him that was immortal, while the rest of his nature was to be given up to corruption and the grave. We foster and inculcate the idea that man was made of the dust of the earth in order to humble him, or teach him to be lowly. This, however, is heathenism, not Christianity. No such sentiment is found in the Word of God.

These observations will suffice to show to what extent the minds of men are still under the influence of that unchristian philosophy, which despises and depreciates this material structure as a part of our manhood—which puts dishonor upon it, as if it were scarcely a worthy partner of the soul: and of a creation so far inferior, as hardly to be worthy of immortality. But these are not the teachings of the Bible. God did not degrade the human soul, when He united it to this material organization. He did not hamper it—did not fail in creating for it a fitting associate, that would be to its honor and glory, or of which it need ever be ashamed. When God looked upon His creation with this crowning work of His power and love, He discovered no incongruity. He said that it was *very good*, and blessed it. He himself was satisfied, while angels rejoiced, and raised their loudest, sweetest anthems of praise.

It is not difficult to explain how this material part of our being has come to be so undervalued. We are now in a dishonored condition as a race, being under the curse by reason of sin; and this body is made subject to disease and pain, to deformity and loathsome corruption, to which we are painfully sensitive, far more than to that moral corruption which deforms and blights the soul. Men are not offended by their inward deformities. These give them little pain or anxiety. They therefore conceive that it might be well with them if it were not for these diseased, suffering bodies, which are ever tending downward toward the grave. The moral perceptions of men being deadened, it is only to the grosser facts of their existence that they are alive: and keenly feeling the ills of the body, they estimate it accordingly, and are ready to pronounce it a cursed thing, imagining that when they can lay it aside, they rid themselves of all ill. But such were not the thoughts of God, when prosecuting His work of creation and following it up age after age to its point of completion. Such are not the views which Christ's work of redemption gives us.

What then are the true relations of this subject?

The teachings of both nature and revelation are, that one of the sources of man's dignity and glory, as a creature of God, is, that he is possessed of a body as an instrument of thought and action, and so identified with this material universe. The Scriptures warrant the idea that in the creation of man, God designed the introduction of a race, upon which He intended to confer especial honor and privilege, bringing it into very peculiar relations of friendship and intimacy with himself, and designing to make it the medium of some of the brightest displays of His glory and love, beyond all that had ever been accomplished through the angelic host. As a fact, we know that our humanity has been carried up to the very right hand of power, far above all principalities in heavenly places, being made head over all. This is the result which has been actually reached. We may readily believe also that this was the place of preëminence originally designed for it, and that it has not come merely by accident, as it were, or as the result of the introduction of sin. It is a mere inference, sustained by no authority of the Word of God, that the exaltation to which our race is destined, and of which we have assurance in the already accomplished exaltation of our living Head, was, as it were, an after thought, and contingent on the existence of sin. We have the same right to *infer* that it was an original design as otherwise, independent of the introduction of sin. God evidently intended, through our race, to make such a revelation of Himself and His attributes, as He had through none other. At this point also, and under such a supposition, we may find a plausible solution of the rebellion and fall of a portion of the angelic host. When they were informed, as we may reasonably suppose them to have been, that there was to be another race created, which God was to bring into nearer relationship to Himself, and upon which He was to confer higher honor, they being invited to become ministers to Him in the execution of this great purpose, we can readily conceive how their jealousy might have been awakened, and they have risen up to resist the plan and decree of heaven. The angels continuing in allegiance, have been, as we well know, ministering spirits in the execution of these very plans of divine love, while those who rebelled were not delivered over at once to their merited doom, but have been *reserved for punishment until God shall have carried through His grand purposes toward our race.* And the angels which kept not their first estate, but left their own habitation, He hath *reserved* in everlasting chains under darkness *unto the judgment of the great day*, Jude vi. It is evident also from the Scriptures that these wicked spirits still roam abroad and occupy this territory, having large liberty for accomplishing their mischievous designs. These are facts, and facts of deep significance, showing clearly that that rebellion of the angelic host has important connections with our history, their final doom awaiting the issue of the problem involved in our humanity. Here, too, upon our territory, God is waging the dread conflict with the powers of darkness; and here those leagued forces of sin are to be forever broken. This view of the subject likewise gives deeper significance to that song, which the sons of God raised with such rapturous delight over man's birth and entrance upon the stage. They had looked forward to the event with thrilling interest, watching the building of earth's mighty foundations through the long ages, until the habitation was complete. They understood that a new page was now to be turned in the history of divine providence, and God's deepest wonders revealed to form the sweetest theme of song that ever broke upon the ear of a listening universe. Herein also may be found the reason of Satan's cursed hate against our race, and his purpose to destroy it, accomplishing thereby, as he verily supposed, the overthrow of the fairest, most cherished designs of Infinite wisdom. Could he circumvent our ruin, he would destroy that race by which God intended most to honor Himself, and make the brightest unfoldings of His perfections. Could he effect this, a blow would be struck, indeed, against the Almighty, a blow which even He would feel. And Satan was blinded and maddened enough to suppose that he could do it successfully.

But to return from this digression to the constitution of our humanity as a union of mind and matter.

When we survey this universe of worlds in its boundless extent, we are overwhelmed at the power and wisdom which can control such a system, and guide its orbs in their endless circuit. We are impressed, too, with the thought, that this array of worlds is designed for the revelation of the Godhead, constituting one of the chief media by which the eternal Infinite unfolds himself to His intelligent creation. Here, plainly, some of His grandest purposes are to be fulfilled. There is a magnificence and wealth of matter which overpowers thought, and we are ready to ask, What is the end of it all? For what is it designed? Not for itself, clearly. Not for mere vegetable and animal existence. It was made as the instrument of thought—to be put under the dominion of mind—to be subject to those who have capacity to rule, and to be subservient to their happiness and will. The connecting link between mind and matter is a mysterious one, which we cannot yet trace out. How mind or the will can move and control matter, we have no knowledge. That it does is obvious. The will, in fact, is the true source of all power—the final cause. All others are but secondary or mechanical, to be traced back through a longer or shorter series to an intelligent will.

What then is the crowning glory of this material universe? Not this magnificent system of countless worlds, but that wondrously skillful organization of matter which God has fitted up as the living temple of the soul—the dwelling-place of thought, the instrument of will—that portion of matter, which God has taken into most intimate relationship to Himself, and owned by eternal covenant in the alliance of sons, stamping it with His own image. *By this God has fixed and settled the continued existence of this material universe.* He has brought it into everlasting and necessary relationship to mind, and so stamped its destiny, making it an essential theatre for human thought and action. Had God created only material globes, He might, perhaps, have blotted them out of being, after having made them subserve His purposes for a season. Had He filled them only with vegetable and animal life, He might have spoken them into non-existence again when they had fulfilled an appointed round. But when He rose to the creation of man, He stamped upon this universe the impress of eternity; for He bound the noblest among His sons by indissoluble ties to this material structure. He was constituted a part of it, and made to have dominion over it. While he continues, therefore, and the dominion which God gave him continues, this material creation will endure. It may be changed and perfected: but change and perfection only insure its continuance the more.

We are strongly inclined to undervalue this creation of God, especially this earth, and look upon it as fit only for the flames. We have undervalued it as we have these bodies, which are so degraded by sin. This earth is indeed now under the curse, yet not always so to remain. Death and the curse are not always to have dominion here. Their empire is to be broken, the last enemy being put under the feet of our conquering Redeemer. This earth is to experience the day of its redemption, entering into the liberty of the sons of God. For this day it waits with longing expectation, travailing and groaning now under its sore and unwilling bondage. This body of flesh is to be raised incorruptible and glorious, in mighty power and eternal beauty, but a body still. It is not to lose its identity, or to be transformed into spirit. It is to continue a material form, and to be the fitting partner and dwelling-place of the glorified, godlike spirit within.

Herein then consists the peculiarity and perfection of our nature, that it is a soul united to a material organization, giving it the widest scope for thought and action, and designed as the noblest instrument for the unfolding of its immortal powers. It is here that this material creation has been carried up to its highest point of honor and exaltation, so that the Son of God himself could take this nature into alliance with himself, and glorify it by a union with the Divine. The Word was made flesh, and dwelt among us; and we beheld His glory, the glory as of the only begotten of the Father, full of grace and truth, John i. 14. Who being in the form of God, thought it not robbery to be equal with God; but made himself of no reputation, and took upon Him the form of a servant, and was made in the likeness of men; and being found in fashion as a man, He humbled himself, and became obedient unto death, even the death of the cross. Wherefore God also hath highly exalted Him, and given Him a name which is above every name, that at the name of Jesus every knee should bow, of things in heaven and things in earth, and things under the earth; and that every tongue should confess that Jesus Christ is Lord to the glory of God the Father, Phil. ii. 6. At the very right hand of power, then, is that glorified, redeemed nature of ours, in the person of the man Christ Jesus. Well therefore in view of this consummation may the Psalmist exclaim, "What is man that Thou art mindful of him, or the son of man that Thou [so] visitest him? Thou hast made him a little lower than the angels [*Elohim*, God] and hast crowned him with glory and honor. Thou madest him to have dominion over the works of Thy hands; Thou hast put all things under his feet."

What was intended by this is explained most clearly in the commentary of the Apostle Paul, when he declares that it was fulfilled in Jesus Christ, who was exalted and made Head over all to His church, destined to share with Him the glory and kingdom forever.

CHAPTER IV.

THE CONSTITUTION OF HUMANITY.

In connection with man's creation, it will be appropriate to consider the constitution of our humanity in the law of its generation, which will throw additional light upon the history of man as related to the material universe, bringing into discussion also that problem of Divine providence, that the sin of Adam involved the entire race.

Why did God frame a constitution of things, which brought such dire consequences? To many it carries the appearance of injustice, as if it were visiting the sins of the guilty upon the innocent. It may not be possible for us fully to comprehend the relations of this subject. The plans of the Divine government may not as yet be sufficiently developed to make all things plain. Being in their incipient stage, they may be necessarily involved in obscurity. It is always difficult for an observer to comprehend a partially finished work or see the wisdom of the architect. It may be impossible, at that stage of the proceedings, for the architect himself to give a satisfactory account of his own work. While, however, God may not now be able to make every thing simple to our apprehension in the working of His grand designs, there is nothing over which our faith should necessarily stumble. God has revealed enough of His ways to satisfy all the demands of faith, and secure our confidence both in His wisdom and integrity.

What then is *the peculiar constitution of our humanity in the law of its generation?*

The law of creation for our race is different from that which obtained among the angels. God gave to each of them a separate existence, creating them all alike upon the same footing, and causing them to stand in the same mutual relations. They know not the ties which bind together parent and child, husband and wife. This fact gives character to their relations under the Divine government, each one being left to fix his own moral standing, which to many seems the only true and proper mode. Some conceive that the moral character and destiny of every being should be determined absolutely by himself, and so determined as not to be affected by influences beyond his own control.

This separate and independent creation of beings is the most simple, demanding the least wisdom and skill. It is *the first or lowest* system—that to which we are necessitated in all our creations by reason of our limited power and skill. In all manufacturing processes we employ the same labor and ingenuity in the production of each separate article. Human wisdom and power are not equal to the production of one parent article, from which others shall flow in an unending series. The separate, independent creation of beings, therefore, is the lowest form for the exhibition of the Divine skill. Our humanity, constructed on a different basis, is a *more perfect system*, calling into requisition higher attributes of wisdom, and more illustriously displaying the Divine perfections.

Again, *the angelic system is more limited in its extent and capacities.*

The angelic host was a limited creation of God,

brought into being by one act and at the same moment. At least such has been our understanding of it, and we cannot reason upon any other. But where is the limit to our humanity to be found? Where is the creation to stop, based upon that constitution which God has here set in operation? We do not assert that it has no limits; but evidently it has capacities and a power of adaptation that are amazing, and may be employed to the accomplishment of the most stupendous results.

Again, *our system gives existence to those multiplied and endeared relations of love, which grow out of our mutual dependencies, and by which God is revealed to us.*

The angels stand in one relation to each other, and to God their creator and ruler. But what sacred and numerous ties bind our humanity, all growing from the fact that God created one man to stand at its head, to whom the rest should owe their existence! How also is our knowledge of God enlarged by this fact, and the means by which He may unfold Himself to us? He is revealed to us as a Father, which conception we readily reach because we have been made to know that tender earthly relation of parent and child in our own experience. How also is Christ's nearest relation to His beloved church brought home to our hearts by the marriage tie, the emblem of that glorious union which is to be consummated when Christ, the true bridegroom, shall take the church as His chosen bride to the embraces of His everlasting love? So Christ is revealed to us as a brother, teacher, friend, our mediator and our King, of which we attain the knowledge through these relationships of earth. And herein are to be found their true significancy and end. They were not primarily made for themselves, but for Christ, and designed to stand as types of those higher, real, and enduring relations which belong to the kingdom of God. The former are temporary, belonging to this present constitution of things, which will pass away. The latter will abide forever to illustrate the Divine glory and perfections; while it is upward to these spiritual relationships in the kingdom of God, that we are lifted by means of the human ties with which we are made so familiar on earth.

These considerations show that our humanity has a capacity for revealing God and unfolding all the depths of His wisdom and love, which the angelic system of creation does not possess. This fact is virtually expressed by the Apostle where he states that he was called to "preach the unsearchable riches of Christ, and to make all men see what is the fellowship of the mystery, which from the beginning hath been *hid in God*, who created all things by Jesus Christ to the intent *that now unto the principalities and powers in heavenly places might be known by* (through) *the church the manifold wisdom of God*," Eph. iii. 9. The church was to be the grand medium of revealing that wisdom. Thus our humanity is a higher system than that of the angels, into which they desire to look. There is no race which God has brought nearer to Himself than our own—none for which He has destined higher honor—none through which He will more gloriously unfold all the hidden wonders of the Godhead. And this, too, grows largely out of the peculiar constitution of that humanity in appointing for it a Head.

If then it be a higher and more perfect system with larger capacities, what have we to object against it? Why should *we* find fault? The jealousy of the angels might have been excited, as we have conceived it to have been in a portion of their number. But our race certainly has no reason to complain at the place of honor and exaltation which has been given us.

But let us look at its workings.

The system involves in its own nature the exercise of

the most powerful formative influences upon all those who are brought within its embrace.

Any relation of moral beings involves a moral influence; and the closer the relation of dependence, the more controlling must the influence be, which is exerted. Mighty agencies are always required to the production of great results; and with the enlargement of the agencies for good, there must, of necessity, be a liability to corresponding evil, if those forces are turned from their legitimate purposes, and employed for mischief. Men, in their wisdom, always aim at the employment of the most perfect machinery, the most powerful forces, which human skill can control. We rejoice in the discovery and use of such forces, regarding them as among the highest evidences of the advancing civilization of our age. True, indeed, there is a liability to more terrible destruction, when these powers are misdirected, or controlled by unskillful hands. But this is no legitimate argument against the employment of the agencies. We should only pity the nervous weakness of the man, who, in this day, would still insist upon travelling by the stage-coach, as in days of old; or cling to the handloom and press, because there is no danger of their explosion. We should not stop to argue with one, who was always dwelling upon the dangers and destruction attendant upon the use of these agencies, and declaiming against it. A weak-minded man might search out the dread history of hurricanes and thunder-storms, and write down the wisdom of God in employing such agencies of destruction as winds and electricity. We seldom find such folly in common things. But in theology men are apt to lay aside their common sense. We fix our eyes upon a limited portion of God's universe, where sin, for the time being, is working out its terrible results, and are lost in wonder that He should ever have permitted it; or that He should have created beings with such capacities for evil and suffering. Their view of Providence and moral government would simply turn back the world to the dominion of fishes and reptiles, which have no such powers liable to abuse. The creation of a moral universe involves the existence of the mightiest forces below omnipotence, with the largest capacities for enjoyment and suffering. It is that creation alone to which God can make Himself known, and which can adequately and intelligently show forth His praises. Yet the creation of such agencies and capacities necessarily involves the liability of their perversion. Sin may enter such a universe; but this proves nothing against the wisdom of its creation, any more than the explosion of a steam engine proves that such a power should not have been employed. The possibility of sin is involved in the conception of a moral system, embracing, as it does, an order of beings, who by their very nature are capable of transgressing—who are subject to temptation and liable to fall. Unless God therefore creates beings at the outset immutably established in holiness (which is inconsistent with the very idea of trial and discipline, from which immutable holiness in all finite intelligences must come), then sin may enter with all its fearful consequences. Neither is its existence any impeachment of the Divine wisdom or goodness. Sin is not beyond the control of the Almighty. He can still hold the empire, and deal with it as justice demands. It will not prevail against Him. Nay, it may be only by God's righteous dealings with sin that all the perfections of His infinite character can be developed. If sin should never enter, it could not be known that God was able to control and subdue it; certainly not, if the ground is taken that He must on no account permit its existence.

With these general observations we may return to our own peculiar moral system.

It was stated that this had a capacity for revealing God and unfolding the highest perfections of His nature, which that of the angels did not possess; inasmuch as there were nearer and more tender relationships embraced in it, and more mighty, far-reaching influences, which in the great purposes of God were designed through coming ages to work out the grandest results. These powers might indeed be perverted, as they have been, and work incidental evil of a fearful character. But that evil is to bear no more proportion to the good to be worked out on this great theatre through the long cycles of the future, than the destruction of the sweeping hurricane, once in a quarter or half a century, is to be compared to the daily and unnumbered blessings which flow from the pure atmosphere, which is our very life. We are now in that stage of our system, where we see the workings of the evil mainly, and only a little of the good; like a child born in the midst of the hurricane, if it could be supposed to take cognizance of the war of elements. It might well suppose that this was a fearful world, into which it had been introduced. But those fierce winds will soon subside, and the skies again be calm. So we are in the midst of the fiercer conflicts of sin, and in the track of the moral tornado, as it is sweeping over these fair dominions of God. To our limited apprehension, as we look back over six thousand years of the past, we may conceive that this is a fearful condition of affairs, and wonder why God should ever have allowed it. But six thousand years is a brief space to Him, with whom one day is as a thousand years, and a thousand years as one day. It is a very brief space in a vast moral system, to which no thought can affix a limit, and where almost interminable ages have been previously assigned to its mere material and introductory stage. It is as brief as the continuance of the fierce tornado which sweeps across the heavens.

Neither are we to forget in the study of this subject that the grand forces involved in this system of humanity *are all to be made subservient to Christ, and employed to work for Him and our redeemed race those blessed, everlasting results, which He intended in its original construction.* We think of Adam standing at the head of our race and pouring in the tide of sin and death upon it in a desolating flood. But have we thought also that the system, which admitted such evil, has the same capacity in the other direction, and was adapted to Christ as the true and heaven-appointed Head of our humanity? Have we thought how He might turn back this tide of woe, and then in His own person pour the endless stream of salvation through that same humanity redeemed and turned heavenward? It is upon this side of the picture that we must look, if we would obtain any just conceptions of the workings of this magnificent system, which infinite wisdom and love have inaugurated. We are now merely in the incipient stages of it—in the track of the brief hurricane, where we hear the howlings of the tempest, and see the desolations which mark its career. Christ has not yet obtained possession of these forces. We have not seen His kingdom in its power, thereby to learn what is in store for our humanity, and what a history is yet to be written of it, when it shall have been redeemed to our Immanuel, and all its mighty elements shall have been turned Godward and heavenward.

One of the chief difficulties on this subject to our minds lies in the fact, that we have been taught to conceive of the largest portion of earth's history as already fulfilled. Our theology has given currency to the idea that the affairs of this world will soon be wound up—that the end is at hand. In this view of the matter, the history of earth is a dark one, which it might be difficult in all respects to explain. It is true the Bible speaks of "the end" as at hand. But by this is meant, not the end of the earth and its inhabitants, but simply, the end of this present dispensation of sin, in which the Prince of Darkness reigns, and earth groans under the curse. A new era will then begin. Then will commence earth's true history under our Immanuel, its real, living Head. The day of its expected redemption will have come, when it shall enter upon its high destiny, to demonstrate what this humanity is capable of as redeemed unto Christ, and made to subserve His grand purposes. The sublime and eventful history of this earth is scarcely begun. Ages have been given, indeed, to the dominion of its fishes and reptiles. But its great lord has but recently been introduced, and his magnificent history has but just begun to be written. The vast capacity of this humanity to illustrate the Divine perfections is yet to be developed. What heights of glory it is capable of attaining we have intimation of in the fact, that Jesus our Head has risen and ascended on high, all power and dominion being given into His hand. We are to share that glory, who have faith to believe in Him; and ere long the joyful hour will come when every enemy shall be subdued under Him, and this earth shall enter upon its new career of redemption.

This is the glorious vision which revelation holds up to our view, and for which it bids us hope and patiently wait.

Here, too, at this point, we may get an insight into the reason for our material organization and its truly exalted nature.

The relations of our humanity spring from the body. It is upon the material part of our oganization that the parental, the marriage, and other relations are founded.

Hence, then, are the higher capacities of our nature for revealing God. Hence are the grand instrumentalities which Christ has employed for unfolding himself, and through himself the infinite Godhead. In this aspect of the subject, this material creation becomes grandly exalted to our apprehension, and this human nature as a constituent part thereof. In our glorified state these present earthly relationships will have passed away and been superseded. But they will have served their high purpose of lifting us up to those nobler and enduring relationships of the kingdom of God, where all the hopes and destiny of our humanity are to be fulfilled. The experience of a child is a rich and instructive one. But he knows little whose experience extends no further than this. True knowledge and blessedness are found alone in the experience of a child of God. The bridal occasion is a happy one. But the truest hour of joy will not come to earth, until that thrilling cry is heard, "Behold, *the* bridegroom cometh, go ye out to meet Him."

CHAPTER V.

THE CONSTITUTION OF HUMANITY.

IN the preceding chapter we dwelt upon the peculiar constitution of our humanity in the law of its generation, attempting to meet the difficulty and objection so often made, that such consequences should flow to a whole race from the sin of one, their constituted head. This was done, by showing that this constitution of our humanity is a higher system than the angelic, possessing more complicated relations—that it has a wider range of being, vaster capacities, a great power for revealing the Godhead, and unfolding all the infinite perfections of His nature. Of necessity, with this augmentation of power, the disastrous results which must flow from the perversion of such a system are increased, which, however, is no argument against it. We showed also that we have not as yet seen the full workings of this system—that we are only in its incipient stages, where we witness its dire perversions by sin: but that ere long Christ will gain possession of all its vast resources, and then through ages this law of production will be made subservient to Him in bringing into existence countless generations of men to show forth His glory. Thus sin is to have *dominion* over our race only in the first stages of its existence; and we are not to form our estimate of the system from this development of it, while we leave out of account those mighty, glorious results which will be achieved by the same, when all its vast resources shall have been subjected to Christ, its true Head, and made to accomplish His gracious designs through ages of uninterrupted righteousness and peace.

We wish to pursue this subject a little further still to illustrate it more fully, and obviate more perfectly the difficulty which has been so deeply felt.

Suppose then that God had placed our race upon the angelic footing, so that its character and destiny should not have been affected by any head, no one can show but that sin would have entered to the same disastrous extent, perhaps even greater, and then possibly without any opportunity for redemption.

When men reason on this subject, and make objections against the present divine economy, they assume that if it had been different, so that each one had been tried by himself, and allowed to stand or fall for himself alone, they would not have yielded to temptation, but have maintained their allegiance to heaven. There is, however, not the slightest evidence of this. The probabilities are every way against it. If our first parents fell with all the weight of responsibility with which they were crowded, no man can assume that he would have stood and passed safely through the ordeal of temptation. No man has any right to make such assumption.

Take the other system, to which many seem to attach such superior advantages. Do away with this parental relation, which necessitates the generation of the race from a single pair, and provides for its continuance through long succeeding ages, of the duration of which we can form little idea, and then bring all these same countless hosts into existence at once by a single act of creating power, each independent of the other, each created from the dust, as was Adam, and breathed upon with the breath of life from God, each to be tried for himself, and to determine his own destiny. This seems to be the arrangement which the abrogation of the other would require. And what have we gained? Who shall tell how many of that entire host shall withstand the temptation of the tree of knowledge of good and evil? Sin may not only make as great havoc in that creation: it may spread wider, and its workings be more dire and uncontrollable; nor might there be any opportunity for the introduction of such a remedial system as has been found under the present economy through a headship to the race. Does any one ask how the effects of sin could be wider than under the present system, where it affects the whole race? We answer: The sin of Adam may extend its effects to the entire race, yet *this present state of things under the dominancy of wickedness* is to continue but a little longer. "*The end*" *is at hand.* This empire of sin is to be broken. The Prince of darkness and evil is to be cast out, and our race is to enter upon its new and redeemed state, in which it is to work out all its blessed results to the glory of the second Adam. It is in that state that the vast portion of the generations of men is to be brought into existence, and prepared for glory and immortality: so that the generations existing during these first six thousand years are but the smallest fraction of our race. Thus this very parental, or federal relation, which has been commonly conceived of as so fearfully disastrous to an entire race, will be made the grand instrument in the hands of infinite wisdom for *limiting and hemming in* the effects of sin—of shutting up its dire results to the earliest and least portions of the system; while, through the second Adam, the blessings of salvation shall flow on to countless myriads of that race through all the later periods of its history, bringing to glory a multitude "which no man can number."

Nor must it be forgotten that it is this very parental and federal constitution that has given Christ the opportunity to interpose, so that He might become the Son of man, as He was the Son of God, and thus be ordained the head of our humanity for its redemption. Who can tell whether it would have been possible, in the nature of things, to have shut up sin within any defined limits, or arrested its progress under the other system? It may not have had the capacity for permitting such divine interference as would be necessary to accomplish the result. We know that God has employed our system for such interposition; that the Eternal One "took not on Him the nature of angels," but did take on Him "the seed of Abraham"—yes, the *seed* of Abraham. It was a *seed*, so that He could take it. And through this strange and wondrous condescension He is to effect not only the redemption of our race, but strike through the powers of hell also, and bruise Satan under His feet, breaking forever his empire, and finally casting him out, with all his infernal legions, down to the pit of destruction. The fact that divine wisdom employs our system to the accomplishment of such vast and glorious results, is evidence enough that it possesses wonderful adaptations, and has capacities beyond any other for the fulfilment of the deepest, sublimest purposes of the Godhead.

The question may be started in some minds, Why was it necessary that the sin of our first parents should essentially affect the character of their posterity, so as to involve their fall? Why might not the parental relation exist, and the moral nature not be affected by it; so that, notwithstanding the sin of Adam, each one of his posterity might have an original trial for himself in his own person under law?

The answer is, that the supposition contradicts the nature of things.

When God bade the earth bring forth its grass, herb, and tree, He proclaimed their eternal law, which was, that every plant should contain within itself *its own seed after his kind.* Each species was to produce its own; and it is this grand law that gives harmony, order, and beauty to the natural world. When the precious seed is committed to the earth, we know what to expect with absolute certainty. We are in no painful doubt as to what the crop will be. The same law of order was given to all the tribes of the animal kingdom in air and earth and sea. "God said, let the earth bring forth the living creature after his kind, cattle, and creeping thing, and beast of the earth after his knd: and it was so." It is a glorious law, fraught only with bounteous wisdom and blessings. This same law God gave to man also. He was to produce after his kind. It is a child in her own likeness that the mother presses to her bosom, and upon which she prints the fond kiss of love.

If this, then, is the wise and beneficent law of man's being, in harmony with the entire creation of God, where does it stop? Does it merely give a body like its parent, and a soul; or does it transmit disposition and character also; not moral character in its strictest sense, as consisting in choice and principle of action, for these belong only to a moral agent; but all that lies back of such moral action in the native dispositions and tendencies of the soul? These must come under the operation of this same law, and necessarily so as part of the human constitution. That constitution, therefore, must necessarily be affected by sin; and these effects must be transmitted in the degradation of the race. It is an inevitable result.

This same law, of which we speak, lays the foundation for the improvments which are made in the cultivation of the fruits of the earth and its living tribes. Not only are seeds and animals perpetuated, but their qualities also; so that, by a careful selection and cultivation, their value may be greatly increased. Some of our most valued fruits were once in a wild, degenerate state, and almost worthless. The law of deterioration implies a corresponding law of progress; and this is the law of our creation. It belongs to all living things connected with this system. Our humanity, therefore, involves the transmission of qualities which affect materially its character and destiny. It would be strange, indeed, and out of all harmony with creation, if it were not so. It would be anomalous if the qualities of the child could be entirely unaffected by those of the parent, either for good or for evil, so that there could be no deterioration or improvement to the race from generation to generation. Yet this unnatural state of things is involved in the objection urged against the fact of a common ruin through our first father. To prevent such a result, would necessitate a radical change in the constitution of this whole economy. Take away that liability or capacity for the degradation of humanity, and you destroy also at the same time its susceptibility for progress, and for the perpetuation of all that is noble and good in our nature. This, moreover, is the side of the picture which is to come into view in the future, when Christ is to have possession here, and work out all His glorious designs as the Second Adam. This law of our nature was a wise and beneficent one, designed to work out the grandest results. Neither are we to pass upon it the sentence of condemnation, because it is now working temporary evil in pouring the tide of sin and death through these first generations. It would be as unwise to judge of the value of our atmosphere by the hurricanes which desolate the earth, or the value of electricity by the lightning bolts which occasionally descend, and make apparent to us what a mighty power is treasured up in that subtle, all-pervading element.

These considerations and arguments may serve to remove some of the objections and difficulties which have been so often made to the fact, that sin entered by one man, and that, through him, the flood-gates of death were opened upon our world. The arguments presented, show that the subject has vast and complicated relations in the economy of God; and that we cannot judge of it by looking merely at one side, or a few isolated facts bearing upon a single point. Even if all our difficulties are not met, we may rest in the conclusion that we do not understand the whole subject, and have yet to learn much respecting it. We can afford to wait for further light before we undertake to pronounce upon God's ways, to condemn them either as folly or wickedness.

CHAPTER VI.

THE TEMPTATION AND FALL.

What are the facts in the fall of our first father?

Our humanity was put on trial, as the history shows, and for this there was a necessity in the nature of things. We always test the capability of a new invention, putting it sometimes to the severest tests, before bringing it into practical use, and risking upon it property and life. The government does not accept a new cannon or rifle without thorough trial. Steam was subjected to many experiments as a propelling power, before it was received to public favor and confidence. Beyond this, however, the trial of humanity is necessary to its own development and perfection, which is not true of machines. The experiment has no effect upon them for good, but only demonstrates what they are. Man, however, cannot attain unto his perfection without trial. It is necessary for his physical, intellectual, and moral nature. His manhood must be developed within himself. This is the law of his being. Heroism is found in resistance to temptation—in triumphing over great obstacles. "Blessed is the man that endureth temptation; for *when he is tried*, he shall receive the crown of life, which the Lord has promised to them that love him." Had our humanity endured the trial to which it was subjected, and proved its own virtue and integrity, as well as its capacity to resist all the assaults of evil, how glorious would it have stood before the universe, admired and honored of all!

Some, however, may still ask, Why was the experiment made with Adam, when it was subject to such a disastrous issue? Why was it not avoided? What, however, would that character be worth, that would not endure temptation? What could it ever accomplish of high ends in the government of God, if it must ever be carefully guarded from evil, and never trusted within its reach? What would a ship be worth for ocean service that must always be kept in smooth water, out of the reach of storms? The very thought of such a thing is her surest condemnation. And must our humanity forever be a weak nursling, upon which no rude wind must blow, that must never be allowed to meet temptation, nor be assaulted with evil? The supposition will show to what an unworthy position man would have been necessarily subjected—that he never could have attained unto any honor, nor been fitted for any high service in the universe of God. The only end he would have answered, would have been for some holiday exhibition. For effective service he would have been of no account.

The fact, also, that our nature did yield to temptation and fall, shows clearly that it needed this very trial and development of which we speak. It was not perfected in strength, nor fitted for the highest moral purposes. It must be made capable of withstanding temptation—able to endure—worthy to be trusted, and so crowned with glory and honor. The aim of every wise parent in the education of his child, is not to keep him forever from all contact with evil; for this cannot be. But it is to instil those principles, and give that stability and strength to his character which will withstand temptation in whatever insidious form it may approach. There was a necessity, therefore, that our humanity should be tried. There was no escape from it, and its fall was a demonstration to this necessity.

The trial was an eminently judicious one in all respects.

There was no positive command requiring the performance of some difficult task. It was a simple prohibition, the fruit of one tree in the midst of the garden being denied, while unlimited access was given to all the rest, and to the tree of life itself. Of the tree of knowledge of good and evil only must Adam and Eve not partake; and, to guard them perfectly, they were informed of the terrible consequences of disobedience, so that they fully understood the matter, stating in the very moment of temptation, the fact that God had prohibited that tree on pain of His everlasting displeasure. There was, therefore, no misapprehension in the case. They could not plead that they were ignorant of the terrible results that would follow from the act of transgression. Eve repeated to the tempter both the prohibition and the penalty attached.

It was, doubtless, only by such a prohibition that the faith and principle of our first parents could be tried. To test character, there must be temptation; and to have temptation, an appeal must be made to some susceptibility of our nature, the gratification of which would lead away from duty and the path of rectitude. We see how this is with men who are placed in easy circumstances, where their every wish is gratified. They enjoy prosperity and meet with no difficulties. Their duties run in the same track with their principal aims. They are successful in their pursuits, and every thing goes well with them. Such men are not tried. They need adversity and difficulty to prove them properly. It cannot be told whether they would abide the hour of temptation. Rough weather and head winds are required to tell what the staunchness and sea-going qualities of a ship are. It is not enough for her to cross the ocean in fair weather and smooth water. She must prove her capabilities amid the storm. So, many a man has a reputation for integrity and worth, simply because he has never been tried. The adversary said this of Job. He insinuated of this servant of God, that he could not be otherwise than a good man, having every desire of his heart gratified. It was his interest to be all that he seemed. "Doth Job fear God for naught? Hast thou not made an hedge about him, and about his house, and about all that he hath on every side? Thou hast blessed the work of his hands, and his substance is increased in the land. But put forth thine hand now, and touch all that he hath, and he will curse thee to thy face."

How might this have been applied to our first parents in their happy Eden! God had indeed made an hedge about them, and hemmed them in on every side, blessing the work of their hands, and increasing their substance until every desire of their hearts was gratified. "Of every tree of the garden thou mayest freely eat." How could they do otherwise than love and serve God? What motive was there to any thing else? Their duty fell in perfectly with all their inclinations and desires.

It is plain that their faith in God and obedience to Him could be tested only by some difficulty or self-denial, out of the ordinary track of this providence. Just this trial was given them through the tree of knowledge of good and evil, by means of which a powerful appeal was made to their nature—the desire of knowledge, one of the strongest and noblest susceptibilities of their being, but which, yielded to in this instance, would lead to disobedience.

The objection, however, may be made, that Eve was deceived by an artful tempter. But this is the characteristic of temptation and sin in all cases. Sin is, in its own nature, a fraud, and can never be committed unless there is deception with it. It is through some delusion, cheat, or lie, that men are always drawn into transgression. Sin is a monstrous imposition; and if it were an apology for it, that the sinner was deceived by false representations, then might iniquity always be defended. The eyes of men are always opened after transgression—and opened to see that they are naked—that they have been made fools of, and deluded to their destruction. This was precisely the experience of our first parents; and this is the experience of a wicked, deluded world now. It is nothing, therefore, against this first entrance of sin, that there was deception practised and false representations made.

It must be conceded, however, that the permission granted Satan to enter paradise and practise his frauds, is a question belonging to a high province of God's government, where we have as yet but limited means of information, and where we must be content to wait for further revelations, which shall show what the relations of these various systems of the universe are. The same objection, doubtless, might be urged against wicked men roaming abroad at will, and cruel seducers entering the abodes of innocence and peace to tempt the unwary to their destruction, and blight all their hopes. This much God would make plain, that virtue cannot be shut out from all contact with wickedness. The nature of the system forbids it. The perfect isolation of moral beings from all temptation and deceit is doubtless impossible in the nature of things, and perhaps would not be desirable, if it were possible, as perfection then could never be attained.

CHAPTER VII.

A REMEDIAL SYSTEM.

Before proceeding to discuss the character of our fallen nature, we shall consider

THE CHANGE MADE IN THE DIVINE ECONOMY UPON THE INTRODUCTION OF SIN.

There is, perhaps, no point where more confusion and error creep into our systems of theology than here—none where more clear and accurate views of the facts embraced in the history are demanded. What those precise facts were, as they occurred immediately after the introduction of sin, it shall be our aim to ascertain.

The first system under which man was placed in Eden was a legal one. In regard to this there is no dispute. The law was given, requiring obedience, and the penalty announced to transgression, which was death. "In the day that thou eatest thereof thou shalt surely die." Death here is to be taken in its highest and most comprehensive meaning, and the most natural to the conception of our first parents, which was, *the loss of God's favor, and His eternal displeasure.* This was death in its proper sense, and that conception of it which they would necessarily form, being the direct opposite of their highest *life*, the love and favor of God. It is not necessary to suppose that our first parents understood all that was involved in such threatening. Experience alone could give such an understanding. Still, the penalty was intelligible in its terms. As God was their life and their heaven, so death was the loss of God and His favor—banishment from His presence. This was the import of that dread threatening to their minds. They understood clearly that they must at once fall under the Divine displeasure and curse, and forfeit every good, if they ventured upon transgression. Accordingly, they were filled with the utmost terror, when they found that the deed of wickedness was done, and sought to hide themselves from the Divine presence.

Did God carry out the law, and execute the penalty as He had threatened?

The answer to this determines the question respecting the nature of the present Divine administration toward our world: and many would answer the question unhesitatingly in the affirmative, pointing for clear proof to the fact that God began to open the tide of woe and death upon our world, dooming the race to the curse which He at once pronounced. We are pointed to this curse immediately put in force, as evidence that God was true to the word which He had spoken, that they should surely die. We are referred to death, and the whole train of evils brought in by sin, as demonstrating that the law was executed upon Adam and his posterity, it being assumed as a point beyond question that these evils were the penalty threatened against disobedience.

We claim, however, that this is a misinterpretation of the facts of the case.

It is clear that God did not pursue the course expected by the guilty pair, and what they had every reason to look for. *He evidently did not shut them out from His favor*, and doom them to His everlasting displeasure. On the contrary, He opened at once the door of mercy and hope to their guilty souls. He spake words of thrilling tenderness and peace, when He announced that a ransom should be provided, and one raised up of their seed who should accomplish their deliverance, and crush the head of the old serpent. These were the first words which fell upon the ears of the trembling pair, as they stood expecting to hear their doom; and instead of being cast down into the depths of despair and wretchedness, they were filled with joy and hope as the unexpected prospect of redemption was opened to their vision, and the attainment of victory over their destroyer.

We might ask of those who claim that God executed at once the penalty of the law, Was this promised redemption from sin, and this triumph over the old serpent, embraced in the threatening against disobedience? Did the penalty, "Thou shalt surely die," contemplate any such results as this? Certainly not. The announcement of a Saviour to be provided was a statement, in so many words, that the execution of the penalty threatened was to be suspended, and an opportunity offered of escaping death, and gaining eternal life. It announced *distinctly the introduction of a new and remedial system*—an economy under which the race was to have a new trial, not under law, but under grace—not where one sin would work out their certain death, but where they might have pardon from many offences through the Redeemer promised.

This was the plain understanding of the case by our first parents. They could make no mistake here, because they knew what death meant, as threatened in the penalty. They saw their nakedness; and when they heard the strange, the wondrous announcement, that they were yet to be continued, and dealt with in forbearing kindness, they understood perfectly that that legal economy had been suspended, and a new one of grace introduced, the workings of which were to be widely different. There was no possibility of their misapprehending the fact, that the law was not executed upon them, while a new system of grace was brought in, which contemplated their salvation, and not their punishment.

It is urged, indeed, that the veracity of God was involved in inflicting the death threatened. He had said, "In the day that thou eatest thereof thou shalt surely die." God's veracity, however, is involved in the same way with every sinner. This same penalty of death eternal lies against every transgressor—against all disobedience. But His veracity is not impeached by the introduction of a remedial system, and the pardon of the repenting sinner; for the system is such that "mercy and truth are met together, righteousness and peace have kissed each other." God's veracity no more compelled Him to doom Adam to perdition, than it does us to-day. Mercy reached him, as it reaches us, while Divine truth and justice still abide forever.

What, then, was the meaning of that curse which followed?

This curse came, indeed, as the consequence of sin, as did the remedial system itself. But no one would thence argue that *redemption* was part of the *penalty* of sin. No more are we necessarily to conclude that the evils embraced in that curse are the proper death-penalty threatened against transgression. It is a mere assumption that they are, and a groundless one. What determines this, is the relation which these evils sustain to the government of God. Evil has, most clearly, other relations in the economy of Providence, beside the single one of penalty to transgression.

The fact that a man is hung, does not of itself determine that he died by the hand of justice as a murderer. He may have committed suicide. It may have been an accident, or he may have been hung by his enemies. We must learn other facts, before we can determine the character of the event, and say that it was the infliction of law and justice. We claim, now, that the evils of this life have their sole relation to the remedial system of grace, and were introduced as a part of such system. They were designed to subserve the great ends of God's economy of redemption, and are so employed, having no proper relation to law as the penalty of death for sin.

All the relations of the subject prove this.

I. *They were introduced in connection with an economy of grace, and not of law.*

God had just announced to our first parents, trembling in their guilt, and expecting to hear their doom pronounced, that a mighty Redeemer should be provided, by whom they might live, and not die; and that the world was to be put under this remedial system for the recovery of the race, the execution of the law being thereby necessarily suspended. In this connection it was that man was doomed to sweat and toil, to sickness and death; and the earth to briers, thorns, and barrenness. This is the relation in which these things stand in the history, and where they were put by their divine Author at their introduction.

II. *They are just such evils as are fitted to a system of grace, rather than of law.*

It was a stupendous work to manage this world of rebellion under a remedial system, in order to bring it back to its allegiance, and establish here again the authority of Heaven, freely forgiving the guilty. The administration of law and the execution of justice would have been a far more simple process. The government that undertakes to deal with a formidable rebellion in excessive leniency and forbearance, hoping thus to subdue it by kindness, rather than dealing with it in just severity and judgment, will be as likely to secure its own overthrow—as that of the rebellion. It is a dangerous experiment to make; and it was a vast undertaking for Christ to deal with the rebellion of this world, backed up by the legions of hell, through a system of leniency and forbearance. Neither did He attempt this work without counting the cost—without a full understanding of the desperate character of this rebellion, and all its resources, as well as of His own ability to control this wickedness, defeat all its schemes, and protect the integrity of His own righteous and everlasting government. It is not in place here to point out the means by which God could maintain the authority of His law while forgiving the guilty: that will be considered in another connection. But it is appropriate now to say, that God did not foolishly undertake to deal with this cruel rebellion according to a system of grace *upon the footing of Paradise.* Such an attempt would have proved a speedy failure. Had man been allowed to continue in Paradise without any curse, sin could never have been kept within control. Even as it is now, hemmed in by fire and sword, by earthquake and tempest, by pestilence and death, it has seemed sometimes as if it would be too strong for God, and His scheme of mercy would be overthrown. Such instrumentalities, then, as these, were essential to the success of this plan of mercy, without which it would have proved an inevitable failure.

The first thing, then, that God did in introducing this new economy of redempton, was to drive man out of Paradise, and rearrange this world after a different model, so that sin might be dealt with and held under control. A curse was pronounced upon the ground, compelling man henceforth to eat his bread in the sweat of his face. The earth was no more to yield without stint, as heretofore. A spontaneous living, now that he was a sinner, would only insure his being an idle, worthless vagabond. He must be subjected to toil, and dig to find a subsistence. This, moreover, in the altered circumstances of the race, is a blessing, sent in mercy and love, not in wrath. It is always in the midst of an industrious, toiling community, that we find the least vice and the most virtue; while, on the contrary, wherever a community, or a portion of a community, is placed above the necessity of that great law of labor, there is a people on the high road to profligacy and ruin.

Such good does not come from the infliction of justice and penalty upon crime; but it is the operation of evil in a remedial system. In itself, toil, or hard labor, is an evil, from which nature shrinks. But in our idle, wicked world, it is a blessing, constituting one of the great regulators of society, a balance-wheel that controls this earth, and makes it, in its wickedness, decent and tolerable.

So sickness and pain, misfortune and evil, in ten thousand forms, with death and the grave, are all a part of the same great economy, and working to the same gracious end. All experience tells us that uninterrupted prosperity—even such prosperity as we may know under this constitution of things—will not answer for this world, either for individuals or nations. They grow proud, haughty, and overbearing under its influence, forgetful of God and all His ordinances. It is hard even for the righteous to withstand the corrupting power of prosperity. But the wicked are carried away with it. Affliction, evil, and sorrow, therefore, are necessary to this present state of things. *The curse is a blessing;* which can never be said of the penalty of the law executed upon the transgressor. That, to him, is a curse indeed, an unmitigated evil. Mark also the bearings of the sentence pronounced upon the woman. It is pain and sorrow indeed; but what a protection to woman, to the household, and to the virtue of the world, has that curse upon her been, even as a wall of fire around, to guard her in the midst of this adulterous and wicked world!

To carry on a scheme of mercy, then, toward sinners, to lead them to repentance, and leave iniquity, for the time being, to go unpunished, God knew well that this must be made a world of sorrow, trial, and bitter disappointment, where there should be no blissful paradise, no continued abiding-place. It must be a world scathed by the lightnings of heaven, rocked by the earthquake, desolated by fire and tempest and sword; while death must stalk abroad in grim form, to fill every soul with trembling, and remind the race that their time was short, their days appointed.

Under these mighty agencies God might hold sin in check sufficiently, and keep it within such bounds that His government would be acknowledged, and the world stand in fear of Him, while He might still deal in tender forbearance with men, to lead them to repentance.

III. *The distribution of these evils shows clearly that their relations are not to law and justice, but to grace.*

This is a consideration of great moment, and is sufficient in itself to decide the point. It is the one fact by which, outside of revelation, we prove that this is a world of mercy and of hope for sinners.

There is but one rule for administering evil as the penalty of crime, and that is justice, or the desert of the transgressor; and if the government undertakes thus to execute law by the infliction of the penalty, *the law must be adhered to strictly, and no departure from justice allowed.*

But there is no fact more perfectly established throughout the entire history of earth, than that men are not dealt with here according to their deserts. Justice plainly is not the rule of the Divine administration in human affairs. This is the positive teaching of the Scriptures. "Thou hast not dealt with us after our sins, nor rewarded us according to our iniquities." As men also have failed to comprehend the plan of God's economy of grace, it has always been among the mysteries of His ways to account for His seemingly strange dealings with them. The wicked are not punished here; the righteous do not receive their reward. We sometimes stand in amazement as we behold the prosperity and triumph of the ungodly, and are ready to ask, Where is the Lord, that He doth not see and regard it? Jeremiah asked of old, "Wherefore doth the way of the wicked prosper? Wherefore are all they happy, that deal very treacherously?" The Psalmist exclaims, "Lord, how long shall the wicked, how long shall the wicked triumph? How long shall they utter and speak hard things, and all the workers of iniquity boast themselves? They break in pieces thy people, O Lord, and afflict thine heritage. They slay the widow and stranger, and murder the fatherless. Yet they say, The Lord shall not see, neither shall the God of Jacob regard it." The wicked thus boast of the fact that God makes no account of their crimes; while the righteous look on, and wonder why He holds back the thunders of His hand. In another place, again, the Psalmist describes the deep perplexity of a good man, as he contemplates this seeming inequality in the Divine administration. "But as for me, my feet were almost gone: my steps had well-nigh slipped." He had well-nigh lost confidence in the wisdom and justice of God's government, and then gives the reason why. "For I was envious at the foolish, when I saw the prosperity of the wicked; for there are no bands in their death." Mark the fact. Their prosperity continues down to the end of their days on earth. "There are no bands in their *death;* but their strength is firm. They are not in trouble as other men; neither are they plagued like other men. Therefore pride compasseth them about as a chain; violence covereth them as a garment. Their eyes stand out with fatness; they have more than heart can wish. They are corrupt, and speak wickedly concerning oppression; they speak loftily. They set their mouth against the heavens, and their tongue walketh through the earth. Therefore his people return hither, and waters of a full cup are wrung out to them. And they say, How doth God know? And is there knowledge in the Most High? Behold, these are *the ungodly which prosper in the world:* they increase in riches. Verily I have cleansed my heart in vain, and washed my hands in innocency." That is, it is all in vain to be good. There is no reward for it. God does not regard it. "For all the day long have I been plagued, and chastened every morning. When I sought to know this, it was too painful for me." It was fearful to contemplate this picture of God's seeming injustice. I was well-nigh overwhelmed. "Until I went into the sanctuary of God." In other words, when I came to see that the Divine plan was a remedial one of grace, and not the execution of law, "Then understood I their end. Surely thou didst set them in slippery places; thou castedst them down into destruction. How are they brought into desolation as in a moment. They are utterly consumed with terrors." This desolation of the wicked, the Psalmist saw by faith in the sanctuary of God. It was not what his eyes beheld through the medium of this world; else he had seen it at first, and had no perplexity or trouble respecting the matter.

This sublime passage tells the whole story. In the sanctuary of God—that is, within the system of redemption—we find an explanation perfectly satisfactory of His ways and dealings, because there is revealed the plan of grace, and not of law. But the moment we measure the Divine administration according to the rules of justice and the execution of penalty, we are involved in endless confusion. The wicked, on the one hand, will boast that God does not know or regard their crimes, while the suffering righteous will look on in wonder and grief, crying, O Lord, how long? how long? when wilt thou arise to judgment? Hast thou utterly forgotten and forsaken us?

The difficulties which men have always had in judging of God's ways on earth, have arisen from the fact that they have measured them by a legal standard. They have conceived that God was executing His law here, when he was but administering a system of grace, which allowed Him to distribute good and evil according to His own pleasure, as he saw would best subserve the ends of that economy of redemption. The execution of the law was suspended, that he might deal with the transgressor in long-suffering patience; allowing him to enjoy uninterrupted prosperity, if need be; while, on the other hand, He might lay affliction and suffering upon the righteous.

Who, moreover, now estimates human character by the Divine dealings? This was, in former days, the ground of judgment. Job was thus judged, and condemned as a great sinner. The disciples thus judged the blind man, though they were at a loss to know whether the iniquity was his, or his parents, as the calamity had been from birth. The doctrine of former days was, that the poor suffering wretch must be a great sinner, who brought upon himself the just punishment of his crimes, while the rich and prosperous were the favorites of Heaven. But who now judges thus? And why not? Simply because this is not a world of retribution—because God does not give the slightest indication of His estimate of men by His distribution of good and evil toward them. A poor, suffering Lazarus at the gate, licked by the dogs, and fed upon the crumbs, may be among His most cherished ones, guarded by the angels; while the man upon whom he has lavished His richest stores of earthly good, may soon lift up his eyes in hell, begging in vain for a drop of water.

This great principle applies also to death, as well as to all other evils connected with this life. Death, as we now witness it, belongs to the system of grace, and not to law. It does not come as the execution of penalty, but is part of this new economy of redemption. It cannot be told, by the event of death, whether a man is a child of God, or an heir of perdition. The doctrine of the Bible is, "All things come alike to all: there is one event to the righteous and to the wicked: to the good, and to the clean, and to the unclean: to him that sacrificeth, and to him that sacrificeth not: as is the good, so is the sinner; and he that sweareth, as he that feareth an oath; Eccl. ix. 2. There is no distinction, at this point, made between the righteous and the wicked, the humble believer and the bold blasphemer. They go down alike into the grave, and the worms cover them. Nor can the wisest tell by any of these things what is their character or destiny, or the Divine estimate respecting them. God will hereafter manifest forth His sons, putting upon them the seal of His everlasting approval, so that they can no more be denied. But He does not undertake to do this now. It would, however, be an anomaly in any human government to attempt dealing with offenders and rebels by meting out justice to them, and yet the result not show which were regarded as rebels, and which as loyal subjects. It is absurd to suppose that God arises to execute His law upon the guilty transgressor, and yet that none can tell in the very transaction whether he is pardoning and saving an offender, or delivering him over to death. Such folly cannot be laid to God's account.

If we measure the Divine administration over this world simply by a legal standard, it must inevitably be condemned as weak, partial, and unjust. High-handed wickedness escapes, while innocence, truth, and piety are trodden down as the dunghill. The wisdom and justice of God's administration can be sustained only on the ground that this is a remedial system, where He is at liberty to deal with men, not according to the claims of law and justice, but as will subserve the high ends of the plan of redemption. And if we concede that this is a gracious and remedial system, it is a contradiction to assert that it is maintained by the execution of the penalty of the law. It may be sustained by evil, but not by evil in its relation of penalty. Evil belongs both to a gracious and a legal economy, and is essential to both. But it is a palpable contradiction to maintain that God administers a gracious system in the pardon and salvation of offenders, by putting the law in force, and dealing with them according to the requirements of justice. In no system outside of theology would such folly ever have been conceived.

CHAPTER VIII.

A REMEDIAL SYSTEM—CONTINUED.

The introduction of a remedial system demands still further consideration, and we allege in evidence that the evils of life stand related to such a system, and not to the law,

IV. *The Atonement of Christ.*

We claim as the facts of the case, that, when sin entered, God did not attempt to enforce the penalty of the law, but suspended its execution. How, then, did He maintain the authority of that law and the integrity of His government? What prevented them from being utterly dishonored before the universe? The obedience and death of Christ were designed to answer this very purpose, constituting a basis for the forgiveness of sin and justification of the transgressor. By that death the authority of the law was fully vindicated, and God was at liberty to offer a free salvation to every believing sinner. Upon this foundation the remedial system was introduced. This was the import of the promise made, that the seed of the woman should bruise the serpent's head. Upon that pledge the execution of the law was set aside for the present, and a system of grace introduced, under which God was at liberty to distribute good and evil, not according to the demands of justice, but as He, in His wisdom saw would best subserve the great ends of His new economy. Under this dispensation, then, it is not necessary for God to inflict evil as punishment, with a view to uphold the authority of His law and maintain the justice of His administration. This He has done by the death of His son. There He has magnified the law, and made it honorable forever, so that He can be just in justifying every one that believeth. The sinner who accepts that work of Christ, and relies upon it for his justification, is freely forgiven. This righteousness of Christ is complete. There is no deficiency in it, to be supplied by the sinner in his tears, or groans, or prayers, or by any thing he may suffer in this world. His justification is complete, while the same free pardon is offered to all.

It would now be a reversal and contradiction of all this, to suppose that God proceeded to inflict the penalty of the law upon this pardoned, justified sinner. Yet what means the fact, that this believer is still subject, as before, to all the evils of life—to pain and sickness, to toil, bereavement, and death? Plainly, these are not penalty. They do not come as the execution of law, and the believer never regards them in this light. He does not look upon them as any evidence of his condemnation, but as part of the scheme of his redemption, belonging to grace, and not to law. These trials are necessary to his discipline, to the development of his faith, his preparation for glory. They all have this one end in view, and so he regards them, counting it his joy that he may suffer with Christ, falling into divers temptations; knowing that these light afflictions, which are but for a moment, shall work out a far more exceeding and eternal weight of glory.

These evils, however, have the same relation to the world at large that they have to the believer. They may not, indeed, have the same beneficent results. But this does not affect in the least their design and relations; and these fix their character. God is laboring to one grand end in this world—its redemption. All His dealings bear upon this point; every thing is made subsidiary to this. The severest Divine judgments are only for the protection and maintenance of this plan of grace. To this end death and the sepulchre are indispensable. So were the deluge, and the storm of fire and brimstone upon Sodom. So are famine and pestilence, fire and sword. These are among God's mightiest remedial agencies, by which He keeps sin in check, and teaches the nations that He still holds the reins of government, though He may long forbear, and permit iniquity to go unpunished. God is at liberty to bear long with the wickedness and rebellion of men, and offer a free pardon to all, because it is backed up by a sin-offering, or ransom, which fully sustains the authority and integrity of the law. The Divine government is not injured by this long delay, nor by the pardon of the worst transgressor. The sinner repenting at threescore and ten has not already suffered a part of the penalty of his iniquities, being for the balance indebted to Christ. He is not like one, sentenced for life to the penitentiary, and pardoned at the expiration of twenty years, his pardon coming in to arrest the further execution of the law, and mitigate its severity. The sinner who believes in Jesus, never regards himself as indebted merely for a mitigation of his punishment. It is a full salvation which he receives, and that because the execution of the penalty of the law has not yet begun.

V. *Another fact proving that the evils of life are not properly penal, is, that the present is a scene of probation for the race.*

There are two kinds of probation for mortal beings—one under law, the other under grace: one as holy beings, with the offer of life; the other as sinners, with the offer of pardon and redemption. Sin ends the first, and eternal life, or the execution of the law, fulfils the second. When a being has sinned, he cannot be tried under law any longer. If he has any further probation, it must be under grace: and if the lawgiver proceeds to execute the sentence of the law, it is simply deciding that there is to be no further trial. The law is to take its course, and the offender is delivered over to just punishment. There is the end of the matter. If our race, then, was put upon a new trial or probation under grace, it was of necessity because the law was not executed. An opportunity was to be offered under a remedial system for regaining the life which had been lost by transgression, and escaping the threatened death. To do this *by the execution of the law* is a contradicton and absurdity. The second trial of a moral being as a sinner to regain his lost liberty and life, is not delivering him to the curse of the law.

Here we may take the opportunity of remarking—though not bearing so directly upon the present, as upon a previous discussion—that this trial of our humanity under grace is more favorable than a strictly legal one. Men object to the present Divine method, as hard and unjust, because we begin our career as depraved beings, with a fallen nature through the sin of our first father. But it should not be forgotten that man is having his favored probation now under a remedial system, where a single failure does not result in inevitable death and ruin, as under a legal one; but where there is, as the Apostle argues in Rom. v., "justification *from many offences.*" Under a legal economy, a single trangression at any point, a yielding to temptation in a single instance, shuts at once the door of hope, and brings swiftly the day of retribution. This is the universal operation of law. If a man commits forgery or murder, though it be but once, yet that seals his doom. He is delivered over to prison or death, no matter what his life previously may have been. The higher his position, and the more exemplary his character, the more certain only will be his punishment, if there be integrity in the government.

Under a system of grace for the recovery of life, this is not so. Here Divine forbearance may be exercised. There may be long-continued and heaven-daring iniquity. Yet the mercy of God may reach to the gates of hell to deliver. The most abandoned and hardened in sin may be restored. Through long years God may employ His varied and multiplied instrumentalities to bring to repentance. If one fails, another may be employed; if one opportunity for entering into life is lost, another may still be enjoyed. Such a probation for sinners under a remedial system has great and numerous advantages, and is perhaps to be preferred to a legal trial of holy beings, where inevitable death follows a single failure. While, to silence forever every objection on our part, God has given our humanity the benefit of both. He tried it first under law, and, on its failing there, He is now giving it a second probation under grace, for the recovery of life, and deliverance from death.

VI. *Our doctrine harmonizes perfectly with the promise of Scripture, that these evils shall ere long be abolished under our Immanuel.*

The ground we have taken, is, that these evils are part of a great remedial system, which has in view the redemption of earth. Instead of executing the law against our first parents, dooming them to His everlasting displeasure, God promised a Deliverer who should triumph over all their enemies, and effect their restoration. Until that day of redemption could be brought in, our earth and race were placed in subjection to certain necessary evils, so that sin might be held in check sufficiently, while the remedial work was carried forward.

There is no theme of prophecy now which is so rich and full as that coming era of the restoration of all things, "which God hath spoken by the mouth of his holy prophets since the world began." It is, beyond all others, the one theme upon which the pen of prophecy kindles. Christ speaks of it as the times of "the regeneration." John describes it as old things passing away and all things becoming new. Isaiah represents it as fulfilling all the fondest hopes—the lion and the lamb lying down together, the child playing upon the hole of the asp—the desert blooming like paradise, death abolished, the curse removed. Paul assures us that this groaning creation is waiting with earnest expectation for that day of "the manifestation of the sons of God," when it shall be delivered from the bondage of corruption. There is such a day of blessedness coming to earth. All the prophets have spoken of it from the beginning.

We can easily understand how such an era may be witnessed on earth, if the curse now resting upon it belongs to this economy of grace; while there is some difficulty in receiving it, if the same belongs to a legal dispensation, and is the execution of the penalty of the law. We can readily see how the sentence of death should have been set aside in the case of such saints as Enoch and Elijah, so that they were translated immediately to glory, if death is part of the economy of redemption, designed to subserve its purposes, and having nothing to do with the law. We can understand, also, how the time may come under our blessed Immanuel, when such translations to glory may become the ordinary mode of the Divine procedure, death itself, the last enemy, being put under the feet of our mighty Redeemer. But if death and sickness, pain and toil, come as the execution of law, we do not see so readily the mode in which they are to be disposed of. May not here, also, be found one of the reasons why Christians have so little faith in that final restoration of all things, of which the scriptures are so full? Their understanding of the matter is, that when sin entered, God proceeded at once to execute the threatening of death, according to His word; and as they conceive He was under the necessity of doing, in order to be true to himself. Therefore they have come to look upon this present arrangement of things not as temporary, but as necessary and unalterable; an essential change of which would involve the very truth of God, and the principles of His government.

When, however, the true relations of all these evils are understood as belonging strictly to the remedial system, and designed to subserve its great ends, we can then see how Christ may bring about the restoration of all things, making new heavens and a new earth, wherein dwelleth righteousness. This view of the subject produces harmony throughout the entire system of the Divine administration, reconciles the difficulties of God's otherwise strange proceedings here, and leaves Him at liberty to distribute good and evil as He sees will subserve best the high ends of His economy of redemption, prospering the wicked and afflicting the righteous. Then in the coming future, when Christ shall have brought the nations into subjection to himself, and cast out Satan, it leaves Him at perfect liberty to make all things new, filling this earth with joy and singing, instead of groans and tears, turning its deserts and howling wastes into blooming gardens, abolishing death itself, if He sees fit, and causing this long-travailing earth to enter into the liberty of the sons of God.

VII. *This view harmonizes with the scriptural doctrine, that the law will be left to resume its course to all such as fail of the grace of God.*

We do not stop here to prove that this is the doctrine

of revelation. We assume it for the present. But it will be seen how perfectly our view harmonizes with such a doctrine of future retribution. We claim the facts to be, that God at the outset suspended the execution of the law, to introduce a remedial scheme, so that we are not now under law, but under grace. Our humanity is having its probation under this new and more favorable economy. That penalty of the law, however, against sin, suffers no abatement of its force. It loses nothing. If this probation fails to any, there remains then, as the Apostle declares, "no more sacrifice for sin, but a certain fearful looking for of judgment and fiery indignation, which shall devour the adversaries. He that despised Moses' law, died without mercy under two or three witnesses. Of how much sorer punishment shall he be thought worthy, who hath trodden under foot the Son of God, and hath counted the blood of the covenant wherewith he was sanctified an unholy thing, and hath done despite unto the spirit of grace!" If the very basis upon which this remedial system is founded is rejected, and trampled under foot, what remains, then, but that fearful judgment and fiery indignation spoken of?

There is a doctrine held by some, that there is no escape from the just punishment of sin—that God cannot, by any ransom or atonement, release the transgressor from the penalty of the law, which must be inflicted here or hereafter. Yet these persons claim to believe that God is most merciful and gracious, pardoning and saving the sinner. In other words, a legal system, in which exact justice is meted out to every transgressor, is a gracious one. To execute an offender, is to pardon him, and show mercy. And a sinner is saved and justified when he is condemned, and suffers the wrath of God to the uttermost. This is a system of contradictions and confusion of ideas, by which it is wonderful that men can be deluded. We need not go to the Bible to disprove such a system, but to the dictionary. If a man does not know the difference between executing justice under law upon a criminal, and showing mercy, the Bible will not help him out. He needs to begin his education anew, and learn the proper use of language. The Bible presupposes that knowledge in every one that reads it. It assumes that men have common sense. If, therefore, a man cannot see any difference between justification and condemnation, between mercy and justice, between pardon and the execution of law, there is no help for him. The Bible certainly will not throw any light upon his path.

We here take leave of this important subject, commending it, as one of deepest interest, to the study of all who would understand the ways of God to man on earth, and assured that it is the key to the system of redemption, opening a large portion of its treasures.

CHAPTER IX.

THE GODHEAD REVEALED.

From the point of creation, we have passed in our investigation down to the introduction of a remedial system for human recovery—the system which embraces the existing plan of Divine providence toward our world.

We pause here for the present, and go back in the history, to take up

The Revelation of the Godhead.

We considered first the creation, because prior *in our knowledge* to God, though not in the order of time or nature; and also because it was the medium through which the Godhead was revealed. This branch of the subject was pursued down to the point where the economy of grace was introduced, upon the basis of which the affairs of earth have been conducted. It is now necessary to study the revelation of the Godhead, which constitutes the substance of all theology, and covers all the Divine economies.

In entering upon this branch of the subject we call especial attention to the plan we are aiming to follow in the development of Divine truth, the peculiar advantage of which will strikingly appear at this stage of our inquiries, and in reference to the present subject.

The ordinary method in our systems of theology is, to begin with the Divine existence as an abstract truth, passing on next to the Divine attributes, showing that God is an infinite, eternal, unchangeable Being, the Maker and Sovereign Ruler over all.

This conception of God now is evidently the most abstract and difficult for the human mind to grasp—the last one which it has reached after long and laborious training. It is that conception to which we have attained, after having the advantage of all the light of Divine revelation going before, and which we find most difficult to bring within the comprehension of our children. It is, in fact, the last and highest conception of theology; and yet at this very point our ordinary systems begin their instruction, from which they pass to the Divine nature and personality as involved in the doctrine of the Trinity, taking up the teachings of the New Testament and the history of Jesus Christ.

This is beginning where God ended with his revelations. We plunge at once into the midst of the most difficult and abstruse parts of the whole science, which God has reached only after ages of careful instruction; and the almost inevitable result is, that we become involved in difficulty, and perhaps change the relations of the whole subject. What would Adam and the first generations have done, if they had been under the necessity of beginning with the Man of Nazareth in order to understand the system of redemption and the Godhead? Revelation certainly did not commence at this point. God did not begin here to unfold himself. He did not intend that we should learn of Him after any such plan; for He has given us another and more simple method, which, if we had been wise to follow, we should have avoided many serious difficulties and errors.

What, then, is the Divine method of revealing the Godhead?

I. *God was first revealed as the Creator of all things.*

Some may perhaps have wondered why the Bible opens with such a minute account of the creation as is contained in Genesis. Such a history might belong to a treatise on geology, astronomy, or natural history. Why it formed part of a revelation from heaven to mankind, is not entirely clear to their apprehension.

The truth, however, is that this account of the creation is most eminently religious in its character and design, conveying the clearest conceptions of an Almighty and Sovereign Deity which it was then possible to convey to the race. It is a most sublime, comprehensive revelation of God, and in a form so simple as to be easily understood.

What have been the conceptions of God which the human mind has always been prone to form, and to which it has tenaciously clung? Is it not, to make deities out of all created objects—the sun and moon, stars and planets—out of men themselves, four-footed beasts and crawling reptiles—out of fire and water, air and sea, and every created thing? Such are the gods which men have always chosen unto themselves, and to which they have bowed down in worship.

What, now, does Jehovah to make himself known?

How shall He give the first and clearest conception of His own nature? He takes up this entire system of creation from beginning to end, and declares that He made it all. He carries us far back to that point when there was no earth, air, or sea, no sun, moon, or stars; when there was no shape or form, and darkness profound rested upon the mighty void. Then He was there, and His Spirit hovered over the face of all that deep.

There is the grand conception of God's eternity, taught not as an abstract truth, but in a tangible, living form, such as the mind can grasp. God was in the beginning, before all things. How far have we progressed with God's eternity beyond that? Yet this conception of Jehovah is simply and beautifully presented by carrying us back in the history of creation to the far distant point when nothing had been done, and telling us that God was there, and that His hand began the work.

Then follows the history of His divine working through the ages. He spake, and the darkness fled before the dawning light. At His commanding word the waters began to separate, and this glorious firmament of heaven was stretched out. Then He called for the earth, and it rose out of the deep, while the waters were gathered to their appointed place. Again God uttered the commanding word, and the earth brought forth every herb and tree. He spake again, and those great lights appeared in heaven to rule the day and night. Yet again, and the waters swarmed with living creatures, and the air with all flying fowl. He spake again, and four-footed beasts of every name walked upon the dry ground. And, last of all, man appeared, to show the brightest image of his Maker.

What, now, is the sublime lesson taught in this thrilling history—taught so clearly, so impressively? It is, that none of these created objects in the heavens above, or the earth beneath, or in the waters under the earth, can be God, but are all the *work* of God. He was before all, and the Maker of all. That fact tells us more of God, and in more simple language, which a child may comprehend, than a volume of abstract statement and argument respecting the infinitude and perfections of the Divine nature. What more can be stated respecting the omnipotence, the omniscience, the omnipresence, the wisdom and goodness of God, than is contained in this vast, this boundless work of creation? That first chapter of Genesis is the truest, the most sublime revelation of God that was ever recorded. It stands forever a living rebuke and protest against all idolatry. It declares man to be the head and crown of all this creation, with none above him but his more glorious Creator, to whom alone he is to bow in homage and worship.

In no equal space, therefore, could more truths be told of God—of His being, His nature, His character, His attributes, and His relations to us, than is contained in that magnificent page of Divine revelation. In no other system can such a chapter be found on the character of its God, as Christianity presents to us at the opening of the sacred Scriptures.

The fact that the record of this history of creation was made by Moses long centuries after, does not conflict with the idea that the same revelation was first given to Adam. We have no question that it was, and it is even possible that a record of it might have been made by Adam, which came down to Moses.

II. *Jehovah revealed himself in some visible, positive manner, to our first parents.*

We enter here upon a point of absorbing interest in our Christianity, to which we invite special attention.

The facts of the history show that God revealed himself to the senses, and in a very familiar manner to our first parents, so that He was in very deed a God at hand, and not afar off. Neither are we to regard this as more strange or startling than that other familiar fact of revelation, that in the new Jerusalem, or Paradise restored, we shall see Him as He is, face to face, and behold the fulness of the Divine glories. This shall be the joy of heaven. This was the bliss of paradise. This is the normal condition of things as respects our race, which sin has obstructed, and for the present rendered abnormal.

It is plain from the narrative that there was the freest intercourse between God and our first parents, and that His manifested glory was entirely familiar to them. He spake to them, and freely communicated His will on every necessary subject. "God blessed them, and said unto them, Be fruitful and multiply, and replenish the earth, and subdue it: and have dominion over the fish of the sea, and over the fowl of the air, and over every living thing that moveth upon the earth. And God said, Behold, I have given you every herb bearing seed, which is upon the face of all the earth, and every tree in the which is the fruit of a tree yielding seed. To you it shall be for meat." There is no reason to doubt that God did literally speak these words to our first parents, as He spake afterwards to Noah and Abraham, to Moses, and from Mount Sinai to the nation of Israel. Again, it is stated that "the Lord took the man, and put him into the garden of Eden to dress it and to keep it. And the Lord God commanded the man, saying, Of every tree of the garden thou mayest freely eat, but of the tree of the knowledge of good and evil thou shalt not eat of it: for in the day that thou eatest thereof thou shalt surely die." This certainly came as a direct command or revelation from God. It was no discovery of reason or dictate of common sense. Neither did it come by dream or vision of the night; for nothing is said to this effect, as is the case when God did reveal His will afterward in such modes. We are left to the natural interpretation of the narrative, which is, that God really spake these words.

All this is made still more clear by the subsequent account given in connection with their disobedience, when "they *heard the voice* of the Lord God walking in the garden in the cool of the day: and Adam and his wife hid themselves from *the presence* (literally, the face) of the Lord God amongst the trees of the garden. And the Lord God *called unto Adam, and said unto him*, Where art thou? And he said, I heard thy voice in the garden, and I was afraid, because I was naked; and I hid myself. And he said, Who told thee that thou wast naked? Hast thou eaten of the tree whereof I commanded thee that thou shouldst not eat?" And so on to the end of the remarkable interview, the woman and man vainly endeavoring to excuse themselves, while God made to them the unexpected promise of a Redeemer, and revealed a new economy of grace, with its varied features of trial and suffering.

The facts here stated respecting the manifestation of the Divine presence in some form are clear and decisive, which we have been wont to overlook, simply because they are unfamiliar to us, and beyond the range of our present experience. The facts are not to be explained upon any supposition of mere mental impressions. Adam and his wife felt the sense of guilt and shame immediately upon their transgression. Their eyes were opened at once, and they saw that they were naked. But they made no attempt to flee from the presence of God, which, as a mere invisible presence, was as near to them then as afterwards. They were concerned at first only in hiding their nakedness from each other by the covering of fig-leaves. It was not till the cool of the day that they fled to the covert of the trees, and then because "they heard the voice of the Lord God," approaching as He was wont, and they "hid themselves from the presence of the Lord God"—which means a visible appearance. "The presence of the Lord" is a common expression in the Scriptures, to denote that visible manifestation of Jehovah which was so familiar afterwards under the economy of redemption. Cain fled "from the presence of the Lord" into the land of Nod. Moses speaks of this manifested glory of the Lord under the same designation. Exod. xxxiii. 14, 15: "And he said, My presence shall go with thee, and I will give thee rest. And he said unto him, If thy presence go not with me, carry us not up hence." That "presence" was the angel, or the glory of the Lord in the pillar of cloud, leading the host. In the same way, "the presence of the Lord" is represented as entering the garden of Eden in the cool of the day (designating a particular hour), from which Adam and his wife immediately fled, though in vain; for they were called from their covert to appear before that offended Divine majesty, and hear their sentence from His lips.

But the evidence on this subject does not end here. We have demonstration of the view thus set forth in the events immediately following, and repeated from age to age.

III. *To these facts of a visible Divine manifestation under the economy of redemption, we now call attention.*

Immediately after the interview above referred to with our first parents, in which they were informed of God's gracious designs, they were driven out of Paradise, a place no longer fitted for them, as sinners, to begin their work of toil, and earn their bread in the sweat of their face; while "cherubim and a flaming sword" were placed to keep the way of the tree of life. This statement is proof that Paradise, and the tree of life in the midst, were preserved after the fall—an important fact, which we shall make use of in connection with another subject. The particular point now before us is, that appearance described as "a flaming sword," meaning a fire or flame in the shape of a sword, the position of which was, not in the hands of the cherubim—for nothing is said to that effect—but between them, no doubt, as afterwards the glory of the Lord, or Shekinah, had its dwelling-place in the tabernacle over the mercy-seat. That glory of the Lord was the manifested presence of the living God of Israel, who is familiarly described as, "Thou that dwellest between the cherubim;" Ps. lxxx. 1. The flaming sword was the same Divine manifestation before the way of the tree of life; for the dwelling-place between the cherubim belongs to our revealed Jehovah, and to none else. The Scriptures make this the place of His abode, which became permanent before the tree of life after the expulsion from Eden, as subsequently over the mercy-seat in the tabernacle. The form of the flaming sword was then doubtless first assumed, though what it had been before in Paradise we are not informed.

Our first parents were no longer to hold familiar intercourse with God, as before in their innocence. Yet His presence was not to be withdrawn from earth. He took up His abode within the precincts of Paradise before the way of the tree of life; and here the sanctuary of Jehovah was first established under the new economy of redemption. Here was the appointed place for worship and sacrifice, and the communication of the Divine will. Here God accepted the offering of Abel, touching and consuming it with His fire, while He rejected the offering of Cain; and from this manifested Divine presence Cain fled into the land of Nod, where, as he says, "from thy face shall I be hid." From the invisible presence of God, Cain was no more hid in the land of Nod, than in that of Eden; but from His visible Divine glory he was separated.

As bearing upon this subject of the Divine intercourse with man, note also the interviews between God and Cain after the murder of Abel—how inquiry was made for the absent brother—the denial of all knowledge on the part of Cain—the accusation and conviction of the murderer—the sentence pronounced upon him, and his own plea for a mitigation of his punishment. All this shows clearly that there was an immediate Divine and personal communication with men, such as is not known in our day. Cain manifested no surprise or alarm at the question put to him by God, as if it was any thing extraordinary, while it seemed altogether natural to him to make reply. There must, then, have been a visible manifestation of Jehovah on earth at that day, as familiar to men, as the Bible is to us.

The fact of the continued existence of this Divine glory with the attending cherubim at the time that Cain made his offering, which must have been at least one hundred and twenty-five years after the creation, Seth being born when Adam was one hundred and thirty, is of moment; inasmuch as, continuing to that point, there is no reason to suppose but that it remained to a much later period. Nor shall we find any cause sufficient for its removal until the event of the Deluge. This point, however, will come up in connection with another subject.

Let us pass forward a little further in the history of the world, to note these Divine manifestations.

Not long subsequent to the deluge, God began again to reveal himself to the race, appearing repeatedly to Abraham, Isaac, and Jacob, not in dreams and visions of the night, but in visible glory, so that they beheld His presence, and heard His voice. Thus we read: "And when Abram was ninety years old and nine, the

Lord *appeared* unto Abram, and said unto him, *I am the Almighty God;* walk before me, and be thou perfect. . . . And I will establish my covenant between me and thee, and thy seed after thee, in their generations, for an everlasting covenant: to be a God unto thee, and to thy seed after thee;" Gen. xvii. 1. "And the Lord appeared unto him in the plains of Mamre: and he sat in the tent-door in the heat of the day;" Gen. xviii. 1. Here we have minute particulars stated of time, place, and circumstances. Then follows a narrative of the entertainment given by Abram—of the promise of an heir, and the approaching doom of Sodom, with his earnest intercesions in its behalf. It is not necessary to enumerate all these interviews between God and His servant Abraham, which also were repeated to Isaac and Jacob. The fact of such visible manifestations is beyond controversy. Stephen so states it in his remarkable address before the Council, when he says, "Men, brethren, and fathers, hearken. The *God of glory appeared* to our father Abraham when he was in Mesopotamia, and said unto him, Get thee out of thy country, and from thy kindred," &c.; Acts. vii. 2. Jehovah is here described as the God of glory, because He appeared in this form, revealed to human sight.

This fact becomes still more clear as we come down to the time of Moses, and behold that same glory of the Lord in the bush at Horeb, to which Moses drew near, that he might see "*the great sight*," and then heard out of the midst thereof the significant words, "Draw not nigh hither: put off thy shoes from off thy feet" (the common method in those days of expressing respect when entering the presence of a superior), "for the place whereon thou standest is holy ground." Moreover, he said, "I am the God of thy father, the God of Abraham, the God of Isaac, and the God of Jacob. And Moses hid his face, for he was afraid *to look upon God.*" Here Moses received his commission to go to Pharaoh to accomplish the deliverance of Israel; and when he asked in whose name and by whose authority he should go before the people, to lead them out, "God said unto him, I AM THAT I AM. And he said, Thus shalt thou say unto the children of Israel, I AM hath sent me unto you. . . . This is my name forever, and this is my memorial unto all generations." Here, then, is the clear revelation of Jehovah himself, and the emphatic statement, "Go and gather the elders of Israel together, and say unto them, The Lord God of your fathers, the God of Abraham, of Isaac, and of Jacob, *appeared* unto me, saying," &c.; Exod. iii. 16.

When, moreover, the hour of deliverance came, and the hosts of Israel were ready to go forth, that Mighty One of Jacob appeared to put himself at the head of their armies, enveloping His glory in a pillar of cloud, and so leading them out. The Divine presence was visible now to all the camp, their guide through the wilderness, their sure defense.

From this point of time the presence of the God of Israel becomes a living, glorious, abiding fact through their history. Arriving at Sinai, He abode upon the Mount in the sight of Israel, whither Moses went up to Him to receive His law, and whence also He spake it in the hearing of all that vast congregation. What a fact of terrible sublimity! From the summit of a high mountain down to its base, no human voice can make itself heard. Yet, from those awful crags of Sinai, God thundered forth the words of His law even to the utmost bounds of the camp, which embraced three millions of people, so that every ear distinctly heard, and every soul trembled, entreating that the word might not be spoken to them any more. Moses, even, familiar as he was with the Divine presence, declared that the scene was almost more than he could endure.

The next step in this marvellous history was the erection of a tabernacle, where Jehovah might dwell; and when it was completed according to His directions, and consecrated, He descended from the Mount in sight of all the nation, and entered His sanctuary, while the cloud enveloped it without. There He enshrined himself within the Holy of Holies, behind the vail, and between the cherubim over the mercy-seat—the identical place which He occupied in the form of the flaming sword before the way of the tree of life. The relation of the cherubim to Him will hereafter be considered.

Here was a marvellous fact in the history of that nation, in regard to which there could be no mistake. They had no idols, as had other nations, none being allowed. The fundamental doctrine of their system was, "Thou shalt have no other gods before me. Thou shalt not make unto thee any graven image." But they had the living presence of their own Jehovah among them. They beheld His glory. They heard His voice, which they could never forget.

Before this tabernacle, also, was the appointed place of worship and sacrifice for the nation. In the first apartment the priests officiated with the shew-bread, the lights, the incense, and the blood; while into the inner sanctuary none but the high-priest could enter; and he only once a year, and never without the sacred blood of atonement. It was too holy a place for any mortal to stand without the blood which taketh away sin.

Here God revealed His will, as was required from time to time in the exigencies of the nation. With Moses He communed face to face, even as a man speaketh with his friend; while His wrath blazed forth at times in consuming terror, as when the two hundred and fifty princes among the tribes assumed to themselves the right to officiate as priests, even as Aaron and his sons. And the fire came out from the Divine presence, and destroyed them in a moment.

Such are the sublime and unquestionable facts of this great history. And if we would get the full and true impression of the way in which God has revealed himself to our race, we must go back, and put ourselves in the midst of them, to see, as it were, that Divine glory, and hear His voice. We read these facts now only as a history of past events, possibly with no little incredulity, and certainly, for the most part, with very faint impressions of the reality. But to the men of those times there was no mistake or doubt. To them, Jehovah was not an abstraction. He was not merely an unseen, invisible Spirit, pervading the universe, or dwelling in the third heavens. *His tabernacle was on earth*, His dwelling place among men. It was no degradation to Him to make this earth His abode, even under the curse as it was. He abode between the cherubim. He spake from the cloudy pillar, or the bush, or as the God of glory to Abraham. It was the most familiar, well-understood, unquestioned doctrine of the nation of Israel, in which they gloried above all others, that they had their God, the living God, the God of the whole earth, dwelling in very deed among them.

Here, then, is the point where God began the revelations of himself to our race, by a visible manifestation of His own living presence and majesty, upon which men could look, and whose voice they could hear. This fact stands out with the utmost prominence in the whole system of revelation from the beginning; and if we would study and understand God's method of instruction, we must begin at this point in the history, and mark the Divine manifestations as they are brought to view. It will be our wisdom humbly to receive and follow His teachings.

CHAPTER X.

THE GODHEAD REVEALED.

In the preceding chapter on the Godhead, we presented two points: 1. That God made himself known as the Creator of all, and therefore in the beginning before all. This involves His eternity, omnipotence, omniscience, His infinite wisdom and goodness; inasmuch as He, who knew all and could do all things, and had all wisdom and goodness, could so create all. 2. That God revealed himself in a visible form to men, so as to be cognizable by their senses, He speaking familiarly to them; they hearing His voice and beholding His glory.

We do not assert that that flaming sword in Eden, or the glory which appeared to Abraham, or the fire in the bush at Horeb, or the pillar of fire in the cloud, was literally God. They were the *manifestation* of God—that manifestation of His immediate presence, by which He saw fit to make himself known to men, and by which they might recognize Him. It is according to the usual method in which we employ language. When we look upon a man, we behold but the outward manifestation of the real man. We take no cognizance of the indwelling spirit, except through the external medium of the body, of which the face is the chief feature. The eye, the lips, the whole countenance speak, lighted up by the divinity within. We look, first and last, to the face, to see and judge the man. His very soul and character are stamped upon those features; and the fixed gaze which the little child fastens upon the countenance, shows what power is lodged there, and what a medium it is for revealing the spirit within.

God has thus manifested forth His glory, and put on, as it were, a face, through which we might recognize His divine presence, and by which He might speak. The form which He assumed was eminently appropriate, and such as would not be mistaken for any mere created object of earth. The thought might indeed be suggested, if God thus clothes himself in some material form, by which to approach us, and cause us to draw near to Him, why might we not mistake it for something created, belonging to earth? To this it is answered, that the very condition of its existence showed that it was not of earth. Take, for example, that flaming sword before the way of the tree of life. All human experience tells us that fire is dependent for its existence on fuel. A flame exists because there is something to burn; and as soon as the fuel is consumed, the fire goes out. Contrast with this familiar fact that mysterious, ever-living tongue of flame between the cherubim—a self existence, as it were, dependent upon no earthly conditions. Though fed by no fuel, it never went out, never waned. What a living representation of a self-existent, unchangeable Deity! How impossible to confound it with any thing of earth!

Notice, also, the fact, so particularly stated, of that appearance of Jehovah at Horeb. "And the angel of the Lord appeared unto him in a flame of fire out of the midst of the bush. And behold, *the bush burned with fire, and the bush was not consumed.*" There was the mystery of the sight. The bush was not the fuel which fed the flame. It was not dependent upon the bush in any manner for its existence; and when the mysterious fire was gone, there stood the bush, green and flourishing as ever. No wonder that Moses said, "I will now turn aside, and see this great sight, why the bush is not burned." So was it with that mysterious pillar of fire in the cloud, and that insufferable brightness ever dwelling in the inner sanctuary over the mercy-seat. There were no windows in that tabernacle of the Lord for the admission of light from without. It was lighted from within, the lamps being kept continually burning in the holy place, while in the Holy of Holies the glory of the Lord did shine. There was the face of the living God himself, a glory above the brightness of the sun. What an unmistakable representation of the self-existent One, dependent upon no earthly conditions! How impossible to be turned into any form of idolatry!

We proceed, upon the basis of these facts, to construct the Scriptural argument of the Godhead.

I. *The facts show that the visible manifestation of God on earth, and His dwelling among men, are the normal condition of things.*

Those early manifestations of the Divine presence on earth, which we have so little appreciated and understood, are regarded as extraordinary and abnormal, aside from all the ordinary methods of the Divine procedure. We look upon the present as the natural condition of things, where God is no longer manifest; while the thought of His ever again taking up His visible abode among men is strange and incredible to most minds, seeming to contradict all the appointed course of nature and providence.

But is this earth, now under the rule of the Prince of the power of the air, in its normal, natural state? Is this course of things, as we witness it, what God made at the beginning—what He wants it to be—what He intends it shall be? Is not the present condition of the earth, groaning under the curse, unnatural? Is not the whole course of Divine providence abnormal? It cannot be denied by those who admit the facts of revelation concerning the apostasy of our race, and the introduction of a remedial system. Yet from this very abnormal condition of earth, we have, to a large extent, judged of God and His ways both in the past and with reference to the future. From the same point of view our philosophers have reasoned, and built up their intellectual systems, assuming that the human mind was in its normal condition, and overlooking the terrible, yet patent fact, that the soul of man was in ruins, under the dominion of sin. But they have gone on, reasoning as if that fact were of no account, and they could study man as still the perfect work of his Maker. A fallen nature has been made little account of by philosophy. In a similar way theology has been studied to no slight extent, on the assumption that what we now see is the true course of nature. As if the curse of God, under which earth groans and travails, were all natural—as if it were natural for man to be in rebellion against Heaven—or for the bride to be clothed in sackcloth, mourning the absence of her beloved!

No, no! It lies upon the whole face of revelation, from beginning to end, that nature is out of course—that God has withdrawn and hidden His face, concealing His glories behind the dark cloud, so that we may no longer behold them. We thus are compelled to walk as pilgrims and strangers here, looking to the future for our glorious city of habitation, where we shall behold His face, with His full beauties revealed to our ravished vision.

The facts of the past, too, if we will but carefully study them, make this all plain.

What was the normal condition of earth, as we find it drawn by the pen of inspiration itself, and left on record for our instruction?

We have shown how God walked in familiar intercourse with our first parents in Eden, revealing His will, and manifesting to them His glory. This was nothing strange, nothing extraordinary, nothing out of the course of nature. God did thus dwell with men on earth, and, even after the fall, did not withdraw himself, although He was not on the same familiar terms as before. Man had now become a sinner, and, as such, was under condemnation, unfit to stand in the presence of a holy God, or speak unto Him. It was necessary that he should understand this, and be made to feel it. His approach to the Divine presence, therefore, was put under restrictions. He was given to know clearly that God had not forsaken him ; for there was His visible, manifested presence, still before the way of the tree of life, now permanently established as in His own sanctuary, and to be approached only by the appointed sacrifice, until the promised day of redemption should be brought in, when all things should be restored again to their natural order. Man was made to understand that he had been widely separated from God by his sin, yet not without hope ; for there was mercy in store for him, and an appointed way by which still he might come and find favor. God was now to manifest himself under the restrictions of an economy of grace, forbidding a near and familiar approach as before, in his state of innocence ; yet holding out the promise that the blessed time should come when his redemption should be effected, and he should know the full joys of God's blissful presence and salvation.

These, clearly, are the facts of the case as they were understood by our first parents ; and we must endeavor to put ourselves precisely in their position, if we would perfectly understand the teachings of God to them. We must go back, and begin with them this great study of redemption and revelation, taking them up in their first elements. If, moreover, there was any fact that was perfectly clear to our first parents, in regard to which it was impossible for them to entertain a doubt, it was that the visible manifestation of God on earth, and their familiar intercourse with Him, were the natural state of things—their normal constitution. It was simply a matter of experience with them. In the entrance of sin, they saw its dreadful loss, and under what restraint they had thereby come in their approaches to God, although He had not entirely withdrawn or hidden himself from them.

We dwell the more on this point, because men have been so much in the habit of reasoning and looking at these subjects from their present position, conceiving it to be the only natural one; and because it is so difficult to carry themselves back to the point where God began His revelations of truth. If the elements of a science, however, as laid down in the beginning of a treatise, are not true and simple, what is a learner to do?

We shall next consider

II. *The personality of this Divine manifestation. Who was He who thus revealed himself to the race?*

Some may be ready here to ask, What room is there for discussion or argument on this point? The matter is plain, beyond all controversy. He who revealed himself to our first parents in Eden, was God undoubtedly, the Creator of the heavens and the earth, beside whom there was none else. To Abraham He said, "*I am the Almighty God.*" To Moses, "*I am the God of your fathers, the God of Abraham, and the God of Isaac, and the God of Jacob.*" And still further, "I AM THAT I AM. That is my name, and this is my memorial unto all generations." To the nation of Israel, Exod. xx. 2, 3, "I am the Lord thy God, which brought thee out of the land of Egypt, out of the house of bondage. Thou shalt have no other gods before me." This, every one will admit, settles the question beyond dispute. The Maker of all things—the God of Abraham, Isaac, and Jacob—the Jehovah of Israel, who thus manifested himself in glory of old, and gave His law from Sinai, is the true

God, the everlasting God, beside whom there is none other. If there is any thing made clear by revelation, that point is. This is the God whom we worship, in whom we believe forever.

This, then, is *a fixed point*, upon which all are agreed —in regard to which no dispute can be raised. It is clear that God made His revelations of himself thus far plain and simple to the race, so that there could be no misapprehension, no mistake. This, moreover, is the advantage which we have in beginning the study of divine revelation where God himself began. The elements are all simple and perfectly satisfactory. Now let us hold on to that fact forever, settled beyond all dispute, *that He, who revealed himself as the God of Abraham, the Jehovah of Israel, dwelling between the cherubim, is the true and living God—our God forever and ever.* If we cannot hold on to that as an established fact, then we may relinquish the hope of settling any truth by the testimony of Divine revelation.

From this fixed starting-point we are prepared to follow this history of the Divine manifestation, as we find it recorded upon the inspired page for our instruction.

This history of Jehovah, God of Israel, we brought down in our last chapter to the point of building His tabernacle at Sinai, in which He took up His abode behind the vail, above the mercy-seat, there revealing His will, as important national exigencies required. When the temple was built on Mount Zion—a more permanent structure than the tabernacle, which had to be accomodated to the journeyings of Israel in the desert, and was so made that it could be taken down and carried from place to place—and was properly dedicated, the Divine presence moved and entered there in all His majesty. The priests brought in the ark of the covenant, containing the two tables of stone. "And it came to pass, when the priests were come out of the holy place, that the cloud filled the house of the Lord, so that the priests could not stand to minister because of the cloud: for the glory of the Lord had filled the house of the Lord;" 1 Kings viii. 10, 11. This occurred at the moment when one of the most magnificent choirs of instrumental and vocal music ever collected was raising its grand anthems of praise and thanksgiving to the Lord; 2 Chron. v. 13. In that band were one hundred and twenty priests with trumpets, beside a large number with psalteries, harps, and cymbals. It was a scene of grandeur never to be forgotten; and could that nation doubt that they had the very presence of their God among them? What if this had been a parallel scene of idolatry? The poor, helpless idol would have been carried in the arms of the priests with the utmost care and reverence, lest he should receive damage, and placed in the new shrine appointed him. But did the priests of Israel have any thing to do with introducing their God? Nothing, but to flee from before Him. He entered of himself, and, filling the whole temple, the priests could not stand to minister there even in their own appointed place. Jehovah God occupied the whole structure with the insufferable brightness of His own majesty. Not only so, but the fire went out from the glory of the Lord, and touched the burnt-sacrifices which had been prepared, and consumed them. Thus that fire was kindled upon the altar by Jehovah himself, which was never suffered to go out. "And when all the children of Israel saw how the fire came down, and the glory of the Lord upon the house, they bowed themselves upon their faces to the ground upon the pavement, and worshipped, and praised the Lord, saying, He is good, for his mercy endureth forever." This was probably the chorus in which the whole vast multitude united with the choir of singers.

We dwell with more care upon these particulars, in order to show that there can be no possible mistake about the Divine manifestation, and because we are so much inclined to overlook it, as not a fact of present experience. But it is a glorious fact of the past, coming home to men of other times as a matter of their experience.

This Divine manifestation of Jehovah continued in the history of that nation, down to the destruction of Jerusalem and the temple by Nebuchadnezzar, six hundred years before Christ. Then the glory of Israel departed. All the sacred vessels of the sanctuary, with the ark of the covenant, were taken to Babylon. But was the God of Israel taken captive? The people, when they returned from their captivity, brought back with them, through the noble generosity of Cyrus, all the vessels of the Lord's house. But did they bring back with them that Divine glory? Alas! the glory of Israel had departed. They rebuilt their sacred temple; but for five hundred years, while that second building stood, there was no manifestation of the Divine presence dwelling between the cherubim. The temple, the vessels, and the worship, were all alike as of old; but the nation mourned the absence of a tabernacling Jehovah.

Thus we have traced down the undoubted history of this Divine manifestation of the God of Israel to the destruction of Solomon's temple. It is a thoroughly connected history from the creation to this point.

Before proceeding further with this history, let us pause to consider

The names by which the Scriptures, and the nation, were wont to designate this presence of the Lord.

We have necessarily mentioned some of these already in drawing out the history. One was, *the Glory of the Lord*—so named because such was its appearance to the eye of the beholder. It was a dazzling brightness, well described by the name of Glory—the glory of the Lord. It was designated as *the Presence*, or *the face of the Lord;* and again, as *the Angel of the Lord.* Thus it is said, "The Angel of the Lord appeared unto him (Moses) in a flame of fire out of the midst of the bush." "The Angel of the Lord, which went before the camp of Israel, removed and went behind them," in the passage of the Red Sea. Isaiah, speaking of these events, says, "In all their affliction he was afflicted, and the Angel of his presence saved them," and in numerous other places. This is slightly varied sometimes by speaking of Him as *the Angel of the Covenant*, because He made the national covenant with Abraham, and was the Author of the same.

The term Angel here does not mean one of the angelic host, nor has it any reference to them. The Bible uses the word Angel to describe any divine messenger—any *object* or *person* which heralds God's approach. The winds are thus spoken of as His angels, or ministers. So it is applied to this Divine glory. That outward manifestation of glory, that fire in the cloud and bush, that flaming sword, was the medium by which God indicated His immediate presence, and made it evident to sight. That, therefore, was the herald of His approach. It was literally the *Angel* of His *presence*—a most beautiful, exact, and appropriate designation of the whole reality. None could be more so.

Again, the same is described as *the Word of the Lord*, or *the Word* simply, representing it to the sense of hearing. It was not only seen, but heard. It spake. Oh, how did it speak from Sinai, so that the whole camp trembled greatly! Nor on that occasion alone, but often did it reveal the Divine will in audible language. If, then, the eye would describe it as the Glory of the Lord, and the Angel of the Lord, the ear would appropriately represent it under the designation of *the Word of the Lord.* This was its outward manifestation to the sense of hearing, as it was Glory to the sense of sight; and this became one of the most common and familiar designations known to the nation; while the name Jehovah was invested with such superstitious sacredness that it was never pronounced. It was regarded as too holy to take into human lips. How common and familiar the use of the Word of the Lord, as the name of God, became to the nation, is strikingly shown by the Chaldee paraphrases of their Hebrew Scriptures, in use after the Babylonish captivity. By a seventy years' residence in a foreign country, during which two generations were born, the people lost the use of their vernacular Hebrew, and returned to their own land speaking the Chaldee, or Syriac, the language spoken by the Saviour himself. The large mass of them could not therefore understand their own Scriptures when read in their hearing. This appears clearly from a fact stated, that when Ezra, and others, selected for the purpose, read the law in the hearing of the congregation, the returned captives from Babylon, "They read in the book in the law of God distinctly, and *gave the sense and caused them to understand the reading;*" Neh. viii. 3. In other words, they translated or interpreted it, passage by passage. There was necessity, however, for something more permanent than such oral reading and extempore interpretation, and translations of the Scriptures were made into the existing vernacular for the use of the nation. Several of these were made, which are now in existence. In these Chaldee paraphrases the fact is made most strikingly apparent, into what familiar use the term *Word of the Lord* had come as the name of Jehovah, inasmuch as it was largely substituted for it. The following are a few out of many illustrations that might be quoted: Gen. iii. 8,

"And they heard the voice of *the Word of the Lord* walking in the garden;" Gen. xxviii. 20, "And Jacob vowed a vow to *the Word*, saying, If *the Word of the Lord* will be my help," &c.; Gen. xxxv. 9, "And *the Word of the Lord* appeared to Jacob the second time when he was coming from Padan-aram, and blessed him." In our Scriptures the name God, or Lord, or Lord God, is used in all these instances, and hundreds of other similar ones might be added, showing incontestibly how familiar this designation of *the Word* was to the Jewish mind, as the name of their Jehovah, who spake from the cloudy pillar, and from between the cherubim.

It will thus be observed that all these designations are founded on the phenomena attending this Divine manifestation to the human senses. As presented to the eye, it would be spoken of as the Glory of the Lord—the Presence or face of the Lord—the Angel of the Lord—or the Angel of His presence; while, revealed to the sense of hearing, it would be, the Word of the Lord, or simply, the Word.

With this statement of fact concerning names, *let us return to the continuation of the history of this Divine manifestation.*

We broke off at its departure from earth, when Jerusalem and the temple were destroyed by the king of Babylon. Of necessity the glory of that sacred temple, built after the captivity, was not like that of the first. The vessels and furniture might have been the same, and the material structure equal to the former; but there was no living presence of the God of Israel there. *The* glory had departed, but not finally and forever. Hear the thrilling words of Malachi, whose prophecy closes the Old Testament. Mal. iii. 1: "Behold, I will send my messenger, and he shall prepare the way before me; and *the Lord, whom ye seek, shall suddenly come to his tem-*

ple, even the Messenger (Angel) *of the covenant, whom ye delight in. Behold, he shall come*, saith the Lord." The minuteness and definiteness of this prophecy are worthy of note. The person designated is *the Lord*, Jehovah, *whom ye seek*, or desire, *even the Messenger of the covenant, whom ye delight in*, who so long dwelt among you in His tabernacle, whose absence ye have so lamented, whose return ye have so desired, *Behold, he shall come*, saith the Lord of hosts. There the Old Testament history of the God of Israel closes. Its last words contain the promise and assurance of the Lord's coming, as does the New Testament also. Both volumes of inspiration are sealed with the precious words, "Behold, he cometh!"

But how does the New Testament resume the history of the Divine manifestation, which the Old left unfinished? Hear the clear and sublime utterances of the beloved disciple, as he opens his revelation. "In the beginning was *the Word, and the Word was with God, and the Word was God.* The same was in the beginning with God. All things were made by him, and without him was not any thing made that was made. . . . And *the Word was made flesh*, and dwelt among us, and we beheld *his glory*, the glory as of the only-begotten of the Father, full of grace and truth." This was written by a Jew to a nation of Jews, familiar with their use of names, and with their glorious history. With such, therefore, there could be no misunderstanding of this language. As a Jew, John knew what was meant by *the Word*, and that all his readers would clearly understand whom he meant. Knowing, too, that this was the name in familiar use by which to designate their Jehovah, we have no hesitation in declaring that it is not possible to vindicate the reputation of John as a man of common sense or honesty, if he employed this term out of its usual meaning, without giving any intimation of the fact. He of necessity used the term in its *common, accepted meaning*, and we have shown how that name of *the Word* was found upon almost every page of the Scriptures, which they read from Sabbath to Sabbath, as the most familiar name of Jehovah. The promise, then, of Malachi was fulfilled. The history was complete. The Divine Word, so long dwelling in His tabernacle, *had returned to His temple.* The Word was made flesh, and dwelt among us in the person of the woman's seed.

Mark, also, the words of Zacharias, the father of John the Baptist, which he spake under the inspiration of the Holy Ghost concerning his own child, Luke i. 76: "And thou, child, shalt be called the prophet of the Highest: for thou shalt go before *the face of the Lord* to prepare his ways." Whom did John go before? Jesus the Messiah, and He was the *Face of the Lord*—the Divine manifestation—God revealed to human sight, and full "of grace and truth." Simeon also designates Him as *the glory of Israel.* As he took the infant Jesus in his arms in the temple from the hands of his mother, he said, under the same inspiration of the Spirit, Luke ii. 29–32, "Lord, now lettest thou thy servant depart in peace, according to thy word: for mine eyes have seen thy salvation, which thou hast prepared before the face of all people; a light to lighten the Gentiles, and *the glory of thy people Israel.*"

When Jesus appeared to Saul, on his way to Damascus, there was the same manifested glory, in which the Divine Word was revealed of old to Abraham, a light shining above the brightness of the sun at noonday, under the power of which Saul was borne to the earth. When Christ, also, is presented in the Revelation of John in His second appearing, seated on a white horse, and all the armies of heaven following, He is described as "clothed with a vesture dipped in blood, and His name is called '*The Word of God;*'" Rev. xix. 13.

If, therefore, there is any matter settled by the Scriptures, it is the fact that the Jehovah of the Old Testament is the Christ of the New—that He, who revealed himself in glory to our first parents, to Abraham, Isaac, and Jacob as their God forever—who dwelt between the cherubim, before the way of the tree of life, and in the holy place of the tabernacle, became flesh in the person of Jesus, so that we now behold God revealed in the face of Jesus Christ. The converging lines of revelation respecting the Godhead, and the woman's seed, the Deliverer of earth, meet at last in the person of Jesus, so that He who spake the promise to our first parents in Eden, of one who should bruise the serpent's head, was himself the seed. He was the coming One, destined to accomplish the mighty work. All this is not so much a doctrine, as it is a simple matter of history, the successive steps of which can be accurately traced for four thousand years, as clearly as we can identify any fact of the world's history. God has revealed himself in visible majesty on earth, dwelling among men; and this is the luminous record concerning these manifestations. Beginning where God began with these instructions, and following His revelations from age to age, the demonstration is complete. Jehovah, the God of Abraham, is our Immanuel Jesus, made under the law, and triumphing over the powers of darkness and hell.

CHAPTER XI.

THE GODHEAD REVEALED.

THE facts developed and established in the chapters preceding, make it plain

That Christ is the revealer of the Godhead.

God is an infinite Spirit, known only as He reveals himself to our apprehension. We cannot comprehend Him, neither can we understand Him except as He puts himself within our reach. What method, then, has God adopted, by which He comes out from His own eternity, and brings himself within the range of His intelligent creatures, so that they may apprehend Him? Jesus answers this question, John i. 18: "No man hath seen God at any time; the only begotten Son, which is in the bosom of the Father, he hath declared him." Paul also declares Christ to be the revealer, or the manifestation of the Godhead. 2 Cor. iv. 6: "For God, who commanded the light to shine out of darkness, hath shined in our hearts, to give the light of the knowledge of the glory of God in the face of Jesus Christ." Christ, then, has undertaken the work of unfolding the infinite Godhead.

As the first step in this process, He created these worlds to be a theatre for the Divine manifestations. This material creation was the first putting forth of the Deity. This, too, as the New Testament distinctly informs us, was the work of Christ. Man was the last link in the creation, and the brightest image of his glorious Creator—the noblest shadowing forth of the great Infinite himself, for he was made in the likeness of God. With man, too, God condescended to dwell, holding familiar converse with, and revealing to him His visible glory.

Who, now, was it that thus clothed himself with an embodied form, and brought himself within the range of the human senses? Not He, whom we designate the Father. He has never thus come out from His own hiding-place. But it was He who was subsequently known as the Christ. He put on that outward glory, clothing himself in flames of fire, and drawing near, so that He could speak to the children of men, and they might behold His face. Sometimes He put on the human form, as when He appeared on one occasion to Abraham, and was entertained by him; and again, to Jacob, wrestling with him to the break of day. In the fulness of time, He condescended to be born of a woman, and come under the curse with us, a full partaker of our nature. In this state He accomplished the work of our redemption, and ascended on high, bearing that humanity redeemed from the curse to the right hand of power, to be constituted head over all. Thus we behold the glory of God in the face of Jesus Christ, which is the fullest, most perfect revelation of the Godhead, full of grace and truth. In times of old, men beheld it only in the face of *Christ*—God revealed in the fire, or the cloud. But the last revelation was in the person of *Jesus*, our elder brother—our anointed High-Priest and King. But it is the same One throughout, as John clearly and emphatically declares, "In the beginning was the Word, and the Word was with God, and the Word was God. The same was in the beginning with God. All things were made by him; and without him was not any thing made that was made. . . . And the Word was made flesh, and dwelt among us, and we beheld His glory, the glory as of the only begotten of the Father, full of grace and truth."

The next point to be considered in connection with this subject, and full of instruction and interest, is

The peculiar name by which God has chosen to identify himself among His people.

Jehovah is the name which God has appropriated to himself forever, and by which He was to be known to His people through their generations. It is His *memorial* name, so declared to Moses, and through him to Israel—that name by which, above all others, the memory of God was to be preserved on earth, and His most sacred relations to His children proclaimed—that name which tells the most of Him, and by which His people know Him best. It was given by God under very peculiar circumstances, and in answer to the request of Moses, that He would designate the name by which He would be known to Israel. "And Moses said unto God, Behold, when I come unto the children of Israel, and shall say unto them, The God of your fathers hath sent me unto you; and they shall say unto me, What is his name? what shall I say unto them? And God said unto Moses, I AM THAT I AM: and he said, Thus shalt thou say unto the children of Israel, I AM hath sent me unto you. . . . This is my name forever, and this is my memorial unto all generations;" Exod. iii. 13.

God thus gave this as a name of peculiar interest and significance, that should ever be dear to His people in their generations. How much significance, now, believer in Christ, does that name convey to your mind? How much meaning has it? Not much, we venture to say. You do not know or appreciate God more by that name than by any other. What, then, is the difficulty? Did God fail to give a name that had significance in it? Or *have we failed to get its true meaning?*

To have this matter understood, we must state some facts familiar enough to Hebrew scholars, but not so well known to others.*

The Hebrew language is peculiar in one respect, in that its letters are all consonants, the vowel sounds being unexpressed and supposed to be understood. In ancient Hebrew writing, therefore, there was nothing to mark the sounds for vowels. There was a consequent liability, as the language became a dead one, that the proper pronunciation of words might be lost. To prevent such a result, about five hundred years after Christ, vowel points were introduced by some Jewish Rabbins, which are not letters proper, but points or marks written above and below the letters to indicate the vowel sounds. These Rabbins fixed the vowel points that we have in the name Jehovah, giving it that pronunciation.

Again, the Jews did not allow themselves to pronounce that sacred name, Jehovah. They looked upon it with such superstitious awe that they would not take it into their lips. If, then, the vowel sounds of that name anciently were neither written nor spoken, the question might well be started, Do we know certainly that we have the right ones?

It is now agreed among the ablest Hebrew scholars, that the vowel sounds attached by the Rabbins are not the correct ones; that, instead of its being Jehovah, it is Yahoch, the consonants being the same in both. It is now admitted that the name is derived from the future tense of the Hebrew word, signifying, to be, the first person singular being *Havah*, I Am; and *Yahveh* is the third person singular of the future tense, formed into a

* This subject has been treated more at large and with great ability by Alexander Mac Whorter in his "YAHVEH CHRIST," the argument of which has not been successfully controverted, and to which the author acknowledges himself much indebted.

noun, and meaning, *He who will be*, or, *Who is to come.* The words, translated, *I Am that I Am*, are properly in the future tense, and should be rendered, *I will be who I will be*, and the *I Am* is, *I who will be.* The declaration of God, then, was as follows, Thus shalt thou say unto the children of Israel, "Yahveh (He who will be), God of your fathers, the God of Abraham, the God of Isaac, and the God of Jacob, hath sent me unto you: this is my name forever, and this is my memorial unto all generations." I will be known to Israel as *He who will be*, or, *Who is to come.* Is there significance to this name—any thing peculiar and appropriate?

Go back, then, to the beginning of the economy of grace and redemption, and mark the import of that great promise written over its majestc portals, and inscribed upon every stone of the structure—the promise which first fell from the lips of God upon the ears of the trembling pair in Eden, as they waited to hear their doom pronounced. Can it be that they are not to die? Yes, verily, there is a reprieve, and the gracious promise is made of One to be raised up of their seed, by whom the salvation should be accomplished. They might prevail yet against their mighty enemy—the tempter. They were taught to look in joyful hope for a deliverer—*the Coming One.*

Of course, our first parents knew at this time nothing of the person or character of this Deliverer, beyond the general fact that he was to be born of them. Neither did they know of the time of his coming, as nothing was indicated in regard to this. There was simply the promise of One, who should bruise the head of the serpent, and He to be of their seed.

What, now, were the thoughts of Eve in that joyful hour when she took her first-born in her arms? Her thrilling utterance was, "I have gotten a man from the

Lord," a translation, however, which does not convey the idea that she intended. The word "from" should be rendered *even;* and the passage would read, I have gotten a man, even Yahveh. If Eve had wished and intended to say that she had gotten a man *from God*, she would not, and could not, have designated him by the name Yahveh. She did not know him by that title. She knew him only as Elohim, God; and speaks of him through all her history only by that name. The term Yahveh, as applied to God to designate Him, was not employed until a later period, as we shall soon show; and the sacred narrative is not guilty of the anachronism of putting this name into the mouth of Eve, as the one by which she would speak of God. She applied it to her child, and not as a *name*, but as describing a *fact*. I have gotten a man, even Yahveh—He who is to be—the promised One. She regarded that first-born child as the predicted Deliverer. This was the one thought which possessed and thrilled her soul, and why not? She had no intimation of the time which must elapse before this promised One should appear, having no instruction on this point. Times and seasons had not yet been revealed. The whole Jewish nation, with the disciples also, were similarly deceived in respect to Christ, when they supposed that his first advent was his coming in his glory and his kingdom, instead of his suffering and humiliation; and this, with all the instruction of the Old Testament before them. They were mistaken greatly as to times and events. So was Eve mistaken in the same way in regard to the coming of the Deliverer, and very naturally, too.

We have still further evidence on this point, in the name she gave to her first-born, which was Cain, signifying, *gotten* or *acquired*, as if she had said, I have *gotten* the promised seed, He who will be. This child is *the possession.* These were the thoughts of Eve, and none need wonder that the first-born of the race awakened them in the breast of that joyful mother. But Eve was doomed to bitter disappointment, the expression of which, perhaps, is represented in the name which she gave to another child, Abel, signifying *vanity.*

May we not also mark a providence in the fact, that Cain proved the character that he was, thereby disappointing the hopes of all, and turning away every expectation from him, that he could be the promised seed?

Passing on now a little further to the days of Enos, the son of Seth and grandson of Adam, we find this statement, in respect to which there has been so much difficulty in determining its precise import, "Then began men to call upon the name of the Lord;" Gen. iv 26. Some have supposed that this refers to the first establishment of public worship. Others to a revival of piety; both of which are unsatisfactory. The present line of thought, however, will throw a clear light upon this passage, making it luminous with instruction. Eve, in the first transports of her joy, had regarded her eldest son as the Yahveh, the promised One, who was to come. This hope she may long have cherished, as others also, relinquishing it only with extreme reluctance. The character and career of Cain, however, at length forced the conviction upon the minds of all that their hope was vain. Cain clearly was not the promised seed. In what direction should they now look? Where should they find this coming Deliverer? For, as yet, they had not the slightest intimation as to the time of his coming. They were, and must have been greatly at a loss, unable to decide this important question. Cain had proved a murderer—the righteous Abel had fallen in death, slain by a brother's hand. The third generation had entered upon the stage, and no indications had yet appeared of the promised Deliverer. Thus disappointed, and guided, in all probability, by some divine revelation, they turned their hopes in a new direction, and "began to call upon the name of the Lord." They began to call upon, or to invoke the name, Yahveh; that is, they applied this name to God, and looked to Him as the promised One—the Deliverer, who was to be. They had known God hitherto only by the name Elohim. Now they began to know and address Him as Yahveh Elohim, or, as in our translation, the Lord God. An examination, also, of the first chapters of Genesis will strongly corroborate this, making the fact apparent that the name Yahveh, or Lord, was not applied to God at first, but was a matter of later knowledge. Through the first chapter the term Elohim, God, alone is used. Subsequently we find Yahveh Elohim, the Lord God; indicating that these are histories belonging to different eras, the first of which might be termed the era of the Elohim—the second, the era of the Yahveh Elohim: and it was in the days of Enos that this latter era commenced. "Then began men" to apply this name to God, thus designating Him as the One who was to come, and setting their hope in Him. For this, doubtless, they had Divine authority. This was one of the important revelations of that period, and marked an era in it.

With these facts before us, we may pass on to that sublime revelation made to Moses at Horeb, where God proclaimed this distinctly as His own memorial name forever. As Moses drew near to see the great sight, why the bush was not burned, God called unto him, and said, "I am the God of thy fathers, the God of Abraham, and the God of Isaac, and the God of Jacob." It will be observed here that He does not designate himself by any name, but only declares himself the God of his fathers. God then told him of His designs in sending him to deliver His people out of Egypt. "And Moses said unto God, Behold, when I come unto the children of Israel, and shall say unto them, The God of your fathers hath sent me unto you; and they shall say unto me, What is his name? what shall I say unto them?" In those days of universal idolatry, when gods were numerous, this was a natural question; and the more natural, too, because the Israelites might be disposed to think that this "God of their fathers" had been very weak, or very negligent, in suffering them to fall into such affliction and bondage, and abandoning them to such terrible oppressions and cruelties. It would not be strange if the nation had lost faith in such a God, which seems to have been the first thought of Moses. He knew that the people would ask to know who this God was, that had done so little for them in the past, and could now effect their deliverance out of the hand of Pharaoh, when all hope seemed extinguished forever. "And God said unto Moses, I WILL BE WHO I WILL BE. And he said, Thus shalt thou say unto the children of Israel, I WHO WILL BE hath sent me unto you. And God said moreover unto Moses, Thus shalt thou say unto the children of Israel, *Yahveh* (He who will be), God of your fathers, the God of Abraham, the God of Isaac, and the God of Jacob, hath sent me unto you. This is my name, and this is my memorial unto all generations."

God thus declares distinctly that He is the Yahveh—*He who will be*—who is to come. He identifies himself as the promised seed of the woman, destined to bruise the serpent's head; for whom the world had been waiting and looking from the beginning with such disappointment. That is *my name*—the name by which I will especially be known to my people. *I am the promised, expected Deliverer.* I am even now come down to deliver them out of their iron furnace of affliction in Egypt, and will go before them to lead them in the way, and to dwell among them. Yet this shall only be a token and shadow of that greater deliverance, which I will yet send to my chosen, and that more glorious day of redemption which earth shall know.

Light also was thrown upon these declarations by the form which the Yahveh here assumed—the wondrous flame in the bush, which still remained untouched. It was the same glorious manifestation of the Divine presence which was made to Abraham, and so long to the first generations of men before the way of the tree of life. It was the same Divine manifestation from the beginning now proclaiming to Moses, in the most unmistakable terms, "*I am Yahveh*, the promised Deliverer. For me is the world to look and wait." This was His memorial name, ever most dear to His people, *The Coming One.*

With this light thrown upon the sacred name of our God, read the exultant language of the ancient saints, as their souls were thrilled with the rapturous thoughts: "Sing unto God, sing praises to his name: extol him that rideth upon the heavens *by his name* JAH" [a contraction of Yahveh], "and rejoice before him;" Ps. lxviii. 4. Isaiah, in describing that future day of blessedness and redemption to earth under the Messiah, when He shall swallow up death in victory, and wipe away tears from off all faces, and the rebuke of His people shall be taken away from off all the earth, bursts forth in the following strain, chap. xxv. 9: "And it shall be said in that day, Lo, this is our God; we have waited for him, and he will save us: this is *Yahveh;* we have waited for him, we will be glad and rejoice in his salvation." In the chapter immediately following, the prophet gives us the song that shall be sung "in that day" in the land of Judah, from which we take the following passages: "Trust ye in Yahveh forever: for in Yahveh is everlasting strength. . . . Yea, in the way of thy judgments, O Yahveh, have we waited for thee; *the desire of our soul is thy name, and to the remembrance of thee.*"

This is the glorious history, complete and continuous from the beginning. All through the Old Testament God revealed himself as Yahveh, and claims it as His memorial name; while the closing words of that first revelation are, "*Behold, he shall come*, saith the Yahveh of hosts," thus, as it were, sealing the sacred book with His own most sacred name.

But pass on still to the New Testament history of Jesus Christ, telling of His advent, and work of obedience and redemption. It might be supposed, now, that after the promised seed had actually appeared, this name of Yahveh would lose its significance to the people of God. But is it so? Is not Christ still the Coming One? Did He not enjoin it on His Church, to look, and wait, and long for His appearing? Is He not still the Yahveh—the expected Deliverer, for whose coming earth travails and waits with earnest expectation? "John to the seven churches which are in Asia: Grace be unto you, and peace from him which is, and which was, *and which is to come.* . . . Behold, *he cometh* with clouds; and every eye shall see him, and they also which pierced him: and all kindreds of the earth shall wail because of him. Even so, Amen. I am Alpha and Omega, the beginning and the ending, saith Yahveh, which is, and which was, and *which is to come*, the Almighty;" Rev. i. 4, 7, 8.

As we pass also to the closing page of Divine revelation, it would seem as if Christ could not too often reiterate the truth, and assure His Church that He was Yahveh indeed, and that they should not be disappointed in the hope of His coming. After having unfolded the whole panorama of the future, to the final consummation of all things, it is added, Rev. xxii. 6: "These sayings are faithful and true. And the Lord God of the holy prophets sent his angel to shew unto his servants the things which must shortly be done. *Behold, I come quickly:* blessed is he that keepeth the sayings of the prophecy of this book." Then again, ver. 12: "And, *Behold, I come* quickly, and my reward is with me, to give every man according as his work shall be. I am Alpha and Omega, the beginning and the end, the first and the last." To this the Holy Ghost and the Church thus joyfully respond, ver. 17: "And the Spirit and the bride, say, Come. And let him that heareth, say, Come." Nor is this sufficient. The sublime truth must be asserted yet once again, and the revelation sealed up with the precious assurance, "He which testifieth these things, saith, Surely *I come quickly: Amen. Even so, come, Yahveh Jesus.*" The New Testament is sealed thus with God's own memorial name, Yahveh. Behold, I come.

Is not this, then, the name by which God has been known to His people through their generations? Was not this the great promise with which the drama of redemption opens—the seed of the woman—He who will be? Did not men in the days of Enos begin to invoke and call upon God by this name? Did not God proclaim this as His memorial name to His chosen Israel. Is not the Old Testament sealed up with the name Yahveh, "Behold, he shall come?" Are not these the last precious words of our Yahveh Jesus, to seal the new revelation? "Surely I come quickly: Amen." What a stupendous history! How luminous every unfolding page with the divinity of our Immanuel Jesus!

Thus do the Scriptures incontestably settle the great question, What think ye of Christ? He is the manifested

God from the beginning, dwelling of old between the cherubim—then tabernacling in the flesh—now exalted to the head of principality and power—hereafter to come in His glory and kingdom.

We close this subject with the remark,

That the great point which the Scriptures labor to establish is the humanity of Christ.

In our systems of theology, which begin at the end of things, we have no difficulty in respect to this. We take up the revealed Godhead at the point where we find Him on earth, and say very satisfactorily to ourselves, Christ was a man. That point is settled. It is plain and simple. We are all agreed here, and there is no occasion for dispute. The next question is the one of mystery and difficulty, to prove that He was more than human, even that He was divine. This, however, is not the way that the subject lies in the Scriptures. The starting-point then, is a simple one, in which all are agreed, is the *the divinity of Christ*—the point of difficulty for faith, His humanity. The history of redemption opens with the glorious promise of the Coming One, *as the seed of the woman*, and the great Deliverer; while a manifested visible Deity was an unquestioned fact of every-day experience on earth, in regard to which there was no doubt or difficulty. From the outset God labors to fix in the minds of men that He himself is that expected One. He takes to himself the peculiar name to designate that fact, Yahveh. In the early days of Enos the thoughts and hopes of men are turned to himself as that promised seed. It was a great mystery, no doubt, to understand how He, who dwelt in living glory between the cherubim, could also be the seed of the woman. But God was educating the race, through long centuries, to the knowledge of the mystery; and the Scriptures contain the history of those two seemingly impossible things, running along in converging lines, the Humanity and Deity of this Yahveh, until we behold them meeting in Jesus Christ, and an inspired apostle sealing forever the fact by the unequivocal declaration, "*And the Word was made flesh*, and dwelt among us." To which another adds, "And great is the mystery of godliness. God was manifest in the flesh." If we, too, begin the study of this mystery where God began it, and follow in His footsteps, tracing it down through its successive stages, until we behold God revealed in the face of Jesus Christ, our wonder may not be diminished, but our doubts will be forever removed: and the fact of the divinity of our Christ will be as clearly established in our minds as any fact which belongs to the history of the world. We may throw away the divinity of Christ and the Bible together, if we deem best; but to deny that the Bible means to teach His true divinity, is to demonstrate our utter ignorance of all the leading facts inwoven with its magnificent history from beginning to end.

CHAPTER XII.

THE TRINITY.

We have attempted to show how the Godhead was manifested forth in creation, and then in a personal form, so as to bring Him within the reach of the human senses and of human faith. We have drawn out the history of this manifested God, showing who He was, and the forms under which He revealed himself until He became flesh and appeared in the person of Jesus Christ, to accomplish in His humiliation the work of man's redemption. The facts of this history show that God revealed himself as fast and as far as the necessities of the case required. He made himself known to men to the extent that they could understand Him, making further and still further developments of His being and relations as mankind were prepared to receive them. God could not unfold himself fully and at once to the world, any more than a mother can reveal herself perfectly to her child in a day or a year. It is only very little that such a child can at first know of its parent; nor, until it has arrived at mature years, can it understand all that is comprehended in that sacred word, mother. From the necessity of the case it must be a gradual revelation. So likewise with God. The relations of His being and the perfections of His nature could be unfolded only gradually, according as the work of redemption was carried forward from stage to stage, and new developments of God's designs were brought to view.

We might now leave the further consideration of the doctrine of the Trinity to a later period of the history of redemption, where it properly belongs. Yet, perhaps it may be best to dispose of the subject here, while we are upon the revelations of the Godhead, and the facts already developed are fresh in mind.

We shall, then, proceed to show

How the doctrine of the Trinity is unfolded in the Scriptures.

The doctrine does not appear in the earlier periods of the history of redemption, and for the reason, just stated, that God could reveal himself only as the race was prepared to understand Him, and enter into His work of salvation. A mistake, however, is made in conceiving that the revelation of God the Father comes first in the order of time. The Son is first presented to our notice and faith, though not recognized in that relation. He was the person in the Godhead first brought to the knowledge of mankind.

We have already shown how God manifested himself

in a visible form to men; how He dwelt between the cherubim before the way of the tree of life, and also behind the vail in the tabernacle; how He revealed himself as Yahveh, God of Abraham, Isaac, and Jacob; and how, as the divine Word, was made flesh in the person of Jesus. The God of the Old Testament, therefore, is Christ the Jehovah from everlasting. He is the revealed God from beginning to end of the Scriptures.

We are now prepared to see where the conception of God the Father passes into the history, and how it is developed.

The earliest presentation of this idea is found in the time of David, in connection with the kingdom of the coming Messiah; this latter idea of the kingdom of Christ being by no means an early revelation, as will be shown hereafter. It does not appear until the erection of the Hebrew commonwealth, and not until an advanced period of the same when the throne was established. Then it began to be revealed that the coming One was to be David's heir, and the possessor of his Kingdom; the same to be established in Him, that He might reign forever and ever.

It is in connection with these ideas that Christ begins to appear in the relation of Son, the promise being made to David, "I will be his Father, and he shall be my Son;" 2 Sam. vii. 14. To this promise reference is had in the second Psalm, "I will declare the decree: the Lord hath said unto me, Thou art my Son, this day have I begotten thee." This is the earliest development of the idea that Christ sustained the relation of Son—the only-begotten. It may also be observed, that this relation is made known to us first by the mention of the Son, the Father's existence or relation being thereby implied. This confirms what has before been stated respecting Christ everywhere appearing as the revealer of the Godhead. The first intimation we have of a Trinity, beyond the use of the plural pronouns as applied to God in the first of Genesis, is by Christ appearing in the character of a Son and the heir of all things, so that our knowledge of the Father's existence comes as a consequence.

This relation is brought out again a little further on in the history of David, where Christ appears with a Divine commission from heaven, accomplishing the will of God. He is represented as one sent, implying the existence of another who sent Him. In the previous history the revealed God of Israel, who is Yahveh, or Christ, appears acting by himself alone, and on His own authority as the Maker and Ruler of all. From amid the smoke and fire of Sinai His language is, "I am Yahveh, thy God, which brought thee up out of the land of Egypt, out of the house of bondage. Thou shalt have no other gods before me." He had revealed himself hitherto as the only living and true God. But now a new relation was to be brought to view, which, from the nature of the case, could not before have been made known, as the way was not prepared. The words of Yahveh now are, "Sacrifice and offering thou didst not desire, . . . burnt-offering and sin-offering hast thou not required. Then said I, Lo, I come; in the volume of the book it is written of me, I delight to do thy will, O my God. Yea, thy law is within my heart. I have preached righteousness in the great congregation. I have not refrained my lips: O Lord, thou knowest;" Ps. xl. 6. These are the words of Christ, the Son, as the Apostle plainly shows us; and they reveal to us this before unknown relation in the Godhead. The reason, too, is plain, why the same begins now to appear. Because Christ's work of obedience as a Son under the law, and His humiliation, are beginning to be unfolded. Yahveh is to be made the seed of the woman; He is to be God manifest in the flesh, and not in the glory or the cloud. Thus born of woman, He is to come under the law and the curse, to obey and suffer, and thereby work out the redemption of our world. To accomplish this work of obedience and suffering, it was necessary that He should be revealed in the new relation —the sent of God, and performing all His Father's will.

It thus appears that our knowledge of this relation in the Godhead grows out of the most practical truths of Christianity—out of the work of Christ as our Mediator. The doctrine of the Trinity is not, as some imagine, a mere abstract, theoretical question having no practical relations, and which might easily have been dispensed with. On the contrary, it grows out of the most vital elements of the system, entering into the heart of Christianity. It is the great channel through which its very life-blood flows. God reveals himself to the race just to the extent that it is necessary for us to know Him, and our relations to Him require ; while He unfolds himself as fast as these necessities demand. When, therefore, in the progress of the work of redemption, it became necessary to bring to light the fact that the God of Israel was to become flesh and place himself under law by His obedience to work out human redemption, then it was needful to disclose the fact that there was such a relation in the Godhead as might be represented by the terms Father and Son.

In what sense are we to understand these terms? Does the title, Son of God, refer primarily to a distinction in the Divine nature, or does it relate only to the Messiahship and humanity of Christ? There is, perhaps, hardly another point in the system of theology that has been more unsettled than this, and upon which it has been more difficult to arrive at satisfactory and definite conclusions. Yet it is one of such importance, that it would seem as if the Scriptures ought to have thrown sufficient light upon it to settle it, and not have left us in darkness and doubt.

Let us, then, attempt a scriptural investigation of this point.

When we speak of a literal Son in the human relation, the original idea of generation belongs to the word, but is necessarily dropped as soon as we pass to a secondary sense. This primary idea, therefore, of generation, has nothing to do with the Son of God as expressive of His Divine nature.

To many minds, however, the term does convey the idea of inferiority, subordination, and difference of nature. When we assert of Christ that He is God, we are met with the reply from certain quarters, No, He is not God; He is the *Son* of God; implying something inferior, and which does not really partake of the Divine nature.

We shall show that this directly contradicts the plain and universal Bible use of this word—*that the term Son is employed throughout the Scriptures to designate sameness and equality; and therefore that the phrase, Son of God, is the appropriate one to express a Divine nature.*

To establish this point, I refer

I. To the common and familiar use of the word Son, for this purpose, in many different connections.

Sons of Belial, is an expression in the Old Testament to designate wicked men; the word Belial meaning unprofitableness, or wickedness. Sons of Belial, therefore, are sons of wickedness—men possessed of a wicked nature, and leading wicked lives. It is synonymous with another phrase, *children of the devil*, which implies neither generation from that wicked spirit, nor inferiority, nor subordination to him; but simply likeness of nature. A child of the devil is one who belongs to the devil by possessing his character. Jesus said to the Pharisees, "Ye are of your father the devil, and the lusts of your father ye will do;" John viii. 44. They were his children, not that they were descended from him, not that they were inferior to or different from him, but simply like him, possessing his nature, as a son bears the image of his father. They claimed to be the children of God, because holy like Him. But Jesus denied this claim, and gave them their true position and character as the children of the Evil One. They bore his image.

Believers are called *the sons, or children, of Abraham*, because they possess his faith and character. This case proves that likeness of nature gives a better, truer title to sonship than even birth itself; for the Apostle denies that the Jews sustained this high relation, though they were his natural descendants, while he gives it to all who possess his faith and character.

There can be no dispute about facts like these; neither are they hidden away in some obscure corner of the Bible. They stand out among its most prominent facts, inwoven with its most essential and familiar truths.

Again, Jesus surnamed two of his disciples, James and John, Boanerges, which is, *Sons of Thunder;* Mark iii. 17—doubtless from their fervid, glowing character, which gave them power, and made them mighty as ministers of the gospel.

Again, believers are designated as *children of the light*, while the wicked are *children of the darkness.* "Ye are all the children of the light and of the day; we are not of the night, nor of darkness;" 1 Thess. v. 5. Here the two classes are contrasted, the one taking their character from the light and the day, the other from the night and the darkness.

Job speaks of the *children of pride*, Job xli. 34, designating those who possess this character or quality.

"The *children of the bedchamber*," mark those who belong to the bridal company.

Joses is spoken of, Acts iv. 36, as one of the converts

to Christianity, whom the Apostles named Barnabas, (which is, being interpreted, the Son of consolation). This surname was given because descriptive of his character, for it is stated how he sold his land and laid the proceeds at the Apostle's feet, a noble offering on the altar of the Lord, and so generous that they conferred upon him the name of Barnabas, Son of consolation.

The Son of Peace, Luke x. 5, describes the character of the house, as one where the disciples and their blessed message would be ever welcome.

Judas is graphically described by Jesus as *the Son of perdition;* and the same is also applied by the Apostle to "That Wicked." "For that day shall not come, except there come a falling away first, and that Man of Sin be revealed, *the Son of Perdition;*" 2 Thess. ii. 3, so applied, because perdition is their portion and end. The term Son embodies the whole thought.

"Then Paul, filled with the Holy Ghost, set his eyes upon him (Elymas, the sorcerer), and said, O full of all subtilty and all mischief, *thou child of the devil*, thou enemy of all righteousness, wilt thou not cease to pervert the right ways of the Lord?" Acts xiii. 11. There is no mistaking the application of such a name. Child of the devil, is not intended to express inferiority or difference of nature, but the closest resemblance possible.

In the following passages the term Son is employed as in those just quoted, but does not appear in our English translation, on account of the peculiar idiom of the Hebrews; and this idiomatic use of the word will serve to show still more strikingly the nature and meaning of the same, and how familiar it was to the Hebrew mind.

"Give unto the Lord, *O ye mighty*, give unto the Lord glory and strength;" Ps. xxix. 1. The Hebrew has *Sons* of the mighty, the word *sons* being superfluous to our language and conception of things.

For "the strangers," Ps. xviii. 44, the original is *sons of strangers.* For "servants," Eccles. ii. 7, the Hebrew has, *sons of my house.* For "the afflicted," Prov. xxxi. 5, *sons of affliction.* For the phrase, "appointed to destruction," Prov. xxxi. 8, *sons of destruction.* "As the Lord liveth, *ye are worthy to die*, because ye have not kept your Master, the Lord's anointed;" 1 Sam. xxvi. 16. The original is, *ye are sons of death.* "My well beloved hath a vineyard in a *very fruitful* field;" Isa. v. 1. "Very fruitful," is the translation of the phrase, *son of oil*, oil expressing the idea of fatness; and the *son of oil*, "fruitfulness." In Zech. iv. 4, for *sons of oil*, we have the translation, "anointed ones." For *sons of valor*, 2 Chron. xxviii. 6, we have in our version, "*valiant* men." "A year old," Micah vi. 6, is *son of a year.* "Arrows," Lam. iii. 13, are *sons of the quiver;* and "sparks," Job v. 7, are beautifully and poetically represented, in Hebrew, as *sons of the burning coal.*

We have been thus minute in developing these facts, because herein lies the force of the argument, in showing how familiar to the Hebrew mind was the term son to express sameness of nature or quality, and employed everywhere and to every object, to designate this idea, where the idiom of our language will not permit its use, and we are obliged to drop the word and express the same in other forms. Nor was this form of speech peculiar to the Hebrews; it was common among the Oriental nations, and is still a familiar phrase in the Oriental tongues. The Arab to this day boasts that he is, "the son of the desert."

If we would read the Bible understandingly, we must study it from this Hebrew point of view. We must go back to those distant times, and learn what was the meaning of language as then and there employed to express ideas. The word *son* may possibly convey to some minds the idea of inferiority and difference of nature. But that is a very slender basis upon which to construct a scriptural argument. The question is to be settled, whether that idea was suggested to the Hebrew mind.

There is, however, still another instance of the use of the word *son* in the Bible, which bears more strongly on our argument than any that have been adduced. The common title by which Jesus designated himself was, the *Son of Man*.

What did he mean by it? Suppose we apply the argument here, which some do to the phrase Son of God. I assert of Jesus Christ that He was a man. No, says my opponent, He is the *Son* of man—that is, inferior to a man—something different from and beneath manhood. Tell us, now, when Jesus called himself the Son of Man, did He mean to *deny* his true manhood, or to *assert* it? Did He not undeniably employ that phrase to convey the idea of sameness of nature—that He was man in very deed—a true man in the highest sense—yea, *the Man*, as none other ever was, the very Head and glory of our humanity?

This settles the question that the term son does not express difference or inferiority of nature, but that it is *the word*, the most perfect word, to convey the idea of identity of nature.

II. We will refer to two passages which show clearly the natural meaning of the phrase, Son of God, and how it is employed to express a Divine nature, as the term Son of Man is used to define a human nature.

"Then Nebuchadnezzar the king was astonied, and rose up in haste, and spake, and said unto his counsellors, Did we not cast three men bound into the midst of the fire? They answered and said unto the king, True, O king. He answered and said, Lo, I see four men loose, walking in the midst of the fire, and they have no hurt;

and the form of the fourth is like *the Son of God;*" Dan. iii. 24. Nebuchadnezzar was a heathen, who knew little or nothing, at this time, about Jewish theology—nothing of Christ, as born of a woman. He spoke from a natural point of view, and wanted to express the idea that he saw a fourth person in the furnace that was not human, but having a Divine nature; and, to convey that idea, he says, "The form of the fourth is like the Son of God." This, therefore, to his mind expressed sameness and equality of nature.

The other passage is found in Mark xv. 39: "And when the Centurion, which stood over against Him, saw that He so cried and gave up the ghost, he said, Truly this man was the Son of God." Here was another heathen, a Roman soldier, who knew little about the Jew's religion, and perhaps cared less. But he had been a witness of that strange and fearful crucifixion, which, before it was ended, made every man return smiting on his breast. This Roman was overwhelmed by the unearthly exhibition of suffering meekness and patience, as well as by the horrors of that darkness at noonday and the rending earth. He was convinced that there was more than a mortal in this strange sufferer; and, unable to contain the bursting emotions of his soul, he cried out, "Truly this man was the Son of God." Yes, "this Man" is not what He seems to be. He is not what His enemies have represented Him to be. He is more than mortal. He is the *Son of God*, by which He intended to express His divine nature.

This use of the term by men outside of the Jewish nation, and without any reference to its religious doctrines, shows how naturally it defines sameness or equality of Divine nature.

III. The term Son is the proper word to define sameness of nature, and not inferiority or difference.

This meaning is founded in the nature of things, and for the reason that God has ordained the great, unalterable law that the son shall bear the likeness of his father. Every parent produces after his kind—every seed after his kind. "Adam begat a son in his own likeness." This is the universal law of God's creation. The cow does not bring forth a beast of prey, neither does the bird produce a scorpion. Every parent produces an offspring in his own likeness. The word son, therefore, involves by necessity the idea of sameness of nature, not something essentially different or inferior. A son of man means a human being. A child of the devil means a devilish being. A son of God means one possessed of a godlike nature. And *the* Son of God is one who possesses that nature in the highest sense possible, as God himself.

We claim, therefore, that there is no term that the Bible could have employed which would so clearly and accurately have expressed His truly Divine nature, as that of Son, and yet, at the same time, imply a distinction in the Godhead. This argument is sufficient to silence forever all objection urged against the true divinity of Christ from the use of the term Son, as implying inferiority or difference of nature, and prepares us to consider positively whether the term is applied to Him in its proper sense as involving equality and sameness of nature.

We shall proceed to show *how and when the term Son originated, in the system of redemption, in its application to Christ; and how it is employed by the inspired writers, as well as the meaning which the Jews attached to the same.*

On opening the New Testament, we find the title, Son of God, in familiar use as applied to Jesus Christ. It is at once appropriated to Him by John the Baptist, by His disciples, and by devils, as His most distinguished designation, beyond all others. It is applied, moreover, as having an established and well-understood meaning among the people. It was not a new term, conveying a wholly new idea, nor invented for this especial occasion and purpose. Its meaning and history were already well understood.

The facts here are similar to those concerning the Logos, which was not something new with John. It had a long history in the nation going before, being the name of their manifested Jehovah, dwelling between the cherubim. When John, therefore, applied this term to Jesus Christ, and declared that that *Word*, which was in the beginning with God, and was God, was now made flesh and dwelt among us, no Jew could be left in doubt as to what he intended.

We apply this same argument of fact to the term Son of God. The object is not to determine what we think, in this country and in this age of the world, it may mean or ought to mean. We want to get at the Bible meaning; and, to obtain this, we must go back and study its history, endeavoring to ascertain when and how it was introduced into the current of human redemption, and what was its inspired use.

This history, too, is very clear and definite. We can go back and lay our finger upon the precise spot where it began. It is highly significant that the history is so perfect, and that we trace it back to a Divine, and not a human, origin. It did not spring up from human use.

This origin was the promise which God made to David concerning the seed which He would raise up to sit upon his throne, and whose kingdom He would establish forever and ever. God had found in David a man after His own heart, who would fulfil all His pleasure; and with him He established His covenant, pledging to him that the Deliverer should arise from his posterity, and be an heir to his throne, which should continue forever. Of that promised seed God says, "I will be his Father, and he shall be my son;" 2 Sam. vii. 14, and 1 Chron. xvii. 13. Here is the point where the idea of the throne and kingdom of Christ first comes to view in the system of redemption—where the seed of the woman is made to appear as having the dominion put into his hands, and reigning forever. David was herein assured that his was a royal house, which should endure, yea, as long as the sun, surviving all the lineages and dynasties of earth. To this promised heir of David, thus destined to hold the eternal dominion, God applies the term son. I will be his father, and he shall be my son." This is the definite starting-point of the whole history.

The question will be, to ascertain what meaning God designed to give this word, and how it was understood among the people to whom He made this promise and revelation.

To show, also, how clearly marked the history of this "Son" is, and within what definite limits it is kept, it may be stated that, except where Nebuchadnezzar speaks of the fourth person in the fiery furnace, which has no relation to the present subject, there are only two references in the Old Testament to this matter, and both relating directly to this promise made to David. These are made by David himself, where he introduces this great promise into the sacred lyrics of the nation in the second and eighty-ninth Psalms. In the former, the words are, "The Lord hath said unto me, Thou art my Son, this day have I begotten thee." In the latter, "He shall cry unto me, Thou art my Father, my God, and the rock of my salvation. Also I will make him my firstborn, higher than the kings of the earth. My mercy will I keep for him for evermore, and my covenant shall stand fast with him. His seed also will I make to endure forever, and his throne as the days of heaven."

This is all that the Old Testament contains respecting the Son of God. The term is not to be found anywhere else. This fact is the more important, because it shows that this inspired use and application of the term fixed its meaning. The word Son, as applied to Christ, means what these passages intended it should. Here we have the origin and history of the whole matter.

The second Psalm opens with a description of the rage of the nations, and the counsels of the rulers against the purpose of God, to exalt his Anointed to the sovereignty of earth, and set his king upon his holy hill of Zion forever. We are then shown how the Lord laughs at all this impotent rage and wickedness of the enemy, which shall not defeat His gracious designs. Then the Anointed One himself speaks, and says, "I will declare the decree: the Lord hath said unto me, Thou art my Son, this day have I begotten thee." The Lord himself hath solemnly declared the decree, which hath made me his Son forever—his only begotten; and at my request, I shall have given me the heathen for mine inheritance and the uttermost parts of the earth for my possession; while I will break the rebellious rulers with a rod of iron, and dash the opposing nations as a potter's vessel. What, then, does this solemn declaration from the Godhead concerning this Sonship of heaven's great Anointed, who was to have universal and eternal dominion, mean?

It does not mean simply that He was to be king upon the holy hill of Zion, for that had been asserted just before. This relationship of Father and Son was another matter, and more sacred. This will appear, also, from the language of the 89th Psalm: "He shall *cry* unto me, Thou art my Father, my God, and the rock of my salvation. Also, I will make him my firstborn, higher than the kings of the earth."

Neither was it the possession of the dominion and sovereignty to the uttermost part of the earth. This sovereignty He was to receive because He was the Son, being founded on this existing relation. This was the inheritance He was to have as Son. "Ask of me, and I will give thee the heathen for thine inheritance, and the uttermost parts of the earth for thy possession."

It is the Godhead who is speaking and declaring His eternal decree or purpose. And what does He say? "Thou art *my* Son," which is to say, thou art possessed of the same Divine nature with myself. This is the natural meaning of the language, as the word is used throughout His Sonship, as was also His conception by the Holy Ghost. But neither of them, nor both together constituted that Sonship. It was predicted of this Coming One that He should be born of a virgin, and be raised from the dead. The fulfillment of these wondrous facts in Jesus, identified Him as this Son of God, who was to be raised up for the redemption of Israel. But it is a mistake to suppose that the Sonship consisted in these facts themselves.

Having thus removed these objections, we proceed to show how the writers of the New Testament apply the term Son of God to Christ.

John opens his gospel, not with an account of the human lineage and birth of Christ, of which he says nothing, but of His Divine nature. He goes back to creation's birth, and tells us of *the Word* that was in the beginning with God, and was God, by whom all things were made. "And the *Word* was made flesh and dwelt among us, and we beheld his glory (the glory as of *the only begotten of the Father*), full of grace and truth." Here he designates this divine and eternal Word, thus made flesh, as the Son of God; and, as if to remove all doubt as to what he intended, and show that he used it in the highest sense possible, as expressing in very truth sameness of nature and equality with God, he adds, "the *only begotten* of the Father." This qualification marks the relation in its highest sense, and makes Son to mean all that it can mean. In ver. 18 he continues, "No man hath seen God at any time; the only begotten Son, which is in the bosom of the Father, he hath declared him." Here is still an additional qualification, "which is in the bosom of the Father," as if he labored to express the perfect intimacy and equality of this relation, and show that this sonship was absolute indeed, without any limit or qualification, and he would leave no room for doubt as to what he intended.

Hear also what Christ himself says in His discourse to Nicodemus. "And no man hath ascended up to heaven, but *he that came down from heaven*, even the Son of man which is in heaven. And as Moses lifted up the serpent in the wilderness, even so must the Son of man be lifted up; that whosoever believeth in him should not perish, but have eternal life. For God so loved the world that he gave his *only begotten Son*, that whosoever believeth in him should not perish, but have everlasting life;" John iii. 13. Whom did God give? Him, who *came down from heaven*. Who was He? His Son—His only begotten—that was in His bosom. It was His Son in His divine nature that He gave; and here was the amazing sacrifice of the gift. God "spared not his own Son, but gave him up for us all." Here, too, was the humiliation and condescension of the Son of God—for it was not a man who thus stooped, but one who "thought it no robbery to be equal with God." "For God *sent not his Son into the world* to condemn the world, but that the world through him might be saved. He that believeth on Him is not condemned: but he that believeth not is condemned already, because he hath not believed in the name of the *only begotten Son of God*," ver. 18. Yes, verily, it is condemnation indeed not to have believed in the very Son of God himself. This is the world's crowning sin that will seal its final doom.

It is worthy of remark, that this expression of the "only begotten" is one peculiar to the Apostle John, in which he seems especially to delight. Excepting as used by Paul in the first chapter of Hebrews, John is the only writer of the New Testament who employs it. This is the more significant, because he, of all these writers, discourses most of the divine nature of Christ.

We pass next to the epistle to the Hebrews, where Paul shows most clearly what idea he had of the Sonship of Christ. This epistle was addressed by him to his own countrymen, to prove the superior glory of the gospel over the covenant of Moses, made by the disposition of angels. Mark the point where he begins his argument. "God, who at sundry times and in divers manners, spake in time past unto the fathers by the prophets, hath in these last days spoken unto us by *his Son.*" He then proceeds to tell us directly who that Son is, so as to place it beyond all question. "*Whom he hath appointed heir of all things—by whom also he made the worlds—who, being the brightness of his glory and the express image of his person.*" Here is the very assertion of sameness of nature in the strongest terms, far stronger than when it is said of Adam, that he "begat a son in his own likeness." "*And upholding all things by the word of his power*, when he had by himself purged our sins, *sat down on the right hand of the Majesty on high*, being made so much better than the angels, as he hath by inheritance obtained a more excellent name than they." The Son of God, then, according to this inspired authority, is the heir of all things—the maker and upholder of all—the very image of the Godhead, and seated on the right hand of the Divine Majesty, with all power in heaven and earth in His hands. If this does not describe sameness and equality with God, it is in vain to attempt it by any language. But listen still further, "For unto which of the angels said he at any time, thou art my Son, this day have I begotten thee? And again, I will be to him a Father, and he shall be to me a Son? And again, when he bringeth in the first begotten into the world, he saith, And let all the angels of God worship him?" Here the Apostle quotes those very Psalms which contained the promise to David of an everlasting heir to his throne, and shows what their meaning is. *We have an inspired commentary on them*, which demonstrates that they have reference to Sonship in the divine nature—that Son of whom the Apostle was now speaking. It was not to any of the angels, even the most exalted, that He made that utterance. For "of the angels he saith, Who maketh his angels spirits, his ministers a flame of fire. But unto the Son he saith, Thy throne, O God, is forever and ever; a sceptre of righteousness is the sceptre of thy kingdom. Thou hast loved righteousness and hated iniquity; therefore God, even thy God, hath anointed thee with the oil of gladness above thy fellows. And Thou, Lord, in the beginning, hast laid the foundations of the earth, and the heavens are the work of thy hands. They shall perish, but thou remainest; and they all shall wax old as doth a garment. And as a vesture shalt thou fold them up, and they shall be changed. But thou art the same, and thy years shall not fail."

There is nothing wanting to this—nothing that can be added. The Son of God is He, who laid the foundations of the earth, and reared the heavens—who art the same yesterday, to-day, and forever—whose throne is established evermore—the brightest and most perfect image of the Godhead.

We will refer but to one other passage to show what is meant by the Son of God. "Paul, a servant of Jesus

Christ, called to be an apostle, separated unto the gospel of God, which he had promised afore by his prophets in the holy Scriptures, concerning *his Son* Jesus Christ our Lord, which was *made of the seed of David according to the flesh*, and declared to be *the Son of God* with power, according to the spirit of holiness, by the resurrection from the dead;" Rom. i. 1. Here He is described in His whole being. As to His human nature, or the flesh, He was made of the seed of David; but powerfully declared to be the *Son of God*, that is divine, by His resurrection from the dead; by which God put His everlasting seal upon Him as His only and well beloved. His two natures are both set forth, and to declare Him the Son of God, is simply equivalent to asserting that He is divine.

We have thus endeavored to develop the scriptural argument on this subject, showing how the word Son properly expresses sameness of nature or quality—then how the term Son of God originated—where it entered first into the system of redemption—what it was understood to mean by the nation of Israel, and how the inspired writers of the New Testament clearly employ it to designate Him whose throne is from everlasting.

This relation is of necessity an incomprehensible one to us. But so is the Eternal Infinite, incomprehensible in all His attributes and relations. At every point He is a mystery beyond all our power to reach. "Lo, these are parts of his ways; but how little a portion is heard of him? But the thunder of his power who can understand?" Job xxvi. 14.

The next point which demands our attention in reference to the trinity is

The doctrine of the Holy Spirit.

The conditions of His revelation are the same with those of the Father and the Son; that is, He is made known to us, when the necessities of the work of redemption require it. We have clear proof in the Old Testament of the work of the Spirit in the sanctification of believers and the inspiration of the prophets. But these are hardly sufficient to establish the fact of His distinct personality. This is not made apparent until the opening of the new economy.

It is not clear to all what is meant by the mission of the spirit under the gospel, or how it can be reconciled with the fact of His previous working under the old economy. If He had always wrought in the conversion and sanctification of men, how could it be said of Him that He should now be sent from the Father, and that the disciples must wait at Jerusalem for His coming? The simple fact of the enlarged scale of His operations would hardly seem to justify such a representation of the matter. We do not, however, regard this increased extent and power of His working as the solution of the question. It is to be found in another fact.

The mission upon which the disciples were sent forth was, that they were to be Heaven's appointed witnesses to to the fact, upon which the whole scheme of redemption turned, the resurrection of Jesus. The rulers had thought by that death to prove conclusively the imposture of His claims. He had died like the rest of the race—died as a transgressor; and there was the perfect demonstration that He was not the Holy One of God—the living Saviour promised to Israel with sovereign power over death and the grave. He could not even keep alive His own soul, much less open the graves of His saints. The fact has been overlooked, that it was the universal belief of the Jewish nation that the Messiah was not to be subject to death. "We have heard out of the law that Christ abideth forever: and how sayest thou that the Son of man must be lifted up? Who is this son of man?" John xii. 34. This shows how the Jews understood their Scriptures.

They expected that the Messiah would continue, that is, live without seeing death; and for this opinion there was no slight foundation. The Scriptures did promise that He should live—that His name should endure forever. "His name shall be continued as long as the sun; and men shall be blessed in him: all nations shall call him blessed;" Ps. lxxii. 17. Numerous statements are found like these. Beside this, also, He was the promised One to prevail against death, and put that enemy, with all others, under His feet. It was not strange, therefore, that the doctrine was accepted by all that the Messiah was not to come under the power of this destroyer. Neither can we properly understand the gospel narrative, without keeping in mind this popular Jewish faith. Here was the incomprehensible mystery of His sufferings and death to the disciples, of which Jesus so often spake to them, which He labored in vain to make them understand, and of which they were afraid to ask Him. When, therefore, He was delivered over to the grave, even they gave up all hope, regarding the matter as settled that He could not have been the Saviour they looked for. "We trusted that it had been he which should have redeemed Israel;" Luke xxiv. 21. But, alas, our fondest hopes have all been blasted. We have seen death triumphing over Him, and His body laid in the sepulchre. We fondly trusted that this was death's conqueror. The joy of the rulers, however, was unbounded. They had proved themselves at last to be in the right. Their triumph was complete.

This argument and demonstration against Jesus must be set aside, and that in the most powerful manner; which was done by His resurrection. God put His seal upon Him as His Holy One and well beloved, by reversing the decree of death and bursting his iron bars. To this fact the disciples were made witnesses. But this was not enough. It was too important a fact to be made dependent upon mere human testimony, which could never have established it to the satisfaction of the Jewish rulers. With their views respecting the exemption of the Messiah from the power of death, together with their embittered hostility to Jesus, it would have required more than human testimony to prove that this crucified Nazarene was the One for whom they had been looking. It was by no means an easy task for Jesus to demonstrate to His own loved disciples the fact that He had come forth from the grave, ready and anxious as they were to believe it, if only they might. How, then, would His enemies ever be convinced? Would they receive the testimony of these Galileans? It is a mistake to conceive that the resurrection of Jesus has been left to be substantiated by the testimony of twelve fallible men. Infidelity has a more difficult task than this in overturning the foundations of Christianity. In addition to this human testimony, there is *the infallible witness of the Holy Ghost*, whose presence was manifested in the church and in Jerusalem, just as clearly as that of the apostles themselves. His presence was the great fact of those days, and His testimony in the case was more than that of the twelve apostles together. They were enjoined by their Master to say nothing publicly about His resurrection, until this other witness should make his appearance, and their words should be backed up by his overwhelming, undeniable testimony. Then they would be endued with power. Then they might stand before Priest and Pharisee, Ruler and Sanhedrim, and proclaim salvation through a *crucified Nazarene*, to the confusion and overthrow of all opposition. They accordingly observed these injunctions, and waited in prayer until the day of Pentecost, when this promised witness did appear, heralded by a terrific sound like that of a hurricane, which startled the whole population of Jerusalem, though the leaves upon the trees were not stirred in the still atmosphere, while to the eyes of men the same Supernatural One was revealed in tongues of fire upon the heads of these Galilean disciples of Jesus, designating them as men approved of heaven—clothing them with the wondrous power of unknown tongues, and enabling them to wield omnipotence itself to attest their divine mission.

Here, beyond all denial, was a new personage upon the stage, substantiating the testimony of these men, that He, whom the rulers had crucified, had come forth from the sepulchre, and ascended on high to the right hand of power; and that remission of sins was to be preached through His name. These were the truths which the apostles were commissioned to hold forth; and every word they uttered was sustained by the power of the Holy Ghost, bearing witness with mighty signs and wonders. When, too, the rulers rejected this testimony, and still opposed the claims of the Nazarene, they committed that sin, of which Jesus warned the nation—that sin for which there was no forgiveness, no remedy, and which swiftly brought the day of destruction. Their sin in rejecting and crucifying the Son of man in His humiliation could have been forgiven. It was forgiven to many, for "they did it ignorantly in unbelief." "Had they known it, they would not have crucified the Lord of glory." But there was no such apology to be offered when they denied the testimony which the Holy Ghost himself bore, in connection with the apostles, to the resurrection of Jesus. There was no denial that these were divine workings; and the rulers were directly charged with blasphemy in doing it.

This was the mission of the Holy Ghost under the new dispensation. He had never appeared before in this relation, nor to accomplish such a work; and it is at this stage of the history of redemption that His personality is clearly made to appear as distinct from that of the Father and the Son. Christ promised that He would send Him from the Father to supply His place for a season on earth. He speaks of Him not as an influence—not as a mere power, but as a person, with a commission to fulfil, just as He speaks of himself as a person sent from the Father. "I will pray the Father, and he will give you another Comforter, that he may abide with you forever, even the Spirit of truth; whom the world cannot receive, because it seeth him not, neither knoweth him;" John xiv. 16. And again, "When the Comforter is come, whom I will send unto you from the Father, even the Spirit of truth, which proceedeth from the Father, *he shall testify of me.* And ye also shall bear witness of me, because ye have been with me from the beginning;" xv. 26. Here the Holy Ghost is spoken of as a living witness, even as the disciples themselves, and sent by the Father. Notice also the following. "Howbeit, when the Spirit of truth is come, he will guide you into all truth: for he shall not speak of *himself:* but whatsoever he shall hear, that shall he speak: and he shall shew you things to come. He shall glorify me: for he shall receive of mine, and shall shew it unto you;" xvi. 13. No language could be more calculated to deceive and lead astray than this, if we are not to understand the Holy Ghost to be a person. A mere influence or inspiration could not be said, "not to speak of himself," but only utter what He should hear and receive.

But we leave the argument for the distinct personality of the Spirit, founded on the language of the New Testament, to the following chapter, our aim at present being to follow the historical development of the Trinity. The facts brought to view show that the triune nature of God is unfolded very gradually in the Scriptures, according to the progress of the work of redemption, and as the necessities of the system required. Our knowledge of the

Divine existence has been growing from the beginning. God has been adding to the manifestations of himself, as the fuller development of the plan of redemption permitted. We cannot assert that that manifestation is yet complete. There may be mysteries in the Divine Being of which we have no knowledge, which, from the necessity of the case, could not now be revealed to us. It might be impossible to make them intelligible. Many reject the revelations which God has already made, simply because they are not conformed to the standard of their own limited being, as though we were to be the line and plummet by which to measure the Infinite. It is true of us that we are made in the Divine likeness. But it is not asserted, neither is it true, that God is modelled after us. We have no right to insist that His infinite being shall be brought down to the limits of our feeble and finite standard. It is difficult for such an one to bring himself at all within our apprehension. Nor has He ever attempted it in the way of dogma or abstract doctrine. God's being and character have always been unfolded in their practical relations, and only as the necessities of our condition required. He has not gone ahead of us and out of our sight, so that we could not follow Him. He has not disclosed truths respecting himself which had no relation to our circumstances, and which were beyond our reach or faith. He has led us along by simple lessons and easy stages. Jesus dealt thus with His disciples. He had many and difficult things to say unto them. But He revealed them only as they were able to bear them. A wise parent or teacher always deals thus with a child, leading him along, step by step, from the beginning. God has so dealt most wisely with our race in developing that profoundest of all subjects, the science of His infinite being.

In following these revelations we have seen how plain

and incontrovertible they were at the outset—how God revealed himself in a visible manner to men, so as not to be misapprehended, while the promise was made of one to come of the seed of the woman. Who that was, God made clear by turning the thoughts and expectations of men to himself, as the One in whom they delighted—for whose return they should hope and wait. Subsequently it was made to appear that there was a deeper relation in the Godhead, which came to light under the terms Father and Son; and that Jehovah, the manifested God from the beginning, was the Son, commissioned by the Father to the work of redemption. Later still, it was made apparent that there was a third relation, represented by the Spirit, to whom was assigned the task of endowing the Church with all gifts and graces, and bearing incontestible witness to the resurrection of Jesus.

Thus does the doctrine of the Trinity enter into the very heart of Christianity, embracing all its great essential truths, denial of one of which carries with it almost necessarily the denial of others. Their relation is so intimate that it is difficult to separate them, or retain one to the rejection of another. It is not a vain thing, therefore, that we hold to the doctrine of the Trinity. The most precious truths of our religion cluster around it. It is a practical doctrine to us of utmost value, connected with all our dearest hopes.

CHAPTER XIII.

PERSONALITY OF THE HOLY SPIRIT.

We have shown under what circumstances the doctrine of the Holy Ghost enters into the system of redemption as a revealed truth. It may be important to present further the argument from the New Testament for the distinct personality of the Spirit, since to many minds this point is not clear and decisive. There is no difference of opinion in respect to the divinity of the Holy Ghost. The only question is as to His personality; whether He is distinct from the Father, or simply His divine agency; while, in respect to Christ, His personality is admitted, and the controversy in relation to Him is regarding His divinity.

Our aim will be TO ESTABLISH THE DISTINCT PERSONALITY OF THE HOLY GHOST.

Those who deny this, hold that, when the Holy Spirit is referred to in the Scriptures, it means simply God working in a specific direction. It would, therefore, have answered every purpose, and conveyed every thought, to have said that God wrought thus and so. In other words, the Holy Spirit, as designating a person, is a figure of speech. It is a mere personification—a poetic license.

We claim that the Scriptures design to convey the idea that there is a distinction in the Godhead, so that the Holy Spirit is not the Father, in a proper sense, but a person. And when we say a person, we do not mean a distinct *being*. It is true, indeed, that the term conveys this idea as applied to men.

But we have no right to assume that the Divine nature is conformed in all respects to our own, though this assumption is commonly made by those who object to and deny the doctrine of the Trinity. We claim that the Deity is not to be measured or tested by the limits of our being; and that we are not to deny the mysteries of His nature, because we do not find any thing corresponding thereto in our own. It is to be supposed that there are elements or features in the being of God of which we have no experience, and no means of fathoming. It is, therefore, only vain presumption in us to sit in judgment upon the revelation of these mysteries, and reject them because they are not conformed to our standard, or within our comprehension. It is the office of faith humbly to receive the divine teachings, not to dictate what they shall be.

The distinct personality of the Holy Ghost then is, 1. *The plain and direct import of the language of the Bible.*

By this we mean that the Scriptures everywhere and abundantly speak of the Holy Ghost in distinction from the Father, and that without the slightest hesitation. The personal pronoun is applied to Him freely as to a person; and these pronouns are *the words*, in our language, to convey the idea of personality. They are for this specific purpose, and have no other use. When, therefore, they are applied to the Holy Ghost directly, and without any qualification, we are authorized to understand that He is a person, or that there is such a distinction in the Godhead, that these pronouns are the only adequate words tc convey it to our minds.

This use of the pronouns, also, is the more decisive, when joined to the fact that the Holy Ghost is spoken of in immediate connection with the Father, and separate both from Him and Christ. If it were the fact that the Holy Ghost was spoken of alone, then it might with more plausibility be maintained that the Father and the Spirit were the same, only described under different names. But this supposition is out of the question when they are both presented to us in the same passages, as, for instance, John xiv. 16: "And I will pray the Father, and he shall give you another Comforter, that he may abide with you forever: even the spirit of truth, whom the world cannot receive, because it seeth him not, neither knoweth him. But ye know him, for he dwelleth with you, and shall be in you." Here are three persons described in this passage: Christ, the speaker; the

Father, to whom the prayer was to be offered; and the Spirit, or Comforter, to be sent from Him. If, however, Christ simply meant that He would pray the Father to come and comfort them himself by His own presence, why did He not so state it? It was as easy, and far more simple, as well as truthful. There was no necessity to confuse the subject, and bewilder the minds of the disciples by an unnatural use of language. If Jesus, therefore, had nothing in His mind beyond the simple conception of God's comforting them by His own presence, or through His truth, He never could have put it in the form in which it stands.

If, however, it is said, that this is rhetoric, personification, poetic license, it is sufficient to answer, that such rhetorical use of language belongs to another class of writing, and is out of place here. Besides, when personification is used by a speaker, there is never a question about it, nor can one possibly be led astray. As this is the turning-point of the argument, let us pause a moment to notice more particularly this figure of personification, what its nature is, and the laws which govern its use.

It consists, then, in this, that a writer or speaker takes an object in nature, or some quality of mind *known to be such*—always spoken of as such, and, for the time being, treats it as a person. It is this known, unquestioned character of the object as an impersonality, that gives the speaker the privilege, in these extraordinary instances, of regarding it as a person, without making him liable to be misunderstood. It is evident to all that he is speaking in a figure. Thus all agree as to what hills, mountains, seas, woods are, the heavens and earth—that they are merely objects in nature. When, therefore, these are addressed as persons, as by the Psalmist, "The sea saw it, and fled; Jordan was driven back. The mountains skipped like rams, and the little hills like lambs;" or by Isaiah,

"Hear, O heavens, and give ear, O earth;" every one sees at once that the writer is departing, for the moment, from the usual mode of speaking, and treating as persons what all his readers know full well are not such, and that he is using a figure of speech. A writer or speaker, therefore, can never be misunderstood in personifying an object. For, to give the representation the force intended, the object must so *manifestly lack personality, and his use of it as a person be such an entire departure from the ordinary mode of speaking*, that every one will see it at once. And if an audience could be left in doubt, debating whether the speaker intended to employ a figure or not, then he has made a sad failure.

Yet just such a failure is involved, in the hypothesis that the Holy Ghost is used in a figurative sense; for the largest portion of the Church has never so understood it. We regard this as entirely conclusive. If Jesus intended merely to personify the power or working of God under the term Holy Ghost, the matter should have been so apparent by all the requirements of language, that no intelligent person could ever have been left in doubt; and if the idea of such personification is suggested only to a few readers, and then to escape a difficulty as to the doctrine taught, it is conclusive that Christ was speaking literally, and that by the Holy Ghost He meant a person, and not an attribute.

II. *Numerous facts are referred to the Holy Ghost as to a person.*

Action is one of the proofs of personality. A person is an agent who carries out designs. The Holy Ghost now is represented as such in the Scriptures, and to Him is assigned a most important and peculiar agency. The whole work of inspiration is referred to Him. "Holy men of God spake as they were moved by the Holy Ghost." By Him the apostles and others were endowed with the gift of tongues and prophecy, of healing and working miracles. He was to teach, to guide, to comfort, to sanctify the Church, and to convince the world of sin. He was to be sent to make His dwelling in the Church, to take it into His own especial keeping, and preserve it unto the day of Christ. He could also be grieved and resisted, blasphemed and lied unto. Some sins committed against Him were of a peculiarly aggravated character, more damning in their nature than those against Christ himself, and less within the reach of mercy.

There is also another work of the Holy Ghost, to which the Scriptures attach peculiar importance, and which, in this connection, is of especial force. He was sent as a *witness* to bear testimony to the resurrection of Jesus. The apostles were witnesses of this same fact. But it was too momentous a matter to be made dependent on mere human testimony. The Holy Ghost himself was commissioned also to bear His witness, and attest it by signs and wonders. John xv. 26, 27: "But when the Comforter is come, whom I will send unto you from the Father, even the Spirit of truth, which proceedeth from the Father, *he shall testify of me.* And ye also shall bear witness, because ye have been with me from the beginning." This too was verified fully by events. The Holy Ghost did come and take up His dwelling in the Church. He came *in a visible form*, even with the appearance of tongues of fire, heralding His approach by a sound from heaven like to that of a mighty wind; and His working in the midst of the Church was on the most stupendous scale. The gifts which He conferred, and the power, were such as could come from a Divine and living One alone; which is the explanation of that fearful charge which Stephen made against the rulers, when they opposed and blasphemed: "Ye stiff-necked and uncircumcised in heart and ears, ye do always resist the Holy

Ghost: as your fathers did, so do ye," Acts vii. 51. They would not receive his testimony; and it was this sin against the Holy Ghost which filled up the measure of their iniquity, bringing upon them the day of desolation. Their sin against the Son of Man, in crucifying Him, could have been forgiven. But when they added to this the denial and rejection of the testimony of the Holy Ghost to the resurrection and acceptance of this Jesus with the Father, the cup of their iniquity ran over.

Who was this witness but a *living person*—one who could bear testimony, and that an effectual one, by mighty signs and deeds! If it was simply the Father, who was doing all this, and exerting His power, it would have been easy so to state it, and the most natural. But the term Holy Ghost is clearly not applied to the Father in the Scriptures, but is employed to designate one sent by and from Him, and must therefore be a third person. Christ never meant that the Father would send himself. If He had so intended, He would have said in simple terms that the Father would come. The Bible is the most straightforward, unambiguous, common-sense book ever written. And the writers of it knew, best of all men, how to use language and make a difficult subject understood. They never used words to cover up ideas. If Christ, therefore, merely had it in mind that His Father would come and work and bear testimony in the world to His resurrection, He could easily have so said, instead of confusing the whole subject by stating that He would send a third party to do it.

As to the idea of personification here, it is an absurdity. What is it that is personified? When the Holy Ghost is said to move holy men to speak—to comfort the disciples—to show things to come, to bring all the words of Christ to remembrance, so that they might record them as inspired history—to convince men of sin, to renew the heart, and to bear witness to the resurrection of Jesus; when the Holy Ghost is represented as doing all these things, will any one tell us, what it is that is personified—what it is that, by force of vivid imagination in the writer, is for the time converted into a living person, that every body knows is not a person, and which same rhetorical use of language, therefore, deceives no one? And will some one also tell us what was the object of such useless personification *at all times, and on all occasions*, so as to destroy its entire effect? We must give up this idea, or renounce all our respect for the writers of the Scriptures as men of common sense.

III. *Believers are baptized into the name of the Holy Ghost, as of the Father and the Son.*

To appreciate the force of this fact—and it is one of conclusive character—it is necessary to have a clear conception of what is meant by being baptized into one's name. Mark it. It is being baptized into the *name of one*—of a person, which is the most solemn form of supreme dedication to another. It is a profession of discipleship to him, wherein the subject engages to receive his teachings—to follow and obey him in all things. To be baptized into the name of Christ is a solemn dedication of one's self to Christ forever, to be His—to bear His sacred name, to receive His doctrines, to follow His commands. What, now, is the formula of Christian baptism? "Baptizing them into the name of the Father, and of the Son, and of the Holy Ghost." Here is the whole Christian doctrine—an epitome of the gospel. Can there be a doubt as to the meaning of this? Here are two persons, beyond question—the Father and the Son. The believer is baptized into the name of God as his Father—owned now as a child, and accepting this filial relation. He is baptized into the name of Jesus Christ, owning Him as his only Saviour, his sacrifice, his

High Priest—his wisdom, righteousness and redemption—the way, the truth, the life. Finally, he is baptized into the *name* of the Holy Ghost. Who is the Holy Ghost? We do not ask, *What* is the Holy Ghost? as if it were something impersonal; but, *Who* is *He?* For it is a baptism into His name. And a name belongs to a person. Is he the Father God? That cannot be. For the believer has been baptized into His name already, receiving Him, and owning subjection to Him in all things. And if it is really the Father that comes to teach, to renew, to guide, to sanctify the Church, and convince of sin, if this is the simple Bible doctrine, then every thing is told when we are baptized into the name of the Father and the Son. As to the *person* of the Holy Ghost, there is no such thing; baptism into His name is a mere delusion.

Are we told that the Holy Ghost is here a personification, and means simply the Divine agency or power? If such a supposition can need refutation, it is sufficient to answer that the *name of a person* would never be given to the mere working or agency of God. Put also the formula into its true construction according to this interpretation. Baptizing them into the name of the Father, and of the Son, and the agency of God. There must be the necessity of maintaining a dogma that will constrain any intelligent mind to such an interpretation of Bible language.

Closely related to this agreement from the formula of baptism, is that which is drawn from the form of the Christian benediction. The Apostle closes his second letter to the Corinthians with these words: "The grace of the Lord Jesus Christ, and the love of God, and the communion of the Holy Ghost, be with you all, Amen." Communion is fellowship, sweet intercourse between friends. Is the Holy Ghost here simply God, the Father?

Why, then, did not the Apostle write, "The grace of the Lord Jesus Christ, and the love and communion of God, be with you," saying nothing about the Holy Ghost? Why did he mislead his readers with the idea that there was a third person in the case? But was Paul here, by a lively imagination, personifying some object which all would know to be such, and not a person? The benediction was no place for the exercise of imagination; and no one could by any possibility know that there was a figure of speech employed.

This is enough to show the absurdity of such construction, or attempting to turn these precious formulas aside from their direct and obvious meaning. Christ must have conceived of the Holy Ghost as a person, when He associated Him with himself and the Father, and commanded that all believers should be baptized into their joint name. The Apostle, too, must have had the same conception, when he prayed that the Corinthian believers might enjoy the communion of the Holy Ghost together with the love of God, and the grace of the Lord Jesus Christ, as if these combined all good that could be conceived of or prayed for.

This leads us to remark,

IV. *That the present language and statements of the Scriptures never could have originated on the supposition that there is no personality in the Holy Ghost.*

In other words, it is the real personality of the Holy Ghost, so understood, that has made the phraseology of the Bible, and its statement of facts, what they are. Language grows out of ideas, and is designed to express them, the same being our conception of things. It is therefore the representative of facts or truths, and modelled after them. It would have been impossible now that the language of the Bible should have been what it is, unless the idea of the personality of the Holy Ghost, as a distinction in the Godhead, had been in the mind of the Author of that book. To make this argument more clear, let us carry our minds back to the simple conception of two persons—God the Father, Christ the Son. God the Father, one, eternal, infinite Spirit—the Creator, Preserver, Sanctifier of all, whose divine working is seen and felt around and within us. Beside Him is the Son, whom He sent to redeem this world. It matters not here, to our present argument, whether Christ is regarded as a *Divine* person or not. All admit Him to be a person. There are, then, simply two persons, and these, by their own immediate agency, do all that is done in heaven and earth in connection with the Godhead; while it is the simple design of the Scriptures, as a revelation, to give us a clear conception of this one infinite Spirit working in and through all, unchangeably the same forever, and securing our forgiveness through Christ.

The presentation of these two persons would have been perfectly simple and easy; and if Christ had nothing beyond this conception of himself and His Father, He could have made this plain without the slightest ambiguity. Nor do we hesitate to say that, under these circumstances, the language of the Scriptures respecting the Holy Ghost would have been an impossibility. There would have been nothing upon which to found it. The reality was not there, and therefore there could be no idea or conception of it as an existence.

Let us imagine Christ to have had the simple conception of God, who, after His own departure from the earth, was to watch over His lonely disciples, and guard, instruct, and sanctify them, and, by signs and wonders which He would do, convince the world that Jesus was the Christ, whom He had sent and raised from the dead. Suppose this to have been the only idea, and how could Jesus ever have said to those sorrowing disciples, mourning His departure, "I will not leave you comfortless?" "I will pray the Father, and He shall give you another Comforter, that he may abide with you forever." "And when the Comforter is come, whom I will send unto you from the Father, even the Spirit of truth which proceedeth from the Father, he shall testify of me. And ye also shall bear witness, because ye have been with me from the beginning." How, also, could Christ have ever prescribed that solemn ordinance of baptism, by which all believers were to be inducted into His sacred body, epitomizing their whole faith by the formula, "Go ye into all the world, and preach the gospel to every creature, baptizing them into the name of the Father, and of the Son, and of the Holy Ghost?" If there is no personality to the Holy Ghost, this formula is a falsehood and deception. If Paul, likewise, had not this same idea of the Spirit's personality distinct from the Father, he never could have pronounced the solemn benediction upon the Corinthians: "The grace of the Lord Jesus Christ, the love of God the Father, and the communion of the Holy Ghost, be with you, Amen." Yes, *Amen;* so let it be to the end. And let us not be told that, while there is boundless truth in the first two thirds of this benediction, the last third is a piece of rhetoric, the omission of which would have detracted not one iota from the truth or force of Scripture, and would have prevented an endless amount of discussion and error. If the Holy Ghost is nothing separate from the Father, then His communion is nothing. Or, if it is the Father's personified power or agency, what respect can we entertain for a revelation which so utterly fails in the attempt at personification, that not one in a hundred ever suspects it? Such a blunder would be unpardonable in any uninspired author, and sufficient to discredit his whole work.

It had been easy for Christ and the apostles not to

have said any thing of the Holy Ghost in distinction from the Father, if so be there is no distinction. There was no necessity for it. It adds nothing to the force or truth of the Scriptures, but only confusion. If we are to accept a revelation from Heaven to man—an inspired volume of truth—it is reasonable to demand that God shall know how to use human language in communicating His will, and that we shall not be under the necessity of breaking down all the rules of rhetoric to obtain its meaning. We could have no respect for a revelation, the writers of which could not be inspired from Heaven, to the proper use of language. If the Holy Spirit, as alleged by some, is simply God himself, or His working, or spiritual influences, then no mention could ever have been made in the formula for baptism; and the benediction of any one but God and Jesus Christ, even if the latter could have been introduced, being no more than a man. The inconsistency, too, of using the name of a mere man in such a connection is so apparent *that numbers of the ministers of this faith drop it out from the benediction, as well as from their prayers.* They do not mention the name of Christ. None, too, would have been so quick to perceive this inconsistency as Jesus himself and His apostles, and to have carefully avoided it. The bendiction, therefore, should have been, "The love, grace and fellowship of God be with you all;" and the formula of baptism, "Baptizing them into the name of God." This expresses the whole, and here the matter should have ended, if there is no trinity of persons.

We are compelled to believe that both honesty and common sense are to be found in the Bible, and that there is, therefore, some mysterious distinction in the Godhead, beyond the reach of our short fathoming line and the grasp of our thought, which is revealed to us in the character and person of the Holy Ghost. As a personal

Agent, He stands forth upon all the pages of the inspired Word. We may not understand it; but this constitutes no reason for denying or rejecting it. Every thing respecting the Godhead is equally incomprehensible. "Canst thou by searching find out God? Canst thou search out the Almighty unto perfection? It is as high as heaven; what canst thou do? Deeper than hell; what canst thou know? The measure thereof is longer than the earth, and broader than the sea." Wilt thou, the poor, blind creature of a day, attempt to sit in judgment upon the Infinite One, and demand that the height and depth, the length and breadth of His being, shall be brought down to the measure of thy little comprehension? Wilt thou require that He shall be made altogether such an one as thyself, and that His incomprehensible being shall contain no deeper mysteries than thine own? Vain man, forbear! Let God reveal himself as He will, without being made subject to the measurement of thy line and plummet.

CHAPTER XIV.

PERSONALITY OF THE WORD.

Before dismissing the doctrine of the Trinity, we wish to consider Christ from the same point of view, and test His personality by the same argument as the one employed in the preceding chapter in reference to the Holy Ghost.

Every reader of the Bible must be impressed with the very different opening of John's Gospel from that of the other Evangelists; and the same will throw a flood of light upon the person of Christ and His mysterious being.

Matthew and Luke begin the history from His advent into our world, tracing out his genealogy as the son of

Mary, and through her as the son of David. They give His history as the seed of the woman, unfolding His human nature, showing that He was a true man, born of a woman, and connected with David's royal line. As such, He had been prophesied of, and it was essential, in order to His reception by the nation, that He should be proved to be their Messiah, by His fulfilling in all particulars the prophesies going before. These historians accordingly give His ancestry, showing Him to be a lineal descendant of David. They then proceed to develop the incidents connected with His birth—the mission of the angel to Mary, with the birth and mission of John, His forerunner, the appearance of the angels to the shepherds of Bethlehem, and the star which guided the wise men from the East to the infant Jesus. In this minute history we have the evidence that the Redeemer of the world was a true man, like ourselves. We are carried back to the days of His helpless infancy, when we see His mother wrapping the babe in swaddling clothes, and laying Him in a manger. We see those parents fleeing with the child to escape the wrath of Herod, and taking shelter in Egypt until the death of the king. He is then brought back to Nazareth. At twelve years of age He goes up to the temple, and thence, through His childhood, He continues subject to His parents, and diligently employed until the time of His public ministry, from which point the Evangelist Mark takes up his narrative. In all this we see the development of a complete human nature from humblest infancy through each successive stage to the close of life. This is the history which the three Evangelists give us. John, too, records the history of our Saviour, but in some remarkable features in striking contrast with the one now delineated. Of the birth and infancy of Jesus he says nothing—nothing of the miraculous events attendant upon His entrance into the world.

Over all these he passes in entire silence, and begins at another point. He goes back of the Saviour's birth, back of His human nature, back of His earthly advent and career, back of creation, and undertakes to tell us what, and who, and where He was "*in the beginning*," before He was made flesh and dwelt among us, permitting us to behold His glory. He opens the history with the sublime statement, full of unearthly grandeur, "In the beginning was the Word, and the Word was with God, and the Word was God. The same was in the beginning with God. All things were made by him, and without him was not any thing made that was made. In him was life, and the life was the light of men." Observe here that John says, "In the beginning *was* the Word." It is the Greek word, ἦν, denoting the fact of existence simply—that He was then in being. Had he designed to express the idea of His coming into being, or beginning existence, he would have used the word, ἐγενέτο. But John does not say that in the beginning *began* the Word; but, in the beginning He *was*. He was then found in existence. This, therefore, is the strongest form of asserting His eternity. He was in, or from, the beginning.

Why did John use this name of the Logos, the Word, to designate Christ? For, as a name, the name of a person, he evidently did use it, since he adds immediately, "And the Word was made flesh, and dwelt among us, and we beheld his glory, the glory as of the only-begotten of the Father, full of grace and truth."

The Evangelist had occasion, by the necessity of his argument and subject, to speak of Christ before His assumption of our humanity, while in that glory which He had with the Father before the world was. What name should he apply to Him? Should he call Him Jesus? and say, In the beginning was Jesus, and Jesus was with God, and Jesus was God? But this was not true. Jesus was the name of a man, born in Bethlehem of Judea, where His mother nursed Him upon her bosom, and bore Him in her arms. As a man, He had no prior existence. Nor did the Evangelist design to carry this human nature back into a past eternity.

Should he, then, designate Him by the name of Christ? But this, also, is a term applicable to His human relations, meaning the *Anointed*, and designates One set apart to the highest and most sacred offices. The High Priest was anointed with holy oil, when inducted into office; so also was the king. And Jesus, being set apart to both these offices, was, in the most emphatic sense, *the Anointed* of heaven, the Christ. But having obtained these offices through His human nature, this term could not be applied to Him to designate His prior existence. Neither could any other name growing out of His human relations.

John, then, by the necessity of his subject, was compelled to employ the name he did, the Logos, to designate the person of Christ in His antecedent relation, before that He became flesh. It was the most appropriate term, and already familiar to his nation as the name of their Jehovah dwelling between the Cherubim. There was no mystery about the name, no question about its meaning or application—nothing strained or forced in its use. The meaning of the Logos, and its appropriation as a name, were perfectly established, as truly so as the Christ; so that, when John applied it to Jesus, or to Him rather who was made flesh, there could not have been the shadow of a doubt as to what the Evangelist intended. Whether John was correct or not in his statement of facts, is another matter, to be debated by those who doubt or deny his inspiration. But as *to the meaning of his language*, there could have been no question in his day. Many might have charged it with blasphemy, and doubtless did. And this was the conclusive argument they would have urged against it.

Having, however, gone over this ground, we will not pursue this point further, but pass to a different argument.

We may suppose ourselves to be ignorant of the Jewish use and history of the name now referred to; and the gospel of John is put into our hands, that we may learn what his view of the person of Christ is. We open his book, and read, "In the beginning was the Word, and the Word was with God, and the Word was God." There are two possible interpretations of this. One is, to take it in its plain, obvious, direct sense, as a literal statement; the other, to make the Logos, or the Word, a personification of some attribute. In other words, the Logos is a real person, declared to be God from the beginning, or something is personified under the term Logos. The question lies between these two. *Is the Logos a person, or a mere personification?*

Recall here the laws of personification as we have defined them heretofore, which are, that a writer takes something which he and every one else knows is not a person; and, for the time being, speaks of it as a person, for the purpose of adding force and impressiveness to his discourse. The use of this figure is founded on the known character of the object described as an impersonality, which is so apparent that no intelligent reader can mistake, and which therefore allows the writer to describe it, for the occasion, as a person, without the slightest danger of being misunderstood.

The Bible surely is not full of rhetorical blunders, that should make us ashamed of it. Its writers do not attempt to personify objects, to add force to their language, and so utterly fail that most of their readers never suspect their design. Such a failure would be without a parallel in the history of literature.

Let us apply these principles to the opening passage of John's Gospel. We are told, by those who deny the true divinity of Jesus Christ, that the Logos is the personification of one of the Divine attributes—the Divine reason or wisdom—and that what the Evangelist designed to say was simply this, "In the beginning was the Divine reason or wisdom. It always existed. It was with God, never having a separate existence. And the reason was God. It was inseparable from his essence and attributes." This is a statement made by a writer representing this side of the question.

Tell us, now, when John thus described the Logos, did he take an object familiar to himself and every body as an attribute only, which he knew no one could suspect of being any thing else; and did he speak of this as a person, knowing that none of his readers could possibly be led into a mistake? *Is* the Logos, described by John, and made flesh to tabernacle among men, *a universally acknowledged attribute only*, destitute of all real personality, so as to be a fitting subject for personification, and therefore liable to no misapprehension? No man will undertake to assert that it is. The faith, of by far the largest portion of the Church, for eighteen centuries, in the real personality of the Logos, is evidence enough that it has not been so understood. Who, also, will presume to assert that John himself *knew* that he was speaking of an attribute only, and not a person, as we dare assert of Isaiah that he knew the heavens and earth were not persons, when he called upon them to listen to him? There is no presumption in asserting this of Isaiah. We know that he did not attach any idea of personality to the heavens and earth. We know that David did not, when he said of the mountains and hills, that they skipped like lambs; or the floods, that they clapped their hands. Do we thus *know* that John did not conceive of the Logos as a person? We certainly do not, and no man will venture the assertion.

But this does not exhaust the argument on this point. We said that the use of the figure of personification is founded on the *previous* known nature of the object as an impersonal thing, so understood by all. For example: We learn the nature of mountains, hills, and floods, not from David's description of them when he represents them as skipping about, or clapping their hands. We are presumed to be familiar with them already from other sources, so that, when we come to these figurative descriptions of them, we shall not be led into any error; as we inevitably should, if we depended upon these for our knowledge. We must have clear and definite information of the objects personified from other sources first, otherwise there is no possibility of intelligibly employing the figure.

We ask, now, Is the character of the Logos (and this argument applies equally to the Holy Ghost) so clearly and unalterably fixed beforehand in the minds of all, as only an attribute of God, an impersonal thing—do we learn this from other sources so absolutely that, when the sacred writers come to personify this Logos, or the Holy Ghost, we understand at once that they are speaking in a figure? Is this the fact? And will our friends tell us what those sources of knowledge are, that settle forever this character of the Logos as an attribute, so that, when personified, no one is deceived? The fact is, that the very passages in the Bible from which we learn the nature of the Logos and the Holy Ghost, are the ones where it is alleged the figure of personification is employed—which involves us in the absurdity of learning the nature of a thing from its personified use only, without any previous knowledge; as if we obtained our only idea of mountains from David's description of them, when skipping like lambs, and others of like figurative character.

This interpretation, then, of the Logos as the reason or wisdom, utterly and hopelessly breaks down, when tested by the unalterable laws of language.

Some may be disposed to ask, "Why did not the Scriptures speak so plainly about the divinity of Christ as to put it forever at rest, placing it beyond doubt?

We reply, that there is no language, no statement of truth, that may not be perverted, when the mind and heart are not in a congenial state to receive that truth; as there were no miracles from heaven, and no testimony of the Holy Ghost to the divine mission of Jesus, that would convince the opposing Jewish rulers that such an one as He was the Messiah of Israel. They did not want to be convinced of it. And their wicked hearts could turn aside all evidence and truth.

But the Scriptures are clear and unequivocal in asserting the divinity of Christ. The statement of John is as conclusive to this point as a mathematical demonstration; from which there is no escape without involving the writer in an unpardonable blunder, which would be fatal to him. And if men had an equal motive for opposing and denying the proposition, that the three angles of a triangle make two right angles, as they have that Jesus is the Son of God from the bosom of the Father, that proposition would find enemies in this world to contradict and blaspheme, just as the doctrine of Christ has done. We repeat, therefore, the statement of John is as conclusive as a mathematical demonstration. Look at the facts.

John was a man of common intelligence. He had ordinary common sense. This is not questioned. He knew how to write, and write intelligibly. He was an able writer, an unambiguous writer, an elegant writer, a profound writer. This is enough, without adding that he was an inspired writer. As such a man and writer, John understood the established laws of personification, which no man ever transgresses. He knew perfectly when an object might be personified—that is, when all his readers would agree with him in regarding the object described as not a person, and when also the subject allowed the exercise of a vivid imagination.

With a clear understanding of this, John takes up the history of his ascended Redeemer. He does not stop to dwell upon His human nature—how and where He was born and cradled. He passes all this by. His mind grasps a vaster conception. He goes back of the Saviour's birth, back of creation's birth, back into God's eternity. He seizes hold of that sacred name, *The Word*, familiar and hallowed to the mind of every Jew, as the name of Him who of old had tabernacled between the cherubim, and been worshiped for ages as the God of Abraham, Isaac, and Jacob. That name, inwoven with all the sublimest facts and associations of Jewish history, John takes as having the closest connection with the history of his now glorified Saviour, and says in a way of plain narrative, where there is not the slightest evidence of imagination, "In the beginning was the Word, and the Word was with God, and *the Word was God* The same was in the beginning with God. All things were made by Him, and without Him was not any thing made that was made. . . . And the Word was made flesh and dwelt among us ; and we beheld his glory, the glory as of the only begotten of the Father, full of grace and truth." Did John, in thus describing the Logos, know that he was speaking of an attribute only of the Deity, which would be so understood by all his readers without a moment's hesitation, and which was so obvious that no one could ever be led into a mistake? No man will assert this. On the contrary, he knew—and we assert this with the utmost assurance—that he was employing a sacred name, identified with the living God of Israel through long centuries, and so found upon almost every page of their vernacular Scriptures.

In these circumstances the personification of the Logos by John was an absolute impossibility, as certain as any mathematical demonstration. We are therefore shut up by the inevitable necessity of language to the literal meaning of the passage. John referred to *a person*, of whom he asserts without ambiguity or qualification, that He was in the beginning with God, and *was God*, the Creator of all things—that He was made flesh and dwelt on earth, revealing to the eyes of men His divine glories.

If, then, we are asked why the Scriptures do not settle the question of the divinity of Christ, we reply, They do settle it. It is plain as language and statement and fact can make it. And the reason why there is controversy still about it, does not arise from any thing that is wanting in the testimony of the Word of God; but wholly from other causes. A blind man may not see the sun, and deny its existence; but it is not for want of any reality or brightness in that luminary. To make the sun visible to such a man, you need to operate; not upon the sun to increase its light, but upon the eyes, to take away their blindness. It is evident, however, from the previous discussion, that many of the difficulties in which this subject has been involved, with the controversies growing out of them, might have been avoided, had we studied this sublime theme in the order and from the point of view in which it is presented to us in the sacred text-book. "Great indeed is the mystery of godliness." God himself knew all its difficulties. He began, therefore, at a point in the history where the elements were simple and indisputable, and, from these, advanced by easy stages to all the profoundest depths of the mystery. Had we followed God in this His own method of instruction, starting with the unquestioned divinity of Jehovah, God of Israel, dwelling between the cherubim, and tracing out the wondrous history until we behold Him as the Woman's seed, the Word made flesh and dwelling among us, there could have been no room left for doubt as to what the teachings of the Bible were on this subject. We should as soon have questioned the true humanity of our Immanuel, as His divinity.

CHAPTER XV.

HUMAN DEPRAVITY.

HAVING studied the revelations of the Godhead, we return to the point where we paused in the history, the introduction of an economy of grace. We are now to take up this system of redemption, and search out its nature, as unfolded in the Scriptures.

The first question that meets us here, lying at the basis of all correct views of a remedial plan for human recovery, is,

What is the character of our fallen humanity? How was human nature affected by the entrance of sin?

This is a question of vital moment, determining by necessity the nature of the whole work of redemption, since that must be adapted to the character of the race—to the nature and extent of their ruin. Accordingly, there is nothing which so shapes the views of men on religion and the doctrines of the Bible, as their opinions upon their own moral condition, and the nature and desert of sin. This is the starting point for all theological systems—the foundation upon which all the superstructures are reared. It is the point from which the Divine plan of mercy began, and by which all its provisions were shaped.

It may be observed, also, that there is no point upon which men are more likely to be led astray—none in respect to which they will more willingly be deluded. There is a powerful, controlling bias of mind which perverts the judgment. The eyes of men are blinded, their hearts are hardened. They are not willing to be convicted of sin. It demands an integrity which does not belong to selfish, unrenewed human nature, and which comes alone from Divine grace, to enable us to sit in judgment here, and study out that which will be to our own condemnation and shame. It is grace alone that can make men willing to know all the truth on this subject. If correct views of the Bible and redemption, then, depend upon a proper estimate of human character, it is not strange that there is a great deal of false theology. When the court and the jury are composed of the criminals and their accomplices, we need not wonder that truth and justice are not maintained. Such men certainly would require grace to administer the law righteously by their own hands.

We add another remark. Neither the Bible nor Christianity is responsible for the doctrine of human depravity.

Christianity does not make the doctrine: it simply finds it in existence. Man is responsible for all there is of truth in it. He made it. The Bible simply states it as a fact. If Christianity were blotted out of existence, human depravity would remain untouched. Man would be just the selfish, sinful being that he now is, and then without any remedy. It is therefore unreasonable to charge this doctrine, whatever it be, upon the Bible, as if it had any responsibility for its existence. Man's depravity and ruin ante-date Christianity, and will continue the terrible facts they are, even if the Christian system were proved a falsehood. We cannot alter in one iota the doctrine of man's utterly lost condition, by proving that the remedy proposed in the Bible is an ineffectual one, and its salvation vain.

These observations will show how appropriate it is to our plan, to take up this subject at this point of the history. That plan is to consider the facts of the Christian system in the natural order of their development. When, then, did the doctrine of sin and apostasy from God meet our first parents? At the very outset, before even they heard the gracious promise of a Deliverer, or knew there was to be any salvation. They themselves discovered this sad truth to their utter confusion and shame, without any revelation from Heaven. They did not need a revelation to tell them they were naked, or lead to efforts to hide that nakedness, or cause them to flee from their Maker's presence. Their knowledge of their own sin and ruin was prior to all their knowledge of the system of grace, and entirely independent of it. The study of it, therefore, is appropriate here.

What, then, is the true doctrine concerning sin, and human nature as affected by it?

In regard to the existence of sin there is no dispute. The only question is as to its *nature* and *extent.*

I. *What is the nature of sin?*

We shall but briefly discuss this point, although there is a wide field of controversy here, upon which we might enter.

Sin is a transgression of the law of God, committed by a moral and intelligent being as a subject of the Divine government; and which, in the nature of the case, cannot be committed by any other. Sin pertains to a moral agent. It cannot be predicated of any other. Whatever is necessary to moral agency, is necessary to sin. If thought, intelligence, will, and choice are necessary to the former, the same also are essential to the existence of the latter. Back of these, and aside from them, there can be no responsibility, no accountability. No man ever regards himself as responsible for a matter in which he had no knowledge, no thought, no choice, no action. You cannot force responsibility upon the mind in the absence of all these. The moral government of God is a government over moral beings—beings subject to moral law—a law revealed to intelligence and choice. God's law, which embraces all of man's duty to the utmost letter, does not extend back of the thoughts and purposes of his soul. It does not attempt to reach or control any thing beyond them. These, with the actions resulting, are all that it does presume to command. "Thou shalt love the Lord thy God with all thy heart, and with all thy soul, and with all thy mind and with all thy strength." "Love is the *fulfilling* of the law;" and common sense teaches that there can be no love aside from intelligence—thought and choice. We should not regard that as love, which had not these elements in it. If, then, the Divine law covers the whole ground of duty and obligation, it does not give any intimation that there can be sin which does not pertain to a being capable of thought and action; and it is certainly useless for us to go beyond that law to search after sin.

That there may be and is a predisposition or tendency to sin lying back of transgression in a fallen nature, is evident enough. The history of the race establishes this. But such tendency *toward* sin is something different from sin itself, because, by the supposition, it precedes sin. That which is prior to sin is not itself sin. That which precedes all moral, intelligent action in the soul, is not itself moral, intelligent action. The moment we get back of the thoughts, the purposes, the feelings of the man, we reach the constitution of the mind, which may indeed be disordered by sin, as belonging to a fallen nature; but there is no thought, choice, action, or any thing else there, upon which the Divine law attempts to lay its binding obligation, or for which that law holds the being responsible. Sin begins when moral action begins; nor would we detract from its exceeding evil, by carrying it back beyond the point of moral agency, and so destroying all the sense of responsibility which the mind must feel respecting it.

Our views of the nature of sin will appear incidentally as we proceed to consider the next point.

II. *Its extent.*

Man is a sinner. But *how much* of a sinner is he? What is implied in being a sinner? What character and standing does sin give to a moral being? These are the questions which men ask, and about which they widely differ.

The doctrine of the Bible, and of common sense, too, is, that sin is an act of rebellion against Heaven, which separates the soul from God—changes its whole moral character and relations, and subjects it both to condemnation and the bondage of evil. This implies the loss of all holiness, of all spirit of obedience and love to God. Thus the *moral* character of the sinner is wrecked.

The sinner himself thinks that this is a great exaggeration of his case—that he is not depraved to this extent—that his moral character is not by any means a wreck; but, like a stranded vessel, can be got off the rocks with more or less damage, and, with some repairs, can be put in good condition again. The sinner thus claims, not that he needs to be born again, or regenerated, but only improved; not that he needs to have an entirely new set of moral principles implanted, but only to develop those which he has already. This claim puts the sinner precisely where the Bible places the believer. The world, in its rebellion, plants itself essentially upon the same high ground which Christ claims for His Church, which He has new-created in himself. If this position of the world in respect to sin and human character is true, there is in reality no need for the Church, no room for it. This Church, according to the Scriptures, is only a partially sanctified body. The work of regeneration is merely begun; a moral principle being implanted, which is destined to prevail, while sin is not eradicated. Yet this is precisely what the world claim for themselves, only that their moral principle or virtue was never totally destroyed. There was always a remnant left, which, fostered and developed properly, will fit them ultimately for heaven. As for the doctrine of regeneration or the new birth, they see no necessity for it, and regard it as a libel on human nature. Accordingly, their moral reformation starts from the same elevated and advanced position, from which Christ's new creation itself begins, and there is a virtual denial of His whole work. It is declared of Him that, after having new-created a soul by the power of the Holy Ghost, and made heaven to rejoice over him, He has not in reality done any thing, or made him essentially different from other sinners, who, unrenewed, possess these same elements of goodness within them. The question, therefore, is a vital one to Christianity, and essential to a knowledge of our true moral standing before God.

What, then, is the true character of a sinner? What effect does the entrance of sin have upon a soul?

The difficulty in estimating the true effects of sin lies in the fact, that God's law is of so small account in our sight, and disobedience thereto such an insignificant matter. If we knew how to estimate the enormity of transgression, we should then no longer be astonished at its results. We may be able to see the subject more clearly in the light of some analogous cases, which will be more readily appreciated.

Let us take, by way of illustration, a man of high standing in the community, of unimpeachable integrity, of large property, and holding important public trusts. His name is a tower of strength, unlimited confidence being reposed in him. That man, in an unexpected moment, to the consternation and grief of the community, falls, betrayed into a flagrant act of dishonesty, which he cannot and does not deny. What is the effect of this deed upon that man's *character for integrity?* It works an entire forfeiture of it. His character is a wreck; and if the man ever establishes another, it must be *another*, built up on a different foundation—that of repentance. He could not regain the confidence lost, by planting himself upon any thing he could gather out of the wreck of his former integrity, without repentance for the crime committed. The very attempt to fall back on his former character, and maintain his good standing still, would only add to the proof of the utter unsoundness of his principles. The one thing demanded by all is repentance. Nothing else will ever restore the forfeited confidence of the community; and that confidence will come back only very slowly, as men have evidence that the repentance is deep and genuine. But mark the fact. This last character and standing are new, built upon a new foundation. The former were wholly wrecked.

Take another case. A man, occupying a high position of trust and power in the country, is found at last, to the dismay of all, plotting with traitorous hands for the overthrow of the government. What is the effect of such an act of treason upon that man's character for *patriotism?* It works, of necessity, an entire forfeiture of it. It destroys all confidence in him in this respect. Neither can he regain that lost confidence of his countrymen, except upon the basis of a new character, built upon a new foundation, that of repentance and the confession of his treachery. The attempt to come back on any other ground would be the deepest insult to his country, and the most perfect demonstration that his patriotism was the purest selfishness—not to be relied upon for a moment.

Woman's virtue might afford another illustration of the same principle. One fatal step taken by her makes a wreck of character, from which there is no recovery, except upon this same basis of deep repentance.

The principle is a clear and obvious one which all understand, that no one questions as thus applied to human conduct. The principle is, that one transgression works the entire forfeiture of character *in the circle to which the crime belongs.* One dishonest act will destroy a character for integrity. One traitorous deed will ruin all claims to patriotism. One fall from virtue will blast all purity in woman.

In the same way sin will work the forfeiture of holiness, and be the ruin of man's allegiance to heaven. Sin affects the entire character within its influence, working the destruction of the principle of which it is a violation. An act of dishonesty is a violation of the principle of integrity. A falsehood of the principle of truth. Treason of patriotism. A traitor is no longer a patriot. A dishonest man cannot have integrity of character.

What then is the principle in human character to which sin stands opposed, and of which it is the destruction? It is holiness—supreme love to God and allegiance to heaven. It is the principle which *the law of God* covers. A violation of that law, therefore, is the overthrow of all holiness, of all righteous allegiance to God and to heaven, making a wreck of moral character over this entire field. This, too, embraces the whole field of moral character. There is no point which the law of God does not reach and cover with its high claims. Other laws and principles are local and limited, embracing only a particular field. But the law of God sweeps the entire circumference of moral obligation, and lays the foundation for all moral character and righteousness. Sin of course, as the violation of that law, is the forfeiture of allegiance to heaven, the loss of all righteousness. The only possible way, too, for a sinner to regain character and reputation is to begin anew on another foundation, that of deep and thorough repentance ; while the attempt to save something out of the wreck of his former self and build on the old foundation, as if there were some truth and virtue and holiness still left, is a deeper insult to heaven by blotting out all distinction between holiness and sin—between allegiance to and rebellion against heaven. God can no more regard a sinner as any thing but a sinner, than we can avoid looking upon a thief or swindler as wanting all integrity. He can no more receive a sinner back to favor without a regeneration of his moral being, than we could admit a dishonest man to our confidence without evidence of his repentance and a change of principles.

Notice another fact of importance in this connection. Whenever a moral being renounces a right principle he adopts its opposite and comes under its power, as he was before under the control of the first. He passes a great gulf in going from one to the other—the deepest, widest gulf to be found in the universe. Between one sin and another there is only the narrowest line, that is easily passed. When a man has put his hand to one deed of iniquity, there is but the shortest step to another. He has then no character to lose, no principle to overstep. But between integrity and dishonesty, truth and falsehood, patriotism and treason, virtue and vice, holiness and sin, there is a great gulf; and a mighty revolution takes place when a man passes from one to the other. When also that fatal, dreadful step is taken, and the hand is reached forth to take the forbidden fruit of sin, the transgressor comes at once under the power of a new principle, which is now his master, to which he binds his soul, and which must rule him until it is renounced and a counter revolution again takes place as great as the original one. When a man goes over to the enemy by an act of treason, he continues a traitor, and treason becomes the principle of his life until it is renounced, if ever it be. He is made by the act an enemy to his country.

Such is the law of sin. When a moral being puts his hand to iniquity he renounces allegiance to heaven—his holiness is gone—he has adopted a new and antagonist principle, that of disobedience and rebellion; and he is necessarily held to that principle, until, by another revolution, equally great, it is broken away from and renounced, and he is restored. Thus when sin enters it becomes a power in the soul to rule there and have dominion. This is the doctrine of all experience. It is the doctrine of the Bible. "Whosoever committeth sin is the servant of sin," John viii. 34. It is his master to rule him.

With these plain facts and principles before us, which no one will controvert, the simple point upon which this question of human character turns is, what is a moral character without holiness—without love to God, without any true allegiance to heaven? How much real moral principle is there to hold one to duty and to right where there is no obedience or love to God? We do not ask here about natural kindness, amiability, generosity, love to kindred and friends, and other similar things belonging to human nature. These have nothing to do with the question. If a man is a traitor to his country it does not affect the matter in the least, or alter our estimate of him, that he is naturally amiable and generous. If a man has betrayed a great trust it makes no difference that he is kind to his family and friends; and no one would think of putting this in as a defence to his moral character. His integrity and character are gone, and public confidence in him is lost.

Moral character has its own peculiar province in human nature and its own laws, and need not be confounded with any other thing, though it frequently is when men wish to make out a case for themselves. Goodness, righteousness consist in principle—hearty allegiance to truth, right, and God—that which will hold a man to duty, which will withstand temptation and all the assaults of evil. Amiability, generosity, or love to friends will not do this. On the contrary, they may be the very things leading to transgression. They may be the occasions of a man's downfall and ruin. Many a one has sacrificed his soul and eternal truth for the sake of a loved wife or child. Love for country is a good thing, and as good, no doubt, for the inhabitants of Great Britain as for the citizens of the United States. Yet that very regard for country, *without any higher principle to control it*, and lead men to regard more what is right and just, might plunge these two nations into a most wicked war, and for the most selfish ends. We never judge of moral principle by these natural qualities and affections of human nature, which are variously distributed, and found indiscriminately among the good and bad. "If ye love them which love you, what thank have ye?" What is it to your credit? For sinners (the most wicked of men) do even the same.

When, therefore, we estimate moral character we demand moral principle—that which will make a man do right, *every thing* that is right—that which will subordinate every minor interest to the eternal law of truth and justice, which is God's law. This constitutes moral character. This makes a good man.

How much of such moral principle does one possess who has no holiness and owns no obedience to God—who has crossed that great gulf between holiness and sin, and become the subject of sin to serve it? What is the moral principle of the man who has always lived in sin against God and never made confession, never received forgiveness? These are searching questions. But just such searching work does the Bible and Christianity make with human character. Sin is an exceeding evil, beyond all the ordinary estimate of mankind. The truth is, all *moral* goodness is holiness. All true, abiding principle that will hold out to the last is allegiance to heaven. The fear and love of God alone can hold men true in every hour of trial, faithful unto death. This is the only rock foundation upon which a building can be reared. All else is sand, and will be swept away when the winds arise and the floods come.

To this world of sinners the love of God comes by repentance and faith in Christ. It begins with the regeneration of the soul. It is a new character built upon a new foundation. And this God requires as essential to securing his favor, even as we demand of the dishonest man and traitor that they shall give evidence of repentance before we admit them to our confidence. God does not demand in this matter more than we do. He acts upon the same principle precisely.

We thus see that the doctrine of regeneration or the second birth is nothing new in the world. It began with the very introduction of a remedial system, offering pardon and life to the sinner and requiring repentance It may not have been stated in the same words as at a later period, after that the Jewish nation had corrupted and denied the truth by the assumption that their natural birth through Abraham was an all-sufficient regeneration for them, enough to separate them from the rest of the sinful race. It became then necessary to assert that that birth through Abraham was of no avail to the end required, and that a second one was needed; the same that had always been demanded of every sinner in order to Divine acceptance. This doctrine of regeneration is laid in the very nature of sin, and Adam could not have been ignorant of it, as part of the system of redemption. He discovered his nakedness in an instant. Sin opened his eyes to the dreadful, irreparable loss of his character and standing in the sight of heaven. He needed no revelation to teach him this; and to coach him also to flee to hide himself from the presence of God. This deep and overwhelming conviction of sin was a matter of experience. Adam knew that his righteousness and innocence were gone—knew that he was *naked*, naked as to his soul as well as his body. The nakedness of his soul was what he learned first and felt most deeply. He had succeeded in partially covering his body; but this did not suffice, as his own statement shows. For, to the question, "Where art thou?" his reply was, Gen. iii. 10, "I heard thy voice in the garden, and I was afraid, *because I was naked;* and I hid myself." The searching interrogatory then came, "*Who told* thee that thou wast naked?" Yes, who told Adam that he was naked? He had suddenly come to the knowledge of the painful fact. Who told him? It was sin that uncovered him. And oh! with what terrific power did that conviction of his destitute condition come home to his soul! It is what every convicted sinner feels, and Adam knew and felt it all. Neither did it require any special revelation to let him understand that he must undergo another change to be restored to his innocence again and the favor of God—that that sin, which was as a separating wall between them, must be taken out of the way. A convicted sinner, pressed down under the heavy burden of his iniquity, and standing at hell's door, is easily taught the truth that he must be born again. That is a simple, elementary truth to the man who has learned something of the extent of sin and the moral ruin which it leaves in its track.

We expect that carnal, worldly men will quarrel with this doctrine of sin—that systems of theology will deny it—those systems which are in league with Satan and shaped to his purposes. Yet the truth of God will stand; while at the same time we can demonstrate to the conviction even of worldly men that this is both the doctrine of Scripture and of common sense; and, however unwelcome to the heart, is in accordance with all the facts of human nature—the only true philosophy, and will stand to the confusion of the sinner and all his self-delusions.

CHAPTER XVI.

BONDAGE OF SIN.

We have dwelt upon the nature and extent of sin, showing, in respect to the latter point, that it makes a wreck of human character, and that the only restoration is by a regeneration, which secures "a new man." We shall pursue this subject still farther in a little different line of thought, and attempt to show

WHAT THE BONDAGE OF SIN IS.

There is a prevalent idea, exerting a wide and powerful influence, that religion abridges the liberty of men—

that they are *free* when they can continue in sin at their pleasure, following the inclinations of their own wicked hearts; but that they at once renounce their liberty and subject themselves to a yoke of bondage when they take upon themselves the obligations of religion, and bind their souls by solemn vows to the service of the Lord. Under the influence of the same thought and feeling many have looked upon the temperance reformation and the pledge of total abstinence as little less than a despotism, by which they were to be robbed of their liberties and subjected to a yoke of bondage. In their view of the subject, the liquor drinkers, sellers, and drunkards are the independent men in the community, who know their rights and stand up manfully for them; while the temperance men have thrown away their liberties, and then turned to wage war upon the rights of others. Thus intemperance with all its deadly train of woes boasts of its freedom, while temperance puts its yoke of bondage upon the necks of men and robs them of their rights. Across the waters, also, we find a class of men who reason and feel in the same way toward republicanism. This to their apprehension is nothing but a brood of serpents—a very cockatrice's den, every egg of which is ready to break out into a viper. It is the very embodiment of licentiousness and anarchy, a contempt of all authority and law; so that if men desire to be free under a good government which shall protect all their most precious rights, let them beware of republicanism and maintain their loyalty to established law and order. Thus are the despotisms of Europe fighting under the uplifted banner of freedom.

This is the defence which iniquity and wrong always seek to make for themselves. It is eminently so in respect to sin. The servants thereof think and claim that liberty and enjoyment are to be found with them alone; while religion imposes a heavy yoke—abridges liberty, denies all rational enjoyment; in short, makes a hard master, to whom they never could submit. The devil thus claims all freedom for his service, and declares of Christ that His yoke is a *yoke* indeed, a yoke of bondage.

This, however, is a fearful delusion and lie. The truth is exactly the opposite. "If the Son shall make you free, ye shall be free indeed," John viii. 36. "Verily, verily, I say unto you, whosoever committeth sin is the servant of sin," viii. 34; becomes enslaved to it, so that it is his master. Nor is there any bondage so dark and terrible as that which sin imposes upon the soul.

This point we shall now endeavor to illustrate so as to make it plain to all, and not to be denied.

I. *By sin a man is sold and bound to the service of Satan.*

We know that many will rebel against this statement. They have never imagined that they were under any such bondage, being sold unto sin and pledged by a covenant which they cannot break, to do iniquity. They flatter themselves that they are free, having the control of themselves, with none to lord it over them. The devil never makes an effort to undeceive them in this. He is willing that his subjects should indulge in this fond delusion. It is a part of his system, by which he cheats men on to their destruction. He is willing that the votary of the wine cup should please himself with the idea that he can innocently indulge his appetite, and stop the moment he sees danger; knowing that he is winding the fatal coil around his unsuspecting victim, and leading him on with syren song to destruction. The votaries of sin are always under a delusion; nor do they discover the fatal cheat until it is too late, and their ruin is secured.

Let us examine now and see if the transgressor, when he yields first to temptation and consents to iniquity, does not, from that moment, surrender his liberty and independence, and covenant with Satan to be his and do his bidding. Although not put into so many words, does not the transgressor find this to be the understanding to which he is compelled to yield his assent, however reluctantly, and to which the adversary sternly holds him as, in fact, part of the bargain? This is the doctrine of Christ as already referred to, "Whosoever committeth sin is the servant of sin."

We shall argue this subject by facts, appealing to human experience.

Let us take those numerous cases so often to be found, where persons are assailed by temptation to commit iniquity, such deeds as they have heretofore not supposed themselves capable of doing. When the crime was first suggested, the tempted one recoiled in horror and refused to listen. But the temptation is renewed again and yet again, until the mind begins to be familiar with it and to parley. The appeals made to passion or self-interest are now listened to, and that with increasing interest, while the ear is being turned away from the warnings of conscience, until at last, in a fatal moment, the consent of the soul is obtained—the mysterious, awful boundary between innocence and guilt is overstepped, and the deed of transgression is done. The man finds himself, to his dismay, on the fatal side of that line, and he awakes, as did our first parents when their eyes were opened, to discover his nakedness—that his character, innocence, and virtue are gone; gone beyond his recall. And what is his situation—what the new relation in which he stands to the adversary? How does that tempter approach now? As he did before, with flatteries and falsehoods to allure and deceive? Ah! he knows the helplessness of his poor victim—knows that he is ruined, that he has sold himself, having parted with his liberties forever; and he comes now as the master to tell the slave what he *must* do—comes to dictate, and obtain a fulfillment of the bargain. He points, it may be, to a repetition of the offence, or to a further step onward in guilt, requiring the subject now to do his bidding. And what can the poor victim of sin do? Can he stand up in the might of his innocence and fling the vile tempter from him? He might once have done this; but that time is gone by. The power with which he could have hurled the fiend from him is gone; and now like a trembling slave he crouches, and begs that he may not be compelled to proceed any further. He asks as a favor that he may not be driven to put his hand again to that deed of shame. But his master knows his power, and is inexorable. He bids his enslaved subject go forward. Nor dare he disobey. He is dragged as with a halter about his neck, and driven on in the way of transgression.

How many sinners are there who, after the first fatal step taken in iniquity, would draw back and place themselves in their innocence, where once they stood, releasing their souls from the covenant of hell into which they find they have entered! But they have put their hands to that covenant, and cannot disown it. They have sold themselves to do evil, and Satan holds them to the engagement. Is this all fiction? Oh! is there not awful truth in it, to which the history of many a transgressor will bear most painful witness?

II. *We see this bondage of sin in the fact that the transgressor is not at liberty to put himself on the side of truth and righteousness, or to follow the call of conscience and duty.*

We assert that the sinner has surrendered his liberty to do what God, conscience, and duty require, and left himself no alternative but to sin and be the slave of sin. Doubtless many will start back at this proposition, prepared at once to deny it; but be not too hasty. The statement is true, and more than this; they who would so readily question and deny it have with their own lips stated the very same thing as matters of their own experience. They have done this scores of times, and never thought that they were uttering any thing strange, any thing different from what everybody knew and believed. We shall convict the sinner by his own testimony, from which he cannot escape, of the truth of our doctrine respecting his bondage under sin. We do not need to appeal to the testimony of the Scriptures. We have sufficient aside from this.

When, however, we speak of the sinner not being at liberty to follow the calls of conscience and duty, we do not mean, of course, that as a *repenting* sinner he might not do this. We speak of him in his present position and character as a servant of sin, without repentance or a new character built up by regeneration. We mean to assert what Paul asserts and what many think to be so severe: "Because the carnal mind is enmity against God; for it is not subject to the law of God, neither indeed can be. So then they that are in the flesh cannot please God," Rom. viii. 7. We are speaking of men "in the flesh" with the "carnal mind." Of them we assert that they are under this terrible bondage of sin, so that they are not at liberty to do right, or obey their own consciences, or perform what they know to be their duty; and we appeal to facts to prove it.

Find a man, then, who is destitute of any given moral principle, and he can never plant himself on that principle as a ground of action. It would be a contradiction and absurdity for him to do it. Take, for example, one who has no regard for the truth, who will utter a lie whenever his interest requires it. This is his known character. If tempted now to the commission of this sin, he may draw back in any particular instance, knowing that it will be of no avail, or that it will be speedily detected. But what an absurdity would it be for him to plant himself on the right ground, on which every honest man would stand—I dare not utter a falsehood. I fear God and must speak the truth. This would itself be the greatest lie he could utter. That man is in bondage to lying. He is not at liberty to speak the truth from principle and a sense of duty. He cannot turn away from temptation here out of any regard to conscience or duty.

Take the case of a dishonest man, who will not hesitate to overreach and defraud when opportunity offers. This is his well-established character. He is solicited to join in a scheme of fraud which promises advantage. He might offer various reasons why he would not embark in this particular enterprise; but how could he say, I am an honest man, and can have no part in the wickedness? Inconsistent with his principles to commit a fraud! Every man knows that it is the greatest of absurdities and falsehoods for such an one to profess to be actuated by principle and a sense of duty—that he must obey God and his conscience. He is not at liberty to profess any principle of the kind. He is shut up to sin.

Take the Sabbath breaker, who will pursue his business, or amusements, or journey on the Lord's day at his convenience. If asked to join in a Sunday excursion, is he at liberty to say, I have too much reverence for the Sabbath, and fear too much to offend God, to have part in this wickedness? Would not the profession of any such principle in his case be an absurdity?

These instances will sufficiently illustrate the principle in this direction. Look now at those of a different character—not where men are tempted to commit sin, but where they are required to perform duty.

Go to a worldly man, and urge upon him the claims and duties of religion—that, for instance, of prayer.

What is the answer which he will give? "I cannot pray." This he says in all truthfulness, not imagining that he is uttering any thing strange. I cannot pray. It would be a mockery of God for me to open my lips unto him. My prayers would be only an abomination to heaven. This is the experience of every worldly man. And the same is true in respect to any other religious duty. There is no heart for any, and none other could be performed more acceptably than prayer.

Is it so, then, by the sinner's own confession, that he is not at liberty to perform any duty which God requires —that the attempt would be but mockery? Is this true, and does the worldly man offer this as a reason why he can make no attempt at the performance of his duty? Is not this, however, a full endorsement of what may have seemed such a startling statement, that the sinner is not at liberty to do right, or follow the dictates of conscience and duty? Is it not precisely the doctrine of Paul, that *the carnal mind is not subject to the law of God, neither indeed can be; so that they who are in the flesh cannot please God?* If a man is destitute of religion, he cannot act from religious principle, and it is vain for him to profess any. If he has not the fear of God in his heart, he cannot act under such fear. If he has no spirit or principle of obedience, he cannot follow any command of God; and he is but uttering one of the deepest, truest convictions of his soul in declaring that he cannot. He thus asserts, concerning himself, that he is not free in this direction—that he has no independence, that he has lost his liberty to follow his own conscience, the voice of God, or his own highest interest. He proclaims himself the slave of sin, able only to do its bidding. He is free to sin, free to follow every evil inclination, which is the only freedom that sinners rejoice in. But to break the fetters of sin—to do what God, conscience, and duty require,—he has no liberty in this direction. Thus is he bound hand and foot under the rod of Satan, the servant of sin.

If sin makes a wreck of moral character, as we showed in a previous chapter, destroying all holiness and allegiance to heaven, we may see what the ruin of a soul is when thus delivered over to the bondage of Satan, and what a wretched delusion it is for such an one to boast of his liberty—his liberty to do wickedness, his liberty to sin against God, to trample upon law, upon truth and justice—his liberty to make war against heaven, and not to be restrained by any regard for God or the great interests of His kingdom of righteousness. That is precious liberty, indeed! Yet that is the liberty which sin offers and of which sinners so often boast themselves.

This subject shows us *how much foundation there is for the boast which the world so often makes of its liberality of sentiment and action.*

The world claims much for itself here, and freely charges the illiberality, narrow-mindedness, and bigotry to the side of Christianity. Some are apt to look upon all as narrow-minded who do not think as they do. But in what does the generous liberality of the world consist? In giving up their own views and principles and coming over to act on Christian ground? That the world never does. It never moves an inch in this direction. It can ask the Christian to abandon his duty, his principles and allegiance to heaven, and come over to its side; and it calls him bigoted and narrow-minded when he does not thus compromise with conscience, duty, and God. But where is the votary of the world that ever does what he asks the servant of the Lord to do? Where is one to be found who abandons for a moment his allegiance to sin, to go over and act for God and righteousness? No one ever does this, until he is prepared to make a final change of masters. Satan does not allow his servants any liberty here. The sinner is a servant to sin—a bond-servant; always such, and under all circumstances. He is never false to his principles. His carnal mind is at enmity with God. It is not subject to the law of God, neither indeed can be. So he never pleases God. His boasted liberality, therefore, is like his boasted liberty, which is nothing but the deepest bondage.

We see again the deplorable wretchedness of the sinner's case and his need of redemption.

The sinner is a slave—the most abject slave to be found; the most ignorant and degraded, and under the worst master. Chattel slavery is not to be compared to it; for such a slave may be one of God's noblest freemen. Political bondage is nothing by the side of it. Both these are but outgrowths from the great overshadowing despotism of sin and Satan. It is the slavery of sin that makes all the other forms of bondage on earth. It is because the Prince of Darkness rules this world that oppression and tyranny and injustice everywhere spring up.

Does any one ask, then, why sinners enjoy so much and feel so little of the burdens of oppression, if indeed they are under such a system of dread bondage? It is because they are within the reach of the sunbeams of Divine mercy, and their dungeon is lighted up and cheered by the sweet influences flowing from the precious liberty of the gospel of Christ. It is Christ and His salvation alone that makes this world tolerable. Sinners owe no thanks for what they enjoy to the master whom they serve, and who claims them for his own. All that he ever conferred upon them was nakedness. He stript them of every thing; and it is only the interposing arm of Divine mercy that is between them and perdition. This bright and beautiful world is not Satan's, but

Christ's; but all the heathenism and wickedness, the despotism and crime in it, are the devil's. It is only because of Christ and His gospel that these sinners are not groaning under the bondage of heathenism, dark as that which covers benighted Africa. Every precious spark of liberty we enjoy we owe to this blessed gospel. It was Christ alone that ever came to open our prison doors and unbind our fetters. It is Christ alone that interposes between any sinner and perdition. The bondage of sin terminates there. That is its legitimate end. The only liberty a sinner has from his master is to sin; and the end of sin is death. It is death always and every where. Sin does not work any thing but death.

It was this spectacle of a world of sinners, under sentence of death and bound in Satan's fetters, that moved the heart of Infinite love and stirred up the Son of God to His divine mission; that in His sufferings and humiliation, His tears and death, He might work out the deep problem of redemption. The language of this triumphing Conqueror is, "I am He, which liveth and was dead: and behold, I am alive for evermore, Amen. And have the keys of death and of hell." Yes, thanks be to Heaven that Jesus, our Immanuel, does hold the keys of death and of hell. That is the reason, and the only reason, why there is any liberty left on earth—why there is a moment's respite or joy to any poor sinner. Christ introduced His remedial scheme of mercy immediately upon the entrance of sin; and this alone has averted hell. The bondage of sin, unmitigated by Christ, is hell—nothing but hell. A sinner will require no other perdition for his soul than to be delivered over to the dominion of sin and Satan, where Christ shall no more interpose for him nor put forth efforts for his salvation. That will be outer darkness forever, even the blackness of darkness.

CHAPTER XVII.

A SIN-OFFERING.

HAVING considered the sinful and lost condition of our world, we pass directly to the study of that system of redemption which God instituted for its recovery; and which of necessity was His work—of His contriving, and made known entirely by Divine revelation. Human wisdom was not equal to its devising; nor human power to its accomplishment, nor human reason to its discovery. It originated in the eternal counsels and was brought down from heaven to men.

It will not be without interest here to study the *method* which God adopted to unfold the knowledge of His will in regard to these matters in the early history of the race; and this investigation may serve to throw new light upon some of the facts recorded there.

The first revelation then concerning the plan of redemption, was in reference *to the way of approach to God, and the terms upon which the Divine favor might be secured.*

This was the point upon which instruction was first demanded. Man could no longer approach God in his innocence to find favor. The question now was, how could he come in his sinfulness? To furnish an answer to this, we have our attention drawn to a most painful and marvellous record—that of the shedding of a brother's blood; a foul murder, committed in the first household, and constituting the opening scene in earth's tragic and bloody drama.

Many, doubtless, may have queried in their own minds, why the record of that fearful crime occupies such a space in the sacred narrative; why such prominence is given to it in a history so exceedingly brief. Why must its memory be preserved to the end in a revelation from heaven, so that every nation should become familiar with the dreadful story? These questions will be clearly answered by a careful study of the narrative.

The history makes it plain that the crime grew immediately out of the subject of religion—a fact which shows the meaning and object of the narrative. There was a controversy between the brothers on the vital question of the way of approach for man to God under a system of grace; a controversy which enlisted the strongest passions of their natures and developed their true principles, and in which God himself at length interfered, becoming a direct partner.

The record runs as follows: "And in process of time it came to pass that Cain brought of the fruit of the ground an offering unto the Lord. And Abel, he also brought of the firstlings of his flock, and of the fat thereof. And the Lord had respect unto Abel and to his offering. But unto Cain and to his offering he had not respect. And Cain was very wroth, and his countenance fell," Gen. iii. 3. The facts are here clearly detailed. The observance of an appointed time of worship, the offerings made by each of the parties, the favor and displeasure which God manifested towards the offerings and the offerers, and the rage which was kindled in Cain's bosom at the rejection of his sacrifice.

The secret and meaning of this striking narrative are, that here was God's attempt to instruct the race on the subject of Divine worship and the way of approach to Him by sinners; not that this was the first instruction given; for Adam had undoubtedly received lessons on this subject already. But here we find the Divine teachings embodied in the lesson which God intended for all after generations, so that they could not forget or mistake them. God would at the outset and forever settle the question respecting the mode in which the guilty were to approach to find favor in His sight and have their sins forgiven. This was a cardinal point, and one on which a revelation was especially demanded; from which He would not withhold his clearly expressed will and decision. This instruction he embodied, not in the form of a doctrine or declaration, but in the shape of a thrilling narrative of facts, which the generations would long have painful occasion to remember. We have the controversy on this subject distinctly brought before us by two opposite and contending parties, resulting in the murder of one of them, with God's decision made in the case. No method could have been conceived better calculated than this to clear the subject from all ambiguity—to arrest attention and make a lasting impression upon the race.

The whole narrative implies, and is based on the fact, that God had made previous communications of His will respecting this matter, and appointed the method of worship and approach to Him by a bloody offering. If we concede the fact of a Divine revelation at all to men, here was the time and the subject for it. It was what Adam needed first of all to know, without which he could do nothing. When we consider also how full and complete revelation has been on the whole plan of redemption in all its parts and relations, it is incredible that Adam should have been without instruction on this vital point—being left, either to do as he pleased and adopt any mode of approach that he saw fit, or to discover God's method by his own ingenuity, a thing plainly beyond his power.

The Scriptures, however, settle this question when

they assert directly, "*By faith*, Abel offered unto God a more excellent sacrifice than Cain," Heb. xi. 4; which means that Abel *believed* God by receiving His instructions on this subject. His sacrifice could not have been made *in faith*, unless God had revealed himself here and required the bleeding lamb. That revealed will, constituted the foundation and object of his faith. Some have understood this faith of Abel, referred to in the Epistle to the Hebrews, as recognizing Christ through the lamb slain and taking away sin. While there may be some truth in this—how much we cannot tell—yet any one who reads the eleventh chapter of Hebrews, will readily observe that the cases there specified are instances of faith in *receiving the Divine testimony*, believing what God revealed to those holy men, however wonderful or strange the same might be. The matter revealed to Abel was that of the bloody sacrifice; and in this he believed God, humbly accepting His teachings. "By faith," therefore, he offered unto God a more excellent sacrifice than Cain. This passage thus settles the positive institution of sacrifices.

It is not an insignificant circumstance also that the record is made in this very brief history that "Unto Adam and his wife did the Lord God make coats of *skins* and clothed them." It is circumstantial evidence to the fact of such sacrifices; and thus did they owe the hiding of their nakedness and shame to the innocence and sufferings of these very slain ones, being clothed in their garments, and obtained only at the cost of their lives.

"And in process of time," which may perhaps refer to the fact of the sons of Adam arriving at such age that the duty of sacrifice was devolved upon them as heads of their own households, and not alone upon their father, "it came to pass that Cain brought of the fruit of the ground an offering unto the Lord; and Abel, he also brought of the firstlings of his flock and of the fat thereof." This difference was not an accident, but clearly a matter of deliberation and design, growing out of settled convictions and principles. Abel's selection from his flock was the result of "faith." He obeyed Divine instruction, discerning also the meaning and appropriateness of such an offering. The manner also in which Cain was offended by and resented the rejection of his fruits, is clear evidence that his selection was one of fixed design, that showed his whole religious character. It was the result of long cherished thoughts and purposes of heart. In truth, here was the culmination of a great and earnest religious controversy on a vital point. Here, therefore, is found the significance of this terrible record of crime in the first household. Had this murder grown out of ordinary causes, such as avarice, ambition, or other passions of like nature, it would never have been deemed worthy of a place in the sacred record. But connected closely with the worship and service of God—growing out of the most opposite religious principles and entering into the vital questions of redemption, it had the deepest significancy for the race through all its generations. "The blood of Abel"—that which he offered in sacrifice—has had a voice of thrilling power to speak from age to age, second only to that richer blood speaking from Calvary. These offerings of the two brothers, then, were matters of deliberation and design—the embodiment of their deep religious convictions.

What meaning, too, to a sinner was there in that bleeding lamb required at his hands, and made the only medium of his approach into the presence of the offended majesty of heaven! That innocent animal, the choicest of the flock, must be taken by the transgressor and bound at the altar of the Lord. Then laying his hand upon the head of that chosen victim *he must confess all his iniqui-*

ties before God, transferring them to this substitute. The solemn confession thus made, with his own hand he must strike the blow which takes its innocent life. He must look upon its dying struggles, and see its life blood poured out. Its body must then be placed upon the altar and consumed, a sacrifice of sweet-smelling savor unto God.

In all this a convicted, humble sinner would see a meaning, which would come home with overwhelming power to his soul. The whole scene would graphically tell of his own forfeited life as a guilty transgressor—that he was the one who merited death, and that only by an atonement made in the blood of innocence could his iniquities be taken away, and he admitted to the presence and favor of God. A transgressor without any sense of guilt might not see this. But he would feel it, upon whose soul lay the consciousness of his sin in the sight of Heaven, and whose burdened thought was, how shall I stand in the presence of an offended and holy God? Thus, too, did Abel receive the truth. He saw the meaning of the appointed ordinance, and with an humble, believing heart entered into it, building here all his hopes as a sinner.

Cain was of a different character evidently, and entertained other views on this subject. He had never been made to see himself as a sinner before God, nor feel the heavy burden of iniquity upon his soul. Consequently, he saw no reason or meaning in that bloody and, to his apprehension, cruel offering of an innocent animal. He could not appreciate its necessity, and, in the pride of his self-righteous heart, contended against it, maintaining, as so many others have done, that God would be as well and better pleased with other sacrifices that were equally valuable in themselves and far more appropriate to His benevolent character. Cain contended, as we have every reason to presume, that these bloody offerings were a libel on the Divine goodness, and that God could have no delight in the blood and sufferings of His innocent creatures. It was unnatural and contrary to all reason. The fruits of the earth were a far more appropriate and acceptable offering, as well as a more fitting expression of man's gratitude for God's overflowing goodness. As soon then as he could have the opportunity he would carry out these deep convictions of his own mind and worship God in the way which he deemed to be most suitable to His perfect nature and all the dictates of sound reason.

It may be, also, that there was another powerful influence operating on the mind of Cain. As shown heretofore, Eve regarded her firstborn as the Coming One, the promised seed, and so named him Cain, or the possession. This of necessity was a cherished idea with her as well as with Adam, and must have been communicated to their beloved child. They must often have talked over that precious promise; and Cain may have grown up under the forming influence of the thought that he was the one destined to bruise the serpent's head and prevail against all their enemies. Many have arisen in the world and claimed a Divine mission to instruct the race, with far less grounds to build upon than this.

Putting this controlling idea into the mind of such a worldly, unsanctified man as Cain was, we can readily understand what a religious fanatic he might become, such as Mohammed and others, who have conceived that they had a commission from heaven to found new systems. Having the preëminence as the firstborn, and as such an anointed one from God, he may readily have cherished the flattering thought that his conceptions of divine things were especially important and to be accepted as the truth. From such a position he would insist upon his own views as possessing peculiar authority, while the race would inevitably look up to him with the greatest confidence and veneration. He was in a situation to command their highest regard. The reason, too, why the most extraordinary success did not attend his career, was because God wisely took the most efficient and summary means to show that he had no authority to reveal truth or instruct mankind, and that his system was all the work of a fool.

With the facts of the case thus explained, look now at the two men, representatives of two great religious systems, appearing before the manifested Divine presence, each with his chosen offering and equally confident of acceptance. In humble faith and deep conscious unworthiness Abel presents himself with his selected lamb, and penitently confessing his sins over the head of his innocent victim, he strikes the blow which causes its life blood to flow out, and then lays its body upon the altar to be consumed.

In the pride of his heart and the assurance which self-righteousness always gives, Cain comes with his chosen offering of fruit, magnificent it may be to all outward appearance and a fitting tribute of thanksgiving to the bountiful Giver—looking upon it with complacency and congratulating himself withal that he had so much nobler views of the Divine character and juster appreciation of His nature than his brother, who so positively insisted that nothing but the blood and suffering of innocence would suffice to appease the wrath of God.

At this point of the history we need to be especially careful that we do not mistake the whole matter by anticipating the character and standing of this firstborn of the race, *as revealed by subsequent events.* We know him as a guilty murderer, driven out from the presence of the Lord. But no one conceived of him thus at this point of time, nor deemed him capable of such a crime. Up to this event his standing and character had been unimpeached. He was a religious man, claiming a knowledge of the Divine will and zealous for its performance, as his sacrifice proved. He was industrious, faithful, laboriously cultivating the earth, honored and loved as the firstborn. At this point of time, therefore, the two had an equal standing and character, the advantage only being on the side of Cain as the elder brother and as the imagined deliverer, who had been promised.

Thus the brothers came and stood before that flaming sword of the Divine presence by the way of the tree of life, the appointed place of worship, to have their principles tested. " And the Lord had respect unto Abel and to his offering; but unto Cain and to his offering he had not respect;" Gen. iv. 4. This respect to one and not the other was manifest and decisive, so as to leave the matter in no doubt; so manifest that Cain's anger was kindled at the slight put upon him, and his countenance gathered blackness at the very altar of God. The form of this Divine approval doubtless was, as in instances occurring afterward, by the fire reaching forth from the flaming sword between the cherubim and touching the sacrifice of Abel so as to consume it, while Cain's remained upon the altar without any sign of recognition. God thus accepted the sacrifices that were presented at the dedication of the tabernacle and the temple, kindling there the sacred fire, which was afterwards carefully kept by the priests and not suffered to go out. The present case, too, was one when Divine interposition was demanded—when God, as we know, did interpose so as to satisfy Cain himself that his offering was an affront, and to demonstrate, likewise, how deeply his feelings and principles had been involved in the success of his chosen sacrifice. Remembering what wonderful calmness and accuracy in the statement of facts pervade the Scriptures, we are authorized to understand that all the strongest passions of Cain's selfish nature were kindled when it is said that "he was *very wroth, and his countenance fell.*" He had evidently been wounded to the vitals. The most deeply cherished principles of his life had been overthrown. The very inspiration which he had claimed from heaven as the Coming One was turned into a lie. Instead of its being manifest that he was acting under a divine commission, it was now apparent that he did not understand the will and teachings of Heaven even as his younger brother, whom he had so often sought to instruct on this subject; and that he could not for himself find access into the presence of God. He stood there rejected and frowned upon, while the fire from the Lord was consuming the bloody sacrifice of Abel, which he had so much despised.

Cain had presumptuously taken it upon him to invade the Divine prerogatives by abolishing God's instituted worship and establishing another system according to his own mind; and the Lord met him at the outset with His deepest frown. As already stated, Cain stood at this time in an assumed position of great importance before the race, where his opinions and action would exert a commanding influence through coming ages. It was necessary, therefore, for God to come out in the most decided manner to establish His doctrine of the bleeding lamb and rebuke this false prophet, putting a mark upon him, so that the world might be undeceived by his pretensions and look elsewhere for a deliverer. This God did; the necessity for such interposition being made still more apparent in the violent wrath which the remonstrance kindled in the breast of Cain. This anger showed how powerfully his own views had taken possession of his mind and how intensely he was attached to them, so that they had become as his very life.

This explanation of the narrative is further confirmed

by the conversation which immediately followed. "And the Lord said unto Cain, Why art thou wroth, and why is thy countenance fallen? If thou doest well, shalt thou not be accepted? [I have the excellency or superiority, that is, over thy brother.] And if thou doest not well sin [a sin-offering] lieth at the door." Such an offering is at hand for thee, by which thou mayest be forgiven and accepted, even as thy brother. He has been welcomed, because he came as a transgressor with a sin-offering. There is the same way of approach for thee. "And unto *thee* shall be his desire, and thou shalt rule over him." Thou shalt still have the place of preëminence and excellency as the firstborn. Cain had evidently claimed this preëminence over his brother, insisting that he had a right to know what the ways and will of God were. And now when it was made manifest that he was in the wrong, instead of humbly acknowledging the fact and taking the means which God pointed out of finding acceptance and maintaining the supremacy which his younger brother was entirely willing to concede, his fierce wrath was kindled. All the pride of his selfish nature had been wounded. God had shown that his claims to a peculiar insight into divine things were false—that he had no authority to declare the will of Heaven, but must humbly receive it even as his more righteous brother, who owned that he was a sinner, condemned before God and needing the blood of innocence shed for his justification.

Cain was not the man to take kindly such a rebuke as this, and all his selfish nature was now roused into intensest action. "And Cain talked with his brother Abel:" by which is implied that he continued the controversy, still endeavoring to justify himself and maintain his own former position. He was not willing even now to bring the required sin-offering and confess himself a transgressor before God, needing atonement. "He talked with Abel his brother. And it came to pass when they were in the field that Cain rose up against his brother and slew him." He was in no mood to listen to argument. God's own decision of the question had only angered him. He was not convinced. He was enraged now against God himself. His wrath was kindled against his righteous brother; but driven from all argument, his only and last resource was violence, and he raised the murderous hand to take that brother's life.

It was a fearful deed. Oh, what sorrow in that first household! The firstborn of the race, thought to be the promised seed, a murderer! His own righteous brother the victim! And the bloody deed committed by the side of the very altar of the Lord, where they had brought their offerings! Yet there was a wise and overruling Providence in it all. Abel was cut off in the midst of his days, when, as it might have seemed, such a man could not be spared. But he had fulfilled his mission; and his death accomplished more for the world than ever his life could have done. "By faith Abel offered unto God a more excellent sacrifice than Cain, by which he obtained witness that he was righteous [justified], God testifying of his gifts; and *by it, he being dead yet speaketh.*" Yet speaketh! Abel's influence and teachings still live. He stood fast by the cardinal truths of redemption —the ordinances of God's own appointment, giving his own life a witness to them. Abel's bloody sacrifice *has* been preaching to the race and testifying to this hour. Cain too! Well was it that he was arrested in his bold and impious career! Better for the world that he should prove a murderer, to go out with the mark of God upon him, than that he should stand forth as the hope and deliverer of earth, to corrupt the knowledge of God and strike down that great vital doctrine of a sin-offering and atonement by the shedding of innocent blood. Cain was a bitter enemy of that doctrine. He denied it and pronounced it a libel on the Divine character. He instituted a mode of sacrifice, a thank-offering of fruits, which he deemed suitable and becoming in all respects; and he "was very wroth" when God rejected him and his sacrifice. We thank God and rejoice unfeignedly, that *Cain, the murderer, stands forever the representative and exponent of such theology*, while the blood of the martyred Abel is an undying witness to the race of the only way of approach for sinners to God, that whosoever doeth not well, for him a sin-offering lieth at the door.

Here then is the deep significancy of that strange and tragic history with which the drama of earth opens. It is God's lesson of instruction to the race respecting a sin-offering and the way of approach to Him for sinners by the shedding of blood, embodied in a form which could not be mistaken. The first instructions given to Adam might, perhaps, have been liable to misapprehension. Cain, at least, did not feel shut up to them, seeming to think that the way was open for him to adopt another and better method. God wisely permitted the attempt and then interposed himself in the controversy, giving his own decision. In that form the lesson stands for the instruction of the race to the end of time. The doctrine was of such vital moment, and withal so much out of the way of men's ordinary modes of thinking, that it was proper and needful that God should make it plain and establish it on a foundation that could not be shaken. Accordingly, we have this thrilling history of Cain and Abel to preach to the end of time, and bear witness to the truth that a sin-offering lies at the door for every transgressor, and that aside from this there is no approach for him to God, nor hope of acceptance.

CHAPTER XVIII.

FAITH.

THE revelation of the system of redemption divides itself into two parts; the first, embracing the divine working, or what God himself purposes to do; the second, human working, or the part man is required to perform. Both are essential. God must devise a plan and open a way, while upon man devolves the responsibility of coöperation and performing his allotted part. In the combination of both agencies the work of salvation is complete.

In the history of Cain and Abel we have explained God's instituted method of worship by a sin-offering, or the way in which sinners might approach to find forgiveness and justification. It is needful, however, to show still more definitely what God requires of the sinner; what he must do to coöperate, so as to make the divine plan effective and complete. The New Testament is full and explicit on this subject; faith being held forth as the great requisite to justification before God. The gospel is declared to be a system of grace, because it is of faith. It does not, however, appear so manifest that this was the one thing required from the beginning; and that it was upon this basis of faith that sinners were always accepted and justified before God. This doctrine *seems* to many to be a newer system, belonging more to the dispensation of these latter days.

What, then, were the early teachings of God on this subject, and where found in the Old Testament?

The Apostle says distinctly that this faith entered into the character of the ancient saints and laid the foundation of their piety. By faith, Abel offered unto God a more excellent sacrifice than Cain, by which he obtained witness that he was righteous, God testifying of his gifts; and by it, he being dead yet speaketh. By faith Enoch was translated, that he should not see death; and was not found, because God had translated him; for before his translation he had this testimony, that he pleased God. But without faith it is impossible to please Him; for he that cometh to God must believe that He is, and that He is a rewarder of them that diligently seek Him. By faith Noah, being warned of God of things not seen as yet, moved with fear, prepared an ark to the saving of his house; by the which he condemned the world, and became heir of the righteousness which is by faith; Heb. xi. 4. So likewise of Abraham, Sarah, Joseph, Moses, and the worthies who followed. The element which entered into the character and lives of these men was faith. By this they were justified and obtained favor with God.

Did they, however, so understand it? Was this made plain at the beginning? And if so, how? The Apostle answers both these questions, when, after speaking of the faith of certain of these saints, he pauses to say, "But without faith it is impossible to please him; for he that cometh to God must believe that he is, and that he is the rewarder of them that diligently seek him." Faith is here founded *in nature and necessity.* It does not require a revelation to make it known. No man *can* come to God with the purpose of seeking Him, unless he believes in the existence of such a being; as no one can write to a friend, except in the assurance that there is such a person. This faith is an essential pre-requisite, and God assumes it in His dealings with men. Besides this faith in the Divine existence there must also be faith in Him as the rewarder of those who seek Him aright in the way of His appointment. God gave men to understand at the outset that He would show favor to sinners —that He would provide a way for their redemption, thus opening the door of mercy and inviting their approach. It needed no revelation to teach men that God would be well pleased with their reception of this, both in believing that what He declared was true, and also in adopting the method which He pointed out—that He would be displeased with their treating it as a falsehood on His part. Faith in God is the strongest dictate of nature. At this very point sin found entrance. Because our first parents distrusted God, and gave a willing ear to the voice of the tempter, they stretched forth their hands to pluck the forbidden fruit. Had their faith in God continued unshaken they had never done that deed of wickedness. What they now needed, too, above all else, was to have that faith restored; and when God revealed the fact that He would be gracious and would save, their simple duty was to welcome the precious revelation, entering into it with fullest assurance. Without such faith it would be impossible to please Him; for "he that believeth not God hath made Him a liar." There is no insult which men more quickly resent than an impeachment of their veracity. It is an equal indignity to God to discredit His word.

The doctrine of faith, therefore, is founded in the necessity of things. It would have been an absurdity for God to have attempted formally to reveal it as something that men did not understand. It would have implied a want of common humanity. Does any one ask then, why so much is said of faith in the New Testament and why it is so often insisted on! We answer, that it is not faith in God as a first principle which the New Testament dwells upon, but the *object* of faith, which is there held forth. The message of the gospel is not simply believe, but believe *in the Lord Jesus Christ.* He is presented as the end of faith. It is the office of the Scriptures to tell us *what* we must believe. This brings us to the next point in our subject:

What was the faith of ancient believers? What did God require them to believe?

We answer in general, all that He saw fit to reveal to them in connection with the plan of redemption. He gave them first to understand, that they were to be placed under an economy of grace with a view to their recovery —that He would deal with them, not according to law and justice, but in long-suffering patience designed to secure their repentance and salvation. They were to receive this precious truth—to look upon themselves as sinners needing redemption, and then humbly believe all that He should reveal from time to time concerning the way in which the work was to be accomplished and their duty relating thereto. They were willingly to accept all the Divine teachings on this great subject.

The first point on which instruction was needed and given, was the way of approach for sinners to God, which brought out so strikingly the faith of Abel. "By faith Abel offered unto God a more excellent sacrifice than Cain." Why more excellent? Because he was willing to receive and follow the Divine teachings, without seeking to find a better way of his own. God had required a sin-offering. By the shedding of innocent blood alone could the guilty approach to find favor. Abel humbly accepted this revelation from heaven and acceded to it, discerning at the same time its true intent and meaning. "Wherewith shall I come before God?" has ever been the great question with a guilty race of sinners, which none, too, but God could answer, and which faith must humbly receive. As sinners, and in their own character, they could not stand before Him. The confession of their sin was but the acknowledgment from their own lips that they deserved death and banishment from the Divine presence. They needed, therefore, to know how they might come with the confession of sin and yet be treated no more as sinners; which was the very thing that God revealed. The offering of a spotless lamb was required, to the head of which they must transfer all their iniquities, and then taking its life, they must offer its blood as an atonement for their souls. It was a most appropriate and significant act, telling, plainer than any words could set forth, their own just condemnation and desert of death and their acceptance of a substitute, upon whom their iniquities might be laid and through whom they might obtain justification. By their own act in laying their hands upon the head of an innocent lamb, with the confession of their sin, they transferred that sin to another, through whom and by whom alone they hoped for justification.

How far the saints of old saw the application of this to Christ, in His being made a sacrifice for sin, it is difficult to tell. It certainly prepared the minds of men and taught them to look for the sufferings of Christ. The Apostle Peter tells us of the prophets, "Searching what, or what manner of time, the Spirit of Christ, which was in them did signify, when it testified beforehand *the sufferings of Christ and the glory that should follow.*" They did not understand clearly how sufferings and glory could thus be united; yet they searched diligently into the mind of the Spirit to learn what the signification was. This much, however, was plain from the beginning, that an atonement was required for the justification of the transgressor, and that nothing would suffice but the shedding of innocent blood. This was the truth lying at the foundation of the system of redemption, which faith must accept. This was the truth which Abel did cordially welcome. He not only received the Divine revelations on this subject as the truth of God, but he also entered into them as the great necessity for his soul, making confession of his own sin, transferring that sin to the head of suffering innocence, and relying upon that shed blood as the ground of his justification with God. Accordingly, he obtained witness that he was righteous, God testifying of his gifts.

But Cain had no such faith. He would not receive the Divine teachings on this subject for the reason, doubtless, that he saw no appropriateness in them; and this he perceived not, because he did not understand his character and condition as a sinner. Cain, so far as he could perceive, had not done any great wickedness. He had been industrious, faithful, obedient, doubtless, to his parents—had submitted to the Divine command in obtaining his bread by the sweat of his face, even as his brother Abel, who devoted himself to the easier task of tending the flocks. It was appropriate, too, as he reasoned, that he should bring of the fruit of his own toil, an offering to the Lord; and fully as acceptable, for aught he could see, as the blood of suffering innocence. Cain thus followed the dictates of his own blinded heart, and undertook to approach God in the way which he in his pride and unbelief thought to be best. When, also, his offering was rejected, and he was told specifically and positively that there was a *sin-offering* lying at the door, through which he would find favor like his brother Abel, all the rebellion of his selfish heart was roused within him. It was not a sin-offering that he cared to make. This it was that offended him, that he should come to confess himself a sinner and acknowledge his own just condemnation. He was ready to make a thank-offering to the

Lord in acknowledgment of His goodness, and that was enough. Thus did Cain show his unbelief and therein stumble to his overthrow and ruin.

The second example of faith given by the Apostle is that of Enoch. "By faith Enoch was translated that he should not see death; and was not found, for God had translated him; for before his translation he had this testimony that he pleased God." The faith of Enoch here described may be taken in two senses; first, in the sense of piety, being descriptive of his character as a saint, and that on account of such faith or piety God translated him. Or, secondly, it may mean that this translation was the *object* of his faith; it having been revealed to him that he would thus be taken from earth without seeing death. This latter we take to be the true meaning, inasmuch as it thus accords with all the other examples given and falls in with the argument. The Apostle's design is to give remarkable instances of the faith of ancient worthies, showing how they believed God and received His testimony in respect to all things in which He chose to reveal His will. Abel received the Divine teachings in respect to bloody sacrifices and presented the required sin-offering. Noah, being warned of God, prepared an ark to the saving of his house. Abraham, when he was called to go out into a place which he should after receive for an inheritance, obeyed; and he went out, not knowing whither. By faith he sojourned in the land as a stranger and offered up his only child of promise. Moses also refused to be called the son of Pharaoh's daughter, and forsook Egypt, enduring as seeing Him who is invisible. So of others, "who subdued kingdoms, wrought righteousness, obtained promises, stopped the mouths of lions, quenched the violence of fire, escaped the edge of the sword, out of weakness were made strong, waxed valiant in fight, turned to flight the armies of the aliens."

These things were the objects of faith to these heroes. The translation of Enoch, therefore, was the object to him which his faith received; not that this was the only thing in which he believed God. He received all the Divine teachings. He brought his bleeding lamb, as did Abel, and offered its blood as an atonement for his soul. But to him in addition were given special revelations in regard to the coming of Christ with His risen saints and for judgment upon the ungodly. These Enoch received and boldly preached, as Jude states, and doubtless amid wide prevailing unbelief, "for he had this testimony, that he pleased God," even as Abel had, that his offering was accepted. Then to crown all, and to seal Enoch's testimony respecting the coming of Christ with His saints, God gave His servant to understand that He would put the extraordinary honor upon him of revoking, in his case, the sentence of death, transferring him from earth without a passage through the grave, thereby anticipating that resurrection state of which he prophesied and giving present demonstration of it to an unbelieving world. Even this did not stagger Enoch's faith. He believed God implicitly in this also; "and by faith he was translated that he should not see death; and was not found, for God took him."

Abraham also furnishes another wondrous instance of faith in receiving all God's testimony, of which we have a full and thrilling record—how he left his own country, not knowing whither the Lord would lead him; how he sojourned in the land of promise as a stranger, having no possession in it; enough to try his faith to the utmost; for to all human appearance at the time it was a signal failure of fulfillment on the part of God. He could not and did not possess the land into which he was brought and for which he had left all. It was occupied by another people, and he was compelled to wander there as a mere sojourner. Yet he still believed God and followed Him implicitly, going down into Egypt and sojourning there for a season—waiting twenty-five years for their promised child, until both he and Sarah had arrived at old age, when all ordinary human hopes would have ceased; and then, when Isaac was seventeen years old, taking him, at the Divine command, a journey of three days to a certain designated mountain, to offer him for a burnt offering. At all this Abraham was never staggered. His faith never wavered. He obeyed without murmur or question, and held on to the promises, not deeming any thing too hard for the Lord. Well indeed might Paul quote Abraham as an example of justification by faith, an illustrious instance of receiving all the Divine teachings. "Abraham believed God, and it was counted to him for righteousness." Yes, verily, Abraham did believe God. He was tried in every possible way, and to the last extremity, in order that the world might see the demonstration, and understand that this was the ground upon which a sinner was to be justified. He must believe God, humbly accepting all His teachings however removed from his own thoughts, and committing himself in full assurance to the Divine guidance.

Under the latter dispensation of the gospel, the special object presented to faith is the Lord Jesus Christ, because in Him all the Divine purposes respecting our redemption are complete. He is the Alpha and Omega, in whom all prophecy and promise are fulfilled. If Abel was required to receive the Divine testimony respecting the bleeding lamb, much more may our faith embrace the Lamb of God. The very fulness of God is revealed in the face of Jesus Christ. When we believe in Him, accepting Him as our only Mediator, our Sacrifice, our Righteousness, our Prophet, Priest, and King, it is enough. We are complete in Him. We have all, and abound. If Christ is ours, all things are ours.

We thus see that there is one uniform principle running through the Scriptures, upon the basis of which God has always justified men. The method of the Divine instruction has varied, as well as the amount of truth revealed. Divine revelation has advanced by progressive stages, and the system of redemption has been more and more unfolded. There are dispensations still in the future, and more glorious than any that have gone before. But all these dispensations are harmonions, being built upon the same everlasting principles. One never contradicts or opposes another. They all belong to one grand and perfect system, one being the outgrowth and development of the preceding, as in the natural world. The seed state is one dispensation of the plant, which passes away to give place to another, in which the blade appears. But this is only preparatory still to a third, when the full corn in the ear is developed. All these are harmonious; and were our power of vision sufficient, we might see in the seed state itself the promise and prophecy of all that is to come. The whole plant with its ear, is really wrapped up in the seed; and that marvellous growth is but a development of the wonders contained within that husk. So in redemption: it embraces numerous stages which outwardly seem very unlike. But they are parts of a great whole, perfectly harmonious, and each necessary to the other. There are differences, but no contradictions.

The doctrine of faith, then, is among the elementary and necessary principles of the Christian system, accepted from the beginning, and so stated by the Apostle Paul. "Therefore, leaving the principles of the doctrine of Christ, let us go on unto perfection [more advanced stage]; not laying again the foundation of repentance from dead works, and *of faith toward God*, of the doctrine of baptisms, and of laying on of hands, and of resurrection of the dead, and of eternal judgment;" Heb. vi. Faith is here classed among the elements of Divine truth, known from the beginning. There has never been any change in regard to it. It was, in fact, assumed as the first element of a Divine revelation. God never placed himself before a race of His creatures in the attitude of attempting to show that they ought to believe in Him, as if there could be a doubt on that point, or he could stop to debate the question. The point is settled at once in the emphatic words of the Apostle, "He that believeth not God, hath made him a liar." Divine revelation is employed in showing *what* men must believe concerning God; and that is grandly summed up in the great requirement of the gospel, "Believe in the Lord Jesus Christ, and thou shalt be saved." That embraces all the revelations of God—is the sum of them all.

Reader, have you faith in God? It is a solemn question—one which will thoroughly test your character and moral standing. The point, too, which will decide this question, is the practical one—whether you believe in the Lord Jesus Christ. Have you welcomed God's testimony concerning His Son, in giving Him as a sin-offering for the world, through whom alone we might have eternal redemption? Have you come to God in this new and living way through Christ? or are you following in the steps of Cain, choosing your own way of approach, rejecting His appointed method, and taking the one which, in the pride, blindness, and unbelief of your heart, you think *he* ought to accept as in all respects most suitable? That history of Cain stands as a faithful warning to the race to the end of time, a beacon-light erected upon the dark shores of unbelief. Dying man, beware of his sin and destiny!

CHAPTER XIX.

TYPES.

No one can have a proper understanding of God's revelations to man, who does not enter into the method of instruction, which *He* so wisely provided for the earlier generations of the race. The Bible was not commenced until the time of Moses, twenty-five hundred years after the creation, and then only the five first books were written. These were added to, from time to time, by other authors for a period of one thousand years, when the Old Testament was closed by Malachi. Five hundred years after, the New Testament was written. The world, therefore, has had the benefit of this complete book of revelation only for the last eighteen hundred years, since the days of the apostles. We should, however, fall into serious error in supposing that the wants of the earlier generations were not provided for in this regard. God has never left himself without witness here. The economy of redemption dates back to the beginning. From the very start God took measures to communicate all the facts therewith connected that were essential to be known in order to the attainment of life. The facts were in the distant future; yet they were revealed beforehand. How this was accomplished, we shall now attempt to point out.

The first Bible given for the instruction of mankind was prepared, not upon a written page, but in a system of types, symbolizing the future events of the kingdom of God, even as the models of the mechanical contrivances of the country are preserved in our Patent Office. An hour spent in that Office would impart a clearer conception of all those inventions than days of study devoted to books. Descriptions of objects by mere words are difficult of apprehension, requiring a closeness of thought and power of abstraction, which are beyond the attainment of the mass of mankind. The most ordinary mind, however, can get a distinct impression from a model, which is simply the thing itself in miniature. Instruction conveyed by this method is simple, effectual and permanent, capable of being transmitted from generation to generation, and not liable to be lost or changed, as abstract truth may be, or a didactic form of words.

God knew well how difficult, nay, impossible it would be, by any written revelation to make men comprehend the events which were to be fulfilled in the coming kingdom of God under Immanuel; and how impossible also to procure such a revelation among men. He therefore adopted a better and more effectual method, which was, to make the types or models of those truths, for the education of mankind. We therefore shall have a clear conception of the true state of the case, if we conceive of the early stages of the world as a magnificent spiritual gallery, in which were placed the models of things pertaining to the work of redemption, as our Patent Office contains the types of material inventions of the country. That this, too, is not fancy but literal truth, the Scriptures themselves distinctly teach. Speaking of the priests of the Old Dispensation, Paul says, "Who serve unto the example and *shadow* of heavenly things, as Moses was admonished, when he was about to make the tabernacle; for, see, saith he, that thou make all things according to the *pattern* [type] showed to thee in the mount;" Heb. viii. 5. Here the tabernacle is stated to be a model, or pattern, of heavenly things; and Moses was enjoined to be exact in the construction, so as to preserve the type. Again speaking of the Mosaic ordinances, he says, "Which are a shadow of things to come; but the body is of Christ;" Col. ii. 17. These institutions of Moses were not the realities of things, any more than the models in the Patent Office are the actual machines constructed for use. "Now these things were our examples [types], to the intent that we should not lust after evil things as they also lusted. . . . Now all these things happened unto them for examples [types], and they are written for our admonition upon whom the ends of the world are come;" 1 Cor. x. 6, 11. It will thus be seen that the Scriptures themselves give this very explanation of the matter, and teach us that the former dispensation was a typical gallery, in which were stowed the models of heavenly truths.

This method of instruction was adopted and introduced in the beginning, long prior to the time of Moses. And here we may find an explanation of that peculiar difference which exists betwen the Oriental and Western mind; the former being of a highly imaginative cast, delighting in allegory, parable, and symbol, and readily apprehending their meaning; while the latter is logical and matter-of-fact. The existence of this characteristic feature of the Eastern nations is often given as the reason why so much of the instruction of the Bible is put into the form of symbol and parable—namely to adopt it to their modes of thinking. This, however, is putting the effect for the cause. The truer solution of the matter is, that God began the religious instruction of the race through type and symbol, and so formed that cast of mind which is impressed upon the Eastern nations to this day. The whole system of Divine truth was embodied in models, and in this great spiritual gallery the nations of the world were taught for ages. Here they received their education in Divine things; and in this mould was the Oriental mind consequently cast. The Western nations have had no such training, and they find it more difficult to enter into the meaning of such symbolical and allegorical language. It is foreign to their modes of thinking, and often a labyrinth of mystery, from which they turn away.

The truths of redemption to be revealed to men, were *facts* or *events* to be fulfilled in the future history of the world. These Divine revelations therefore were, in reality, prophecies; and types are prophecies set in symbols instead of words. The future event to be accomplished was represented to the minds of men by a model, and thus kept before them continually for their instruction. The object selected for such model was, in many cases, something which fulfilled a present useful purpose, which the models in the Patent Office do not, they being preserved to this end alone. Many of the types of revelation were events or personages of their own day, fulfilling at the same time their own special mission, as well as representing also the future. Melchizedec was a great and good king, as well as a representative of Christ, and must have been so in order to be a type of Him. Canaan was the actual inheritance of Israel, as well as a type of the future rest. So of other things. This typical method of presenting truth was the foundation of the bloody offering required in worship, as discussed in the previous chapter; the bleeding lamb setting forth the future events of the shedding of Christ's blood as the only means of taking away sin, and so prepare the world for His atoning work.

Having thus shown what God's method of instruction was in the beginning, we proceed to particulars, calling attention, first, to *the inheritance, which was promised to our redeemed humanity.*

The promise of redemption having been made, and a remedial scheme introduced to effect the end, it became necessary to set before the minds of men, as distinctly as possible, the fact of that future restoration, as a reality and an object of earnest hope and effort. The danger was imminent that the race, now degraded and blinded by sin, would be content with the little earthly good they might enjoy here under this present system of grace, without looking to any thing beyond, or hoping for any better portion than earth under the curse could offer. How, then, did God carry the minds and hopes of men forward to the restored inheritance of the future?

To obtain the true impression of this subject as revealed in the Scriptures, we must necessarily go back, and mark how God himself unfolded this subject to the first generations, listening to the elementary lessons which they received, and which were adapted to their understandings. We must commence at the beginning, and follow the Divine instructions.

The most prominent and impressive fact of those early days was the existence of *Paradise*—a word still precious in human ears, and that gives the promise of all that is glorious in the future. The memory of that forfeited inheritance has not faded away from this sin-cursed world, nor the hope of its restoration gone. There was such a place as Paradise—the home of our first parents in their innocence—the spot which God selected and fitted up with especial care in a creation which was all fair and beautiful. It was a garden which He planted eastward in Eden, and which He adorned as His hand alone could fashion it, and fill with all delights that were pleasant to the eye, and good for food. Human skill has made fairy spots on earth, even since the curse came; but never such an one as this—never one that made any approach thereto. It was worthy of the Divine handiwork. There God caused the tree of life to grow, from which man has never plucked, since those gates of paradise were closed upon him; and there also God walked in familiar intercourse with our first parents, revealing His visible presence, and comunicating all His will. Their cup was full: it ran over. There was nothing wanting of all their hearts could desire.

This paradise of beauty was an actual possession and enjoyment, having the tree of life itself, to which they were allowed free access. It was their present inheritance, and at this point of time does not appear to have been a type of any higher truth. There is no evidence of any such thing.

But the glorious inheritance was lost. Man sinned, and although an economy of grace was introduced to effect his restoration, yet he was driven out from paradise and doomed to live where he might feel the curse, until the promise of redemption to earth could be fulfilled. From this point of time paradise subserved its grand purpose as a symbolic institution under the new economy to prophecy of the inheritance to come through the promised Seed. And here it is necessary to call attention to the fact that *that garden in Eden continued in its integrity after that the curse was pronounced upon the earth.*

Of this there is sufficient evidence, and it is a fact of great importance as proving the method of Divine instruction in the things of redemption during the first ages of the world. Mark, then, the statements in the narrative; "And the Lord God said, Behold, the man is become as one of us, to know good and evil; and now, lest he put forth his hand, and take also of the tree of life, and eat, and live forever; therefore the Lord God sent him forth from the garden of Eden, to till the ground from whence he was taken. And he placed at the east of the garden of Eden cherubim, and a flaming sword, which turned every way, to keep the way of the tree of life;" Gen. iii. 22. What are the facts embodied here? "God drove out the man." This involves the continuance of the garden; for, if the curse had fallen upon this spot as upon the rest of the earth, there would have been no occasion to drive out the man and prevent his return. Another fact is, that the tree of life continued as before in the garden, and the man was driven out, "lest he should put forth his hand, and eat, and live forever;" while the cherubim and the flaming sword were stationed on the east of the garden "to keep the way of the tree of life." The subsequent history also shows that this flaming sword, which was none other than "the presence of the Lord," was in existence when Cain and Abel brought their offerings, one hundred and twenty years at least after the creation. And if they continued to this point of time, they evidently belonged to the system of instruction which was designed for that age, and no doubt lasted through the same until swept away by the deluge.

Paradise then stood in the midst of the earth untouched by the curse. And what a solemn lesson of instruction to our first parents and their posterity! From the midst of their sweat and toil, surmounted by briers and thorns and barrenness, by sickness, death and the grave, they might still gaze in the distance upon that blessed inheritance, now lost to them, but still preserved under the guardianship of the cherubim and the flaming sword, in the assurance and hope that through the coming One they should again have access to the tree of life, and enjoy the blissful smiles and presence of their God. These teachings were plain and unambiguous. Paradise stood to the antediluvian age as the type of the promised inheritance, even as Canaan symbolized to Israel the same rest for which they were taught to hope and wait. The curse had indeed fallen upon the earth. Man had been driven from his blissful abode in Eden, being no longer allowed to have familiar access to the Divine preserver, nor partake of the tree of life. In toil and sweat and pain must he now, as a sinner, eat his daily bread, and go down to the grave. But there was the inheritance still, and needing no toil of his to make it smile in all its loveliness. It was a lesson which he could read and understand—a lesson which told him of an inheritance lost by transgression, but to be regained by redemption. It told of the work to be achieved by that mighty One who should restore the ruins of the fall, conquer death, and deliver the earth from the curse under which it was now travailing. Many, perhaps, can hardly credit the fact that this great truth was thus so vividly set before the minds of men and so easily comprehended at this early age. But if we have the Bible with its marvellous history and the words of the Son of God from heaven, why should we doubt that paradise should be permitted to stand with its tree of life, and cherubim and flaming sword, to teach men that this groaning earth was not their rest, but that they must aspire to a better inheritance, a nobler destiny?

Consider, next, *the character of the inheritance, which was held out to faith.*

The entire work of creation from the beginning proves that this earth was made for man. It bears his image through its whole structure. The successive creations from age to age show how God was gradually approaching and preparing for the advent of man, the lord and crown of all, on reaching whom his work ceased. Neither is it in vain that revelation describes this process day by day, until it was finished. God intended that we should understand how He had prepared this earth for His chosen sons, designing it as their habitation, and adapting it peculiarly to them, so that He was pleased with it in all respects, and saw that it was very good. It was a perfect work of God. We are not to forget, also, that there was a most intimate and fitting relation between man and this creation, he being closely allied to it in his own person, and constituting a part thereof. His own perfect body was formed of the earth, not, indeed, to teach us of our lowly origin. Such theology is not derived from the Bible. This body is not a degradation to us, or clog, which we are to deliver over to corruption, and leave forever buried in the grave. The Bible honors the body as truly as it does the soul. One is destined to incorruption, as the other is to immortality; and man is not complete without both. Herein is the glory of our humanity, being so constituted, that through this material organization our race might be perpetuated from age to age, and all bound in one blessed brotherhood.

There is no evidence either that Adam had any other thought than that God was satisfied with his own creation, and with this earth as a fitting abode for him. "God saw everything that he had made and *behold it was very good;* Gen. i. 31.

Man, indeed, had come under the curse, and this maternal creation was made to groan with him and travail in pain, until the appointed day of redemption, when the enemy should be cast out, and the work of restoration effected. The promise held out was *the restoration of all things*—the bruising of Satan, and subjection of every enemy—the removal of the curse—the regeneration, when all things should be made new again; while paradise, untouched by the foe, stood before the eyes of men an evidence and representative of what earth would be when that blessed time of restitution should come. Adam was never taught to look and hope for deliverance *from* earth, as if it were a prison in which he was now confined, and to regard escape from it as his only salvation. He was not taught to look for escape either from his own body or from this earth. Such ideas have sprung from heathenism, not from our Christianity. It was the curse simply that was to be removed, and earth restored again. Man was taught to look forward to a day when such a triumph should be achieved, and the enemy vanquished upon this very arena where, for a time, it seemed as if he had defeated God's grandest purposes. The result, however, would prove that this was the scene of hell's most signal overthrow. Here the terrible warfare with the powers of darkness was to be waged. This earth was to be made forever memorable by the travail and sore conflict of the Son of God, by the sorrowing footsteps and tears of Him who empties himself of divinity and the glory which He had with the Father, humbling himself unto death. Yes, this earth is dear to the heart of God. It is a portion of His creation, which He has especial cause to remember—over which He has bent with the deepest solicitude—where He has made the largest sacrafices, achieved the sublimest wonders, and where He will witness the most stupendous triumphs. God does not intend to give up this earth to destruction. He designs to redeem it. The time is to come when "the tabernacle of God shall again be with men, and he shall dwell with them and be their God, and they shall be his people."

All the teachings of Scripture run in this channel; and the hope of believers has been directed from the beginning with the most earnest expectation to the coming of such a day. Their steadfast eye was fixed upon another and different dispensation for earth, when "the seed" should come. The scriptural idea is one of *ages*, or *dispensations*, God's work being carried on by these successive eras. It was so in the creation of earth. Long ages antedated man's appearance upon the theatre; and these were but the preparatory stages to the grander dispensations of wisdom, power, and love, when the great lord of creation should appear to act His part. This working by ages or dispensations enters so essentially into the Divine plan, that the word itself passes into the meaning of "worlds." The work of creation, in the language of the Bible, is the arranging of these dispensations, as when it is said of Christ, "By whom also he made the *worlds* (or ages); Heb. i. 2. Revelation points us forward to these ages to come in the history of earth, when Christ shall fulfil all His gracious designs. We speak according to our modern ideas of looking "beyond this world," meaning another sphere, away from earth, and having no connection with it; whereas, in the theology of the Scriptures, "beyond this world" means beyond this dispensation to another succeeding, but one belonging to earth as much as the other. "This world," and the world to come, represent simply differing periods of time, through which the earth is passing. The Jewish nation looked forward to the times of the Messiah as the consummation of all hope and desire, not misunderstanding in this their own Scriptures; and that future blessed era was "the world to come," in contrast with this present evil world, where sin abounds. Thus it was literally the world or age *to come;* not a world already in existence, upon which we might at once enter, if only released from the body. It had no being as yet, except in the promise and purpose of God. In the strictest sense it was the *future* world, the world *to come.* This is the thought which runs through the Scriptures, but which we often overlook because our minds turn away from earth to some far distant sphere. "But God, who is rich in mercy, for his great love wherewith he loved us, even when we were dead in sins, hath quickened us together with Christ (by grace ye are saved); and hath raised us up together, and made us sit together in heavenly places in Christ Jesus: that *in the ages to come* he might shew the exceeding riches of his grace in his kindness toward us, through Christ Jesus;" Eph. ii. 4–7. "Having made known unto us the mystery of his will, according to his good pleasure, which he had purposed in himself; that in the *dispensation of the fulness of times* he might gather together in one all things in Christ, both which are in heaven and which are on earth;" chap. i. 9, 10. The times, therefore, are not complete. The ages are not finished. There are eras or dispensations in the future, when the grandest purposes of God shall be fulfilled, and He shall reveal all the marvellous riches of His grace to His believing ones, even "an exceeding weight of glory."

Notice, again, *the manner in which the Scriptures speak of the righteous inheriting the earth.*

The promise of redemption, made in the beginning, belonged to the righteous. They were the heirs of the inheritance, and died in the full faith that it would be theirs. "These all died in faith, not having received the promises [the things promised], but *having seen them afar off*, and were persuaded of them, and embraced them, and confessed that they were strangers and pilgrims on the earth;" Heb. xi. 13. Notwithstanding their death and departure, they believed that they should still inherit these promises. The same thought is presented in the 37th Psalm: "Fret not thyself because of evil-doers, neither be thou envious at the workers of iniquity. For they shall soon be cast down like the grass and wither as the green herb. . . . Rest in the Lord, and wait patiently for him: fret not thyself because of him who prospereth in his way, because of the man who bringeth wicked devices to pass. . . . For evil-doers shall be cut off: but those that wait upon the Lord, *they shall inherit the earth.* For yet a little while and the wicked shall not be: yea, thou shalt diligently consider his place, and he shall not be. But *the meek shall inherit the earth;* and shall delight themselves in the abundance of peace. The wicked plotteth against the just, and gnasheth upon him with his teeth. The Lord shall laugh at him: for he seeth that his day is coming. . . *Wait on the Lord, and keep his way, and he shall exalt thee to inherit the land.* When the wicked are cut off, thou shalt see it." Have these promises been fulfilled? Who has seen an end to the prosperity of the wicked, or of the righteous patiently waiting upon the Lord for the accomplishment of this very word? Who has seen the earth yet put in possession of the meek, that they might inherit it? Is not the condition of things described by the Psalmist precisely what we witness to this hour? Do we not need to be cautioned still not to fret because of evil-doers, nor to be envious of the workers of iniquity, while we trust in the Lord, and wait patiently for Him, until we see the wicked cut off, and the righteous put in possession of this earth as their inheritance? This was the very promise made in the beginning—the redemption ever held forth as the object of faith. This earth is to come into the possession of the saints. The wicked have held it hitherto, since sin extended; which has been the occasion of wonder, and sometimes of fretfulness and envy to God's children. But it is not always to be so. The wicked are not always thus to triumph and plot against the just. Their day will come ere long, and the righteous shall see it. Christ declares the same truth in His sermon on the mount; "Blessed are the meek, for they shall inherit the earth." They do not inherit it now. The wicked are exalted, riding on the high places. It was no idle boast of the Adversary, when pointing to the kingdoms of the world and the glory of them, he said to Jesus, "All these are mine, and to whosoever I will I give them." There was too sad truth in this. The kingdoms are his. The world has undergone no radical change, no regeneration, since David's time. But there is a restoration promised; and those who *wait patiently* for the Lord, trusting in him, shall see it. The meek shall inherit the earth. Christ, the promised seed, shall give it to them as a possession forever. This is the consummation held up to faith, and long waited for. And though it has seemed to delay, and the suffering people of God have oft cried, "How long, O Lord, How long!" yet the Lord is not slack concerning His promise as some men count slackness, even though a scoffing, infidel world does ask, "Where is the promise (evidence) of his coming?" The Apostle declares how the very creation itself is waiting with earnest expectation *for this day of the manifestation of the sons of God*, while it now travails in pain and groans under the curse. Thus the promise of redemption is not only to the people of God, but also to the creation. Peter and John both describe the new heavens and the new earth, which are to be, wherein dwelleth righteousness, when old things shall have passed away, and all have become new.

Thus do the teachings of the Scriptures from the beginning agree as to the redemption of earth from the curse, and the final restitution of all things, paradise standing for centuries before the early generations, a living type and demonstration of that truth as Canaan did at a subsequent period. Thus Paradise and Canaan have both become sacred names to the Church of God, burdened with hallowed associations. Believers have not yet "received the promises," but die in faith, counting themselves strangers and pilgrims on the earth, and looking for the rest remaining for them. And the day shall come that shall see all their hopes fulfilled.

CHAPTER. XX.

THE TREE OF LIFE.

"And out of the ground made the Lord God to grow every tree that is pleasant to the sight, and good for food; the tree of life also in the midst of the garden, and the tree of knowledge of good and evil;" Gen. ii. 9. These two last were evidently special creations for paradise, not found without its sacred precincts, and sustaining the most important relations to our race. To this one, Adam and his wife were allowed free access; the other was forbidden them on pain of death. What terrible reality, too, there was in this prohibition, our ruined race has had most painful experience of. We may believe, therefore, that there was no less a reality to the other.

The designation of the trees was significant. That applied to the forbidden tree was taken from the fact that the eating thereof through the transgression of God's commandment led to the knowledge of evil, or the difference between good and evil. The temptation, as presented by the Adversary, was that it would lead to knowledge, exalting them almost to the place of Divinity, fulfilling the destiny for which God created them: "Ye shall be as gods," or, more properly, *as God*. The Adversary here held out the attainment of that preëminence and glory which were designed in their creation, and which he knew were intended for them, which also may have been promised as the reward of their obedience. The Tempter pointed to this magnificent tree as the means of securing all that had been revealed to their faith—all that they desired and hoped for; and expressed his surprise that God should have prohibited them from partaking of this fruit.

We need also to bear in mind the fact, that Eve was at this time entirely ignorant of the true character of her tempter, and knew not that such a malignant being existed. He came in the guise of a friend and well-wisher—as every tempter does—anxious to promote her best welfare, and wondered that that tree of knowledge, which God himself knew to be the means of their highest advancement and glory, should have been forbidden them. Under this delusion they plucked and ate, but found to their bitter sorrow, that the knowledge acquired was that gained by transgression—the knowledge of good lost, of evil experienced. The tree of life, however, was not a forbidden tree, but one that was given them freely to enjoy; and so called, doubtless, because it had power to preserve the body in undecaying vigor; and here was the assurance given to man, that, while he continued in obedience, enjoying the Divine favor, no change should pass upon him such as he might witness in the creation around. To him was given the pledge of incorruption, and the tree of life was both the seal of that covenant of God with him, as as the means of securing it. Accordingly, where sin entered, and man was placed under a remedial system of which death and the grave were a necessary part, he was driven out of paradise, "lest he put forth his hand and take also of the tree of life, and eat *and live forever;*" Gen. iii. 22. The tendency to change and decay was not to be interfered with: and not only so, this change and decay were henceforth to be humiliating and painful in the highest degree. They were to be a curse in the ghastly form of death and the grave: yet under a remedial system, where God might work for human recovery. Thus, while death reigned, man must be shut out of paradise, and debarred all access to the tree of life.

Yet the way thereto was still kept, committed to the

guardianship of the cherubim and the flaming sword; and now, under the new economy of grace, it became a symbol and pledge of that life promised through the seed of the woman, when He should come to put all enemies under His feet, conquering death itself and the grave. Paradise was not utterly and forever lost. Man was driven out for the present, while it still stood before his eyes the pledge of the inheritance to be restored through the coming One. There was the tree of life still blooming, the way thereto kept by the cherubim and the flaming sword of the Divine Preserver, the assurance to those who believed that there was a victory to be achieved over death and the sepulchre, and that, in the day of the coming Deliverer, they should again be permitted to eat of its fruits, and "live forever." Accordingly we find in those new heavens and new earth, described by John in Apocalyptic vision, this tree of life growing upon the banks of the river of life, whose "leaves were for the healing of the nations; *and there shall be no more curse.*" "And God shall wipe away all tears from their eyes; and there shall be no more death, neither sorrow, nor crying, neither shall there be any more pain; for the future things are passed away." The tree of life thus stands in the Scriptures set over against the curse. While man is shut out from access to that tree, the curse is to continue, and the sepulchre is to be his portion: but when under the promised redemption by the seed of the woman, he is again permitted to take of the tree of life, "there shall be no more curse."

We may be certain, also, that these lessons of instruction were much plainer to our first parents, and to their posterity, than they have been to us. We have not carefully studied them, and they have been to us for the most part a neglected page. They were also especially adapted to those early ages. Adam in paradise knew by experience what the tree of life was. He had plucked of its precious fruit or leaves, for we know not in which its virtue lay. It was no mystery to him, but the most simple reality. When, therefore, he was driven from paradise, and death appointed as his lot, that tree of life, from which he was now debarred, was no unmeaning symbol, neither was it difficult of apprehension. It told in unequivocal language of the time to come when the dread decree of death and the curse should be abolished, and their forfeited lives restored—when God should again dwell with them as of old, and free access be had to the tree of life. The truth revealed in this symbolic form was simple, easy of comprehension, and precisely adapted to their necessities.

The expression used in Scripture concerning the cherubim, that they were appointed "to keep the way of the tree of life," is worthy of being more particularly noticed, and will serve to throw light upon the point now under consideration. The idea more commonly attached to this, is that of guarding, so as to prevent approach. The original, however, expresses another idea of equal if not greater importance—that of *preserving*. Our translation of *keeping* expresses very accurately both ideas. It was not the office of the cherubim and the flaming sword merely to guard the tree of life so as to prevent all approach; they were also appointed to preserve or keep the way open thereto. The tree of life was put under their care so as to be protected, until, in the fulness of time, access might again be had to its precious fruits. Until that appointed time of the opening of the gates of paradise, the cherubim and the flaming sword were charged to keep the way; and herein was assurance given, to the sinning race of man, now under the curse, that there was a day of deliverance and restoration in store for them. The decree of death was to be reversed and the restitution of all things to take place. In this view of the subject it was not designed that those cherubim and flaming sword should be looked upon with awe and terror as dread sentinels of justice. They were, on the contrary, the best friends of our humanity—the guardians of its choicest treasures. They were preserving the way of the tree of life to our redeemed race—standing watch over paradise, not to thrust us out, but to guard the way of return. Thus most appropriately did the Divine Presence, in the shape of that flaming sword, station himself at the gateway to paradise, before the way of the tree of life, inviting a sinning race there to approach to find acceptance and favor. It was emphatically saying, what Jesus Christ afterward said of himself, "I am the way;" "I am the door; by me, if any man enter in, he shall be saved, and shall go in and out, and find pasture." And when men came, as Abel did, with their bleeding lamb and humble confession of sin, the manner in which the offering and worshipper were received told plainly that for such the way of the tree of life was kept, and the inheritance preserved.

We have thus erred not a little in our estimate of the condescension, grace, and winning tenderness toward sinners of those earlier manifestations of the Divine Presence. They have been clothed with an awe and terror which they were not intended to bear, while we have greatly failed to appreciate the blessed work which was performed in keeping the way of paradise and the tree of life for our apostate race.

CHAPTER XXI.

THE CHERUBIM.

"AND he placed at the east of the garden of Eden cherubims, and a flaming sword, which turned every way to keep the way of the tree of life;" Gen. iii. 24. Very imperfect and erroneous conceptions have prevailed respecting these cherubim, as is shown by the ordinary representations of their pictures in the form of angels. Tnis is the more strange, as the Scriptures give accurate and full description of them, so as to leave no question in regard to their appearance and form. They occupy, also, a very prominent place in the Bible, and are evidently designed to embody some highly important truth.

Let us first give attention *to their history as found in the Scriptures.*

They are brought to our notice at the opening of the drama of redemption, having their place in closest proximity to the Divine Presence within the precincts of paradise before the way of the tree of life. No description, however, is given of them here that would be of any assistance to us. Moses speaks of them, as if those to whom he wrote knew what they were, and nothing more need be said. They were familiar objects to the nation of Israel and a description of their appearance would be superfluous. The next mention of them is in connection with the tabernacle at Sinai, where they are associated with the most sacred features of that holy place. Two figures of these cherubim, wrought in gold, were placed in the Holy of Holies immediately over the ark of the covenant, and between them the glory of the Lord took up His abode; whence originated one of the designations of the God of Israel, "He who dwelleth between the cherubim." Figures of the same, also, were wrought in richest needle-work over the inner curtains of the sanctuary, and the veil separating its two apartments. These cherubim met the eye of the beholder whithersoever he turned in the tabernacle of the Lord—a fact certainly of no mean significance, and not to be overlooked in our study of the system of redemption. It was not in vain that such a conspicuous and extensive place was given to these figures in the sanctuary of the God of Israel. They have a meaning there. Yet neither here do we find any description of them, except that allusion is made to their wings and faces. This omission is the more remarkable, because every other part of the tabernacle is so minutely described, and Moses was so particularly enjoined to make every thing according to the pattern shown him. The omission, therefore, is clear evidence that the nature and form of the cherubim were familiar to Moses, so that a description of them would have been superfluous. It was only necessary for God to direct in regard to the material of which they were to be made, and the position in which they were to be placed. Had Moses been directed to place the figure of an ox in the tabernacle, it would not have been necessary to show him a pattern of this animal, or to have described it, as if he could have been ignorant in the case. To name the animal would be all sufficient. In the same way, Moses needed no description of the cherubim.

Whence, then, did Moses obtain the familiar knowledge of the cherubim? The answer to this question will throw much light upon the earlier history of Divine revelation and redemption.

The matter can only be explained in the existence of these cherubim before the way of the tree of life, and their continuance to the time of Noah, when that first system of types, as connected with paradise, was swept away by the flood. During that period of sixteen hundred years, the form of these living ones was continually visible to men, thus becoming familiar, like any other object on earth. They were precious, too, to the men of faith in those days, and carefully studied as embodying revelation from heaven. They must have been familiar objects to Noah and Shem, the former of whom lived till within two years of the birth of Abraham, while the latter was contemporaneous with him for one hundred and fifty years. Thus Abraham might easily have learned from Shem directly all that was known to the antediluvian saints of God's revelation to them, and of the system of instruction by which He communicated the facts of redemption. As set forth as symbols, also, the system was easily understood and preserved. It could not readily be lost. These facts are more worthy to be dwelt upon, inasmuch as they give us an insight into the profound wisdom of God's early revelations to the race, and the method of those revelations—how wisely adapted they were to all the necessities and difficulties of the case, and how admirably the knowledge of divine truth was preserved and handed down through these appointed types. One system God carried down to the time of Noah. Another of similar character He began with Moses; while Shem, who was familiar with the former, was for one hundred and fifty years contemporary with Abraham, and died only twenty-five years before him. Many have wondered that Abraham should seem to know so much, as he evidently did, of God, and was so ready to obey and follow Him. They find it difficult to account for his extraordinary faith, and knowledge of Divine truth, called out, as they conceive, from the midst of heathenism. We, however, have underrated the means of instruction enjoyed in those early ages. There was a complete and permanent system of revelation in the form of types, transmitted from the antediluvian age to the next succeeding, through the family of Noah. A great and sacred trust was committed to them in this particular, and nobly did they fulfil it. Before that Shem had passed away, who was personally conversant with the first system of types, God began again to reveal himself in a visible manner to Abraham, and renew the covenant made with Adam respecting the promised seed. Thus, between Abraham and Moses, there was but a brief interval of less than four hundred years; and filled, in part, by such saints as Isaac, Jacob, and Joseph, through whom the knowledge and blessed memories of paradise could be most easily preserved. It is not difficult, therefore, to understand, with these facts before us, how Moses was familiar with the story of those bright cherubim before the way of the tree of life; so that, when God directed him to make the figures of these living creatures for the tabernacle, it was superfluous to give a description of them, as if he were ignorant of their form and nature. The absence of such description is the very evidence which we now need to establish the important fact, that the knowledge of the cherubim had been preserved and handed down from the days before the flood, thus opening to us all the history of those early Divine revelations.

But the knowledge which was taken for granted in Moses, is wanting still to us. This is supplied at a later period in a vision which Ezekiel describes at the river Chebar, in the land of Chaldea. This vision was one of singular magnificence, and impressive in the highest degree. It is found in the opening chapter of his prophecy. The first thing which attracted his attention, was a whirlwind from the north, and a great cloud, and a fire (suggestive of the pillar of fire and cloud going before the host of Israel), from the midst of which appeared four living creatures, having in general the human form, but each with four faces and four wings. The front face was that of a man; on the right was the face of a lion; on the left that of an ox; on the back that of an eagle. Their feet were straight, and cloven like those of an ox, thereby classing them among the clean, and not the unclean living creatures; while they sparkled and shone like burnished brass or coals of fire. Their motions were inconceivably swift, like a flash of lightning, and the noise of their wings in flight was as the noise of great waters, or of a mighty host. In immediate connection with these glorious living ones, and over their heads, was a magnificent firmament like crystal, and above the firmament was seen a throne as of sapphire stone, and on the throne the Divine glory in the likeness of a man, as the color of amber and the appearance of fire, and brightness round about, like a rainbow. "This," adds the prophet, "was the appearance of the likeness of the glory of the Lord." The fact here stated, that this glory of the Lord upon the throne above the crystal firmament "was the likeness as the appearance of a man," is to be noted as showing the intimate connection between this glory of the Lord, and our humanity, in the person of our Immanuel. Subsequently the prophet saw this same splendid vision repeated in the temple at Jerusalem, the account of which will be found in chap. x. In this second vision he says: "And the cherubim lifted up their wings and mounted up from the earth in my sight. . . . And the glory of the God of Israel was over them above. This is the living creature that I saw under *the God of Israel* by the river Chebar; and *I knew that they were the cherubim*." They had not been designated by this name before, only their appearance had been described. But the prophet knew that they were the cherubim, because he was familiar with their form as found in the tabernacle. It was not a matter revealed to him, but one of his own observation. "I knew that they were the cherubim." Here, then, we have arrived at the desired description of these living ones full and accurate, and abundantly satisfactory. But this is not the only one.

They are presented in a similar scene in Rev. iv. 6. John in vision beheld a throne encircled by a rainbow, and one seated thereon glorious to look upon as a jasper and sardine stone. And round about the throne were four living creatures, full of eyes, having the same four faces described by Ezekiel, with six wings. And they rest not day and night, saying, Holy, holy, holy, Lord God Almighty, which was, and is, and is to come. With the four and twenty elders also they fall before the throne, and sing that new song, "Thou art worthy to take the book, and to open the seals thereof: for thou wast slain, and hast redeemed us to God by thy blood out of every kindred, and tongue, and people, and nation."

Such is an outline of the history of the cherubim as found in the Bible. They are the same throughout, occupying the same essential position in connection with the Divine glory, performing the same part and exalted most evidently to a place of very peculiar honor and privilege.

That they are typical or symbolic beings, designed to set forth some great truth in the system of redemption, is evident. There are no such living existences in the universe. They belong clearly to the economy of redemption, being introduced at its opening scene and associated therewith through all its history. They formed a part, and conspicuous part, of both systems of types, and are presented to us in the same associations in the visions of John in connection with our redeemed humanity. Here we are manifestly to look for their meaning and design. But we must leave the development of these to another chapter. A single point here, however, is worthy of a moment's consideration. In the visions of Ezekiel and John, the cherubim are presented as living creatures, possessing life, activity, and intelligence in their highest possible forms. In the tabernacle there were only the *figures* of cherubim, those over the mercy-seat wrought of gold, those on the hangings wrought in needle-work by the hand of man. What were those before the way of the tree of life? Were they living creatures, as seen in the visions of the prophets, or were they merely figures, inanimate representations of such beings? The more natural supposition is, that they had the same *appearance* of life as in the visions of Ezekiel. The narrative would imply this. Moses was directed to make the *figures* of cherubim for the tabernacle. They were the work of human art. But Adam had nothing to do with the construction of those in paradise. They were the Divine workmanship; and we can hardly conceive that God would make an inanimate figure, and place under its guardianship the future inheritance of our race with its tree of life. Beside this, the nature and design of the symbol, which we shall hereafter consider, would seem to require in this instance that it should have all the appearance of life in very deed, with such powers as those presented in the vision of the prophet.

Realize, then, in imagination, the fact of the appearance of such wondrous living forms, so strange, and with such transcendent powers, standing within the precincts of paradise, before the way of the tree of life. How would they arrest attention and impress the mind! We have often read the statement of the presence of these cherubim there: yet how little meaning have we given to it! How little have we thought that they were a living reality to the men of those generations? And in the failure to appreciate these facts, to what an amazing extent have we lost a knowledge of the Divine revelations, by which God instructed those ages of the past, and opened to them the future mysteries of redemption! We have passed this portion of revelation by as an unmeaning myth, which, even if understood, could add little or nothing to the Word of God, and of which we have been content to remain in ignorance. We have conceived, perhaps, that the cherubim were an order of angels, having no relation to us or to our system, never suspecting that they embodied a precious Divine revelation. In the further development of the subject, we may learn how much this ignorance has cost us, and how it has thrown obscurity over a large portion of the work of redemption.

CHAPTER XXII.

THE CHERUBIM.

HAVING traced out the history and connections of the cherubim in the Scriptures, we shall now consider

THEIR DESIGN AND MEANING.

Symbols are designed to represent not the same, but analogous objects in another sphere. A lamb, as a symbol, does not represent itself, but an analogous character in a higher system—that is, the human. The inanimate objects of nature, such as the sun, stars, mountains, islands, represent analogous objects in the sphere next above them, the political world. The heavens are the political fabrics of earth, with their orbs and luminaries. The beasts with their heads and horns are the reigning dynasties of the kingdoms. Apply this simple principle to the cherubim. These are creatures, or living ones, in the form of humanity in combination with the highest excellencies and powers selected from all departments of the animal kingdom.

First, they have the godlike human form, the noblest of all the Divine creations. But, added to this, are the grandest features, which can be found in the other creations of God, making a combination which could not be surpassed.

They had four faces, of which the fronting one was human, setting forth the highest idea of intelligence, and fitted for God's noblest service. But this was not enough. A mere human face might not have indicated any thing beyond what we see of humanity in this world. Our conceptions must be carried beyond this. Three others therefore are added. On the right was that of a lion, a beast which has ever been the fitting representative of majesty, power, and dominion, ruling the acknowledged lord of the forest. This is the chosen emblem of Britannia's rule.

The left face was that of an ox, which stands foremost among all the domestic tribes, and has ever been esteemed the most essential to human industry and comfort, and therefore regarded among all the nations of the ancient world as the symbol of creative or productive industry. This was the animal chiefly employed in husbandry, venerated and valued beyond all others, and primarily instrumental in developing the productive powers of the earth. On this account, in the earliest forms of idolatry, God, as the Author of all good, was worshiped with highest honors, under the form of an ox. This was the great Egyptian divinity, the same which the Israelites demanded of Aaron at Sinai, and with whose worship they were so intoxicated—the same, also, which was set up by Jeroboam in Dan and Bethel as rivals to the temple in Jerusalem, and which were deemed so sacred that not even Jehu, with all his zeal to destroy idolatry, presumed to touch them. This has been the divinity of the nations; and, because so patient of labor, and submissive, and withal so powerful, he ever stands as the acknowledged symbol of the noblest traits of character, unwearied toil, patient endurance, submission to authority, and productive industry.

The last face was that of an eagle, the king of all the feathered tribes, our own chosen national emblem, as well as that of the old Roman empire. The Roman eagles were for many long centuries known everywhere as the emblem of dominion and irresistible might. The range of vision of this proud bird, and the power of his flight, as well as his boldness and courage, are unequalled. He can soar on loftiest pinion, and gaze upon the sun in his unclouded brightness. Such a bird is a fitting symbol of the far-seeing intelligence, and the heavenward tendencies of the highest forms of created mind. On the loftiest crags he builds his nest, and looks down upon all earthly things.

Combining these symbols together, we have the highest possible conceptions of life, with the noblest characteristics which can belong to created intelligence. But these were only the head of this living creature. It had other features equally striking. John represents them, in his vision, as full of eyes before and behind, denoting their ceaseless vigilance and exalted capacities for knowledge. They were clothed, likewise, with numerous wings, the noise of which was like many waters, or a great host. These were designed for rapid, lofty flight, and showed that they were intended for a higher, wider sphere than merely to tread upon this earth, as man now does. They could soar upward on tireless pinions, while their motions were swift as the lightning. In addition to this, they always went straight forward, never turning in their course. With one face alone we must necessarily turn our bodies, but with four faces, the cherubim could go in any direction, and yet always move forward in the direct line of vision, never turning to the right or the left. This denoted their superior spiritual natures, and their undeviating integrity in the service of God. Lastly, their appearance was exceedingly glorious, like burning coals of fire, and sparkling as the color of burnished brass.

Where, now, according to the principles of symbolic interpretation, are we to look for the realization of all this? They were living creatures, it will be observed, taken from the departments of human and animal life. Where is the analogous sphere, in which we may find their fulfilment—the sphere next above the present human one? The only answer is, our redeemed humanity, delivered from the curse and restored by the woman's promised seed. These cherubim stood forth before the eyes of men the embodiment of that glory to which our humanity was destined in its resurrection state, when it should realize all the highest, grandest conceptions of life and immortality, with the development of all the noblest excellencies of character. In that redeemed state, there should be found a combination of powers and excellencies such as could now be set forth only by such a wondrous living creature as the cherubim. All nature must be laid under contribution to produce the grand conception. They were emphatically *living ones*, creatures preëminent for life, which rest not day nor night, but are unceasingly employed without weariness in the high service of God—beings of ceaseless activity and energy, whose powers never faint or fail. And *what* powers! what intellect and capacities for fathoming all the deep mysteries of God! On what lofty pinions can they soar! For what dominion and rule are they qualified, as well as submission to all righteous authority! With what mighty productive energy are they endowed! What straightforward integrity of purpose and character, which never turns to the right hand or the left! How boundless is the range of their being, and on what lightning wing do they move to execute all the commands of Heaven! How resplendently glorious their appearance, like burning coals of fire, and dazzling as the light!

Such were the primary and essential ideas set forth in the cherubim, all perfectly natural and easily understood. Beyond this, also, their associations and connections showed still farther that this was their intended meaning.

They stood within the prohibited bounds of paradise.

They did not, therefore, belong to this present economy of things, while the curse prevailed, and man was shut out of his inheritance. In the same way the principal seat of the cherubim in the tabernacle was within the Holy of Holies, into which there was no entrance for men now, not even for the people of God; and which symbolized that future, perfected state, when the glory of the Lord should be revealed, and the new Jerusalem should descend to earth. This fact clearly told where men must look for the realization of that which was shadowed forth in these glorious living forms. They belonged to the new creation—to paradise restored—to the inheritance kept in reserve.

Again, their intimate connection with the Divine Presence was a fact of great significance.

That Divine Presence had, since the entrance of sin, withdrawn himself from all *familiar* intercourse with men, no longer walking with them as in their innocence in paradise. He had not, however, withdrawn from earth, but fixed His abode in paradise, the gateway to the tree of life, where He might be approached and His favor secured. This indicated that the familiar intercourse of God with men was now obstructed, and would not be known again until the curse should be removed and paradise restored. But mark the intimacy of the cherubim with the Divine glory. They had their dwelling in paradise, and there kept the way of the tree of life. The flaming sword of the Divine Presence dwelt between them. So was it in the tabernacle. Their privileged place was in the Holy of Holies over the mercy-seat, beholding the very glory of the Lord. In Ezekiel's vision, likewise, above the heads of the cherubim was a crystal firmament, on which was a bright throne, and seated there the glory of the God of Israel in a human form. When John beheld these same cherubim, it was round about the throne in heaven, on which One sat, that was to look upon like a jasper and a sardine stone, over-arched by a rainbow like unto an emerald. Here was the same Divine glory in the person of the Lamb slain, who was worthy to take the book, and open the seals thereof.

The fact of the cherubim always being found in immediate connection with and surrounding the Divine Presence, is one of deep interest and significance, and declares plainly, that those whom they represent have a right within the paradise of God, where they may look upon the unveiled Divine glories, and behold Him face to face, which is the blessed promise held out to our redeemed humanity.

But there is one further argument, if any more is needed, which settles this question, and determines the character of the cherubim—*It is the song, which John in vision hears them singing round about the throne, the new song to the Lamb.* Rev. v. 9: "Thou art worthy to take the book and to open the seals thereof: for thou wast slain, and *hast redeemed us to God by thy blood*, out of every kindred, and tongue, and people, and nation: and hast made us unto our God, kings and priests: and *we shall reign on the earth.*" It is the four living creatures, with the four-and-twenty elders, which unite in this song, and so describe themselves as the company redeemed from earth. This forever removes all possible doubt from the subject.

To such a clear and satisfactory conclusion do the Scriptures bring us in this matter. It should also be remembered that these types were more simple and intelligible to those ancient saints of the East than they are to us. We have not studied them, nor felt the necessity of doing it, having the words of the Lord Jesus himself, which to us are more intelligible. Types are foreign to us and to our modes of thinking. But nothing was more familiar to the Oriental mind. In these was contained the whole system of revelation to the early ages. They were carefully studied by the saints of old, who understood that they were looking at the models of heavenly things, to be revealed in the future history of earth. If, therefore, these things are strange and wonderful to us, we are not to suppose that they are really new discoveries. They are, in fact, old things, and long laid aside because they were antiquated, which we have imagined ourselves to have outgrown.

Let us now bring before our minds distinctly that group of types which God established for the instruction of the first generations of men, and see what they were, and what they foretold. There was Paradise, the blessed inheritance, from which the race was for the present shut out, and doomed to toil and sweat, to pain and affliction, and the grave. Paradise was not forever lost, or destroyed. There it was still in all its glory and loveliness, untouched by the curse. But under an economy of grace it stood as a prophecy and promise of the future inheritance, when the curse should be removed. There was the tree of life, whose precious fruit could arrest the work of decay and death in this body, and confer immortal youth. They could not be plucked now; but the way of the tree of life was kept for the race, until the time appointed.

There also were the magnificent forms of the cherubim, with their more than mortal powers, standing in the immediate Divine Presence, and ministering to Him, revealing thus to the very eyes of men the unearthly splendor, dominion, and power, to which these now fallen natures were to be raised in that coming period of earth, when the woman's seed should accomplish all His promised work, and the head of the old serpent should be crushed. Here was a model of our risen and glorified humanity, as complete as it could be presented to the minds of men.

But did the saints of those days so understand it?

We cannot question it; and the demonstration of the fact will open a page of the work of redemption in the past, which has been strangely dark to the Church. The question is even now discussed by Christian writers, as if it were not yet perfectly settled, whether the doctrine of immortality is revealed in the Old Testament, and was apprehended by the saints of former times. Some seem to suppose that the Old Testament is silent on this subject, and that this doctrine was not revealed until Jesus Christ brought it to light, the former ages being left in darkness and doubt as to a future life. There are few, also, who would be able to state satisfactorily to their own minds, or to others, where, and how precisely, the ancient Scriptures do establish this truth. They may find some glimmerings of it in various passages. But where it is clearly unfolded, and at what point *revealed* in the system, they would be at a loss to state.

Let us hear first what the apostles say concerning the knowledge and faith of ancient believers, and their understanding of the doctrine of immortality. After describing the faith of Abel, Enoch, Noah, Abraham, and others, Paul says, Heb. xi. 13: "These all died in faith, not having received the promises, but having *seen them afar off, and were persuaded of them, and embraced them*, and confessed that they were strangers and pilgrims on the earth. For they that say such things declare plainly that they seek a country. And truly, if they had been mindful of that country from whence they came out, they might have had opportunity to have returned; but now they desire a better country, that is, an heavenly; wherefore God is not ashamed to be called their God, for He hath prepared for them a city." The fact is here stated, that, though these patriarchs died without having received the inheritance, yet they went down to their graves in the assured faith of realizing it still. They looked forward to the fulfilment, confident that they would yet enter into the possession of the promised country. But how could this be, when they were dead and buried? They knew that they should rise again. They did not regard death as any obstacle to their inheriting the promises. They "died in faith;" not faith in the sense of piety, but faith in this particular truth—that is, their possession of the inheritance, and therefore of their resurrection to a life beyond the grave. Death was no bar to the promise. This the apostle declares distinctly to have been the faith of these ancient believers. He never once imagined that those noble men were ignorant of the doctrine of immortality.

Jude gives information to the like effect, when he informs us of the doctrines which Enoch taught in his day. The grand, inspiring theme of his ministry was, "Behold the Lord cometh!" Cometh with "ten thousand of his saints"—that is, an innumerable host: and if He brought them with Him, He must bring them from the dead; for they had gone down to the grave. They must, therefore, be His risen saints. This, too, was precisely Enoch's doctrine; while he declared also that Christ would come to execute judgment upon the ungodly who had uttered against Him their hard speeches. Thus Divine revelation settles the question that the doctrine of Christ's coming, and the resurrection of the saints, was understood and preached boldly in the days of Enoch. It was not guessed at, or speculated on as a possibility: it was proclaimed as the clear and settled faith of God's people. The Lord would come—come to bring His saints with Him, and to execute long-delayed judgment upon the world of the ungodly.

Notice, also, the statement in Heb. vi. 1, 2: "Therefore, leaving the principles of the doctrine of Christ, let us go on unto perfection; not laying again the foundation of repentance from dead works, and of faith toward God, of the doctrine of baptisms, and of laying on of hands, and *of resurrection of the dead*, and of eternal judgment." Here the apostle classes the doctrine of the resurrection among the elementary principles of the Christian system, which the least should understand. How different is this from the position we have ordinarily given it, when we have questioned even whether the ancient saints knew or ever heard any thing about it?

But there is another fact which is decisive on this question, placing it beyond all controversy. It is, *that the doctrine of the resurrection was a settled article of the orthodox faith when Christ came.*

This was part of the national Jewish faith, being denied only by the limited sect of the Sadducees, as they denied also the existence of angel and spirit. Christ did not introduce the doctrine. He found it in existence, as the popular and cherished faith. There were imperfect and erroneous views in regard to the resurrection-state, as there were in respect to all matters relating to the coming and kingdom of Christ. But as to the doctrine itself, the faith of the nation was settled. There was no necessity for Christ to reveal it as an original truth.

Who now will go back in the history of that people,

and tell us where this great doctrine first began to enter into the national life? Where is the prophet to whom it was first communicated? Where does the little stream begin to rise, which expanded into such a broad and swelling river of truth? Where are the teachings of the Old Testament, upon which such a firm national faith was founded? An adequate cause must exist. The doctrine must have been revealed at some point. Yet these teachings, in *a didactic form*, are not to be found: and here it is that we have so stumbled on the subject. We have not understood, as we ought, God's great method of instruction, which He ordained from the beginning. This doctrine of the resurrection goes back to the very beginnings of the Jewish nation—yea, is even older than that nation. It dates back to paradise, being among the elementary principles of God's work of redemption, at the very foundation of the system, classed, as Paul states, with such simple elements, as faith in God, repentance for sin, and baptisms or purifications. Believers were made to understand from the outset that their promised inheritance lay in the future beyond the grave, death being no bar to the fulfilment. Accordingly they "died in faith," having the assurance that the promise was still theirs in all its integrity. They expected, therefore, to rise again. The way of the tree of life was kept for them; and in the magnificent forms of the cherubim, they saw the type and demonstration of that higher state to which our redeemed humanity was destined to attain, when the woman's promised seed should complete His work of conquest.

We cannot, therefore, but regard it as a deep reproach to our systems of theology to start the question, or permit its discussion, whether the doctrine of the immortality of the soul is revealed in the Old Testament. A doubt on this subject only betrays our ignorance of that grand and lucid system of instruction which God, for sc many centuries, followed up, and with such wonderful success, for the education of the race. We say, with such wonderful success; for the national faith of the Jews in the doctrine of the resurrection before the coming of Christ, is demonstration absolute on that point. While all heathen philosophy laughed to scorn the idea of resurrection, as the most absurd and offensive of all doctrines, the nation, which had been trained under the Divine tuition—cherished it as one of the simple elements of their faith, as undoubted as the existence of angel or spirit, and no more to be denied. The Scriptures start out from the very beginning with the doctrine of the resurrection, as with that of repentance for sin and faith in God. It was necessarily involved in the promised inheritance. The saints could not conceive of their entering into that inheritance except by coming forth from their graves; for they expected to return to earth again, and that here should be their promised abode. They had no reason to think of or look for any thing else. It was perfectly natural for them, therefore, to hope for their resurrection. From the foundation of the economy of grace God has taught men to look for the redemption of this body, as also of the earth itself. In the faith of this, patriarchs and holy men have died. It has been in-wrought into the whole fabric of our Christian faith. It is time, therefore, that we had left these first principles, which long since should have been understood, and gone on unto perfection. Paul's reproof on this point, which he gave to the Hebrews, is not without its force now. Had we studied God's method of instruction, beginning when He began, and following up His easy lessons, we should not be discussing first principles, and feeding still on milk.

Nor is this all. There are those still in our day, claiming the Christian name, who really deny the resurrection of the body, converting it into something else, we cannot undertake to tell what. As to any recovery of these bodies from the dust of the grave, they have no expectation of it. They regard them as forever consigned to corruption, no more to be redeemed. Such are under the power of that old heathen philosophy, which has so long ruled the world, and whose dominion has not yet passed away, the essence of which is, that this body is a dishonored work of the Creator, of which He himself may be ashamed, and upon which He will put the seal of His reprobation by delivering it over to the eternal silence of the sepulchre. There were such notions in Paul's day, growing out of the wide-prevailing heathenism. But he evidently regarded a denial of this doctrine of the resurrection as involving a denial of the whole gospel. "For if there be no resurrrection of the dead, then is Christ not risen [and His, beyond all denial, was a resurrection of the *body*]: and if Christ be not risen, then is our preaching vain, and your faith is also vain. Yea, and we are found false witnesses of God; because we have testified of God, that He raised up Christ; whom He raised not up, if so be that the dead rise not. For if the dead rise not, then is not Christ raised. And if Christ be not raised, your faith is vain: ye are yet in your sins. Then they also which are fallen asleep in Christ are perished. If in this life only we have hope in Christ, we are of all men most miserable;" 1 Cor. xv. 13. Mark these last words: If there be no resurrection of the body, "then they which are fallen asleep in Christ are *perished*"—there is no life beyond the present. That is the way the apostle reasoned—the way the saints of old reasoned. They said, If there is to be no resurrection, then we perish when we die. The grave is the end of us. There is no inheritance, no life beyond; and we are of all men most miserable; for we have rejected this life as our portion; and having none in any life to come, we are miserable creatures indeed. But if there be an inheritance and life in the future, then must we come forth from our graves to enter therein. These bodies must be restored, if man, as *man*, is to be redeemed and live forever.

This is the Bible doctrine. This is the faith of the Scriptures, taught from the beginning, as among the first elements of the system of Divine truth: and this was the earnest hope and desire of Paul, to which he looked forward with the most intense longing. "If by any means I might attain unto the resurrection of the dead;" Phil. iii. 11.

CHAPTER XXIII.

DOCTRINE OF A REMNANT.

We have called attention to the fact, that Divine and human coöperation was essential to the completeness of human redemption—that while, on the one hand, God must arrange a plan of justification for sinners, and open a door of mercy and hope for them, they, on the other hand, must accept the offered terms, and, by humble faith, enter into His gracious designs, thus becoming believers, or justified sinners. Unbelief, then, must of necessity have a controlling influence upon the administration of this economy of grace; and we shall consider its bearings as related to what we may denominate

THE DOCTRINE OF A REMNANT.

There were those from the beginning who understood God's plan of grace, and heartily entered into it, knowing that it was theirs humbly to receive all the Divine teachings relating thereto. Abel, and others of like character, saw this truth plainly. They perceived that forgiveness, justification, and final salvation, were held out to such as complied with the offered and appointed means—to those who brought the bloody offering as an atonement for their souls; and thus reconciled to God, followed Him in all the ways of holy obedience. These were the spiritual, holy men, who walked with God, and died in the faith of the promised inheritance. But the history of Cain shows that there was another class of men, who took different ground, and maintained a very different doctrine. Abel was the representative of a class. His faith and principles lived in a body of noble men following after, and continuing to this day. The same is true of Cain. His history had not been preserved, if he had stood merely as a solitary, exceptional case. But he was a representative man also. His views and character have lived in a distinctive class following in his footsteps, and maintaining essentially his principles.

Cain was a religious man *in his way*, and zealous in the maintenance of his principles—a fact not to be overlooked in the history. A careless neglecter of religion would never have taken the deep offense that Cain did at the rejection of his offering. He was an intense religious bigot, like Saul of Tarsus. But he took his own way to serve the Lord, the way of his own blinded, perverse heart; and when God gave him to understand how plainly that such was not the way of His appointment, and that He would not recognize or sanction it, all the deep perverseness and rebellion of that heart were stirred to its profoundest depths. He raged in the fierceness of his anger against God, and against His appointed ordinances. He raged against his more righteous brother, until that brother's blood was found upon his hands. Nor did the sight of his murdered body cause his heart to relent. He looked upon it still in wrath, as his insolent reply to the

Lord shows, when inquiry was made concerning his brother. These facts show how deeply Cain's passions were enlisted in his religious principles, and that he clung to them against the Divine teachings and rebuke, and over a brother's murdered body. The same facts show also that Cain expected the Divine favor and approbation, and, of necessity, a part in the promised inheritance. He claimed that his religion was as good as Abel's, and even preferable—his sacrifice being more appropriate to the Divine character and consistent with reason—consequently he claimed to himself all the benefits of redemption, even all that was held out to faith in the future, promised inheritance.

Have we not here, then, a clue to the prevailing type of religion in the antediluvian period, outside of the faithful company who adhered to the Divine instructions, and looked for justification by faith in the shedding of innocent blood?

No age, so far as our knowledge extends, has been wanting in forms of religious faith. The experience of the world has demonstrated that religion, in some shape, is a necessity to man; and we have no reason to suppose that the antediluvian era was any exception to this rule. The only question would be, what was it? What form did it assume? Cain's history throws light on this point. In him we have an authentic statement of the point of departure from the true faith, and the false system introduced. While paradise was continued, and the living presence of Jehovah in the flaming sword before the way of the tree of life, it is not probable that the world would fall into the gross idolatry of subsequent ages, the worship of stocks and stones, and beasts of the earth. They would be likely to recognize this living presence of God, yet adopt their own methods of worshiping Him, as Cain did; or if they retained the bloody sacrifice, it might be with no proper conception of its intent and meaning. Fire-worship may have existed during this period, originating, as we have no doubt it did, from the manifested presence of Jehovah in the flaming sword, and the fire in the cloud. Cain, when he fled from this "presence of the Lord," may have sought to make up for the loss by the substitution of material fire, answering somewhat to the higher conception of heathenism, that the idol is not the god, but the form in which the spirit of the divinity dwells. It was in living flame that the infinite and eternal One did manifest His presence on earth; and hence might easily and naturally have originated the fire-worship of the early ages. But whatever particular form the religion of the antediluvian age might have assumed, this thought would enter into it, that the service rendered was acceptable, and *would secure the promised inheritance.* They lost sight of the truth that God must be sought by sinners in the way of His own appointment. How easy, too, this was, is shown in the history of Cain. Neither is it likely that his pernicious error was arrested by the rebuke which it met from heaven. He himself evidently did not accept the Divine decision, notwithstanding its unequivocal character. "He was very wroth, and his countenance fell." There was no teachable, submissive spirit. The decision made served to guide and enlighten the few who were willing to be taught of God. But the subsequent history shows that the masses followed the lead of Cain. He was a type and fitting representative of the age. The violence which he inaugurated became the leading characteristic of the period. The earth was filled with it, and every imagination of the thoughts of man's heart was only evil continually. Intensity of meaning would be given to the portrait of that wicked generation, should we apply this statement to their perverse views of religion and the

Divine teachings, and not simply to ordinary evil thoughts and desires, as found in the hearts of men. Such a statement would well have described Cain's character. All the imaginations of the thoughts of *his* heart, even in regard to God and religion, were only evil continually. His views were false and pernicious in the extreme, and corrupting to the whole man. The first foul murder on earth grew directly out of this religion. Here the violence began, and hence it spread. Yet with all this wickedness and rejection of the Divine teachings in the matter of faith and justification, men still clung to the idea of their acceptance with God, and their participation in the promised blessings of redemption. It is the idea which enters into every false religion. All systems of error cry, peace, peace, to the wicked, and flatter, with the fond hope of salvation.

Could we also gain an insight into the preaching of that age by any of the faithful servants of God, this would serve to throw light upon our present subject, and show what the tendencies of those times were. This very desired information is furnished us. Enoch was raised up to be a faithful witness for God, and a preacher of righteousness; and we have a brief, but very clear statement of the doctrines which he held forth, as demanded by the times. His theme was the coming of Christ, to give reward unto *His saints*, and execute judgment upon *the ungodly*. This was a fuller development of the truth contained in the promise concerning the woman's seed, and a clearer statement of Abel's doctrine of justification by faith—that they alone were God's people who accepted the Divine teachings, coming in His own appointed way, and that such alone would the Lord bring with Him at His appearing, to share the glory and inheritance. This was the doctrine held by the saints, and which Enoch was commissioned especially to preach, declaring as emphatically that the wicked were reserved unto judgment, however they might seemingly prosper now, and claim for themselves the Divine favor. For all their ungodly deeds and hard speeches spoken against the Lord, they should assuredly be called to account. What, moreover, were the "hard speeches" of those times against Christ, if not such doctrines as Cain inaugurated, which struck a fatal blow at the whole system of salvation by faith, and opened wide the door of entrance to heaven for every unsanctified sinner? To make God the author of such doctrines was uttering against Him hard speeches indeed.

The mission of the prophet Enoch was, undoubtedly, an opportune one—such as the exigencies demanded. It reasserted the great promise, made in the beginning, of earth's Deliverer; and then defined more accurately than ever, the line intended to be drawn between the righteous and the wicked, reward being given to the one, and judgment reserved for the other. It is to be borne in mind that God was now dealing with a world in rebellion, to secure the repentance and salvation of transgressors, while yet His character was not understood, nor the terms upon which His favor was to be obtained. The effect was to make wickedness bold and defiant, even to claiming God himself on its side, with the benefit of all His promises. It is the nature of wickedness and rebellion to secure its own selfish ends, to the overthrow of all truth and righteousness, the breaking down of the authority of all law, and the utter defeat of justice. Such was the impious development of sin in these first ages, when men wholly misinterpreted the Divine forbearance; and here was the significance of Enoch's mission and preaching. But however his testimony might have been a witness for the truth, and blessed, doubtless, to some, it did not stay the wide-prevailing error and ungodliness of men. These increased more and more, until they threatened to sweep the truth utterly away, leaving not a vestige behind. The time was approaching when God must interpose, or give up *His* system of redemption, to adopt one of human devising. He began, therefore, to make preparation to bear His testimony in a manner not to be misunderstood even by the wicked, that His doctrine was that of the salvation of the believing, even though but a remnant; and Noah was raised up to preach it faithfully for one hundred and twenty years more, while at the same time he was taking means to save himself and his household from the gathering storm of wrath. His preaching, however, made no impression, showing how utterly the world had apostatized from the truth, and from all faith in God, being given up to their own wickedness and delusions. The time, therefore, had fully come for God to vindicate himself from the hard speeches which ungodly sinners had so long spoken against Him, in claiming that He was on their side, and that they, too, might hope for His salvation. They laughed to scorn the doctrine of Noah, that God was about to destroy the world; for had He not given assurance of its redemption? Did not paradise remain as a type of the restoration of the earth from the curse? Was there not still the tree of life standing there, guarded by the cherubim, to tell of the deliverance of the race from death? Noah, therefore, was a narrow-minded bigot and fool, misrepresenting the Divine character and government, and setting up his wisdom, not only against the world, but the Divine teachings also. This position of the antediluvians would be no more strange than that of the Jewish rulers and nation demanding for themselves the kingdom, because of their descent from Abraham, and regarding Christ as a Samaritan and devil, because he denied their claim. It was time, therefore, for God to appear and show himself on the side of truth, and preserve it from utter overthrow.

By an awful stroke of desolating judgment, too, He did reveal himself for the deliverance of *a remnant*, bearing witness that the universal salvation of the wicked was no part of His gracious plan. This was a terrific confirmation of Enoch's preaching, that the Lord would come *with His saints*, and for their deliverance, but for the overthrow of the ungodly. It was a lesson, too, which the world would not soon forget.

May we not find, at this point, the significance and meaning of that first dispensation of the world? It has been for the most part a very dark one, ending, as it did, in such a dreadful and almost universal overthrow; and causing the Lord, in His own expressive language, to "repent that he had made man upon the earth." Was that dispensation, then, a failure, so that God accomplished nothing by it in furtherance of His great work of redemption? Was not that antediluvian age an important and necessary one, having an end and meaning of its own, and working out great results? The dispensations succeeding, as we shall show, had their peculiar mission, and carried forward the work of redemption toward its fulfilment. Did not the antediluvian era fulfil its part? We cannot doubt it, and believe that the doctrines and history of Cain and Abel are the key of explanation to that period. The men of faith, such as Abel, Seth, Enoch, Noah, and others of like character, clung to the bleeding lamb and the blood of atonement as the only way of approach for sinners to God, while an unbelieving race followed in the way of Cain, rejecting such sacrifice, yet claiming all the benefit of the Divine promises, without any confession of their sins, or acknowledgment of their condemnation. Such a fact will help to explain the fearful aboundings of wickedness in this period, and the necessity for an overflowing deluge to sweep away a race of impious sinners. The fact may also be noted, that, since that terrible overthrow of impiety, the doctrine of bloody sacrifices has been accepted by the world. When God began a new dispensation in the person of Noah, He had secured the permanent establishment unto the end of that central doctrine of all religion for a world of sinners, *a sin offering by the shedding of blood.* Henceforth men were to confess themselves transgressors. However false their religion in other respects, and however debasing the forms of idolatry into which they might sink, this point at least was settled, that men were under condemnation, to hope for pardon and acceptance only through an atonement for their souls. Nor is it without its significance that we have this record immediately after Noah came forth from the ark. "And Noah builded an altar unto the Lord, and took of every clean beast, and of every clean fowl, and *offered burnt offerings* on the altar. And the Lord smelled a sweet savor; and the Lord said in his heart, I will not again curse the ground any more for man's sake, for [though] the imagination of man's heart is evil from his youth; neither will I again smite any more every living thing as I have done. While the earth remaineth, seed time and harvest, and cold and heat, and summer and winter, and day and night, shall not cease." God had carried that doctrine of a *burnt offering* over the heads of an ungodly world, and contended for it to their destruction, establishing it upon an immovable foundation, as *the doctrine* which must belong to all religion.

This grand lesson, worked out in the providence of God in that first dispensation, was the more impressive, because the remnant, for whom the deliverance was wrought, was so small, while the ruin was so wide-spread and overwhelming. God had been gathering out a remnant of believing ones all through this period, who died in the faith, and whom He was keeping unto His heavenly kingdom. But this was unnoticed and unregarded by a wicked world. Something more positive was needed which would convince not faith, but unbelief itself, silencing rebellion and the hard speeches of ungodliness. It was a mercy to the world for God to do it. When, therefore, the righteousness of the earth was reduced down to the smallest limits possible, and seemed on the point of extinction; while wickedness and unbelief were nearest to the point of triumph, then did God come out to teach the world a lesson respecting the nature of His present economy of redemption, showing that His plan was to save the righteous, even though they were but a remnant, while the unbelieving multitude should be reserved for the day of destruction.

The world, however, needed further instruction still on this subject, and God began the inculcation of another lesson by choosing out a nation, and setting it apart as a holy people unto himself, with whom He might establish His covenant and promises, and among whom He might dwell to reveal all His will. The first system of types connected with paradise had been swept away by the deluge. It might have seemed as if this was an irreparable loss. But before the death of Shem, God began to provide another, more complete than the former, embodying fuller revelations respecting the coming One, and the promised redemption of earth. In the introduction of this new system, connected with the land of Canaan and the chosen people, it is to be noted with what remarkable prominence God made the doctrine of *faith* to stand out in the history of Abraham, the great founder of the nation. In commencing a new system of instruction and types for the race, God would leave no room for doubt in respect to that fundamental doctrine which had been so misrepresented and denied in the age preceding. Accordingly, God raised up that wonderful man, Abraham, in whose character and life the doctrine of faith was made to stand forth in all its magnificent proportions. God tried Abraham—tried him in every possible manner, and to the utmost extent of endurance. He intended that this doctrine should occupy the forefront of the picture, drawn in living lines in the sublime history of this man of God. It was because Abraham believed God—believed implicitly and fully, that the covenant was established with him and his posterity, that the Lord should be their God, and they His people.

Here, then, in the choice of this nation to be the recipients of God's covenant and promises, was the doctrine of the salvation of a remnant embodied in a permanent form in a system of instruction, as it had never been before. God intended that it should be—intended that the race should understand that His covenant was with His people—those who would believe His word, receive His teachings, and obey His commandments, and that He would gather out such a people unto himself. This point was not embodied in any type connected with the first system in Eden, though God did teach it most emphatically in the overwhelming waters of a deluge. It was, however, directly embraced in the second system, and made to occupy there a very prominent position. So did the nation of Israel understand it, beyond question. They recognized the fact, that *they* were God's peculiar people, whom He had owned by covenant, and that to *them* belonged the promises and inheritance. No truth connected with the system of redemption was more thoroughly wrought into the Jewish mind, and all their modes of thought, than this very one. Yet we shall see how even they prevented it, and turned it aside from its true intent, as did the generations before the flood. God intended that faith, like that which Abraham so illustriously exhibited, should be the foundation of His covenant with

Israel, and that they should so understand it; for He told them distinctly again and again, that if they were disobedient and unbelieving, so as not to hearken to His voice, He would cast them off, and give them over into the hands of their enemies, to become a byword and hissing in the earth. The nation, however, was too sensual to understand the true system of faith as the basis of salvation. There were some, indeed, taught of the Spirit; men of faith and piety, who embraced the Divine teachings, and discerned their spiritual import, looking beyond the shadows to the substance. But, taken as a whole, the nation was perverse and rebellious, walking in the way of its own lusts and self-righteousness, clinging to birth, and circumcision, and observance of the law, but neglecting still the *righteousness of faith*, while the doctrine concerning a chosen, covenant people, according to their carnal construction of it, fell in with all their selfish views and desires, even as the antediluvian world had claimed the benefit of the promised inheritance. Yes, verily, said Israel, God has made His covenant forever with us, declaring himself to be our God, and that we are His people. The kingdom belongs to us. Messiah, the Prince, is to come and take possession of the throne, and reign over the house of Jacob forever, and ours shall be the glory of all lands. For us the kingdom and blessedness are prepared. These were the ideas embodied in the proud, carnal Pharisee, whose religion has now become, under the teachings of Christ, but a synonym for hypocrisy.

Here then, again, was the doctrine of faith and the salvation of a remnant to be vindicated anew under different circumstances, and the world once more taught the great lesson on this subject. There was, however, an important difference between the controversy here and that of the preceding age, showing an advance in the progress of truth and redemption. In the former, the whole race claimed the benefits of salvation in virtue of God's promises. In the succeeding dispensation, the covenant was with Israel, the nation understanding by this that they were constituted into a grand, spiritual aristocracy, with all the rights and privileges of the kingdom of heaven conferred upon them. This was congenial to the pride of their carnal hearts, and they grasped the fond idea, cherishing it with the most intense enthusiasm. The doctrine of a remnant was held firmly, yet turned virtually into the doctrine of universal salvation; universal, so far as their own nation was concerned. The doctrine of faith was thrown out and lost sight of, while descent from Abraham and circumcision were substituted in its place; and thus an aristocracy of birth, race, and blood built up, with which the covenant of God and redemption was established.

CHAPTER XXIV.

DOCTRINE OF A REMNANT.

It is a prevalent idea, that the gospel is a narrow and exclusive system, wanting in all large and generous views—that it has a narrow door of entrance, shutting out the great mass of mankind from its blessings, and imposing a hard yoke of bondage upon the necks of men, which is difficult to bear. Not only does the world entertain such thoughts respecting the plan of redemption, but too often are the minds of Christians influenced by them, so that they fail to grasp the grandeur and freeness of this system of Divine grace.

In prosecuting further the study of the doctrine of a remnant, it becomes necessary to take up these prevalent ideas; and in demonstrating their error, we shall be able to show more clearly what this doctrine of the salvation of a believing remnant is, and how it has entered into all the plans of Divine providence thus far developed.

There has ever been a fierce ambition among men to gain possession of the places of emolument and power, in which the few have been successful, while the many have been their tools and victims. When the prize, too, has once been gained, the means were always at hand to secure it not only to the fortunate possessors, but to their posterity. Men have ever sought to transmit their names and titles, their honors and privileges, their power and wealth, their estates and kingdoms, to their children after them. Thus have aristocracies grown up, and chartered monopolies of hereditary privilege and power. The world has been ruled, not by the best men, but the most ambitious and daring; who have seen, too, that their power was transmitted as a chartered right to their successors. To this system the world has submitted, because it had not the virtue or intelligence to maintain its rights against such aggressions; and under it the nations have been robbed and spoiled from age to age. It is the ambitious few that grasp after the rule in our own republican country, in spite of the fact that this Government was founded to the end that the many should hold the power here. But democracy does not banish ambition and selfishness from human hearts; the few still covet the monopoly of power, and will drench the land in blood to obtain the prize. Liberty has been secured only at the price of blood; and by precious blood alone can it be preserved. The nations of Europe are passing through these same struggles, contending for their liberties, and slowly making head against those huge monopolies of rank, wealth, and power, which have for so many ages ruled them with a rod of iron. What such monopolies are, we ourselves have had most vivid demonstration in that gigantic system of oppression which has grown up in our own republican country, impiously claiming the right of property in a fellow man, and denying all the rights of humanity. Fearful as is such a system of robbery and wrong, yet what demonstration have we of the sacredness which it may assume in the eyes of its apologists, so that they will cling to it, fight for it, and overthrow liberty and Christianity to maintain it; seeking to build up their confederacies upon it as the chief corner-stone? Such are the systems of injustice and oppression which have prevailed from the beginning; and under these the places of power and emolument have been monopolized to the privileged few. The world has always had its favorites—*its chosen, elect numbers*—to whom the fortune and power have belonged. Theirs have been the rank and high-born blood; and their privileged aristocracies have been surrounded by all the bulwarks which law and hereditary custom could erect for their defence. These, too, for the most part, have been the cruel and haughty oppressors of the race, under whose iron heel every vestige of liberty has been crushed, and earth has been made to sigh and weep, to groan and bleed.

God has ever contended against these systems of pride and injustice, declaring himself emphatically "no respecter of persons." He has never shut himself up, in His dealings with the race, to these selfish distinctions, as if He had not "made of one blood all nations of men;" but has dealt with all men alike, upon the same broad principles of eternal justice and truth; and His has been the only really effective blow that has ever made the slightest impression upon the buttressed fortresses of human pride and selfishness.

But has not God also had His favorites, upon whom He has delighted to bestow His love? It could not be otherwise. But who are these chosen ones of Heaven, and upon what ground are they recognized? Does God show respect for persons, and confer the honors and privileges of His kingdom, because of blood or rank, of wealth or learning, or any of those distinctions of which the world makes so much account? He has never made himself liable to this charge; but has, on the contrary, kept himself independent of all these human distinctions, and pledged His favor forever to the penitent and believing. Upon what grounds God may go before in leading men to repentance, we have no knowledge whatever, neither has He revealed himself. There is a province of the Divine administration which is beyond our reach. But upon this one point, that faith is the essential requisite to acceptance with Him, God has never left himself without witness. Whosoever believeth, shall be saved. This truth God made clear from the beginning, and upon this broad basis the door of mercy was thrown open alike to all; justification and eternal life being made free to every sinner upon the same equal terms. Thus the covenant was established with Israel. "Abraham believed God, and it was counted to him for righteousness; and he was called the friend of God." This illustrious example of faith was made to stand out with such prominence, that the world should understand beyond question what was the method of the Divine procedure, and upon what grounds men were to find favor and acceptance before God. Israel were to be His people, if they would be obedient, and hearken to His voice; while, if they were unbelieving and rebellious, He would cut them off, and count them as His enemies. This was the foundation-principle entering into the constitution of that chosen nation.

It was, however, a remnant only of the nation that thus accepted the covenant. The mass were unbelieving and disobedient, rejecting God's prophets, and, last of all, His Son, while they still sought to appropriate to themselves all the rich blessings of the covenant, basing the same on the new ground of birth, blood, and circumcision. They thus claimed a superiority of race, and on this ground separated themselves as a holy people from all other nations. This was the cherished national idea in the time of Christ. To be an Israelite, was title sufficient to the kingdom of heaven; while the Gentile nations were counted but as dogs.

God also well understood from the beginning how the nation would run naturally toward this error, as the antediluvian generations had done, perverting His whole system of grace and salvation; and He sought, as far as possible, to guard them against it, and make them understand that His covenant was never based upon a preeminence of birth or blood. Thus God asks, "Was not Esau Jacob's brother? Yet I loved Jacob, and hated Esau, and laid his mountains and his heritage waste for the dragons of the wilderness;" Mal. i. 1, 2. The argument is, Esau was the first-born, and so entitled, *as men judge*, to the preëminence. God ought to have preferred him, according to the birth-right. "Yet," says God, "I chose Jacob." So, also, at a subsequent period, He set Ephraim before Manasseh; and, through them, gave Joseph, although among the youngest of his house, a double portion in the two tribes of Ephraim and Manasseh. God would not sanction the aristocratic doctrine, that the first-born among men must necessarily take the precedence, and be thereby entitled to all Divine favor. True, indeed, He chose Israel to be a peculiar people unto himself, establishing with them His gracious covenant; and He knew how this action would be misunderstood and perverted—how this people, in their perversity and blindness, would change the whole covenant, and claim a title to the kingdom of heaven simply because descended from Abraham; thus building up their nation as a vast religious monopoly. God knew that men, in their pride and unbelief, would seek to force even His economy of grace on to this very ground, setting up an aristocracy of race and blood, with Heaven's own seal attached, and a title to everlasting life.

Before the nation, therefore, was organized, God entered His solemn protest against any such doctrine; declaring that such was not the meaning of His covenant, nor so to be interpreted. While He had a first-born, chosen race, it was not based upon their little human distinctions of rank and descent, nor to be converted to mere selfish purposes. This principle, too, God carried out through the entire history of the nation with the most unswerving purpose. What though He did redeem them out of Egypt with a mighty hand and an outstretched arm, and with great judgments, feeding them with bread from heaven in the wilderness? Yet but the smallest remnant—even Caleb and Joshua alone, of all that unbelieving generation—entered the promised land. In the time of Elijah there was a remnant of but seven thousand who had not apostatized unto Baal. At a subsequent period, ten tribes forsook the Lord, and were carried away unto a strange land, so that no man knoweth of their dwelling-place. Of the two tribes remaining, but a remnant also were found faithful. Expostulations and warnings were employed in vain. They gave no heed; and they, too, were driven into captivity, Jerusalem being made a desolation, and their temple burned with fire. After seventy years' exile, God again gathered a remnant, and brought them back to their inheritance. Yet, when Christ appeared, how small the number to be found who were willing to be taught of God, and receive the Lord's Anointed! The nation scorned the thought, that they were not fit for the kingdom in virtue of their birth and circumcision; or that they needed a second birth, as did the uncircumcised heathen; and still more, that these unclean Gentiles and sinners were to be welcomed to sit down with Abraham, Isaac, and Jacob, upon the simple ground of faith. Upon this broad platform Christ designed to offer a free salvation to every tribe and kindred and people under the whole heaven, to Jew and Gentile alike. But the pride of the Jew was mortally offended at this, and he fought against it with the most determined hostility. The Scribes and Pharisees, the chief priests and rulers, all combined to resist such an invasion of their chartered rights, as they regarded them. They raged against it, crucifying the Son of God, and blaspheming against the Holy Ghost. At this very point, the fiercest warfare was waged that earth ever witnessed. The nation was agitated to its foundations, contending desperately for their monopoly of the kingdom, while God would not yield one jot or tittle. He vindicated His right to justify men everywhere on the broad ground of faith alone, defending thus the claims of our universal humanity; and this, too, though the victory was achieved in the overthrow of the covenant nation, and their dispersion to the ends of the earth. Here was the very Malakoff of the enemy, the mightiest spiritual monopoly that human pride and self-righteousness had ever built up; and never did the religion of Christ perform more illustrious service than when it stormed and carried this citadel, breaching its frowning walls and razing them to the ground. There was no attempt to evade the issue. The direct question was, whether men were to be justified by circumcision and the law, or by faith in Christ simply. And that was but the statement of the question, whether God was shut up to confer His spiritual blessings upon those of a particular race and birth, or whether He was at liberty to bestow them wherever He pleased, upon Jew and Gentile, on the broad ground of faith. God intended, moreover, that this question should be settled in Jerusalem first, under the very shadow of the Sanhedrim, where the high churchism of the Pharisees and rulers had entrenched itself within its strongest bulwarks. The apostles were not sent off to distant and unknown heathen tribes, to preach this doctrine of faith. They must begin at Jerusalem. Here must it win its first and glorious triumphs. Here must it be sublimely held forth as the power and wisdom of God unto salvation, to which the Jew himself must cheerfully bow. Within the sacred precincts of the temple, before priest and Pharisee, Sadducee and Sanhedrim, must this broad doctrine of faith be preached, and the chosen nation be told that they had no exclusive title to the kingdom of heaven, and no title whatever, except as they, too, were justified by faith in the Crucified of Nazareth.

This truth, in its fulness, burst with astonishment upon the minds of even the most enlightened and spiritual men at that day. The disciples of Christ were amazed to discover the breadth and magnificence of the Divine operations here, and the amazing sweep of those principles which the gospel was now inaugurating. Even they had not understood them hitherto. The Holy Ghost opened the subject to their apprehension, when He imparted His miraculous power to Cornelius, the Roman centurion, and his Gentile friends. Peter beheld this Divine working with astonishment, exclaiming, "Of a truth, I perceive that God is no respecter of persons: but in every nation, he that feareth him and worketh righteousness, is accepted with him;" Acts x. 34. The apostles themselves had not understood, until this hour, that the gospel was to be preached unto Jew and Gentile alike, both being placed upon the same equal footing, and both alike acceptable to

God—the circumcision and the uncircumcision—if only they believed. If the apostles, too, could scarce credit such a truth, and could be convinced only by the miraculous demonstration of the Holy Ghost given to the Gentile even as to the Jew, putting no difference between them, we need not wonder that such men as the Scribes and Pharisees, with the unbelieving mass of the nation, should contend for their supposed and cherished monopoly of the Divine favor. God's doctrine of saving whom He would, through faith alone, was the most radical, revolutionary doctrine that was ever started on a mission against the gigantic monopolies of this world. It quailed not before the high places of power and pride, but went forth upon its Heaven-appointed errand of mercy, to take our wide humanity by the hand and lift it up from the dunghill, vindicating its common and equal right to the favor of God against all privileged classes of every name and character. Its sublime, heroic language was, "Where there is neither Greek nor Jew, circumcision nor uncircumcision, Barbarian, Scythian, bond nor free; but Christ is all, and in all;" Col. iii. 11. On this ground did God gather an elect people to himself, setting a wide and open door of mercy to the entire race. Yea, if God has seemed to lean in any direction in this matter, it has been toward the poor, the neglected, the outcast and down-trodden. So apparent, too, were the overflowing sympathies of Christ's nature in this direction when on earth, that the proud rulers stigmatized Him as "the friend of publicans and sinners." It was a reproach of damning shame in the eyes of all. But little did those men dream that it would carry His name down through the centuries, and become the most glorious title of honor ever conferred upon any of the sons of earth, beyond all the stars of nobility and the decorations that were ever boasted of.

To carry out these broad and noble principles of freedom and righteousness, it was necessary to take out a remnant again from the Jewish nation, which had become as Sodom and Gomorrah, filling up the cup of their iniquities. The nation had abandoned the fundamental principle upon which the covenant was originally made with them—that of faith—and were seeking utterly to overthrow it, even as our own nation had, for some years past, come to regard the preservation of slavery, and not liberty, as the law of its life, and the spirit of its constitution, to mould all its administration and policy. Israel had departed so far from the true meaning of this sacred covenant, that they were found contending at length against the most cherished ordinances of Heaven, and seeking to confine to themselves, and their race, all the blessings of salvation, which God had designed for our wide humanity, and which He had based on faith alone, that thus it might be unlimited in its influence and operations. The doctrine of salvation by faith was the only one which could possibly make a free salvation for all. To reject this, and substitute any other ground, was to make a narrow, selfish monopoly, which would shut up salvation to the few, and those the unbelieving and wicked. Nay, these would neither go in themselves, nor suffer them that were entering, to go in. The doctrine of justification by faith is the broad ground of universal pardon and salvation, of universal truth and right, and the overthrow of all wickedness. Justification on any other ground—of race or blood, or circumcision, or righteousness of men—is giving a monopoly of heaven into the hands of the wicked, and making it a matter of odious favoritism, without any truth, justice, or humanity. God accordingly overthrew that aristocratic system of the Scribes, Pharisees, and rulers, and dashed the nation in pieces, in order to give the free offer of mercy and salvation to the entire Gentile world.

God has thus proved himself to be no respecter of persons, making that fact so simple to us that we can hardly realize how any other idea should ever have been entertained. The doctrine of faith is the grand principle which characterizes and controls the work of redemption. It is the salvation for sinners—sinners of every name, and of the deepest dye, and adequate to meet all the woes of our ruined humanity. It does not monopolize the favor of God to the few boasting righteous, who claim that they have never been enlisted in the great rebellion against Heaven. Christ told the Pharisees emphatically, that He came to call sinners to repentance—that His mission of mercy was to them. These weary ones He invited to come to Him. For these He has stood up a bold, fearless champion, contending unto the death for their sakes, that the door of heaven might be open to them also—yea, that the publicans, harlots, and Gentiles might sit down with Abraham in the kingdom of God.

Away then forever with the idea of the various exclusiveness of the gospel of Christ. It is the only system that has ever possessed the least liberality or spark of generous spirit. It is the only power on earth which has had the nobleness, the enduring courage and might, to stand up and encounter all the tallest systems of human ambition and pride. It is the only system that has had the hardihood to espouse the suffering cause of our universal humanity, and assert its equal rights against every chartered monopoly of human selfishness. Christianity has never quailed at any point upon this wide field. She has marched up in steady column to the most formidable batteries of the enemy, and stood the hottest of their fire; and she will carry every one of them by assault. She never has been defeated. She never will be. Christianity has never taken back the sublime, though to many, deeply offensive, declaration she put forth at the outset,

"Neither Greek nor Jew, circumcision nor uncircumcision, Barbarian, Scythian, bond nor free; but Christ is all, and in all." To maintain this doctrine, the opposing Jewish nation was dashed in pieces from the place of their pride and glory, a remnant only being saved; even as God rescued the same truth with a small remnant in the days of Noah over the heads of an ungodly race, who were making shipwreck of all truth and righteousness, and aiming to overthrow the whole covenant of mercy and redemption. The doctrine of a believing remnant is thus the doctrine of the world's salvation; for, "had not the Lord left unto us a very small remnant, we had been as Sodom, and been made like unto Gomorrah."

God's doctrine of a chosen people, therefore, is a solemn and eternal protest against all favoritism and class distinctions of this selfish world, asserting the broad and everlasting principles of truth and righteousness in the kingdom of His grace.

CHAPTER XXV.

DOCTRINE OF A REMNANT.

We have studied the history of two dispensations—the antediluvian and the Mosaic—in the light of our present subject, and have seen how they both terminated, beyond all controversy, in the deliverance of a believing remnant. The antediluvian age ended in sweeping away the entire world of the ungodly with a flood of waters, Noah and his family alone surviving the dreadful wreck; while the succeeding Mosaic period closed with the overthrow of the covenant nation in their unbelief and wickedness, a remnant of faithful men alone being gathered out, upon whom the Holy Ghost had set His seal.

It remains to consider

The character of the present dispensation, and the principles on which God is now dealing with the Gentile nations, to whom the word of life is come.

There is no more difficulty in determining this, than in settling the facts of the dispensations going before. They are all alike open to observation. Eighteen centuries of this period have already rolled by, and whatever of doubt there might have been in the beginning as to what it would be, there need not be any question now, as to what it has been.

The disciples of Jesus, in common with their nation, were, at one time, expecting something very different from what has been realized. They supposed that the time had come for the introduction of that blessed era of righteousness and peace under the Messiah, of which prophets had been speaking from the beginning, having entirely overlooked Christ's first advent of humiliation and suffering. That had virtually dropped out of their scriptures, and their thoughts were fixed only upon the revelation of His kingdom and glory. Through all His ministry, Jesus sought to correct this misapprehension in the minds of His disciples, though He was obliged to approach the subject with extreme caution, and was then rebuked and contradicted by the impetuous Peter, who took upon him to assert that such things should not happen unto him. The matter of His sufferings and death was one of utmost difficulty to break to their minds, being at the farthest remove from all their thoughts, and, in spite of all His repeated instructions, beyond their comprehension. Nor did they get an insight into its meaning and relations until they beheld their risen Saviour, and their minds were opened to understand the Scriptures, "how that Christ ought to have suffered these things, and enter unto His glory." Instead of His death, they therefore were looking constantly for His ascension of the throne of David, not necessarily or precisely in that carnal sense which the worldly Jewish rulers expected; but in the fulfilment of what David, Isaiah, and all the prophets had foretold concerning it. Christ, however, gave His disciples to understand that that event, and the blessed era therewith connected, were still in the future—that He was now, in His humiliation under the curse, to make himself a sin-offering; that He was to depart for a season in order to receive that kingdom, and to return, for which they must wait, and look, and pray. He informed them, likewise, that the interval between His departure and return would be an uninterrupted period of great trouble and conflict of abounding wickedness and apostasy, during which the people of God would scarcely be able to endure, and hold fast to their faith. On this point Christ gave most careful and repeated instructions, knowing well how different the real facts were from all their anticipations, and warning them with emphasis not to be deceived—that they must not be disappointed at what should befall them; because the dispensation and events, which they hoped for, were still in the distance, and that a period of sore trial and tribulation must first intervene. They were to be His witnesses to testify to His resurrection—that, though crucified and now absent, He was a living Saviour still, who would, ere long, come in His glory and kingdom. They were to go forth with their lives in their hands, to preach the doctrine of the cross, and offer salvation to all upon the same broad foundation of faith, their commission, "Go ye into all the world, and preach the gospel to every creature. He that believeth and is baptized, shall be saved; but he that believeth not shall be damned;" Mark xvi. 15.

Mark here, again, *the basis upon which the covenant of mercy and salvation with men was established under this new dispensation.*

It is most distinctly and emphatically stated, so as to leave no room for doubt. It is the same condition affixed to the covenant in the beginning, and upon which Abel, Enoch, and Noah were justified; the same that was made with Abraham, and counted unto him for righteousness. God never made a covenant with unbelief and disobedience—never. When, therefore, at last we come to the new dispensation, under which the great sin-offering was made, by the shedding of whose precious blood the way was open to offer a free salvation to all in His name, we find the condition of the covenant the same as ever, and held forth in still more emphatic terms. The door was wide open for every tribe and kindred, Gentile and Jew alike. The glad tidings were to be preached to every creature; but, "he that believeth and is baptized shall be saved; and he that believeth not shall be damned." That is emphatic and unambiguous. The blessings of redemption were no more to the wicked and unbelieving than they had ever been; and the great question was now to be tested, whether men would receive this risen Jesus as their sin-offering, owning Him as their Messiah and Prince. That question was speedily decided in respect to the Jewish nation, as we have already shown. A remnant believed, and were taken out, to be kept unto the day of redemption; but the nation, raging against the Crucified, and blaspheming against the Holy Ghost, was dashed and broken in pieces. But how was it with the Gentile world? The glad tidings of great joy came to them, even a wide and open door of mercy. Did the Gentiles enter into the privileges which the Jews in their blindness and sin had rejected?

This is a question of fact and plain Scripture testimony combined, concerning which there need be no doubt. The same development of unbelief and wickedness has been made under this dispensation, notwithstanding all the increasing light and power of the Divine workings, as in those preceding. Christ and the apostles foretold of apostasies and unbelief, of persecutions and monstrous delusions, of forms of impiety and wickedness, such as the world had never seen before. Scoffers would appear, walking after their lusts, and defiantly asking, "Where is the promise [evidence or assurance] of his coming?" 2 Peter iii. 4. Christ put the question in respect to that return, "When the son of man cometh, shall he find faith on the earth?" Luke xviii. 8; thus declaring in the strongest manner possible that it would be a time of abounding unbelief, when faith would be well-nigh extinct. He asserted likewise of His coming, that it would take the world by surprise, as the flood in the days of Noah, and the storm of fire upon Sodom. He should come as a thief in the night, overtaking the world in its wickedness. The facts hitherto have been in exact fulfilment of these predictions. The Gentile world has not owned Christ. The nations have not bowed to His sceptre. The governments have not acknowledged Him. The rulers have "taken counsel together against the Lord, and against his Anointed, saying, Let us break his bands asunder, and cast away his cords from us." The Prince of Darkness still claims the kingdoms, and they own the allegiance. They are all controlled by the same selfish, worldly, self-aggrandizing and ambitious policy that spurns subjection to the law of Christ. This is the fact now, at the distance of eighteen centuries from the ascension. Through that period, not one nation or government has really bowed to the authority of our Immanuel Jesus. The only thing effected is that which has been done from the beginning, though to a larger extent. God has been gathering a remnant, not from one nation, as formerly, but from the East and the West, the North and the South, from every kindred, and tongue, and people, and nation. Christ has had His Church—nothing more—a body chosen out of the world—in it, but not of it. "I have given them thy word; and the world hath hated them, because *they are not of the world*, even as I am not of the world. I pray not that thou shouldest take them out of the world, but that thou shouldest keep them from the evil. *They are not of the world, even as I am not of the world;*" John xvii. 14. Christ speaks of His disciples as a "little flock," but bids them not to fear, for the kingdom was theirs, and would come into their possession, even though they were small, and despised, and down-trodden. The flock of Christ is small—has been small. It is a remnant gathered out from the midst of wide-prevailing unbelief. This also will be the characteristic feature of this Dispensation unto the end thereof, as it has been of the preceding.

The unbelief of the antediluvians continued down to the last moment, when judgment overtook them. The unbelief of the Jewish nation continued, until the cup of their iniquity was filled to the brim, and the hour of their desolation came. "So shall also the coming of the Son of man be. For as in the days that were before the flood, they were eating and drinking, marrying and giving in marriage, until the day that Noe entered into the ark, and knew not, until the flood came, and took them all away; so shall also the coming of the Son of man be;" Matt. xxiv. 37. Thus does Christ positively teach that the nations will continue in their unbelief, disregarding all warnings, as in the days of Noah, until the time of their judgment shall come, and the Son of man shall be revealed in flaming fire from heaven. There is to be no radical change in the character of this dispensation. The flock of Christ is to continue small. The world is to persevere in its unbelief and rejection of Him unto the end; and He will come as a thief in the night, to surprise it in all its ungodliness, and to gather His elect, the remnant of believing ones, from the four winds. These facts are most clearly and forcibly set forth in the parable designed to illustrate this very subject, and spoken *to correct the misapprehensions which then existed*, in supposing "that the kingdom of God should immediately appear. He said, therefore, A certain nobleman went into a far country to receive for himself a kingdom, and to return. And he called his ten servants, and delivered them ten pounds, and said unto them, Occupy till I come. But his citizens hated him, and sent a message after him, saying, We will not have this man to reign over us. And it came to pass, that *when he was returned, having received the kingdom*, then he commanded those servants to be called unto him, to whom he had given the money, that he might know how much every man had gained by trading;" Luke xix. 12. Christ is that nobleman, *absent now on that journey*—gone to obtain the kingdom, which He does not possess until His return. The Church is the company of His servants entrusted with His interests, while the world represents His enemies, who will not have Him to reign over them—the former to be richly rewarded, and the latter to have judgment meted out to them. For their Lord's return those faithful servants, above all things, anxiously watch and wait; nor do they anticipate any change in the aspect of affairs, neither can there be, until He does return with authority to take the throne and possess the kingdom. Through all His absence, also, until the very hour of His unexpected appearance, His enemies will continue to assert that they will not have Him to reign over them, even as they now do, and have done since the day of His departure. These are the obvious facts of the parable, the very facts which Christ intended to set forth, and which cannot be controverted.

According, then, to this statement of facts, the history of the world thus far from the beginning is characterized by one leading feature, which so far constitutes it one dispensation. That feature is prevailing unbelief and wickedness, from the midst of which *a remnant* is gathered who are kept through faith unto salvation. This feature of the world has never changed. It runs through the entire history of the past, and will continue unto the time of "*the end*," so often spoken of. Then there will be a change, and that a radical one. The righteous shall thenceforth be no more a little flock and feeble remnant, gathered out of all nations. The wicked shall then no more be in the ascendancy. But Christ shall have returned to possess the kingdom, even the greatness of the kingdom under the whole heaven. The termination of this long reign of wickedness, and the supremacy of Satan's power, is what the Scriptures mean by "*the end*," and which they declare to be now at hand. The introduction of the gospel dispensation did not essentially change the character of the world. It is hostile to Christ and the truth as ever it was; and through the eighteen centuries past the opposition to God's method of salvation has been more determined and violent than in any age preceding. Error and wickedness have had the ascendancy all through, and the truth has maintained its foothold only by the most desperate conflict; while the cry of God's suffering, persecuted ones has continually gone up, O Lord, how long! how long! But there is to be an end. This long night of the Church's sorrow is to be over. The way for Israel through the wilderness was a long and weary one, and their hearts oft fainted. But there was an end to their pilgrimage. And the Church now shall enter into her rest. She shall soon lift up her head with joy, beholding her redemption nigh. But that which she longs and waits for is her Lord's return.

Having thus developed the character of this dispensation, and the principles of the Divine administration entering into it, let us consider more especially *the character of the unbelief now manifested by the world.*

It has been shown heretofore how the Jewish nation rejected God's covenant, as based on faith and obedience, and sought a monopoly of the Divine favor and the kingdom on the ground of birth and blood, as the seed of Abraham, for which they contended desperately unto their overthrow. In a similar way have the Gentile nations dealt with Christ and His covenant of mercy, aiming to secure a selfish monopoly of them to their own wickedness.

The ground of justification revealed in the gospel for sinners was through a bloody sacrifice, Christ himself being made the sin-offering. His blood alone could cleanse from sin, and to this end was the faith required. The sinner who would approach God and hope for His favor, must come in this new and living way, accepting Christ as his only Mediator, and relying upon His blood shed as an atonement for his soul. Here was a wide and open door of mercy, through which a sinning world might enter. But how has this gracious offer of salvation been met? A few have been taught of God, and, as condemned sinners, have trusted their whole salvation here. But the mass have followed in the steps of the unbelieving Cain, and rejected Christ as a sin-offering for their souls. They have been willing to take Christ as a thank-offering, as Cain was ready, in the pride of his heart, to bring of the fruit of the ground, and as the Scribes and Pharisees were ready to present their abundant service and righteousness. Multitudes have been willing to do penance for the kingdom of heaven, and mortify their bodies, thus, by their own sufferings and self-denials, making atonement for their sins, but denying the Lord that bought them. There was no faith in Christ here.

Multitudes, again, rely upon their morality and good character, and make these their only saviour. They have no wickedness to confess before God. As for their few faults and shortcomings, God can easily overlook them. This is a salvation clearly for the righteous—not for sinners. And this is the monopoly which the Gentile world has sought to make of the kingdom of heaven to themselves. But how large a portion of our race will be admitted to the Paradise of God on the ground that they have never done any harm—have never been in the league with hell against the throne of Heaven, and can stand before God without any need of blood shed to wash away their sins? How many are there whose character is so high and pure that it would be an insult for God to offer them a gracious pardon through the righteousness of His only Son? For if a man is not a transgressor, under condemnation, it is the deepest insult to offer him a pardon and free justification through the merits of another, which he is humbly, thankfully to accept, singing forever of the grace that has saved him. How large, now, is the class in this world whom God would insult by such an offer of undeserved mercy and salvation? Christ declares emphatically, that His mission from heaven to earth was to save *sinners*, calling them to *repentance*, even them that were lost. The theory, therefore, that makes religion to consist of human virtues and exemption from sin, is at war with all the declarations of the Bible and the facts of human history; and if the righteous only are to be saved, what is to become of the sinners, whose iniquities are multiplied as the sands, and who have no holiness in the sight of Heaven? The religion demanded on earth is a religion for sinners—sinners of every grade—sinners of the blackest dye—sinners on the verge of damnation, and who see not how even the infinite mercy of God can reach to snatch them from perdition. If you would have a religion broad as the race and deep as the woes of ruined humanity, you must not begin to speak of virtuous lives, and human excellencies, and exemption from sins. You must bring a religion which can justify the guilty; that can make clean the vile, washing the foulest clean. It is sinners that need to be saved, not the righteous. Any religion, therefore, which does not provide for these, is narrow, partial, exclusive. A religion of human virtue would never carry one poor sinner to heaven. Go, tantalize such an one with the doctrine that a blameless life on earth is essential to an admission to the Paradise of God. His answer at once is, "Then is my perdition sealed forever; for mine is only a life of continued iniquity from beginning to end." Will you tell him, then, that henceforth he must lead a blameless life? "Ah! that," says he, "seals my damnation just as surely. I'm a captive, sold under sin. I have no power to break these cords of iniquity, which are bound fast about me. I have no strength to contend with and prevail against sin. And if this is all the promise you bring, you open no door of hope to my despairing soul. Tell me, oh! tell me, how a sinner may live and be justified with God! That is what I want to know. Tell me how my iniquities, in all their number and aggravation, may be freely forgiven; and then, how such a sinner as I, sold under the power of sin, may lead a new life unto God. Give me a religion to answer these ends, and then, and then only, you open the door of hope and heaven to my guilty soul."

This, too, is the very thing that the gospel does. To effect this very redemption, Jesus Christ came down from above, and made himself a sin-offering; and His blood can wash away the deepest, foulest stain of sin. "Though your sins be as scarlet, they shall be as white as snow; though they be red like crimson, they shall be as wool;" Isa. i. 18. It is the glory of our Immanuel that He saves sinners, even the very chief. He has prevailed to conquer hell, and all our foes. He can therefore save unto the very uttermost, to the last one, all that will come unto Him. Put, too, upon the simple condition of faith, it becomes a universal religion, confined to no favored, select class, but offered freely to all upon the widest terms possible; which are, that "*whosoever believeth in him* should not perish, but have everlasting life."

But there is no system of salvation against which the world, in its pride and selfishness, has contended so desperately, and opposed at every point, as this very one. By the grace of God a few have been led to accept it, and rejoice in it, and sing the new song of redemption. But the world has persistently opposed, denied, and blasphemed. The nations have united with the Jewish rulers in crucifying the Son of God. Jew and Gentile were both joined in that foulest deed of earth; and it is still required at their hands. It has brought the day of judgment to the Jew. It will, ere long, bring the hour of avenging wrath to the Gentile world; and that will be *the day*, the great day of God Almighty, such as earth never witnessed before. For eighteen centuries God has now been delaying, and testing the nations, to see whether they would bow to the authority of Christ and accept His offered grace. That experiment is going on to its tremendous issue, as in the antediluvian age, and under the Mosaic covenant. A remnant was gathered out in each of those periods. A remnant is being gathered now. And "as the days of Noe were, so shall also the coming of the Son of man be. For as in the days that were before the flood, they were eating and drinking, marrying and giving in marriage, until the day that Noe entered into the ark, and knew not, until the flood came, and took them all away; *so shall also the coming of the Son of man be.* Then shall two be in the field; the one shall be taken and the other left. Two women shall be grinding at the mill; the one shall be taken, and the other left;" Matt. xxiv. 37.

To interpret all this as meaning that God designs to save the wicked as the righteous, and to put no distinction between faith and unbelief—between an acceptance and rejection of God's covenant—but that both alike are kept for the kingdom of heaven, is an insult to common sense, as well as the whole system of the Divine teachings. The doctrine of the universal salvation of the wicked and unbelieving, *as a doctrine of the Bible*, is, in the light of this history, an absurdity; and the maintenance of such a doctrine as God's truth, after such a history of the past, is one of the crowning evidences of the world's stupendous unbelief, and its ripeness for the last day of avenging judgment, that shall sweep such ungodliness from the earth. If God has not settled the question by this time, that there is a day of wrath in store for the wicked, there is no use in His attempting to convince unbelief. Nothing will do it but the very day of wrath itself, which shall burst upon a deluded world, and surprise it in its wickedness.

Oh, dying man, where shall that fiery day of judgment find you? Are you reckoned now among that faithful company who have been taken out from the world, and have been justified through Christ, rejoicing to enter this wide and open door of mercy by which every lost sinner of the race may find a welcome? Or have you rejected this free salvation by grace, and are you clinging to some old monopoly of the kingdom; expecting to gain heaven because you have not been much of a sinner—have never done any wickedness that you cannot offset by your own righteousness, and have no need of any sin-offering such as Christ provided for a world of sinners? Oh! man, you are clinging to a lying delusion, against which God has fought from the days of Cain to this hour—a delusion which once swept the earth with the waters of a deluge—which dashed the covenant nation in pieces, and which will bring in the last great day of wrath upon an unbelieving world. God will stand fast by the great doctrine of faith and a sin-offering to the last; and this dispensation, in its issue, will prove the perfect truth of the words of Christ, when He sent forth His disciples on their high mission, "He that believeth and is baptized, shall be saved: and he that believeth not shall be damned."

CHAPTER XXVI.

THE DAY OF THE LORD.

To complete the study of God's revelations respecting the doctrine of a remnant, it is necessary to consider more particularly *that day of the Lord*, which marks the close of this present dispensation and which is described with such impressive grandeur in the Scriptures. The history of Divine providence, as developed in God's dealings with the wicked and unbelieving in this world, is a thrilling one, and worthy of our most attentive study.

The work of redemption hitherto has been carried forward in distinct eras, or dispensations, marked by their own peculiarities, and each one being an advance upon that going before. Through all these eras of the past sin has been in the ascendant; and what God has done in the way of salvation, has been in gathering out a remnant from the midst of the prevailing wickedness—a remnant kept unto the day of redemption to come. Another fact connected with these eras is, that they have all terminated in signal disaster and overthrow, and, in a certain sense, failure; not failure of God's purposes or plans —for He has been continually advancing His great work —but *failure to men in entering into the grand arrangements of God's grace.* God has not been disappointed. Nothing has turned out differently from His anticipations; and yet there is a truth of weighty import embodied in the idea of failure in these dispensations. It is that very one which God himself expresses in such strong language, when He says, "*And it repented the Lord that he had made man on the earth, and it grieved him at his heart;*" Gen. vi. 5. The prevailing tendency in each dispensation has been downward to disaster and overthrow; and the way that God has succeeded in His enterprise has not been by persevering in the policy of a particular period, or pushing the experiment farther—for that would have resulted in utter ruin—but in saving what he could out of that era, and then abandoning it to bring in a new one, with higher agencies and better adaptations to the accomplishment of His ends. In our development of the doctrine of a remnant, we have seen that each dispensation of the past has closed with the salvation of a faithful few, and a day of dreadful overthrow and judgment to the unbelieving multitude, who would not enter into God's gracious designs.

As far back as the days of Enoch we find this principle distinctly embodied in his preaching, and the fact stated that the Lord's coming would be both with salvation and judgment. "Behold, the Lord cometh with ten thousands of his saints, to execute judgment upon all, and to convince all that are ungodly among them of all their ungodly deeds which they have ungodly committed, and of all their hard speeches which ungodly sinners have spoken against him;" Jude 14. But the world did not receive this doctrine. They rejected the testimony of God, not deeming it necessary to follow the Divine teachings, and live a life of faith and godliness in order to secure salvation. They followed in the perverse way of Cain, yet still claiming for themselves the Divine favor and promises. Thus wickedness grew at a fearful rate, while faith and piety diminished, until they were threatened with extinction. Then came the crisis, when Heaven must interpose to vindicate the Divine administration, and introduce another and higher dispensation, in which the truths of redemption might be set forth in a still clearer light. There was no object in prosecuting the existing experiment farther. Accordingly, a remnant was preserved in the righteous family of Noah, while dreadful judgment overtook the world of the ungodly. Here were salvation and judgment in a way not to be misunderstood. It was an unmistakable and most impressive commentary upon Enoch's preaching, and the days of Noah thus became a striking type of the greater day of the Lord, when He should come with ten thousand of His saints.

The period intervening between Noah and Christ might appropriately be divided into two parts: the first embracing the patriarchal, down to the time of Moses. This dispensation issued in salvation and judgment—a small remnant only of the generation brought out of Egypt entering the promised land, while the unbelieving and stiff-necked multitude were overthrown in the wilderness. Judgment after judgment, through forty years, overtook them. Their carcasses fell in the desert, and they saw not the promised land, Caleb and Joshua alone, of all the adult population, being permitted to enter into the inheritance of Canaan. Fire and sword, pestilence, earthquake, and serpents' poisonous fangs, consumed them, it being reserved to the next generation to behold the fulfilment of God's promises.

Passing still onward, we find the history of the next succeeding dispensation, commencing with the possession of Canaan, terminating in the same manner. Israel did not enter into God's gracious designs of mercy. They would not receive His Son, although raised from the dead and exalted to the right hand of power. They not only crucified Him, but blasphemed against the Holy Ghost when He appeared bearing witness to His resurrection. Thus did the nation *fill up the measure of their iniquity*, and bring swiftly the day of their desolation. A remnant was saved, but terrible judgment overtook that unbelieving people; and that, too, while holding firmly to God's covenant, and pleading the impossibility of any such destruction falling upon them. They perished with the covenant of Heaven in their hands. God made them a monument of His wrath, a hissing and byword among the nations.

The next dispensation commenced with the proclamation of the gospel to the Gentile nations, to continue until Christ's return to claim the kingdom, as unfolded in the parable of the nobleman taking his journey into a far country; Luke xix. 12. For that return the faithful servants are waiting, and they are occupying till He come. There is to be no change until He does return to relieve his servants of their charge, and to possess the kingdom which He has gone to secure.

What is to be the issue of this period? This the Scriptures must decide: and they make it clear that it is to be with salvation and judgment precisely as heretofore, although on a grander scale, and ushering in a brighter, more glorious day than earth has ever yet witnessed. That coming of Christ is the one described by Enoch, not as a sin-offering, but bringing salvation to His saints and judgment to the ungodly foe. And if Christ's first advent in His humiliation, to accomplish the work of His priesthood, was attended with salvation and judgment to the covenant people, much more may we expect the same developments when He shall appear in His glory to take the promised kingdom, and put down all opposing rule and authority, subduing every enemy under His feet, and calling to account His enemies who would not that He should reign over them.

How, THEN, DOES THE WORD OF GOD DESCRIBE THAT DAY, AND THE ATTENDING EVENTS?

We are not now speaking of the final day of judgment, when the books are opened, described in Rev. xx. 11. That day closes a still future dispensation in the drama of earth, and is different from the vials of wrath which are to be poured upon the living nations at the close of the present dispensation, and the ushering in of the day of millennial glory. It is nothing new that that day is to be introduced by terrific judgments. The fact is put beyond question by the Scriptures, and falls in with the entire history of God's providence in the past. He has never yet introduced a brighter day to earth without delivering up the preceding economy, and saving a remnant out of the wreck of the wicked. We have shown heretofore how He is gathering that remnant of faithful ones now, and "when the Son of man cometh, shall He find faith on the earth?" The issue of this dispensation is to be a failure, in the sense we have described, as the other dispensations going before: otherwise God would not now be gathering a remnant. The salvation of "a little flock" does not indicate success in respect to this adulterous and sinful generation. The Gentile nations are not entering into God's gracious designs, any more than Israel did; and the prosecution of this dispensation, in gathering a remnant only, will end in ruin to the world, not in salvation. "The end" is at hand—the end, which closes all the dispensations of the character now described, ushering in another era, when Christ, and not Satan, is to have the supremacy—when righteousness, not sin, is to be triumphant—when "the meek shall inherit the earth," and abundance of peace prevail so long as the moon endureth. The day that fulfils this work is "the day of the Lord." "That day," as if every reader of the Scriptures, conversant with its prophecies, understood what day was intended. It is "the great and notable day of the Lord"—"the great day of His wrath"—"the day of Christ." When the Scriptures thus single out a future day by such expressions, and make it stand apart from all others, as *the day* of the Lord emphatically, we may not doubt that there are events to give it all this preëminence.

What, then, is the testimony of Scripture on this point?

We have already referred to the preaching of Enoch, and need not here repeat again.

In the second Psalm, allusion is made to it, when, after declaring God's purpose to set His Son, as King, upon His holy hill of Zion, giving Him the heathen for His inheritance, and the uttermost parts of the earth for His possession, it is said of the kings and rulers, who rage against this decree of Heaven, "Thou shalt break them with a rod of iron; thou shalt dash them in pieces like a potter's vessel. Be wise now therefore, O ye kings. Be instructed, ye judges of the earth. . . . Kiss the son, lest he be angry, and ye perish from the way, when his wrath is kindled but a little." This is not conversion; it is judgment, even with a rod of iron; and thus shall the opposing rulers be dashed and broken. Isaiah portrays these judgments upon the nations in the most vivid language, in close and striking contrast with the peace and blessedness which are immediately to follow under the reign of Christ. This fact is to be especially noted, that all these descriptions of judgment and overthrow *stand in immediate connection with earth's promised day of redemption under our Immanuel.* Hear, then, how the prophet portrays that day of vengeance: "Come near, ye nations, to hear; and hearken, ye people; let the earth hear, and all that is therein; the world, and all things that come forth of it. For the indignation of the Lord is upon all nations, and his fury upon all their armies; he hath utterly destroyed them, he hath delivered them to the slaughter. Their slain also shall be cast out, and their stink shall come up out of their carcasses, and the mountains shall be melted with their blood. And all the host of heaven shall be dissolved, and the heavens shall be rolled together as a scroll: and all their host shall fall down" [a symbolical description of the political powers, and the rulers, kings, and princes], "as the leaf falleth off from the vine, and as a falling fig from the fig-tree. For my sword shall be bathed in heaven; behold, it shall come down upon Idumea" [that powerful kingdom standing as a symbol or representative of the enemies and persecutors of the Church of God], "and upon the people of my curse, to judgment. The sword of the Lord is filled with blood; it is made fat with fatness, and with the blood of lambs and goats, with the fat of the kidneys of rams; for the Lord hath a sacrifice in Bozrah" [the chief city of Idumea], "and a great slaughter in the land of Idumea. And the unicorns" [the princes and great ones] "shall come down with them, and the bullocks with the bulls; and their land shall be soaked with blood, and their dust made fat with fatness. For it is the day of the Lord's vengeance, and *the year of recompenses for the controversy of Zion.* And the streams thereof shall be turned into pitch, and the dust thereof into brimstone, and the land thereof shall become burning pitch. It shall not be quenched night nor day; the smoke thereof shall go up forever; from generation to generation it shall lie waste; none shall pass through it forever and ever." Following immediately upon this is an equally vivid description of the blessedness and joy of earth under our Immanuel, when we behold the wilderness and solitary place made glad, and the desert rejoicing and blossoming as the rose; when that highway shall be there, the way of holiness, over which the unclean shall not pass: no lion shall be there, nor any ravenous beast shall go up thereon. But the ransomed of the Lord shall return, and come to Zion with songs and everlasting joy upon their heads; they shall obtain joy and gladness, and sorrow and sighing shall flee away. No one questions that this last is a description of the restoration of all things under the reign of Messiah. The judgments, therefore, described in immediate connection, relate to the same period of the world's history; and thus are judgment and redemption brought into closest proximity, fulfilling "the day of the Lord's vengeance, and the year of recompenses for the controversy of Zion." "Who is this that cometh from Edom" [taken again as a symbol of the ungodly nations and persecutors of the Church], "with dyed garments from Bozrah? this that is glorious in his apparel, travelling in the greatness of his strength? I that speak in righteousness, mighty to save. Wherefore art thou red in thine apparel, and thy garments like him that treadeth in the wine-fat? I have trodden the winepress alone; and of the people there was none with me: for I will tread them in mine anger, and trample them in my fury; and their blood shall be sprinkled upon my garments, and I will stain all my raiment. *For the day of vengeance is in mine heart, and the year of my redeemed is come.* And I looked, and there was none to help; and I wondered that there was none to uphold: therefore mine own arm brought salvation unto me; and my fury, it upheld me. And I will tread down the people in mine anger, and make them drunk in my fury, and I will bring down their strength to the earth;" Isa. lxiii. 1. Here Christ is represented as taking, at length, the work of vengeance into His own hands, and returning from the slaughter of His haughty foes—a mighty conqueror, His garments rolled in blood, as they that tread the winepress. In immediate connection also with this day of recompenses, there is the thrilling announcement, "Behold, the Lord hath proclaimed unto the end of the world, Say ye to the daughter of Zion, Behold, thy salvation" [Saviour, it might be rendered] "cometh; behold, his reward is with him, and his work before him. And they shall call them, *The holy people, The redeemed of the Lord; and thou shalt be called, Sought out, A city not forsaken;*" Isa. lxxii. 11. Thus does the day, which bringeth redemption unto Zion, bring also the day of dread vengeance, long delayed, to the proud foe: "Behold, the day of the Lord cometh, and thy spoil shall be divided in the midst of thee. For I will gather all nations against Jerusalem to battle; and the city shall be taken, and the houses rifled, and the women ravished; and half of the city shall go forth into captivity, and the residue of the people shall not be cut off from the city. Then shall the Lord go forth, and fight against those nations, as when he fought in the day of battle. And his feet shall stand in that day upon the Mount of Olives, which is before Jerusalem on the east; and the Mount of Olives shall cleave in the midst thereof toward the east and toward the west, and there shall be a very great valley; and half of the mountain shall remove toward the north, and half of it toward the south . . . *and the Lord my God shall come, and all the saints with thee.* . . . And it shall be in that day, that living waters shall go out from Jerusalem; half of them toward the former sea, and half of them toward the hinder sea; in summer and in winter shall it be. *And the Lord shall be King over all the earth: in that day there shall be one Lord, and his name* one. . . . And this shall be the plague, wherewith the Lord will smite all the people that have fought against Jerusalem; Their flesh shall consume away while they stand upon their feet, and their eyes shall consume away in their holes, and their tongue shall consume away in their mouth," [indicating the effects of fiery eruptions]. "And it shall come to pass in that day that a great tumult" [panic] "from the Lord shall be among them; and they shall lay hold every one on the hand of his neighbor, and his hand shall rise up against the hand of his neighbor. And Judah also shall fight at Jerusalem; and the wealth of all the heathen round about shall be gathered together, gold, and silver and apparel, in great abundance. And so shall be the plague of the horse, of the mule, of the camel, and of the ass, and of all the beasts that shall be in these tents, as this plague;" Zech. xiv.

Ezekiel gives a thrilling account of these scenes of judgment, in the overthrow of Gog and Magog; chaps. xxxviii. and xxxix. We quote only a portion of it. "And it shall come to pass at the same time when Gog shall come against the land of Israel, saith the Lord God, that my fury shall come up in my face. For in my jealousy and in the fire of my wrath have I spoken, Surely in that day there shall be a great shaking in the land of Israel; so that the fishes of the sea, and the fowls of the heaven, and the beasts of the field, and all creeping things that creep upon the earth, and all the men that are upon the face of the earth, shall shake at my presence, and the mountains shall be thrown down, and the steep places shall fall, and every wall shall fall to the ground. And I will call for a sword against him throughout all my mountains, saith the Lord God: every man's sword shall be against his brother. And I will plead against him with pestilence, and with blood; and I will rain upon him, and upon his bands, and upon the many people that are with him, an overflowing rain, and great hailstones, fire and brimstone. Thus will I magnify myself, and sanctify myself; and I will be known in the eyes of many nations, and they shall know that I am the Lord." Further on, the prophet, in describing the terribleness of this overthrow of Gog and Magog, states that it shall require seven months to bury the slain; and the weapons of war left upon the field, the shields, the bows and arrows, the handstaves and spears shall furnish fire-wood for seven years to the inhabitants; while the feathered fowl and beast are invited to the feast in these words; chap. xxxix. 17—22: "Speak unto every feathered fowl, and to every beast of the field, Assemble yourselves, and come; gather yourselves on every side to my sacrifice that I do sacrifice for you, even a great sacrifice upon the mountains of Israel, that ye may eat flesh, and drink blood. Ye shall eat the flesh of the mighty, and drink the blood of the princes of the earth, of rams, of lambs, and of goats, of bullocks, all of them fatlings of Bashan. And ye shall eat fat till ye be full, and drink blood till ye be drunken, of my sacrifice which I have sacrificed for you. Thus ye shall be filled at my table with horses and chariots, with mighty men, and with all men of war, saith the Lord God. And I will set my glory among the heathen, and all the heathen shall see my judgment that I have executed, and my hand that I have laid upon them. *So the house of Israel shall know that I am the Lord their God from that day and for-*

ward." This last statement identifies clearly the time of these events as the period when "the vail shall be taken from the hearts" of this people, and they shall recognize their Deliverer, and welcome Him as King in Zion forever.

"For, behold, in those days, and in that time, *when I shall bring again the captivity of Judah and Jerusalem*, I will gather all nations, and will bring them down into the valley of Jehoshaphat, and *will plead with them there for my people and for my heritage Israel, whom they have scattered among the nations, and parted my land.* . . . Proclaim ye this among the Gentiles: Prepare war, wake up the mighty men, let all the men of war draw near; let them come up. Beat your ploughshares into swords, and your pruning-hooks into spears; let the weak say, I am strong. Assemble yourselves, and come, all ye heathen, and gather yourselves together round about; thither cause thy mighty ones to come down, O Lord. Let the heathen be wakened, and come up to the valley of Jehoshaphat, for there will I sit to judge all the heathen round about. Put ye in the sickle, for the harvest is ripe; come, get you down; for the press is full, the fats overflow; for their wickedness is great. Multitudes, multitudes in the valley of decision; *the day of the Lord* is near in the valley of decision. The sun and the moon shall be darkened, and the stars shall withdraw their shining. The Lord also shall roar out of Zion, and utter his voice from Jerusalem; and the heavens and the earth shall shake; but the Lord shall be the hope of his people, and the strength of the children of Israel. So shall ye know that I am the Lord your God dwelling in Zion, my holy mountain; then shall Jerusalem be holy, and there shall no strangers pass through her any more. And it shall come to pass in that day, that the mountains shall drop down new wine, and the hills shall flow with milk, and all the rivers of Judah shall flow with waters, and a fountain shall come forth of the house of the Lord, and water the valley of Shittim. Egypt shall be a desolation, and Edom" [the two mightiest kingdoms then known taken as a representation of all] "shall be a desolate wilderness, for the violence against the children of Judah, because they have shed innocent blood in their land. But Judah shall dwell forever, and Jerusalem from generation to generation. For I will cleanse their blood, that I have not cleansed: for the Lord dwelleth in Zion;" Joel iii. 1.

These descriptions combine all the most terrible imagery that thought or language can furnish to represent the judgment of that great and notable day of the Lord, when He shall come to be glorified in His saints, and bring the hour of dread recompense and vengeance to the insulting foe. The day here described is clearly not the day of final judgment, when the wicked dead are called to account. It is the living wicked who are brought before us in these scenes—the nations and their haughty rulers, who have long shed the blood of the saints, and for whom there was none to interpose. The Lord had looked in vain for help, "and wondered that there was none to uphold; therefore mine own arm brought salvation unto me, and my fury it upheld me." It is, therefore, the Lord's year of recompenses for Zion; and she is to be redeemed with judgment—terrific, overwhelming judgment. The sword of the Lord is to be drunk with blood, and the iron rod of his wrath is to come down upon the haughty rulers who have said in their pride, "Let us break his bands asunder, and cast away his cords from us," and they shall be utterly dashed like a potter's vessel. Let it not be forgotten, either, how intimately these scenes of judgment are connected with and immediately precede the day of millenial glory described by the prophets. The day of vengeance and redemption go together. It is so expressly declared, "The day of vengeance is in mine heart, and the year of my redeemed is come."

Passing to the New Testament, we find Christ and His apostles taking up this same theme, and making it still more clear and emphatic. They look forward to these same scenes, and confirm all that prophets before had spoken. The disciples came to their Master privately as He was seated upon the Mount of Olives, saying, "Tell us when shall these things be? and what shall be the sign of thy coming, and of the end of the world," [the age or dispensation, not the earth or time]; Matt. xxiv. 3. The inquiry of the disciples was more specifically for the *time* of these great events, and the signs which should mark their approach. These Christ undertakes to point out; neither did He fail in the attempt. He gave a most graphic picture of the times that were before them, and the character of the period unto the end thereof. He told them that it was to be a period of trouble, persecution, and sore tribulation to His Church; that error, wickedness, and apostacies would prevail; that the kingdoms were to be powerfully agitated; that wars and earthquakes, famines and pestilences, were to be experienced. There was to be commotion and trouble everywhere. Yet these were to be but the beginning of sorrows—the common experiences of the times, at which they were not to be alarmed or disappointed. They were not to look for the triumph of truth and righteousness. If the people of God should be able to endure to the end, it would be all that could be expected. They should be brought before kings and rulers, called to witness for Him, and lay down their lives. Whosoever killed them would be esteemed as doing God service. At length, however, after these ordinary days of tribulation, toward the latter end there was to be an hour, by the terrors of which the very sun should be darkened, and the moon should not give her light; the stars should fall from heaven, and all the powers of heaven should be shaken. There should be distress of nations with perplexity, the sea and the waves roaring, men's hearts failing them for fear, and looking after those things which are coming on the earth. And when these things begin to come to pass, *then look up, and lift up your head, for your redemption draweth nigh.* And then shall they see the Son of man coming in a cloud with power and great glory. When these dreadful terrors are abroad, and it would seem as if all things were dissolving, the very day of God's avenging wrath on the nations having come, then look up, for your salvation is hastening, even as the budding leaves tell of the near approach of Spring. "Take heed to yourselves, lest . . . that day come upon you unawares. For as a snare shall it come on all them that dwell on the face of the whole earth. Watch ye, therefore, and pray always, that ye may be accounted worthy to escape all these things that shall come to pass, and to stand before the Son of man;" Luke xxi. 34.

In his Epistle to the Thessalonians, Paul spoke of the speedy coming of Christ, and in such a way as to lead them to suppose that the event was immediately impending, or rather had already been realized—which is the true idea involved in the word translated "is at hand" in 2 Thess. ii. 2. The word occurs seven times only in the New Testament, in five of which it is translated to denote *a present and existing state of things*, while in the sixth the same is clearly the meaning, as anyone may observe. "This know also, that in the last days perilous times *shall come;*" 2 Tim. iii. 2;—that is, shall be. The perilous times belong to those last days. They shall not be near or approaching, but actually existing. From this uniform use of the word, then, we are authorized to give it the same meaning in the seventh instance, when the Apostle beseeches the brethren in Thessalonica, "by the coming of our Lord Jesus Christ, and by our gathering together unto him, that they be not soon shaken in mind, or be troubled, neither by spirit, nor by word, nor by letter as from us, that the day of Christ *is at hand*"—that is, has come—being an event already realized. This was the impression which the Thessalonians had received from the Apostle's first epistle, and were much "shaken in mind" and "troubled" thereby, so that he found it necessary to write a second letter to quiet their minds and correct their error. In this he informs them that that day of Christ has not transpired, and "shall not come except there come" —what? The millenium? By no means; "but a falling away first, and that Man of Sin be revealed, the son of perdition, who opposeth and exalteth himself above all that is called God, or that is worshipped, so that he as God sitteth in the temple of God, shewing himself that he is God. *Remember ye not, that when I was with you, I told you these things?* . . . And then shall that wicked be revealed, whom the Lord shall consume with the spirit of his mouth, and destroy with the brightness of his coming." This apostacy was thus to continue until overthrown by the outshining revelation of Christ's second coming, bringing to the blaspheming foe the hour of avenging judgment.

The above passage is of great value in marking, with the utmost clearness, the time of the second advent. There is no question as to the period of the revelation of "That Wicked" and his destined overthrow, as being connected with the present dispensation. And his destruction is stated to be "with the brightness of his coming"—not simply with His coming, but "the brightness of his coming"—literally, the epiphany or bright shining of His coming. It is the word applied to Christ's personal advent in every instance of its use in the New Testament, and to nothing else. The expression, therefore, is the strongest employed in the Bible on this subject, and puts the meaning beyond question. It is not merely the epiphany or appearing of Christ, nor the coming of Christ; but the epiphany or bright shining of His coming, making it doubly sure, and marking His own personal revelation in the most positive terms. By this outshining revelation of His glorious presence, then, is "That Wicked" to be consumed. He of necessity is to continue unto that event.

Peter declares here, in the last days—that is, in the end of this period of Satan's power—men will arise to deny the Lord's coming, scoffing at the idea, and appealing to the uninterrupted course of nature, hitherto, to prove that all things will continue as they are—that there will be no change of the present dispensation, and that the personal coming of Christ is an absurdity and a lie. This, too, is most strikingly realized in our day, when the profoundest philosophy teaches that nature itself is God, without any personal being above to control it. "But, beloved, be not ignorant of this one thing, that one day is with the Lord as a thousand years, and a thousand years as one day. The Lord is not slack concerning his promise, as some men count slackness; but is long-suffering to us-ward, not willing that any should perish, but that all should come to repentance. But the day of the Lord will come as a thief in the night; in the which the heavens shall pass away with a great noise, and the elements shall melt with fervent heat, the earth also and the works that are therein shall be burned up;" 2 Peter iii. 8. This description of judgment is so terrific, that many have been led to suppose that it is the end of all things indeed. Yet we cannot but conclude that it refers to the same hour of avenging wrath, which is coming on the earth to close up this present period of unbelief and apostacy, and overthrow that blaspheming infidel power which denies God himself, and scoffs at the doctrine of Christ's coming. There will be fiery irruptions of wrath on the earth, not universal, but partial, though very extensive, that shall meet this very description. The prophecy of Zechariah, already quoted, would seem to correspond very closely with this of Peter. We repeat his words: "And this shall be the plague wherewith the Lord will smite all the people that have fought against Jerusalem. Their flesh shall consume away while they stand upon their feet, and their eyes shall consume away in their holes, and their tongues shall consume away in their mouths"—representing the effects of fiery irruptions which consume men while they stand upon their feet. "And so shall be the plague of the horse, of the mule, of the camel, of the ass, and of all the beasts that shall be in these tents, as this plague." It shall sweep every living thing within the reach of its fiery breath. To show, however, that this is not to be the end of all things, Peter describes in immediate connection, and as the result of this day of avenging wrath, the redemption then to be ushered in. "Nevertheless we, *according to his promise*, look for new heavens and a new earth, wherein dwelleth righteousness. Wherefore, beloved, seeing ye look for such things, be diligent that ye may be found of him in peace, without spot, and blameless." Here is the same intimate connection between the day of promised redemption and avenging judgment to the proud foe, which we found in all the prophets. Throughout the entire revelation of God one follows immediately upon the other.

In the opening of the sixth seal, the same scene of judgment is brought to view. The fifth seal unfolds the events preceding, and describes the suffering martyrs of Christ, crying unto God for the long-delayed hour of vengeance against their cruel persecutors. "And when he had opened the fifth seal, I saw under the altar the souls of them that were slain for the word of God, and for the testimony which they held: and they cried with a loud voice, saying, How long, O Lord, holy and true, dost thou not judge and avenge our blood on them that dwell on the earth? And white robes were given unto every one of them; and it was said unto them, that they should *rest yet for a little season, until their fellow-servants also and their brethren, that should be killed as they were, should be fulfilled.*" The judgments of the sixth seal were not to open until the cup of the nations was full, and the number of Christ's martyrs was complete. This is that period of trial and persecution to the Church of God —that time of tribulation of which Christ spoke to His disciples—the time of great Babylon, drunk with the blood of the saints. The martyred ones of the Lord are now crying to heaven for the day of recompense, and they are to "rest yet but a little season," when the hour of retribution long delayed, and the day of redemption shall come. "And I beheld when he had opened the sixth seal, and, lo, there was a great earthquake; and the sun became black as sackcloth of hair, and the moon became as blood; and the stars of heaven fell unto the earth, even as a fig-tree casteth her untimely figs, when she is shaken of a mighty wind. And the heaven [the symbol of earth's political fabrics] departed as a scroll when it is rolled together; and every mountain and island [the empires and kingdoms] were moved out of their places. And the kings of the earth, and the great men, and the rich men, and the chief captains, and the mighty men, and every bond-man, and every free-man, hid themselves in the dens and in the rocks of the mountains; and said to the mountains and rocks, Fall on us, and hide us from the face of him that sitteth on the throne, and from the wrath of the Lamb: for the great day of his wrath is come; and who shall be able to stand?" Rev. vi. 12.

Again, the doom of great Babylon is described when she came up in remembrance before God, to give unto her the cup of the wine of the fierceness of his wrath. "Therefore shall her plagues come in one day, death, and mourning, and famine; and she shall be utterly burned with fire: for strong is the Lord God who judgeth her. And the kings of the earth, who have committed fornication and lived deliciously with her, shall bewail her, and lament for her, when they see the smoke of her burning, standing afar off for the fear of her torment, saying, alas, alas! that great city, Babylon, that mighty city! for in one hour is thy judgment come. . . . Rejoice over her, thou heaven, and ye holy apostles and prophets; for God hath avenged you on her. . . . And after these things I heard a great voice of much people in heaven, saying, Alleluia: Salvation, and glory, and honor, and power unto the Lord our God; for true and righteous are his judgments: for he hath judged the great whore, which did corrupt the earth with her fornication, and hath avenged the blood of his servants at her hand. And again they said, Alleluia. And her smoke rose up forever and ever." Then follows immediately the triumphant shout of joy over the kingdom of our Immanuel, bringing the same two events together as before. "And I heard as it were the voice of a great multitude, and as the voice of many waters, and as the voice of mighty thunderings, saying, *Alleluia: for the Lord God omnipotent reigneth.* Let us be glad and rejoice, and give honor to him: for the marriage of the Lamb is come, and his wife hath made herself ready. And to her was granted that she should be arrayed in fine linen, clean and white: for the fine linen is the righteousness of saints. And he saith unto me, Write, Blessed are they which are called unto the marriage-supper of the Lamb;" Rev. xviii. Thus the downfall of great Babylon, the coming of the bridegroom, and the marriage-supper of the Lamb are brought into immediate juxtaposition, one following upon the heels of the other.

The same terrible day of the Lord is described with graphic power at Rev. xix. 11, where Christ himself appears, beyond all question, a glorious conqueror upon a white horse, attended by His saints, and bringing judgment to the proud foe. "And I saw heaven opened, and behold a white horse; and he that sat upon him was called Faithful and True, and in righteousness he doth judge and make war. His eyes were as a flame of fire, and on his head were many crowns; and he had a name written, that no man knew, but he himself. And he was clothed with a vesture dipped in blood: and his name is called THE WORD OF GOD. And the armies which were in heaven followed him upon white horses, clothed in fine linen, clean and white. And out of his mouth goeth a sharp sword, that with it he should smite the nations: and he shall rule them with a rod of iron: and he treadeth the wine-press of the fierceness and wrath of Almighty God. And he hath on his vesture and on his thigh a name written, KING OF KINGS, AND LORD OF LORDS. And I saw an angel standing in the sun; and he cried with a loud voice, saying to all the fowls that fly in the midst of heaven, Come, and gather yourselves together unto the supper of the great God; that ye may eat the flesh of kings, and the flesh of captains, and the flesh of mighty men, and the flesh of horses, and of them that sit on them, and the flesh of all men, both free and bond, both small and great. And I saw the beast, and the kings of the earth, and their armies, gathered together to make war against him that sat on the horse, and against his army. And the beast was taken, and with him the false prophet that wrought miracles before him, with which he deceived them that had received the mark of the beast, and them that worshipped his image. These both were cast alive into a lake of fire burning with brimstone. And the remnant were slain with the sword of him that sat upon the horse, which sword proceeded out of his mouth: and all the fowls were filled with their flesh."

These are the more prominent descriptions which the Word of God gives of that great and terrible day of the Lord, which is to be the issue of this present dispensation: and they show clearly that it is to be *the day* emphatically—the great day of His wrath, and the fierceness of His anger. That these sublime prophecies have not been fulfilled by any events of the past among the nations, is clear, and so almost universally conceded by the commentators. That they have no reference to the day of final judgment, when the dead are raised, is equally evident. There is no difficulty, therefore, in identifying them as the judgments which are to overtake the unbelieving rulers and nations for their wicked, persevering rejection of Christ, and their cruel persecution of His suffering Church. It is "the year of recompenses for the controversy of Zion," "the year of my redeemed," when Christ shall come up a mighty conqueror from Edom, "glorious in his apparel, travelling in the greatness of his strength." They demonstrate, therefore, that this period is to close, like those going before, in judgment and salvation—a judgment more terrible and a salvation more glorious far than any preceding—ushering in at the same time that new era for which this groaning creation has long been travailing in birth. This present dispensation is not to change its character. In the end thereof, scoffing, baspheming, infidelity, and opposition to Christ are only to grow more bold and impious, so as to demand the interposition of heaven, and call down those terrible judgments which can alone vindicate the course of Divine providence, and prepare the way for the next scene in the drama of redemption. Each period of the past has continued until the cup of the nations' iniquity was filled to overflowing, and the righteous retribution of heaven came, a faithful remnant only being gathered out. The covenant nation itself stood defiantly in the very pathway of the Divine purposes of mercy, and the only remedy was to strike them through with vengeance. The Gentile nations are pursuing precisely the same course. It is their declared purpose that they will not have "this man" to reign over them—this their determinate counsel. We speak primarily of the rulers—those who hold the high places of power, and control the governments of earth. Not one of these kingdoms, in eighteen centuries, has bowed to the authority of Jesus. There is not one now in existence that gives any signs of such submission. Individual men are converted, and Christianity is a power in the earth. We concede this fully. But Satan rules still in every government under heaven. He can go to the mountain-top, and thence surveying all the kingdoms of the world, and the glory of them, say, as he did long time ago, "All these are mine." It was no vain, braggart boast of his then, and Jesus so well understood it. He knew what a desperate conflict was before Him, when He refused that proffered compromise with the adversary, and undertook to fight His own way to the empire of earth. He knew that it would be by a pathway of sorrow and tears, of blood and terrible judgment: and the devil is going to fight it out to the bitter end. This dispensation is proving that the nations will not bow to Jesus. They will compel Him to "rule them with a rod of iron," and smite them with the sharp sword which goeth out of His mouth. Thus will they force His judgments, which, in truth, is the way that God's judgments have always come. He does not delight in them. He has ever been slow to wrath, ever backward to unsheath His sword of vengeance, and has done it only in the last extremity, when even His patience was exhausted. We should never have been as slow to lay hold of the bolts of wrath, to hurl them at the impious wickedness of this world, if they had only been within our reach. We should have opened the windows of heaven, and let loose the storms of fire and brimstone upon the ungodliness of men, far oftener than God has done, if they had been within our control. God has been slow to wrath. But there is a point where Divine vengeance delays no longer; and the time is coming again, when the very "wrath of *the Lamb*" shall be kindled, and it shall be "the year of vengeance;" when He shall gird on His sword, and be "red in His apparel," and his garments like him that "treadeth in the winefat." This is not our language, but the very words and representation of the Divine record itself.

Nor let any be startled at the idea of the bolder development of impiety and blaspheming infidelity in these latter days, instead of the wide increase of truth and righteousness. Truth and righteousness may spread in the conversion of individual souls to Christ, as in the days of the apostles, when tens of thousands believed, and yet only a remnant was gathered out of Israel. This, however, does not convert the governments and rulers to Christ. Notwithstanding the wonderful success and spread of the gospel in the beginning, the covenant nation was cast off and scattered with terrible judgment. Their unbelief and blaspheming opposition to Christ drew upon them the righteous retributions of heaven, and their "house was left unto them desolate." So will it be with the Gentile nations. Christ will gather His chosen remnant, but infidelity will still rage and blaspheme, and "the rulers take counsel against the Lord and against His Anointed."

In this connection it is important to mark the inspired prediction of the coming of THAT WICKED, ανομος, *That Lawless*, whom the Lord shall consume with the spirit of His mouth, and destroy *with the brightness (epiphany) of His coming;* even Him, whose coming is after the working of Satan. "*Who opposeth and exalteth himself above all that is called God, or that is worshipped; so that he, as God, sitteth in the temple of God, showing himself that he is God;*" 2 Thess. ii. 4. This description has been, for the most part, referred to the Papacy. But that apostacy has never reached the point of atheism and blaspheming wickedness here represented. "The great Whore" has enough to account for, without attributing to her sins of which she has not been guilty. She acknowledges both God and Christ, claiming to derive from them all her authority; while "*That Wicked*" is an infidel, atheistic power, exalting itself above God and every object of Divine worship, sitting in the temple of God, and claiming that *He* is God. It is thus emphatically THE LAWLESS, arrogating to itself the very throne of heaven, and denying all power above and beyond itself. Neither is it difficult to discern the fearful elements of evil which may enter into and constitute this last gigantic development of wickedness and opposition to Christ, which He will consume with the spirit of His mouth, and destroy with the brightness of His coming. The popular mind of christendom is deeply poisoned with the spirit of infidelity and atheism, that is secretly but surely sapping all the foundations of society. The large mass of the Protestant population of Europe has gone over to this infidelity, the very clergy occupying their pulpits being the expounders of it; while the multitude upon whom the Romish supersititon has lost its hold, is swept into the same devouring vortex. Men are putting a living, personal God out of th universe, and resolving all into materialism. This is philosophy—the highest reach of science—the profoundest, truest solution of the mysteries of the universe. In accordance with this, faith in Christianity as a supernatural power, or having a supernatural history, is swept away at a stroke, and the entire system is reduced to the level of naturalism. Jesus Christ being esteemed but a man, and a man too not necessarily free from mistakes and imperfections. Christianity itself is being finally converted into the service of infidelity and atheism. The system is no longer opposed as once it was, when religion was denounced as weak superstition, and Jesus despised as its author. That was the infidelity of a ruder and less scientific age. The more refined and subtle skepticism of our times claims Jesus Christ as its own, the Sent of God, the great inspired One of heaven, and His doctrines as the true teachings of philosophy and nature; while it denies all that was supernatural in His life and work. It was a grand achievement of Satanic strategy to secure possession of the *Church*, and subsidize the same to its purposes, making it "a cage of every unclean and hateful bird," as it did in the Papacy. But it is the last and most distinguished achievement to claim Jesus Christ as its own, making Him the great Apostle and High Priest of infidelity and atheism. This is the blaspheming infidelity of these "last days"—the development of its perfected wisdom and science. These are the scoffers who may well ask, "Where is the promise of His coming?"

A powerful movement has begun in Europe toward popular freedom; but it is a most painful fact, yet indisputable, that that freedom involves, to a very large extent, the renunciation of all moral allegiance to a Higher Power. How deep-seated and extensive this idea is, strikingly appears in the manifesto of the principles of European democracy put forth by the Executive Council of German Radicals, appointed by that memorable body, the Frankfort Diet, which sat in 1849, representing all German liberalism. The following is an extract from that document: "We declare *the supreme power of the state, over all economical and social relationship, as a ruling principle.* Education and instruction must therefore be stripped of all religious doubts and superfluities [by which is meant religious faith and obligations]. The sole object is to make men fit companions for each other. *Religion, which must be banished from society, must vanish from the mind of man.* Art and poetry will realize the ideals of the true, the good, and the beautiful, which religion places in an uncertain future. *The revolution generally destroys religion by rendering hopes of heaven superfluous*—by establishing the liberty and welfare of all on earth. We pay attention, therefore, to religious struggles and contentions (the formation of free congregations, and so forth) only so far as we may, under the phrase of religious liberty, *understand freedom from all religions. We do not desire liberty of belief, but the necessity of unbelief. In this, as in all other respects,* we wish to break entirely with the past. We do not wish to engraft a fresh branch upon a rotten stem: we in no respect desire reform, but everywhere revolution."

Such an open, unblushing, authoritative avowal of blank atheism by the friends of what is called liberty in Europe; such a renunciation of all the claims of religion, of all allegiance to a higher Power, and the assertion that this life contains the only and supreme good, is startling and alarming in the highest degree. This terrible revelation, too, could not have come from such a source without its being well understood that the public mind was prepared to receive and sustain it. That "Executive Council" knew the character and views of their constituency. The following statement, also found in one of our own religious journals, furnishes circumstantial evidence to the truth of the state of things here developed:

"We do not believe there is any press in the world so utterly radical and destructive as the German newspaper press of the United States. Of some sixty journals, the majority assail every form of church institutions, make light of historical Christianity, in notorious instances deny the personality of God and the immortality of the soul, and teach the most thorough-going Epicurianism. Of four daily papers, published in a single city, three ridicule every form of church association, deride those who support any clergy, and more than hint that material interests are our only reasonable concern."

Nor is Germany alone involved in this dreadful vortex of infidelity and atheism. It is spread widely through the nations of Europe. Lamartine wrote, after the failure of the revolution in 1848, that the fatal defect of French character, which made a permanent French republic impossible, was lack of conscience. Casimir Perier, one of their most discerning statesmen, said, in 1832, "The thoughts of this people are not the thoughts of a civilized race; their imaginations are those of a savage tribe." They have, indeed, attained an outward civilization of the highest elegance; but the everlasting foundations of truth, religion, and morality are wanting, and the current is sweeping on with irresistible power to a gross sensualism, which is undermining the whole framework of society. Niebuhr, the great historical critic of modern times, and an earnest lover of liberty, wrote from Rome, in 1830: "It is my firm conviction that we, particularly in Germany, are rapidly hastening toward barbarism, and it is not much better in France. That we are threatened with devastation, such as that two hundred years ago, is, I am sorry to say, just as clear to me; and the end of the tale will be despotism enthroned amid universal ruin. *In fifty years, and probably much less, there will be no trace left of free institutions or the freedom of the press, throughout all Europe, at least on the continent.* Very few of the things which have happened since the Revolution in Paris have surprised me. Constitutional forms are of no use among an enervated or foolish nation. I know how to prize a free constitution, and certainly am better acquainted than most with its worth; but of all things the first and most essential is, that a nation should be manly, unselfish, honorable."

The European mind is thus rushing downward to the grossest materialism and sensuality, as it inevitably must without the restraints which the obligations of religion, and a sense of responsibility to a living, personal God must impose. Wickedness has maintained its supremacy in the world through its past history, under all the restraining power which the acknowledgment of a higher ruling agency in the affairs of men has brought to bear upon their minds. It may be reserved to the "last days" to show what the world will be when it casts away all idea of God and religion, and *That Wicked* is revealed, who opposeth and exalteth himself above all that is called God or is worshipped, so that He, as God, sitteth in the temple of God, showing himself that He is God. Facts, which might be adduced in abundance, show clearly that an utter debauchment of the public morals is taking place under this obliteration of all conscience from the minds of men—this godless, Christless rule—this reign of materialism.

There is portentous evil in the rule of such a godless democracy as is here described, beyond any thing that the world has ever realized. Through the centuries past, the kings and potentates have enjoyed the empire, and have had the opportunity of showing whether they would bow to the supremacy of Jesus Christ. The people themselves, too, are rendering their verdict upon that point, by denouncing the rulers as usurping tyrants, who have trampled upon all human rights, and are unworthy to be trusted more with such precious interests. Their language now is, Give us the power, to whom it rightfully belongs. We can govern ourselves. We may be trusted. The great heart of the people is always right. *Vox populi vox Dei.* God is suffering this last experiment to be made. He is giving the world full and fair opportunity, under the rule both of kings and people, to show what its spirit is, and whether it will own subjection to Jesus Christ.

We have seen somewhat of the spirit of this godless democracy in these United States, spurning the control of all higher law, and grasping after the empire with the most desperate and malignant purpose, ready to adopt or renounce any principles that may but give it the ascendancy. The gigantic war, waged through four years for the overthrow of free institutions and the permanent establishment of slavery, is a terrible demonstration of the character of this democracy, beyond all that we could before have deemed possible. It boldly sets up the claim, also, that it shall not be interfered with by the law of Christ—that politics have been properly divorced from the religious element. The care of government has been committed to the people and the politicians—religion to the churches and ministers. The sphere of each is fixed, from which it must not depart to interfere with the other. Thus does this ungodly democracy demand that they shall not be interfered with from the pulpit, by any of the claims of religion, or the obligations of the Divine law. They resent it as an ecclesiastical usurpation, asserting that they are supreme in their own sphere, and that politics are to be divorced from religion. It is claimed, too, and believed by vast numbers, that *the will of the people is the fundamental law*, not qualifiedly in subjection to Christ as supreme over all, but absolutely. The doctrine is that the people are the ultimate source of sovereignty, and that their decision, whatever it be, makes fundamental law, beyond which you cannot inquire further. Christian ministers from the pulpit have, in some instances, defended this position. The language of the European democracy is unqualifiedly, "We declare the supreme power of the State, over all economical and social relationships, as a ruling principle. Education and instruction must, therefore, be stripped of all religious doubts and superfluities." The doctrine has not, indeed, been so broadly asserted here among us. Public opinion would not permit it. Yet this is its intent in the minds of multitudes, and this its practical operation.

Every mind, too, must be filled with deepest anxiety and alarm, in view of the growing demoralization of our government, which is manifest in the extensive bribery of legislators and officials—the frauds and robberies on the part of public men, and the desire to obtain office and rule, in order to participate in such plunder, which is fast becoming the great end of all political strife, the corruption of justice, the impunity which is allowed to crime, and the breaking down, in the public mind, of the everlasting principles of justice, which prevents the execution of law, and tolerates the most enormous offences. National corruption must end in national destruction, more swiftly and surely, too, in a republic than in any other form of government, because least fitted to withstand such shocks. However it may be with a monarchy, a republic cannot continue without virtue and religion. Anarchy must follow in the track of lawlessness, and despotism must then be sought unto as a refuge.

It is sometimes asserted that if our free institutions

prove a failure, the world will be put back many centuries amid the darkness of past ages. But God's providence does not move backward. The pathway of His chariot is onward, and it will be onward over the fall of republicanism, as well as of monarchy. The hopes of earth are not involved in the rule of the democracy any more than in that of the kings. They both may fail, and yet God not be disappointed in His plans. We cannot but think, too, that the Church has put no little dishonor upon Christ, her living Head, in relying to such an extent upon a form of human government, and placing her dearest hopes there. The issue of the ages, according to the word of prophecy, is whether Christ shall have the rule. The doctrine of our Christianity is, that Jesus, our Immanuel, is the supreme ruler of this world—the source of all government and power; that He puts the sword of jussice into the hands of rulers, and that to Him they must be held accountable for its administration. He has ever asserted this supremacy; asserted it over the heads of kings, asserted it over the people. That sovereignty He will defend to the last, never yielding one jot or tittle thereof, however the heathen may rage, or the rulers take counsel together, or the *people* imagine a vain thing. It is the determinate counsel of heaven that Christ shall have the dominion over this entire earth. "Yet have I set my King upon my holy hill of Zion;" Ps. ii. 6. That is the decree, that the problem which is being worked out in Divine providence, and the final issue to which all things are tending. It is not the rights of kings, nor State rights, nor the rights of the people; but sublime above all is the question of Christ's rights. "Sit there on my right hand until I make thine enemies thy footstool." The power now that arrays itself against this sovereignty of Christ, whether it be kings or people, shall be broken and dashed, and "perish from the way when his wrath is kindled but a little."

If such, too, be the alarming tendencies and developments of this godless rule, as we have most painful experience of in these United States, where Christianity exerts such an influence, what may we look for in Europe, when the great democratic idea rises there to assert and claim the dominion? Nor is the circumstance to be overlooked that the Emperor of France, under the Napoleonic dynasty, glories in the fact that he is the true exponent and representative of that very democratic idea—*being elected to the empire by the voice of the people*—and the advocate of their rights. There is no legitimacy to his rule, according to the European doctrine of legitimacy. He holds the sovereignty by the voice of the sovereign people, and thus stands as the embodiment of that modern idea of the democracy, behind whose will there is no rule, no allegiance—beyond which there is no appeal.

When, therefore, the dreadful shock of revolution shall come in Europe, as come it must, sooner or later; when thrones and powers, civil and ecclesiastical, shall be tossed like drift-wood upon the raging elements, how easily and almost necessarily may "THAT WICKED" arise, which the pen of inspiration describes! How will the way have been prepared for His advent by the destruction of all sense of responsibility to a living, personal God, and the conversion of Christianity itself to mere infidelity and materialism! It is in the midst of these convulsions, and as part thereof, that great Babylon is to fall, cast like a millstone into the sea, and the smoke of her torment is to go up. And when that cruel despotism is cast down, buried in the deep, the infidel, atheistic masses, craving, by the very necessity of their nature, some object which they may exalt to the throne and worship, yet without any conception of, or sense of responsibility to, a spiritual power above themselves, may force the coming of "the man of destiny"—the destined or divine man, who alone can represent humanity, and take the empire and sovereignty into His hands, seating himself in the temple of God, and showing himself that He is God. It is most evident that when the idea of a living, personal God is effectually uprooted with all the old superstitions connected therewith, there is nothing then to interpose between humanity and the eternal throne. Man himself becomes God. And *The Man*, or *That Wicked* will be called for as a necessity, and will be revealed. When, too, the world, in its profoundest wisdom, has reached this pitch of infidelity and wickedness, then will it be time for Christ, the rejected and crucified, to appear, to assert His sovereignty, and put His insolent enemies beneath His footstool. As in the days of Noah, there will be no object in carrying the experiment of Divine forbearance further. The world will have acted out all its folly and madness when it has attained this point of daring blasphemy, and stretched forth its impious hand to seize the eternal throne itself, proclaiming its own godhead. The time for judgment will then have come; and come it will, swift and dreadful. It will be the day of vengeance and recompense. It will be time for Christ, the second Adam, the true man, to show himself, and prove His right to the throne. And well may the very "*wrath of the Lamb*" be kindled, so that the rocks and mountains shall be sought unto for a refuge from the fury that shall come up in his face. John in vision presents to us the scenes and events of those times. "And I saw three unclean spirits like frogs come out of the mouth of the dragon, and out of the mouth of the beast, and out of the mouth of the false prophet. For they are the spirits of devils, working miracles, which go forth unto the kings of the earth, and of the whole world, *to gather them to the battle of that great day of God Almighty. Behold, I come as a thief.* Blessed is he that watcheth, and keepeth his garments, lest he walk naked, and they see his shame. And he gathered them together into a place called in the Hebrew tongue Armageddon. And the seventh angel poured out his vial into the air; and there came a great voice out of the temple of heaven, from the throne, saying, It is done. And there were voices, and thunders, and lightnings; and there was a great earthquake, such as was not since men were upon the earth, so mighty an earthquake, and so great. And the great city was divided into three parts, and the cities of the nations fell: and great Babylon came in remembrance before God, to give unto her the cup of the wine of the fierceness of his wrath. And every island fled away, and the mountains were not found. And there fell upon men a great hail out of heaven, every stone about the weight of a talent: and men blasphemed God because of the plague of the hail; for the plague thereof was exceeding great;" Rev. xvi. 13. Prophecy is thus clear and emphatic in regard to the coming of that great day of God Almighty, when the kings of the earth and all the allied powers of wickedness are to be gathered to defeat the everlasting decree that places Christ upon the throne, and gives the dominion into His hand. This is the issue of this present dispensation. Armageddon is the field for the settlement of this long controversy, "the valley of decision," and there will these confederate hosts be broken with God's iron rod, and all the feathered fowl of heaven, and the beasts of the earth be gathered to feast upon the carcasses of the mighty. The antediluvian world forced the judgments of heaven to its overthrow. The generation which came out of Egypt compelled judgment after judgment for forty years, until they were consumed. Israel was struck down in wrath, clinging to God's covenant, yet raging in blasphemy against Christ and the Holy Ghost. But when the Lord shall tread the great winepress of the wrath of Almighty God, well may He be presented red in His apparel, and His garments like him that treadeth in the winefat; for blood shall there flow to the horse-bridles. We have seen God arise to plead the controversy of His despised poor in *this* land, who, through weary years, cried unto Him from the house of their hard bondage in bitterness of soul; and how, to vindicate their cause, He suddenly gathered such hosts as modern times have never witnessed, and the dread thunder of the battle was heard from afar. The terrible iron rod of His anger was seen here uplifted, and His cruel enemies were dashed like a potter's vessel. But *the day, the great day, the great and notable day of the Lord* is yet to come, when "the kings of the earth, and the great men, and the rich men, and the chief captains, and the mighty men, and every bond-man, and every free-man shall hide themselves in the dens and in the rocks of the mountains; and shall say to the mountains and rocks, Fall on us and hide us from the face of him that sitteth on *the throne*, and from the wrath of the Lamb: for the great day of his wrath is come; and who shall be able to stand?" Rev. vi. 15. Hasten, Lord, the day, when thine enemies shall be driven like chaff before the whirlwind, and the long-delayed hour of redemption shall come to thy suffering Church.

CHAPTER XXVII.

THE PRIESTHOOD.

We pass to the point in the history where God began to unfold the next important truth in the work of salvation, found in the doctrine of

THE PRIESTHOOD.

We have shown already how God revealed the way of approach to Him for sinners by means of a sin-offering, so clearly set forth in the tragic history of Cain and Abel. It does not, however, appear from their history, or others recorded through that period, that there was any regular and established priesthood. The facts narrated are against it. Adam undoubtedly offered these sacrifices, although the fact is not specifically stated. He did not, however, perform the part of a priest for his children, since the duty was devolved upon them, when arrived at suitable years, of bringing the required lamb, and officiating at the altar for themselves, even as their father had done; which is sufficient to indicate the established practice of that age. Cain and Abel assumed nothing unbecoming in attempting to minister at the altar. The sin of Cain lay wholly in the nature of his offering, and in that was his condemnation.

Melchizedec is the first priest of whom we have mention. He is recognized in this official capacity, being acknowledged by Abraham, and receiving from him the appointed tithes; showing that there was then an established practice on this subject. Mention is also made of Jethro as the priest of Midian. These facts would indicate that the office originated soon after the Deluge. The matter was probably revealed to Noah, or Shem, as one of the new features to characterize the age then commencing. The office evidently did not originate with men. The priesthood, throughout its history, has been so sacred, and connected so indissolubly with the system of redemption, as well as jealously guarded by Divine authority, that we cannot imagine it to have originated with men. The Aaronic priesthood, we know, was or dained of God, and consecrated in the most solemn manner to their sacred functions; while the prior priesthood of Melchizedec was owned of God, as superior in some respects to that of Aaron, and more immediately representing the ever-living priesthood of Christ. It is certain that God would never have sanctioned this office as a mere human device; nor would human ingenuity have been adequate to contrive an institution which should so clearly and fully have set forth our Redeemer in one of the most momentous relations which He sustains to our race. God has ever been most jealous in regard to all interference with His instituted modes of worship, as may be seen in the matter of Cain's offering, and the attempts made at different times to invade the priest's office by unauthorized persons, such as Korah, Dathan, and Abiram, and King Uzziah, whom swift judgment overtook for their presumption. The priesthood, therefore, most manifestly was not instituted without Divine sanction, any more than sacrifices themselves. They were both the appointment of God. The history also shows that, soon after the Deluge, a class of men was set apart and consecrated to this sacred office of mediatorship with God, which is the essential idea of a priest—one to whom the offering of sacrifices is especially committed, that he may intercede with Heaven in behalf of the guilty, who themselves have no access into the Divine presence. Thus not only must a bloody sacrifice or sin-offering be made, but made by certain persons who have been clothed with this special authority to act for others. They are appointed mediators between God and man, through whose intercession, by the offering of blood, atonement is made, and justification obtained for the transgressor.

The promise in the beginning, which constituted the basis of the entire system of redemption, was that of the woman's seed destined to bruise the serpent's head.

How or when He should come, or how accomplish His work, did not then appear. The general fact only of a coming Saviour was held forth, and made the object of earnest hope to the race. His character and work were to be the theme of future revelation, unfolded from time to time as the world should be able to receive the instruction. As the first step in this development, the bloody sacrifice or sin-offering was appointed, and sinners were taught that this was the only way of approach for them to secure the Divine favor. The connection between the promised Saviour and this sacrifice may not then have been apparent, though we can now easily see what that connection is, and what a work also this typical, bloody rite achieved, in schooling the race into the nature and necessity of an atonement for sin. Faith, too, accepted the Divine teachings on this subject; and when the humble soul believed God, and obeyed, to the extent of the revelations made, he was justified. It was not essential that he should comprehend fully the Divine method. It was his to believe and obey to the extent that God revealed truth and duty, and by such faith he was justified. When he, therefore, came with the bleeding lamb, and confessing over its innocent head his own iniquities, in the assurance that he should find mercy, he was accepted. This, however, was but the beginning of the Divine revelations on this theme. We come now to the next step in advance, where a new phase of the subject was opened, presenting a fuller view of the Coming One.

This was the ordaining of an established priesthood, to whom the offering of these sacrifices was committed.

As already stated, we find the beginnings of this in the period immediately succeeding the Deluge, in which event God had taught the world that grand lesson of the salvation of a believing remnant. This, too, was a fitting time for the introduction of some further truths in the plan of redemption. The righteous family of Noah stood ready to receive all the Divine teachings; and the terrific judgment through which the earth had passed, would tend to impress those teachings, whatever they might be, deeply upon the minds of men.

It would appear from the history that the rise of the priesthood was somewhat gradual. In other words, God did not make a sudden transition from the practice of the antediluvian age, in this particular, to the one succeeding. The transitions of all God's dispensations are, to a certain extent, gradual. The Jewish overlapped the Christian. Jewish believers were not required at once to abandon circumcision and the observance of their ritual. These were tolerated for a period, though no more essential, and not to be laid as a burden upon the Gentile convert. His liberty was earnestly defended; while the Jew was allowed to cherish those things which had been so long dear to his nation, and which God had instituted, but now laid aside for a richer dispensation of grace. The antediluvian age may thus have overlapped the next succeeding in the matter now under consideration. In the early part of the latter, we find both practices prevailing in the offering of sacrifices. We discover clearly the new office of the priesthood, designed to be the permanent institution, while the practice of the former period was still allowed for a season. Noah offered sacrifices, as did Abraham, Isaac, and Jacob. But Melchizedec was a recognized priest of the Most High God, to whom especial honor was due in this official character; and as soon as the priesthood could be established in the nation of Israel, it was ordained in the house of Aaron, and to them the work of sacrifice was then exclusively committed.

From this time the office and work of the priesthood occupy a place of great prominence in the history of redemption: and constituting, as it did, part of an extensive typical system of instruction, it could not be understood otherwise by those who were enlightened to know the things of God, than as pointing forward to a grander work and office to be fulfilled in earth's coming Deliverer. God intended to make the race familiar with the idea, not only of a sin-offering, and blood shed for the remission of sins, but also that a mediator was required, by whom this atonement for the transgressor should be made. The sinner was given plainly to understand that he could not come himself to plead his own cause before God, and stand in His holy presence. A mediator must be found to intercede for him, and to this office the priest was solemnly and forever consecrated. It was his prerogative to enter the sanctuary of Jehovah, and minister there at the altar, while all others were forbidden access. The transgressor brought his selected victim to the door of the tabernacle of the Lord, but went no further. There confessing his sin, with his hand laid upon the head of the innocent animal, he struck the blow which ended its life. The priest then took the slain lamb, and went within the tabernacle to make the atonement by the presentation of the body and blood in the appointed manner before the Lord. Some tell us that atonement means reconciliation simply: and the doctrine with them is merely the reconciliation of a sinner to God. But such an idea of atonement most clearly is not derived from the Scriptures. As presented there, the sinner has no agency in the work, except the mere preliminary step of bringing the animal as the victim to be offered, which is the expression of his desire that an atonement may be made for him, and his concurrence therein. He is the guilty party needing to be reconciled, but he does not make the atonement, nor have any agency in it. It is made by the priest, who, as a third party, mediates in his behalf, interceding for him by blood, and thereby obtaining his forgiveness and justification. No fact in the institutions of the Old Testament is plainer than this. Take a single passage out of many, where the whole congregation have become involved in transgression. A young bullock is, in such case, required to be brought before the tabernacle. "And the elders of the congregation shall lay their hands upon the head of the bullock before the Lord; and the bullock shall be killed before the Lord. And *the priest that is anointed* shall bring of the bullock's blood to the tabernacle of the congregation: and the priest shall dip his finger in some of the blood, and sprinkle it seven times before the Lord, even before the vail. And he shall put some of the blood upon the horns of the altar which is before the Lord, that is in the tabernacle of the congregation, and shall pour out all the blood at the bottom of the altar of the burnt offering, which is at the door of the tabernacle of the congregation. And he shall take all his fat from him, and burn it upon the altar. And he shall do with the bullock as he did with the bullock for a sin-offering, so shall he do with this: *And the priest shall make an atonement for them, and it shall be forgiven them;*" Lev. iv. 15. What the priest therefore does, constitutes the atonement. It is his intercession, by means of blood, that secures the forgiveness and justification of the transgressor. The nation of Israel, through their history, had no other conception of the matter. There could be no mistake on this point, that only through a mediator and a sin-offering could they approach to God, while atonement was the exclusive work of the priest. The people could not pass beyond the door of the tabernacle. There the anointed priest must meet them, and enter in to plead with blood in behalf of transgressors—that blood being the only argument which he might present—the blood of innocence shed for the guilty, after that the confession of sin had been made. It will be seen from these facts, also, that atonement was not made when the animal was slain. His life was taken by the hand of the sinner at the door of the tabernacle. But the atonement was the work of the priest, when he had carried the slain beast within, and there presented it before the Lord in the required manner as an offering. This is an important fact, the bearings of which will hereafter be considered.

Now, if there was any thing marked with peculiar prominence in the nation of Israel, it was this matter of the priesthood. It was their great institution, preëminent above all. For five hundred years of their history they had no king. But they were never without a priest. The tabernacle was the centre of attraction to the nation, whither all their deepest interest turned. Here was the dwelling-place of the God of Irsael—the holy place of His tabernacle, where He abode in glory. Here the priesthood officiated with their solemn rites, and the nation assembled three times a year to worship before the Lord. The priests alone were allowed to go in and stand in this holy place; while to one of their sacred body—the high-priest, and to him only once in a year, on the great day of atonement—was the exalted honor given of entering within the vail, to stand in the Holy of Holies, where abode the Divine glory itself between the cherubim. This distinction put upon the priesthood, and especially the high-priest, invested them with preëminent sanctity and power, even as God intended they should be. This office was identified with the nation's entire history, the throne and monarchy entering at a later period, and under very different circumstances.

What, then, was the meaning of this?

It was part of God's great system of instruction, designed to unfold the character and work of the promised Deliverer—a shadow of things to come, as were the tabernacle, the people of Israel, and the land of Canaan. They were types of heavenly things; and so the spiritually instructed men of those times understood it. It was not possible for the blood of bulls and goats to take away sins. These very priests, who interceded for others, needed to have atonement made for their own cleansing, before they went in to minister for others. The tabernacle itself must be sprinkled with the blood of atonement. These, therefore, were but the shadows of nobler realities to come; and the nation was taught by these earthly models to look for the heavenly things in the future, when the woman's seed should come to bring the promised redemption. It was not in vain, therefore, that God arranged that vast system of sacrificial worship, and established the priesthood long prior to the introduction of the throne in Israel; causing the nation, in the person of their great patriarch and founder, Abraham, to bow to the higher office of Melchizedec, the priest, to pay tithes to him. We shall show hereafter how the idea of *the kingdom* of Christ was introduced—a truth of subsequent revelation, and based upon the more fundamental doctrine of the priesthood and sacrifice. By the arrangement of the latter, God intended to establish Christ's great office of the priesthood, and His work of atonement, making them familiar to the minds of men. In this character the Coming One was first to be presented to human faith, occupying the priest's office and performing the work of mediatorship belonging thereto. This was the import of Christ's first advent. He came then to execute the priest's work, and prepare the sacrificial victim, which accounts for the fact that it was wanting in all regal honors and power, and characterized only by humiliation, obedience, and suffering. Christ has not yet taken the promised throne and kingdom of David, as we shall show hereafter. This is the period in which He is accomplishing the work of His priesthood; having gone in, as the Apostle tells us, behind the vail, where he is no longer visible, to make intercession, even as the priest of old went within the sanctuary out of sight of the worshipper at the door of the tabernacle. Jesus, our forerunner, is now in the sanctuary above, accomplishing His great and effectual priesthood for us, and by His own blood making atonement for our souls.

This explains also the prophecies concerning the sufferings of Christ, which were, at the time, so difficult to reconcile with His promised glory, and kingdom, and power, and which were so extensively overlooked by the nation. It was not made plain to them of old that the prophecies concerning the Messiah were to be fulfilled in two separate advents—the one, when He should come to accomplish the work of His priesthood, the other, when He should take the throne and reign over the house of David. The line was not drawn then between the prophecies, as it now is by the actual first coming of Christ, and the appropriation thereto of all those prophecies which relate to His humiliation, His obedience, and sufferings. It is now made clear that He came then to fulfil His priesthood, making himself a sin-offering; while the other prophecies respecting His glory, dominion, and kingdom, remain to be fulfilled in another advent, for which we wait and pray. The Apostle Peter tells us how the prophets inquired and searched diligently of this salvation, who prophesied of the coming grace: "searching what, or *what manner of time* the Spirit of Christ which was in them did signify, when it testified beforehand *the sufferings of Christ, and the glory that should follow;*" 1 Peter i. 10. The Jewish nation did not understand that first mission of suffering and humiliation. Jesus found it extremely difficult to make His disciples comprehend it; and for the reason that they were looking in another direction, having their minds exclusively occupied with His throne and kingdom. It is only wonderful that their faith adhered to Him still through that dreadful hour of His crucifixion. But the whole truth burst upon their astonished vision after the resurrection, when their minds were opened to understand the Scriptures, and see how Moses and all the prophets had told of the sufferings of Christ, as well as the glory that was to follow—how He was first to accomplish His priestly work by being made a sin-offering, thereby preparing a people for himself; then, subsequently, to come a second time in His kingdom and glory, to fulfil all that was foretold of His dominion and triumphs.

But why did not Christ, as the great High-Priest of men, come of the tribe of Levi, to which this work and office pertained in Israel?

Because His priesthood was superior to theirs, it being predicted of Him, that He should be a priest "after the order of Melchizedec;" Ps. cx. 4. The superiority of this priesthood over that of Aaron consisted in two things: one was, that the priesthood of the former was combined with the kingly office, Melchizedec being both priest and king, as Christ was designed to be, and as Aaron was not. In the Jewish system these two offices were most carefully kept distinct. The other point of superiority was, that the priesthood of Melchizedec was designed to represent a perpetual, ever-living intercessor. This it did in the fact that he stands alone, without any connection with a line going before or following after; or, as described by the Apostle, "without father, without mother, without descent, having neither beginning of days nor end of life; but made like unto the Son of God, abideth a priest continually;" Heb. vii. 4. We have no account of any beginning or end of his priesthood, or of its transmission to a successor. It stands, therefore, a more fitting type of Christ's ever-living priesthood than Aaron's, of which we know the entire history—the beginning, succession, and end. Had Christ come of Aaron's line, it would not have been consistent for Him to hold the kingly office and occupy the throne of David, the same being forbidden to his priesthood; while the succession in that line implied a termination. Christ therefore came of another priesthood, one which involved the kingly office, and of which there was to be no termination.

The Revelation of John, which gives us the future of the Church, is deeply significant and instructive on this subject. The scene of those wondrous visions is laid in the tabernacle, as the whole scenic representation of the book shows. The opening vision presents Christ to our view standing by the seven golden candlesticks, and therefore in the first apartment of the sanctuary, or holy place, where He was performing His priestly work in taking care of the lights, and keeping them continually burning. In his epistle to the church of Ephesus, he describes himself, Rev. ii. 1, as He who "walketh in the midst of the seven golden candlesticks"—the priest of His Church. Here, as seen by John, He was clothed in the priestly robes—a white garment, flowing to the feet, and bound with a girdle. This is the character in which our Redeemer now appears—this the work which He is now executing. This solves the meaning of the dispensation of grace through which we are passing. The scene of the present economy is laid in the holy place of the sanctuary, where are the altar of incense and the candlesticks, of which Christ has the care. At a later period of those visions of John, we behold the inner apartment of that sanctuary opened, and the mysteries of the most holy place exposed to view, when we see Christ revealed in His kingly office, and coming to occupy the throne. This was the typical meaning of that tabernacle with its two apartments. The Church of God is the true tabernacle, which the Lord pitched, and not man. The first apartment, with its altar, candlesticks, and table of shewbread, presents the history of the Church under Christ as its High-Priest, making intercession. The second, or most holy place, shows us Christ upon His throne, revealed in His glory between the cherubim. The opening of that apartment is yet a future event. We are now in the first tabernacle, where Christ is in the midst of the candlesticks. This is stated to be the summing up of that whole system. "Now of the things which we have spoken, *this is the sum:* We have such an high-priest, who is set on the right hand of the throne of the Majesty in the heavens; a minister of the sanctuary, and of the true tabernacle, which the Lord pitched, and not man;" Heb. viii. 1. Our Immanuel Jesus is both High-Priest and King.

How vain, then, for any to think of knowing Christ in His glory and kingdom, who have not known Him first in the fellowship of His sufferings, and secured His mediation as their High-Priest! Here the foundation is laid for the whole superstructure of redemption. Here is the corner-stone laid in Zion; and if this is rejected, there is salvation in none other. There is no other mediator to go in to plead for the sinner; neither can the transgressor find entrance himself. His place is at the door of the tabernacle; and if he refuses the mediation of God's anointed High-Priest, there is no forgiveness, no redemption for him. And when He comes to reign in His glory, it will be His then to say of all such, "I never knew you."

CHAPTER XXVIII.

PRIESTHOOD OF CHRIST.

HAVING shown how and when the doctrine ot mediator was introduced, we proceed to take up *the facts as connected with the mediation of Christ, as fulfilled in His first mission.*

I. *Christ, then, is presented as the spotless lamb of God.*

In all mediation for sinners, a clean animal, free from every blemish, and a firstling of the flock, was required, the very choicest being demanded for this sacred service. In this peculiar relation Jesus Christ is distinctly brought to our notice; and by the man sent of Heaven to herald His approach, and especially endowed to present Him to Israel, as well as to prepare His way. John appeared in the spirit and power of Elijah to announce the coming of heaven's great Anointed. His representations, therefore, are invested with peculiar significance and value. The character in which this new Elijah would hold Him up to His expectant nation, is to be unhesitatingly accepted; and the moment his eye fell upon Him, he exclaimed, "Behold the Lamb of God, which taketh away the sin of the world."

What, now, did a Jew mean by a lamb taking away sin? He meant, beyond denial, a lamb offered in sacrifice —a lamb over whose head confession of sin had been made by a transgressor—whose life had been taken and His blood shed in expiation of guilt. *This was its uniform, unquestioned meaning.* There was no other way in which a lamb had ever been known to take away sin; and this was the way of God's appointment, into which

He had been educating the race from the time of the martyr Abel, the blood of whose innocent victim had continued to speak and testify through all the generations, until the blood "which speaketh better things" was shed.

When John, therefore, under Divine inspiration, held forth Jesus as the lamb taking away sin—the sin of the world—he could be understood to mean only one thing: that here was the victim, the true Sacrifice appointed of God, by the shedding of whose blood expiation was to be made, and the forgiveness of sins obtained. The question here is not, what construction *we might* put upon these words of John, or what they might possibly bear in our day, when institutions and modes of thinking are all changed. They were not spoken in this nineteenth century, but in another age, and to a different people; and the only question is, What meaning did the author attach to them? *In what sense did he know that they would be understood and accepted by those who heard him?*

We often hear Christianity reproached because of the uncertainty of its doctrines, and the Scriptures for their Sibylline character, as if they could be made to teach any system. What, however, shall be said of the intelligence or honesty of those who change the position of words by eighteen centuries of time, placing them also among an entirely different people with other institutions and modes of thought, and yet never stop a moment to ask what their meaning was in the mouth of him who gave them utterance, or in the ears of those who heard? Under such treatment it is certain that the Bible can have no fixed meaning; God never could have given a revelation to mankind to be interpreted upon such principles, because its teachings would only change with the changing sentiments of every generation; and not only so, but with every nation in each generation. Every people would make the Bible to suit themselves. Men never deal thus with other books and subjects, yet they do thus strangely deal with the Word of God, attaching modern and possible meanings to its statements after the revolutions of many centuries, and then imagine that they have the import of its words as they were originally uttered. God is not to be held responsible for any such folly as this; nor is the reproach of ambiguity to be laid to His revealed system on this account. His Word has a clear and well-defined meaning, which can be ascertained if the book is only fairly dealt with. It is not a trumpet with an uncertain sound. Here, too, we set up our defense for that divine and inspired record, charging it upon human ignorance and dishonesty as the responsible cause why its plain teachings have not been understood and accepted. The man who reads a book eighteen hundred years old, as if it were written yesterday, needs to begin his education anew, starting from the alphabet. He needs to lay aside all the opinions which have been formed upon such principles of interpretation, and, begining again with the simple elements, try to ascertain what meaning the Scriptures were intended to convey when written, and which, by the eternal laws of language, they must continue to convey till time shall be no more.

Guided now by these undeniable principles, we assert that there cannot be a shadow of doubt as to the meaning of the words of John in his own lips, and in the ears of his nation, when he described Jesus Christ as "the Lamb of God taking away the sin of the world." That people had been too long and faithfully trained under the influence of bleeding lambs, and expiation thereby made for transgressors, to leave the matter in any doubt. We do not hesitate to assert that John intended to mislead his nation, if he employed this language out of its accepted meaning without giving the slightest intimation of the fact, since every honest man is bound to use words in the sense in which he knows they will be accepted. We have a right to speak strongly here, for it is a plain case; and it is time that the question was settled, that the Bible is a book written to be understood, and whose meaning can be authoritatively established. It is time that the deep reproach of the Scriptures' teaching any and every doctrine—of their serving God and the devil—were taken from them, and placed where it properly belongs. It has too long lain at God's door, and men have not been backward to place it there. It is time that the Divine name and honor were vindicated.

If any, indeed, are not satisfied with the doctrines which a fair interpretation will thus evolve from this revelation, claiming to sit in judgment upon and condemn the same, that is another question, which may be discussed in its own place. The one now before us is simply as to the meaning of God's Word. We assert that its teachings are unambiguous, and need not be in eternal doubt and controversy—that God was capable of writing a book containing His will, that would be intelligible to honest men. If we cannot stand upon this ground, then a revelation from Heaven to mankind is out of the question, and we may as well abandon all attempts to study the Scriptures.

It is worthy of further observation, that the language and description of John respecting Jesus are the most remarkable, inasmuch as this was not the character in which the nation was looking for Him, nor in which human wisdom would have thought to exhibit Him. It was not the human conception of the expected Christ; it did not, therefore, originate with John. He was taught it from above, even as Peter was, when he was enabled to say concerning Jesus: "Thou art the Christ, the Son of the living God," while the words addressed to the latter would have been as applicable to the former: "Flesh and blood hath not revealed it unto thee, but my Father which is in heaven."

Jesus Christ, then, was a *spotless* lamb, and the only human being that ever realized this character of stainless purity. He was the only one placed under the law and the curse with us, who was entirely exempt from sin, being subjected, too, to temptation in all its severest forms. He was not spared in any particular, though an only Son, and well-beloved—was not hedged about from evil, with an easy lot chosen for Him. On the contrary, He was subjected to the hardest conditions, and met all the fiercest assaults of temptation, being the object of hell's special malignity. He submitted to all the will of Heaven, even when others' sins were laid to His account—the severest form of trial to which our nature can be subjected, and which will test to the utmost all its integrity. Yet Christ was victorious, submitting without a murmuring word, even when the trial wrung the gory sweat of agony from His body, and fainting nature was ready to sink. He still meekly bowed, and said, "Thy will, not mine, be done." Thus one at last was found, whom Satan could not move from His allegiance to Heaven—one man, who passed successfully through, with no guile found in His mouth. He was a spotless Lamb, and set apart to a holy priesthood; for He needed no blood shed for His own cleansing, to take away His sins. This trial of Christ was very different from that to which our nature was first subjected in paradise. There it was in a state of innocence. Here it was under the curse, Christ assumed our fallen humanity. Not that He was himself stained with sin; but He took our nature as it now is under the curse, subject to all the trials, suffering, and temptation which belong to our present lot. He came into this world, not in its paradisiacal state with God's blessing upon it, but resting under the curse. He took our nature, with all its present liabilities—doomed to toil, to suffering, to reproach, to death. He claimed no exemption from any lot or trial to which man might be subjected, as a test of His obedience and faith in this world of temptation and sin. He, therefore, took a servant's place—a place of humblest ministry, to serve the race, and bear all the odium, the rebuke and contempt, which such a position and work would necessarily call forth from the high places of power and pride; for they who have been in honor here have not been those who have served, but those who have ruled. The servants—the men who have put their hands to toil—have always been the class to be despised and trampled on by the haughty sons of power. Christ knew well what His task would be when thus He condescended to be the woman's seed, and came under the law and the curse with us, to endure and suffer all—to refuse no duty or trial that His lot might demand, and meet every assault which the malice of hell could invent. We have been slow to concede this position fully to Christ—that He was *verily a man like ourselves*, with all our liabilities upon Him—"tempted in all points like as we are." We have allowed His divinity to hold Him above such real condescension, hardly conceiving that the Son of God could truly perform a human part, engaging in the great battle of life with us. Accordingly, we have failed in no slight degree to enter into this life of our Redeemer on earth, and realize that in very deed He did achive the victory—that He met the foe, and triumphed, prevailing by obedience as a perfect man, and that in our present circumstances. "Who in the days of his flesh, when he had offered up prayers and supplications with strong crying and tears unto him that was able to save him from death, and was heard in that" [in respect to that which] "he feared. Though he was a son" [on that account not liable to toil as a servant] "yet learned he obedience by the things which he suffered. And *being made perfect*, he became the author of eternal salvation unto all them that obey him ;" Heb. v. 7.

According to this view of the facts, Christ redeemed first His own humanity, by taking it out from under the curse, and carrying it beyond the power of death and the grave to its glorified state, where alone He was properly qualified to be a Saviour. While under the curse, and a servant himself, subject to the law, He was not in a condition to redeem ; or, in the language of the Apostle, "made perfect." He must pass out of this state of humiliation. He therefore redeemed our nature, as it were, in himself, taking it up to the right hand of power. "And now, O Father, glorify thou me with thine own self, with the glory which I had with thee before the world was ;" John xvii. 5. This prayer was for the exaltation of His human nature—that nature in which He had obeyed and suffered—which He had humbled himself to take, and made worthy of this exalted honor. The prayer, too, was answered. That man has been raised from the dead and glorified, all persons in heaven and earth being put into His hands.

In this way a perfect offering was prepared, free from every blemish, the Lamb of God which might take away sin.

Some claim that the end of Christ's mission was to set us an example. But this was merely incidental. The Scriptures never speak of it as the work which He came to fulfil. So neither was His great object to reveal the will of God. Others could have been inspired by the Holy Ghost to do this as fully as did Christ. Moses and Paul are as reliable for truth as He. It is an impeachment of God to assert that He could not have revealed all His will through such inspired men. But no other one was ever sent, or could be sent, to fulfil the whole law, and prevail against all the power of sin, so that God might bend over him with deepest joy, and say, "This is my beloved Son in whom I am well pleased." This honor forever and alone belongs to Jesus Christ. He is *the man* who has prevailed to conquer hell. Therefore is He the spotless lamb of God, upon whom the sins of the world may be laid.

II. *The next fact in the mediation of Christ is the death of the victim.*

The lamb selected for sacrifice was brought to the door of the tabernacle, and slain—which was done by the hands of sinners. So must the death of Christ be accomplished, and that by the hands of men who were the transgressors. We find Him thus speaking of His death, and the necessity of it, as no other man ever did. He refers to it as if it were the chief event of His life—the end which He kept in view, and at which He was aiming. The great object with men ordinarily is, to *live*. With Jesus, death seemed to be the goal toward which He was pressing. The prominence, however, which is thus given to His death is not to be understood as arising from the fact that this one event constituted the sole ground of the atonement; but simply, that this was the consummating act which crowned the whole. It is according to a common law of thought and language. We speak of our patriot soldiers as shedding their blood and giving their lives for their country. We thus specify this particular act because it is the greatest of all their sacrifices, but necessarily including the rest—their absence from home, their marches, wounds, imprisonment; their hunger, cold, and nakedness—in short, all their privations and sufferings. All these are summed up in the one fact that life itself is given. In like manner, the whole of Christ's humiliation and obedience entered into and formed a constituent part of His mediatorial work, making a basis for atonement. "God sent forth his Son, made of a woman, made under the law;" Gal. iv. 4—the moral law, the ritual law, the law of the curse, of toil, suffering, and death. "And being found in fashion as a man, he humbled himself, and became obedient unto death, even the death of the cross. Wherefore God also hath highly exalted him, and given him a name which is above every name;" Phil. ii. 8. Here the obedience of Christ is recognized as embracing every thing; and the completeness of that obedience is shown by the fact that it was even "unto death." It failed in no particular.

Into this mystery of His obedience and sufferings Christ labored to instruct His disciples—a task of extreme difficulty. They did not know that He was thus to be first under law, before He could be "made perfect" and enter His glorified state. They had no conception that the Messiah of Israel could be subject to death. When, however, the appointed hour came, He delivered himself into the hands of His exultant enemies without a show of resistance, and was led as a lamb to the slaughter. He meekly bowed to death, crying with His last breath, "It is finished." It was finished—the work of obedience and suffering. He had drained every bitter cup of sorrow. The Son of God had humbled himself even unto death. The Lamb had been slain.

III. *The next fact in this mediation of Christ is His priesthood.*

Christ's priesthood properly commenced with His resurrection, or His ascension to heaven, and His entrance there within the vail to make intercession for sinners. It has been common to consider the atonement as made by the death of Christ, and at the time of His decease; and the question has been here earnestly debated whether it was universal, or limited. But we have shown, in the preceding chapter, that the atonement was not made by the death of the victim at the door of the tabernacle, but by the priest, when he took the slain animal, and went in to present his blood before the Lord, thereby making intercession for the transgressor. That innocent blood in the hands of the priest, and presented by him, was the means of mediation. The blood was the life of the animal, and with this he made atonement. The death of Christ on the cross corresponded to that of the animal at the door of the tabernacle, which was accomplished by the hands of sinners. The atonement was not made until Christ entered the tabernacle, there to appear in behalf of the guilty, and intercede for them by blood. There must be found one qualified to go in behind the vail, and stand in the immediate Divine presence, where our Jesus accomplishes the work of His priesthood. This was not His work when suffering on the cross. There He was the victim slain. Herein is the peculiarity of Christ's mediatorship, that He unites in himself *the victim and the priest*, which could not be carried out in a typical priesthood. The two things must necessarily be separated there.

The fact of Christ's fulfilling both these offices is distinctly stated in the Epistle to the Hebrews, where the Apostle is discussing the meaning of the Old Testament types. "But Christ being come an high priest of good things to come by a greater and more perfect tabernacle not made with hands, that is to say, not of this building; neither by the blood of goats and calves, but by *his own blood, he entered in once into the holy place*, having obtained eternal redemption for us;" Heb. ix. 11. "For Christ is not entered into the holy places made with hands, which are the figures of the true: but into heaven itself, now to appear in the presence of God for us: nor yet that he should offer himself often, as the high priest entereth into the holy place every year with blood of others: for then must he often have suffered since the foundation of the world; but now once in the end of the world hath he appeared *to put away sin by the sacrifice of himself.* And as it is appointed unto men once to die, and after this the judgment: *so Christ was once offered to bear the sins of many;* and unto them that look for him shall he appear the second time without sin" [sin-offering] "unto salvation;" chap. ix. 24. "For it is not possible that the blood of bulls and goats should take away sins. Wherefore, when he cometh into the world, he saith, Sacrifice and offering thou wouldst not, but a body hast thou prepared me. In burnt-offerings and sacrifices for sin thou hast had no pleasure. Then said I, Lo, I come to do thy will, O God . . . By the which will we are sanctified through *the offering of the body of Jesus Christ once for all.* And every priest standeth daily ministering, and offering oftentimes the same sacrifices, which can never take away sins. But this man, after he had offered one sacrifice for sins forever, sat down on the right hand of God; from henceforth expecting till his enemies be made his footstool. For by one offering he hath perfected forever them that are sanctified;" chap. xi. 4. These passages are clear and unequivocal, describing Christ as the priest and the victim, entering in with His own blood to make intercession.

When, then, was, or, more properly, is the atonement made? Not until the priest enters within the tabernacle, to present the blood in the holy place before God, thereby obtaining forgiveness for the repenting sinner. The atonement is the work of the priest—his mediation with blood. It is not his prayers, nor entreaties, nor arguments. He offers none such. *He offers innocent blood,* which is his only plea for the guilty; and with that argument he prevails. God accepts this innocent blood as an atonement for the transgressor.

But when does Christ thus intercede, or make atonement for the sinner? Whenever that sinner humbly applies for His mediation, making confession of his sin. Christ is now officiating in the work of His priesthood; He is now within the vail in the most holy place, ready to make intercession—ready to undertake the cause of every penitent, believing sinner, even as the priest of old was at the door of the tabernacle in his appointed place, to meet every applicant who brought his victim to have atonement made for his soul. So the lamb has been slain which can suffice to take away the sins of the world. It now remains for the sinner to accept this as his sacrifice—to apply to Christ as his high-priest, and, with humble faith and confession of his sin, ask His intercession. According to these facts, the work of atonement is now being accomplished. Christ is fulfilling His priesthood, ever living to make intercession for us. His mediation or intercession is by atonement. He prevails to obtain forgiveness and justification only by presenting His own blood as our defense, while we secure His interests for us by faith.

This view of the subject avoids all the controversy respecting the extent of the atonement, whether it is universal or limited. That controversy need never have been started, and never would have been, if the facts had been understood. Of course, Christ intercedes only for those who apply in humble faith to Him, and accept His blood of innocence, shed as the ransom for their guilty souls. But here is a lamb which taketh away the sin of the world; and every sinner may avail himself thereof to his eternal salvation. In this light the apostles present the subject. They represent that Christ is now officiating in the great work of His priesthood; and the Bible knows of no mediation or intercession for sinners except by blood. "Who shall lay any thing to the charge of God's elect? It is God that justifieth. Who is he, that condemneth? It is

Christ that died, yea, rather, *that is risen again, who is even at the right hand of God, who also maketh intercession for us;*" Rom. viii. 33. "But this man, because he continueth ever, hath an unchangeable priesthood. Wherefore he is able also to save them to the uttermost *that come unto God by him, seeing he ever liveth to make intercession for us;*" Heb. vii. 24. "And if any man sin, we have an Advocate with the Father, Jesus Christ the righteous. And he is the propitiation for our sins; and not for ours only, but also for the sins of the whole world;" 1 John ii. 1. Christ, then, is our Advocate with the Father—that is, our High-Priest or Mediator, who pleads our cause; and not only so, He is our propitiation also—that is, the offering by which propitiation is made for our sins. He is the victim whose blood is shed, and of such wondrous efficacy, that it can take away the sins of the entire world. Yet it does not avail to any sinner until by faith he applies to this Advocate, and thus secures His intercession. He saves to the uttermost "them that come unto God by him;" but He, as plainly, does not mediate for such as do not come.

This gives a clear and consistent view throughout of Christ's first mission to earth, and the work which He is now carrying forward, in the accomplishment of His priesthood. He prepared himself first as the spotless lamb for an offering, and then was led to the slaughter without a murmuring word, being made sin for us. But this victim slain was to be the priest also, to go within the sanctuary, taking His own blood wherewith to make atonement. He was therefore raised from the dead, and, after remaining a sufficient time to furnish the demonstration of that fact to enable His disciples to bear witness to the same, He ascended on high, entering within the vail to perform His priestly office in pleading for all who will come unto God by Him.

This subject shows us what an everlasting foundation is laid for the work of redemption, and the sanctification of a chosen people unto the Lord.

The first work to be performed by the woman's seed in order to His triumph over the foe, was to make a sin-offering, and be constituted a priest or Mediator, by whom forgiveness and justification could be obtained. To this end, He appeared first to fulfil all righteousness. But in this character He was not known or recognized, notwithstanding all the evidences He gave of His divine mission; and for the reason that men were looking for Him as a King, not as a victim for sacrifice—as one to make law, not to be under it himself as a servant. So they turned away and hid their faces from Him. These, however, were the first prophecies to be fulfilled. In order to forgiveness, there must be blood shed. In order to reconciliation with Heaven, there must be a Mediator appointed. In order to the justification of the guilty, there must be atonement made. In this way was a holy people to be prepared for the Lord, even as Israel must first be sanctified, and have intercession made for them by blood, before they could be accepted as a people unto God. So, by faith in this one living Mediator, were sinners to be restored to the Divine favor. They could never come to plead their own cause, for they could obtain no entrance to the presence of God in their defilement, neither could they present any plea which could avail in the least for their justification. They could only confess their iniquity, and desert of just condemnation. But a Mediator appointed of heaven might make a plea in their behalf: and that, His own blood freely poured out.

This subject also shows *how admirably God prepared the way for the coming of Christ, and instructed the race in the great doctrine of a sin-offering and mediatorship.*

For long centuries did altars stream with innocent

blood, and transgressors lay their hands upon the heads of their substituted victims, and mediators go in to plead before the Lord, and make atonement for their souls. Long were the generations of men trained to the idea that without the shedding of innocent blood there was no remission; and that they, in their pollution and guilt, could not enter into the sanctuary of the Divine presence to obtain audience. None but a consecrated, appointed Mediator could enter there.

At length, too, appeared the One constituted a priest forever—the one ever-living Mediator with God, who had authority and was sanctified to enter the sanctuary above to plead for sinners; not with the blood of goats and calves, but with His own precious blood—His effectual plea His own obedience and sufferings. With these He undertook the mighty work of mediation. This doctrine of mediatorship is thus the central truth of the system of redemption. There is no way to God except by Christ—not Christ as a teacher, not Christ as an example, but Christ as a *Mediator*. No sinner can know Christ truly, until he knows Him as his High-Priest to make atonement for him—his Advocate to intercede. Neither does Christ plead for any but those who ask His mediation, and rely thereon—those who make humble confession of their sin, and accept Him as their only Advocate before the throne, having no righteousness or plea of their own. And blessed forever be His name, He rejects no sinner who will come, however numerous his sins, however aggravated his guilt. "Him that cometh to me I will in no wise cast out." Sinner, will you come?

CHAPTER XXIX.

CHRIST A SIN-OFFERING.

JESUS CHRIST is the grand living problem of the age —the problem of all the ages; and the great question concerning Him is, What were the end and meaning of His life? What of His death? Did His life and death sustain the same relations, and accomplish the same ends in Divine providence with the lives and death of other men? The Scriptures must decide these questions, and they alone must be the arbiters in the case.

It is evident enough that the nation failed to understand this subject aright, and so fearfully failed that they crucified the Lord of life. They continue, too, to crucify Him to this day, spitting upon His name and all His pretensions. The disciples, also, much as they loved and trusted in their Master, failed to understand the matter, until after His resurrection, when their minds were opened to see the wonderful relations of this subject, and take in the grand designs of heaven in the mission of Jesus. He had told them before of His approaching death, and sought to prepare their minds for the event; but it was not until after His resurrection that He attempted to explain its end and relations. On the first occasion that He met them all together, after His crucifixion and return from the grave, He said unto them, "These are the words which I spake unto you, while I was yet with you, that all things must be fulfilled, which were written in the law of Moses, and in the prophets, and in the Psalms, concerning me. Then opened he their understandings, that they might understand the Scriptures; and said unto them, Thus it is written, and thus it behooved Christ to suffer, and to rise from the dead on the third day: and that repentance and remission of sins should be preached in his name among all nations, beginning at Jerusalem;" Luke xxiv. 44. Here we have Christ's own authoritative explanation of His mission to earth—the design of His sufferings and death, even as it had been written of Him in all the Scriptures from the time of Moses, and as it behooved Him that He should suffer, and rise from the dead. What, then, is this explanation thus given by Jesus himself—the doctrine *of repentance and remission of sins in His name?*

Does it mean that He simply brought down to the world and taught the doctrine of repentance and remission of sins, and the love of God in the bestowment of such mercy?

Many assert this, claiming that this is the sum and substance of the doctrine of Christ. They tell us that He brought down the love of God to this ruined world, revealing the grand truth of the remission of sins.

But who, that has learned even the alphabet of Christianity, does not know that this doctrine of the love of God toward men, and the remission of sins, is as old as the Bible, going back to the very beginning of all Divine revelation—that it is found upon every page of the Old Testament, and belongs to the simplest elements of a gracious economy toward a world of sinners—yea, is embraced in the very conception of a remedial system? God held out the sceptre of love and mercy to a sinning world from the moment that He established His covenant of grace with man, and announced the coming of that seed of the woman who should bruise the serpent's head and accomplish the work of deliverance; while the streaming blood from every altar of sacrifice through four thousand years was a faithful witness for God that He was merciful and gracious, slow unto wrath, abundant in pardons, and could be sought unto in hope by every humble believing soul. Is it to be insinuated that patriarchs, prophets, and righteous men of old from the days of the martyr Abel, were ignorant of the doctrine of Divine love—love that would reach unto the forgiveness of sins? Is it to be insinuated, and are we to be told, that God never proclaimed himself, until the coming of Jesus, "The Lord, the Lord God, merciful and gracious, long-suffering, and abundant in goodness and truth, keeping mercy for thousands, forgiving iniquity, transgression, and sin?" Exod. xxxiv. 6. What, we may well ask, is the Old Testament worth, as a revelation from heaven, if it does not tell us of the love and mercy of God to sinners, and that He can be sought unto by them, that they may receive the forgiveness of sins? Where is any religion to be found in those Scriptures, any piety, any faith, if men were ignorant of these first elements of all religion for a world of sinners? Yet there are those who would make us believe that this was the great truth that Jesus Christ brought down from above, it being the end of His life and death to reveal this grand mystery. Away with such ignorance and folly. The man is not fit to be an expounder of this Christianity, who has no deeper insight into its meaning than this. Every prophet that was ever sent from heaven preached of the love of God, of repentance, and faith, and remission of sins. They were proclaimed from the very beginning, before that man was driven from paradise; and upon these elementary principles this entire Divine economy has been built. A remedial system never could have been introduced, without a revelation of the love of God and the doctrine of the remission of sins.

If Jesus Christ, then, taught nothing beyond these elementary facts, which had been taught by all preceding prophets, His mission was a failure. He need not have come from heaven to begin again the revelation of a system under which God had already been training the race for four thousand years. He need not have come to teach the alphabet of a religion which had been taught through long ages from the times of Abel, Enoch, Noah, Abraham, and Moses. And they utterly fail to comprehend the mission of Christ, who do not discern therein any thing beyond this. None, indeed, may question that Jesus Christ came to make a great advance upon all God's previous revelations. His mission changed the whole aspect of affairs, terminating that ancient economy under which God had unfolded himself so wondrously to His people of old, redeeming them out of Egypt by a mighty hand, and abiding among them by His own visible presence. Glorious as was that former dispensation, it was all eclipsed by the brighter effulgence of that new dispensation introduced by Christ, even as the rising sun hides every bright star in night's magnificent canopy. And yet, there are those who would now begin this grand dispensation of the rising sun of righteousness at the very point where God began His older dispensation of the night. "The evening and the morning were the first day." It is time that the world had learned that "the evening" is past, and that the day has dawned.

Does any one either suppose that the simple preaching by the apostles of the love of God, of repentance and remission of sins, would have produced any disturbance in Jerusalem, or excited any opposition and alarm? Could this have aroused the nation to frenzy, causing the rulers to rage and blaspheme against God and the Holy Ghost, until they filled up the cup of their iniquity, and brought on swiftly the dreadful day of their desolation? Surely, we need to find some more adequate cause, some newer and more profound truth than this involved in the doctrine of Jesus, thus to fire the nation to madness, and convulse it to its deepest foundations, causing them to be driven out from their inheritance, a hissing and byword to the ends of the earth.

What, then, was the new doctrine of Jesus?

This will be seen by marking more particularly His words as spoken to the disciples, in explanation after His resurrection. "And that repentance and remission of sins should be preached in his name among all nations, beginning at Jerusalem." *In His name.* There was the marrow of the doctrine. Remission of sins in His name. For His sake—He himself being the primal cause and ground of the same to every man to earth's remotest bound, and until time should end. Every sinner was to owe his pardon and justification directly and immediately to Him. In His name the remission of sins was to be offered—in His name it was ever to be sought and obtained, while there was a sinner to be forgiven and saved; and none other plea was to be of slightest avail to any.

And did Jesus claim that no sinner could ever obtain the remission of his sins, and stand in covenant relation with God, except in His name, and by virtue of what He had done? This, then, was a new doctrine indeed, in advance of the dispensation going before. The rulers and the nation verily did not understand that they were to be indebted for their justification, in the sight of heaven, solely to the Nazarene—His merits and work being the only ground of their defense, the only basis of their standing before God. It was no wonder that Scribe and Pharisee and chief priest raged against such a doctrine, even to madness. They had crucified the Nazarene as the wicked subverter of their faith—the enemy of their law. And now to be told that through Him alone, and in His name, they could stand in covenant with God and be counted the children of Abraham—well might they be filled with wrath, and blaspheme even against the Holy Ghost.

But mark another fact. *It was only this doctrine that could ever reconcile the mind of a Jew to accept the fact of the death and crucifixion of his Messiah.*

Deny this relation of Jesus' death, and then let any tell how it was that Jesus, as the Messiah of Israel, was delivered over to this destroyer.

Death is the sentence of God against sinners, and the demonstration that they are such. It is the curse under which this world lies because of sin. "Death hath passed upon all men, because that all have sinned." Subjection to this curse is conclusive evidence against any one that he belongs to an apostate, sinful race. This, also, was one of the mighty foes from which the promised One was to deliver our groaning earth—the last enemy that was to be put under His feet—enabling the ransomed ones to sing that song of triumph, "O death, where is thy sting? O grave, where is thy victory?" This was the last stronghold of the powers of darkness to be carried by our great Immanuel.

Did Jesus now fall before this enemy? Then He, too, was a transgressor, as others, and under the same condemnation. Death passed upon Him, because He, too, was a sinner. Heaven's dread curse was upon Him—the curse which sin brought. Not, indeed, that He was necessarily guilty of the particular crimes alledged by the rulers. But His death proved unanswerably that He was liable to the same condemnation under which the whole race lies. Nor did Heaven interpose for His rescue, but gave Him into the hands of the destroyer. That argument, too, was, for the time being, conclusive. None could reply, or rebut the terrible testimony. Death, in all the past history of the world hitherto, had been the final arbiter, from which there was no appeal. It was the stern, unalterable decision of Heaven against a sinning race.

How, now, is the character of Jesus to be vindicated from that condemnation? How is it to be proved that He was not a sinner like other men, going down to the grave, because He was such as the rulers asserted? If, moreover, He was an innocent, spotless one, how are the Divine character and government to be vindicated, in suffering the powers of darkness to prevail against Him, and not lifting a finger for His rescue? Is this the way that heaven can be relied on to defend the cause of innocence and right? This the way it stands by its own to vindicate their cause, and bring the power of its sublime sovereignty for their defense and support? What is God's government worth—what confidence can be placed in it, if it will not, to the last moment, and the utmost of its resources, stand up for innocence, protecting its own, and never give him up to the howling beasts of prey to tear and devour? If it will not do this, I cannot trust it. Nor can any other man. Its integrity is gone, and every ground of faith in it, as a righteous government, is destroyed. The argument of the Jewish rulers at this point was a valid one beyond doubt or denial. They said, "If he be the king of Israel, let him now come down from the cross, and we will believe him. He trusted in God." Yes, He said that He was the well beloved, the chosen of God, doing all His Father's will, in whom no sin had ever been found, and, as such, He committed His cause to the righteous vindication of heaven. He boasted that His trust was in God, who would never forsake Him, but would deliver His darling from the power of the dog. "Let him, then, now deliver him, if he will have him; for he said, I am the Son of God." But heaven did not come to the rescue. There was no interposition, no hand stretched out for His deliverance. God appeared of old for the rescue of His chosen sons; and, to accomplish it, arose upon Egypt in the might of his wrath, and made it a desolation, until the wailing cry of agony went up from every habitation to the farthest limits of the land, and until proud Pharoah and his princes, his chariots, and horsemen, were all buried deep at the bottom of the Red Sea. Yet when Jesus made His appeal to heaven, there was no answer, no interposition. He was abandoned to His fate, and yielded up the ghost, the agonizing words falling from His dying lips, "My God, my God, why hast thou forsaken me?"

Upon what ground, then, will you place the vindication of Jesus? How is His name to be rescued from the deep ignominy of that death, and the grave? How was a dying man ever to be offered to a Jew, to be accepted as his messiah, hope, and deliverer?

There is no explanation of this, except on the one ground that He was made sin for us, our iniquities being laid upon Him, He being delivered the just for the unjust. If He was not a sinner himself, bearing His own sins, then He bore ours. We must accept one or other of these positions, or abandon all faith in the integrity of the Divine government. There is no escape here; and those who deny that Jesus was made a sin-offering to bear the iniquities of others, are inevitably forced by the stern logic of the facts to the position, that He was a sinner himself, bearing the curse, as we do, for His own transgressions. We insist that this is the only alternative, that one or the other of these positions must be accepted. Death, here, is a terrible reasoner, aud there is no escape from his inexorable argument. His witness lies against Jesus in all the fearfulness of his condemning power.

We accept now for ourselves the solution which the Scriptures give of that death. We maintain that He was still the Holy and Just One, the well beloved of heaven, upon whom our sins were laid. Let those who choose, deny this, accepting the only other solution, that Jesus was a transgressor like other men, belonging to an apostate race, and therefore coming under the same curse with them, and sharing their condemnation. The former solution is the one which Jesus himself gave after His resurrection, and which the disciples joyfully accepted, "That repentance and remission of sins should be preached in his name among all nations, beginning at Jerusalem." When this grand solution of the death and humiliation of their Master was presented, their minds being opened to understand the Scriptures and see that it behooved Christ thus to suffer, and to rise from the dead on the third day, that repentance and remission of sins might be preached in His name, they sprang at once from the depths of despair to the highest pitch of enthusiasm, wonder, and joy. They were no longer cast down by the death of their Jesus. They were not ashamed of His sepulchre—not even of His cross. They could now stand up in Jerusalem, within the sacred court of the temple—under the very shadow of the Sanhedrim, and proclaim their faith still in the Nazarene, that He was the looked-for Messiah and Deliverer. They could boldly declare and prove that He was not a transgressor, whom Heaven had forsaken and disowned; but that He was the anointed One from the bosom of the Father, who was delivered for our offences, being the Lamb slain which taketh away the sins of the world, through whom alone is the remission of sins and eternal life. Here is the precious blood in which the new covenant is ratified forever. Here is the door by which every sinner must find entrance into the kingdom. There was power here. It was a new doctrine, which demanded the mission of the Lord from heaven to unfold—which no prophet before had ever made the mighty burden of his discourse, except as he looked forward to and anticipated this day of Christ. Nor were the disciples now afraid or ashamed—although, at first, they timidly assembled in an upper room, and locked themselves in for fear of the Jews—to stand up before their nation—before Scribe and Pharisee, Priest and Rabbi, and demand their faith in this Crucified, as the One whom God had raised up and anointed to be their Deliverer and hope.

But, aside from this, the doctrine of a dying Messiah was one of infamy. It was an absurdity that no sane man could accept or believe in. It was an insult to any man to offer such a Messiah to his faith; for it was nothing else than presenting before him a sinner, no different from the rest of the race, who could not deliver his own soul, but must bear his own iniquity, and go down to the grave accursed. The doctrine was full of stupidity, and could never have been started in Jerusalem. It never could have found an advocate, never a convert.

But there was power, yea, the omnipotence of heaven, in the doctrine of the remission of sins *in his name*—Christ a sin-offering—the Lamb slain from the foundation of the world—God so loving the world as to give His only begotten Son, that whosoever believeth in him should not perish, but have everlasting life. It electrified Jerusalem, heaving its population as under the treadings of an earthquake. It sent home awful conviction of guilt to the minds of that nation; for they had condemned to death, and crucified, not a vile sinner, as they in their blindness and wicked folly imagined, but the Son of God himself, the very Lord from heaven. And no wonder that they cried out in the sore agony of their minds, "Men and brethren, what shall we do?" while the answering response of Peter was, "Repent, and be baptized, every one of you, in the name of Jesus Christ for the remission of sins." This was the doctrine accepted by the converts to this faith. It was reliance on Jesus, the crucified, for the remission of sins—justification by His blood. It was a new doctrine, bringing in a new dispensation, against which the rulers raged and blasphemed to their own eternal confusion and overthrow. It was a stumbling-block to the Jew, and well it might be, if he did not see therein, as, of course, he did not, the doctrine of a sin-offering. "This was the stone set at nought of the builders, which is become the head stone of the corner; neither is there salvation in any other: for there is none other name given under heaven among men, whereby we must be saved;" Acts iv. 11.

The facts thus brought to view show us that the doctrine of the Bible respecting Christ is clear and unequivocal, so that there need be no controversy among those who admit that He was the Anointed One of heaven.

There is no ambiguity in the Bible on this great subject. God has not left this vital doctrine in doubt, nor any room for question respecting it. We speak strongly here, and we have a right to. We mean to say that the facts are plain and undeniable, so that a wayfaring man, though a fool, need not err therein. We assert that there are only two sides to the question respecting Jesus—the same precisely that were maintained and fought out to the terrible issue by the apostles and the Jewish rulers—one maintaining that Jesus was a sinner himself, who bore the burden of His own iniquity; the other maintaining that He was the Holy and Just One from heaven, who bore the sins of the world, and through whom we have pardon and eternal redemption. It was on this ground that the great and decisive battle of Christianity was fought out in the days of the apostles. There was none other. When those men preached the resurrection of Jesus, the reply of the enraged rulers was: Ye "intend to bring this man's blood upon us," as if we had been guilty of putting a righteous man to death. The answer was, "The God of our fathers raised up Jesus, whom ye slew and hanged on a tree. Him hath God exalted with his right hand to be a Prince and a Saviour, for to give repentance to Israel, and the forgiveness of sins. And we are his witnesses of these things, and so is also the Holy Ghost, whom God hath given to them that obey him;" Acts v. 30. The only question here at issue was, whether Jesus was a sinner himself, or the Anointed spotless One of God. That was the point to be settled. We accept the doctrine of the apostles, that He was raised up "for to give repentance to Israel, and the forgiveness of sins," being delivered for our offences. Let those who will, take the other, and bear the responsibility which the Jewish rulers assumed, when they gave Him to death as a transgressor who was not worthy to live.

The modern doctrine concerning Christ, which denies Him to be a sin-offering, and yet claims Him as the world's Saviour and hope, is one that really stultifies its adherents. It holds up as a great deliverer one whom Heaven disowned, and demonstrated to be a sinner, even as others of the race, by His subjection to the curse; while it scornfully rejects the only possible vindication that could be made in His behalf, that He was delivered for our offences. The first thing demanded of Jesus, after passing under the power of death, was His own complete vindication—the demonstration that He was not a sinner; and then the explanation of the mystery how He, if free from all sin, was subjected to the curse of sin. The Scriptures place that vindication in His resurrection, by which He was powerfully declared to be the Son of God; while the satisfactory explanation of His death was, that He was made a propitiation for us, our iniquities being laid upon Him, so that with His stripes we are healed. There is, there can be no other explanation of His death under the government of God, except that of being a transgressor himself. Let us not, then, be insulted by the offer of one, as a Saviour, in whom we are to trust our eternal all, who could not even save himself from death and the curse, He appealing to heaven in vain for help, and admitting, with His own dying breath, that He was forsaken of God as surely He was of men—while His own vindication of himself, that He was made sin for us, is scornfully rejected.

Is it not time, then, that this controversy about the object of Jesus' mission to earth, and the nature of His work, were ended? Time that those who accept and love the great doctrine of the shedding of blood for the remission of sins, understood that the question respecting the Man of Nazareth was narrowed down to the single point, whether He formed a constituent part of a fallen race, against which the curse justly lies, or was delivered for our offences, the just for the unjust? Is it not time that the matter were settled, that there is no ground for any man to have the slightest faith in Jesus who denies His having been made a sin-offering; and that the doctrine of the Bible on this point is plain beyond all controversy or denial? Is it not time that the Church of God took shame to herself that she has been so blinded to the facts of the case in the death of her Lord, and allowed the enemy to cast insult upon her by offering one as a Saviour who could not save His own soul from death, and for whom Heaven would make no interposition? We think the time has come for it to be conceded that the Bible is a plain book, which was meant to be understood, and that there is no necessity for this endless controversy respecting its teachings. The Word of God should not be a continual reproach to its Author, in being a Sybilline oracle that may mean any thing or nothing, as may suit those who consult its shrine. The Bible is not ambiguous. The great truths which it was given to make plain are not left in doubt. The fact of Christ being made a sin-offering can be established with the certainty of a mathematical demonstration; and the enemies of this doctrine should be pushed to the wall by the stern alternative, either this, or the doctrine that Jesus was a transgressor himself, falling under the curse like other men.

Regarding Christ, too, as a sin-offering, we may then understand how Jesus brought down the love of God to men as never it had been before. "Herein is love, not that we loved God, but that He loved us, and *sent His Son to be the propitiation for our* sins;" 1 John iv. 10. This was a new unfolding of the Divine love, as only such a mission of the Son of God from the bosom of the Father could have brought to light. Even now an unbelieving world can scarce accept the fact that heaven was equal to such an amazing sacrifice as this. It does exceed all human thought. "As high as the heavens are above the earth, so far are God's thoughts above our thoughts, and his ways above our ways." And nothing short of such a mission as that of the Son of God could ever have demonstrated the fact, or convinced men that the Divine love reached to a height and depth like this. That mission, therefore, formed a new era in the Divine purposes of mercy, bringing in a brighter day to earth, and commencing a new period in its history.

CHAPTER XXX.

ATONEMENT AND JUSTIFICATION.

In connection with the doctrine of the priesthood, it remains to consider more particularly *the nature of an atonement for sin.*

The term "atonement" was formerly used in the sense of agreement or reconciliation between parties offended. With this meaning, the preposition "between" is employed as above. When, however, we use the preposition "for," as making atonement for sin, it then means, as defined by Webster, "expiation; satisfaction or reparation made by giving an equivalent for an injury, or by doing or suffering that which is received in satisfaction for an offence or injury." Expiation, the same lexicographer defines as follows: "The act of atoning for a crime; the act of making satisfaction for an offence, by which the guilt is done away, and the obligation of the offended party to punish the crime is cancelled. . . . Among Pagans and Jews, expiation was made chiefly by sacrifices. Among Christians, expiation for sins of men is usually considered as made by the obedience and sufferings of Christ." This is decisive authority as to the meaning of terms.

Moreover, the idea of atonement or expiation for sin is deeply laid in the constitution of the human mind; and a religion for this world of sinners, which does not furnish this conception, meeting this necessity of our nature, is worthless. It can never abide, or satisfy the wants of the soul. This is the grand idea which almost every religion from the beginning has aimed to meet—the furnishing of an adequate expiation for the sins of men, through which the justice of the Divine government might be maintained, while iniquity is forgiven. The solemn question ever rising from the depths of the human soul in the consciousness of its sin and ill-desert, has been: "Wherewith shall I come before the Lord, and bow myself before the high God? Shall I come before him with burnt-offerings, with calves of a year old? Will the Lord be pleased with thousands of rams, or with ten thousands of rivers of oil? Shall I bring my first-born for my transgression, the fruit of my body for the sin of my soul?" Micah vi. 6. These questions have meaning. They stir the profoundest depths of our nature; nor can the soul ever be satisfied until they are answered.

The Apostle also, in the clearest terms, presents this idea of atonement or expiation, as the specific one which constitutes the doctrine of redemption by Christ. "Being justified freely by his grace through the redemption that is in Christ Jesus, whom God hath set forth to be a propitiation" [an expiatory offering] "through faith in his blood, to declare his righteousness for the remission of sins that are past, through the forbearance of God; to declare, I say, at this time his righteousness, that he might be just, and the justifier of him that believeth in Jesus;" Rom. iii. 24. This statement of the atonement is as definite and complete as language can make it. Christ was set forth as a propitiatory offering, to declare God's righteousness in the remission of sins; or, stated in another form, that God might be just in justifying the sinner who believes in Jesus. This clear and unambiguous statement settles the question as to the relation of the death of Christ in the intent and meaning of the Scriptures. Men may still dispute, if so inclined, whether their teachings are to be received. But as to what those teachings are, and what significance they attach to the death of Jesus, there need be no question. It was to declare God's righteousness in the forgiveness of sins, so that "he might be just, and the justifier of him that believeth in Jesus." No theological statement of the doctrine of the atonement could be clearer; and that is Bible truth. Men may reject the Scriptures because such doctrine is found in them. But God himself could not have given a revelation to the world, in which the doctrine of the expiation and forgiveness of sin by the shedding of innocent blood could have been more clearly set forth. If the Bible, therefore, does not teach it, it could not have been revealed by any method.

The necessity for such an atonement is laid in the eternal principles of truth and justice, which are ever embodied in righteous law, and every true government.

It must ever be a deep problem in government, most difficult of solution, and most dangerous to be tampered with: How can crime and treason be forgiven? How can the righteous penalty affixed by law to transgression be remitted, and the criminal restored to good standing, without endangering the stability of the government, and all the best interests of society?

In the definition given by Webster of expiation, it is said to be "the act of making satisfaction for an offence, by which the guilt is done away, and *the obligation of the offended party to punish the crime is cancelled.*" If an atonement does this, it accomplishes all that can be required; the great ends of law and justice are met, and the way is open not merely for the pardon, but the *justification* of the transgressor. An atonement becomes thus a substitute for the penalty, answering all the high ends which it has in view, being a satisfaction rendered to justice. He, too, who has a clear understanding of what penalty is, what its nature and end are, can have no question as to the necessity of an expiation made for sin in a perfect government, when the transgressor is released from punishment. Law requires penalty, and can have no existence without it. No man can ever properly issue a command without having something by which to enforce and make it good to every jot and tittle. Penalty is that thing—the infliction of suffering or evil which sustains authority, and maintains the supremacy of government. Advice cannot be enforced. It may be followed or not, at the pleasure of him to whom it is given. But law is *command.* It comes with authority;

and for the reason that there is power behind to make it respected by bringing every offender to condign punishment. We say, offender; for such he is who transgresses law—a guilty man—guilty in his own eyes—guilty in the eyes of the community for whose protection the law was made—guilty in the eyes of the rulers who are set for the defence and maintenance of law. This sense of guiltiness and obligation to punishment show, beyond all question, what the necessity for that punishment is; and that its infliction is the only means of maintaining the supremacy of law. Let crime go unpunished and there is an end of government. Law is prostrate in the dust, and wickedness supreme. Nor can imagination conceive what such a triumph of sin would be in the universe of God. It would be infinitely worse than hell itself, inasmuch as hell is the triumph of law and justice over the wicked; while the overthrow of law would be the triumph of the wicked over God and the universe.

Penalty, then, is the power which guards the throne—that by which the lawgiver maintains his authority in spite of all the wicked opposition which may be arrayed against it. His is the everlasting right to punish, ac knowledged by the guilty parties themselves. They own their sentence just, and dread their righteous doom.

The highest and most sacred of all duties, too, is that which rests upon a ruler to maintain this integrity and supremacy of law. To his hands are intrusted interests such as are committed to none else. A great crime may be committed by one who violates law—a crime which may demand death as its only just punishment. But crime does not destroy government—does not impair it in the least. It may only be the occasion on which its integrity, its righteousness, and its power shall shine forth with new radiance, awakening the admiration and joy of every true heart If that government is true to itself, dealing with iniquity according to its deserts, no evil can befall it. Government is destroyed when its own appointed guardians prove false to their trust, and, through weakness or want of integrity on their own part, fail to execute its high sanctions, and maintain its supremacy. Then the highest crime is committed; for in the overthrow of law, justice, and government, all is lost; and such a government ought to be blotted out of existence. The death penalty ought to be executed against it; for it is not fit to live. The universe cries out against it, as the greatest of all criminals, and demands its overthrow.

We may see also here, at this point, the folly and madness of that philosophy and theology, which makes the great end aimed at in the penalty of law, to be the good of the offender; and punishment a disciplinary process designed for his reformation. It is an utterly false view of the whole nature of penalty, and would subvert any government under heaven, or in it. The primary end of *penalty* is the maintenance of law, the protection of government, the establishment of the authority of the lawgiver. It is that by which he makes his will respected and authoritative. It says to the disobedient, "Thou shalt surely die;" and its language is *wrath*, wrath only—wrath forever. The first duty of a government is that which it owes to itself—its first law that of self-preservation. It is bound to maintain its own existence, because it is the supreme interest, paramount over all, and involving all others. The penalty now is that by which the lawgiver does assert his supremacy and the integrity of his government against every wicked offender rising up against them—by which he vindicates his authority, and makes his law respected. The punishment, too, required, is just that which is necessary to secure this end, whatever it be. If the death of the transgressor is necessary, then death must be inflicted.

His good is not an element now to be brought into consideration. He has forfeited all his rights as an obedient subject, and the one simple question is, What are the sufferings necessary on his part to vindicate the majesty of the law, and reassert its violated integrity? This is the one sole end of penalty, and by this is the degree of punishment to be determined. *The law never contemplates the reformation of the criminal—never provides any means to that end.* This end may be aimed at from other quarters and through other channels; but *penalty* never contemplates it. When a criminal is sentenced by a judge at the bar, he is never sentenced *to be reformed*, or to have any means employed for his reformation. He is sentenced to be punished. And that punishment, whatever it be, is evil inflicted—wrath—wrath only—wrath to the end. It never changes its character. Reformatory influences may be brought to bear upon that criminal; but the penalty does not provide them. When a man is sentenced to the Penitentiary, it is *to hard labor or confinement* within its walls; not to be taught in a Sabbath school, or to listen to preaching, or to read good books. These are no part of the punishment of his crime. The judge does not sentence him to these. The law does not contemplate these, or provide them. The law, the judge, and the penalty, have only to do with the infliction of evil. With that their province begins and ends; and if any good comes to that guilty man, it cannot come through them. They were never designed to be the channel of good to the violator of law, but only evil.

The fatal mistake made on this subject, is in confounding a gracious and a legal system together—one, contemplating the punishment of the transgressor; the other, his reformation and pardon. God's system over this world, since the entrance of sin, has been a gracious or remedial one, framed with a view to redemption, and administered wholly on the principles belonging to such a system. He did not execute the law against our first parents in dooming them to death for their disobedience, but announced to them at once that He would provide a Deliverer, through whom they might be justified and saved. The legal system, therefore, was suspended, to introduce this economy of grace. In the same way the family is administered as a gracious, and not a legal system, patterned after the Divine economy in this world. Under these gracious systems, discipline is exercised with a view to the reformation and good of the offender. That is the end of the entire plan. But to confound this with a proper legal administration, is a sad and fatal error, subversive of all law and government.

The great question now involved in the atonement is, upon what ground God could, as a righteous moral governor, set aside for the time being a perfect legal system, to introduce a gracious or remedial one. This question, of course, has no force to the man who does not distinguish between the two systems, and utterly confounds them by the fatal dogma that the end of law and penalty is the reformation of the guilty—in other words, that a legal system, or the administration of justice, is a gracious one; and that God seeks to pardon and save the sinner through the infliction of punishment. The Bible is not guilty of revealing such nonsense and falsehood. It assumes that men know what law and punishment are, and what it is to deserve death, standing guilty and condemned before a holy God, bound to maintain forever His own authority and the integrity of His government.

JUSTIFICATION.

At this point we are met by the fact that the Bible treats of justification as its grand, leading theme—a fact which no one will deny The subjects discussed in it are of a legal nature, involving obedience and transgression —righteousness and wickedness—reward and punishment —pardon and acceptance with God—justification and condemnation—eternal life and eternal death. These are the questions connected with law and moral government; and the one theme treated in the Scriptures, which may be said to embrace all these, is that of *justification*. This covers the whole field.

Another fact equally unquestioned is, that the Bible treats of the justification *of sinners, the ungodly*, undertaking to reveal a peculiar plan by which such a result can be effected. The Scriptures take the broad ground that there are none other than sinners in this world—that "there is none righteous; no, not one; they are all gone out of the way." If God justifies any, then, it must be transgressors, deserving of condemnation. Such, too, is the fact—a fact which demands especial attention.

No book in the world insists so strongly upon integrity, truth, right, and justice in all their relations, as the Word of God. It claims throughout to abhor wickedness, to oppose it at every point, and to love and approve only righteousness and truth. "*He that justifieth the wicked, and he that condemneth the just, even they both are an abomination to the Lord;*" Prov. xvii. 15. What is said here of the Lord, too, is true also of man. Such perversion of truth and justice is abomination in the eye of God and man. Let a judge upon the bench, who is set for the maintenance of justice and the vindication of the right, throw himself on the side of the wrong, prostituting his sacred office to the defense of crime, so that the guilty shall escape and the righteous be condemned—so that the wicked shall look to him as their protector, and the innocent regard him as their worst enemy, and where is the vile criminal that is a greater abomination in the sight of heaven and earth than he, or more deserving of the severest retributions of justice? Or let any one attempt to justify the wrong-doer, and we as instantly condemn him as the very author of the sin himself. He who justifies the wicked, shows plainly his own sympathy with the wickedness, and that he would not hesitate to put his hand to the deed of evil, if only the opportunity were presented.

But what is justification?

It is a legal term, and represents that act by which one is shown, or pronounced, to be right in law or equity, so that he stands acquitted, the law having no claims against him. The ground of such justification, in all ordinary cases, must of necessity be the innocence of the party. He is justified by being proved to be righteous or just; while condemnation follows necessarily upon the proof of guilt. If, however, a wicked man, deserving of condemnation and punishment, is justified, it is still his vindication. He is pronounced to stand right before the law, and placed under its protection so as to enjoy all its immunities as an obedient subject. It is, therefore, putting a guilty man in the place of a righteous one to receive his deserts; while to condemn a righteous man, is to treat him as if he had committed a crime, and doom him to punishment. Such justification of the wicked, and condemnation of the righteous, are both alike abomination in the eye of God and man.

It is now an undeniable fact, lying upon the whole surface of Divine revelation, that *God justifies the ungodly*, doing the very thing that is represented to be such an abomination in the sight of Heaven when done by men. The Bible claims, in behalf of God, that He can justify the sinner—not that he can prove his innocence or righteousness; but taking him in all his vileness and guilt, justify him—acquit him—set aside all the claims of law and justice against him—free him from condemnation—restore him to Divine favor—shield him from all accusations, and pledge himself as his best and everlasting friend to plead his cause against every enemy. The Bible claims that God does this very thing, releasing transgressors from deserved punishment, and cancelling all claims of the law against them. In accordance also with this, there are multitudes who assert that God has done this very thing for them. They make no denial of the fact that they are transgressors. They confess their own iniquity and desert of damnation, making no pretence to any thing else. Yet they claim that God has justified them—freed them from all condemnation—released them from all obligation to punishment—cancelled every demand of law against them.

There may be those who have never had any such understanding of the facts of the case—never so realized them. Yet who can deny them? Who will deny that the doctrine of *justification*, and the justification *of sinners, the ungodly*, is found in the Bible? There can be no dispute here as to the meaning of terms. There is no loop-hole of escape at this point. All are agreed as to the meaning of justification and condemnation. That meaning is clear and unquestioned. Justification sets the party right with law, so that all its righteous claims are met or cancelled, and the accused has nothing more to fear.

We assert then, again, beyond denial or contradiction, and as an amazing fact, that *God* justifies sinners. Such, at least, is clearly the doctrine of the Scriptures. The fact is asserted in such passages as these: "Therefore, being justified by faith, we have peace with God through our Lord Jesus Christ;" Rom. v. 1. "Moreover, whom he did predestinate, them he also called: and whom he called, them he also justified: and whom he justified, them he also glorified. What shall we then say to these things? If God be for us, who can be against us? He that spared not his own Son, but delivered him up for us all, how shall he not with him also freely give us all things? Who shall lay any thing to the charge of God's elect? It is God that justifieth. Who is he that condemneth. It is Christ that died, yea, rather, that is risen again, who is even at the right hand of God, who also maketh intercession for us;" Rom. viii. 30. Here the facts are stated in the most unequivocal terms possible—and stated as the unquestioned doctrine of the Bible—as its great, leading doctrine.

How, then, can a perfect and righteous God do that which He himself declares to be abomination in His sight when done by man?

How does He vindicate himself—how proclaim His own righteousness? Why is not the character of God forever destroyed in the eyes of the universe by such transactions? Why is not all hell in a jubilee of triumph, rallying to His defense? The entire volume of revelation was written to be that vindication. God himself confesses to the fact, that it was a strange and wonderful proceeding beyond all the ordinary reach of thought, and demanding explanation and justification. He admits that He needed to *justify himself in justifying the ungodly*, and place His righteousness therein before the universe beyond all question or cavil, so that all hell would be forever silenced. To this end He gave His own revelation, that men might understand what His plan was for effecting the justification of sinners, declaring His righteousness forever in the same. In this volume He sets forth His everlasting love to this world of sinners—how His heart yearned toward them, and how He gave His only Son a ransom for their souls, upon whom their iniquities might be laid. "Whom God hath set forth to be a propitiation through faith in his blood, to declare his righteousness for the remission of sins that are past through the forbearance of God. *To declare*, I say, at this time, *his righteousness, that he might be just, and the justifier of him that believeth in Jesus;*" Rom. iii. 25. Here God distinctly declares that Christ, *as a propitiatory offering for sin*, was His everlasting vindication before the universe, in justifying the ungodly, who believe in that Saviour Jesus; and that He was set forth to be a propitiation to this very end of declaring the eternal righteousness of God in this transaction. It needed, too, to be thus declared. If God, in very deed, does justify the wicked, there is an absolute necessity that He should show that He has no sympathy with the wickedness itself and the violation of law—that He is not breaking down law and trampling truth and justice in the dust to give free license to iniquity. Nor did God fail in this matter. He did proclaim His everlasting righteousness, proving, in the sacrifice of His innocent Son, that He did hate sin, and love His holy law to the uttermost; and that, in the justification of the sinner on this ground His character could never be misunderstood, nor compromised to the slightest extent.

This work, too, is the sublimest wonder of our God, standing forever without a parallel, where all the depths of His infinite wisdom and love are brought to view, and into which the angels desire to look, as the field where they may make their profoundest discoveries.

It is thus made apparent that *the justification of the ungodly under the government of God is more than their pardon or release from punishment and their restoration to the Divine favor.*

A criminal may be pardoned—that is, released from the righteous claims of law, and restored to its protection —while he is very far from being justified. The executive of our government might pardon one who has forfeited his life to his country by his crimes—that is, he might release him from the grasp of the law, restoring him again to the privileges of citizenship; but he would not be justified thereby. The traitor or the murderer could not, by any executive act, be placed right before law and justice, so that their claims would be met, and they unite in acquitting the criminal, being satisfied with his release. The pardon is effected at the expense and sacrifice of law and justice. Their righteous claims are not met or cancelled. They cry out still for his condemnation. They demand his punishment and are not satisfied with his release. *He has escaped justice.* Jefferson Davis might be pardoned and set at liberty; but it is beyond all the power of man to justify him. Law and justice, truth and right, God and humanity, can never be made his friends and protectors to pronounce their blessings on his guilty head, in his release from human law. He cannot be set right with them. They will to the end unite to to condemn, and demand his punishment.

When God, however, undertakes for sinners, He does not violate truth and justice to set them free. He does not merely reverse the sentence of condemnation; He justifies them also. Through Christ as their propitiation, He magnifies the law and answers all the ends of justice, maintaining His own honor and the perfect integrity of His government. It is made apparent to the universe that these transgressors, even though they be the chief, are pardoned in the most honorable manner; yea, with glory to God and perfect safety to every righteous interest, so that nothing suffers, and none has cause to complain. Those pardoned, justified sinners, might be raised to the very throne to reign with Christ and administer the government over this redeemed earth, as they will be; and who shall rise up to utter one word against it?

"Who shall lay any thing to the charge of God's elect? It is God that justifieth. Who is he that condemneth?" Not a devil in perdition shall stand up to charge God with the slightest wrong in this matter, or the infringement of the least righteous interest. "Mercy and truth are met together, righteousness and peace have kissed each other." The character and government of God are forever clear. Not only is He free from all blame, but His highest glory is found in these very transactions. The loudest notes of praise which the intelligent universe will raise to His name, will be on account of this very salvation; while those who shall forever stand nearest to the throne to enjoy the warmest smiles, and receive the highest honors which infinite love can bestow, will be those sinners who have been taken from the horrible pit and the miry clay, being raised from the very gates of hell. 'Tis a great, a wonderful redemption, that can accomplish such ends as these! "Oh, the depth of the riches both of the wisdom and knowledge of God! How unsearchable are his judgments, and his ways past finding out!" Divine wisdom has solved that strangest, deepest problem of the universe, the justification of the ungodly.

It is apparent, again, *that the justification of the ungodly under a perfect moral government is impossible in the nature of things without an atonement.*

It cannot be conceived of. A sinner may be pardoned or released from deserved punishment, being restored again to the protection of law; but if that is all, it is by a violent act of authority, which may involve as great injustice as the original crime. There is no peace made. Another wrong only has been added to the first. Every reason that existed for the condemnation of that sinner, exists still. The facts of the case have undergone no change. If he was guilty, and justice at first demanded his punishment, it demands the same still. If it was right to doom him to death, it is an equal wrong now to reverse that sentence; and it can be done only at the sacrifice of justice, and the destruction of an eternally righteous government. That pardoned criminal would ever carry about with him a sense of condemnation in the deep consciousness that the claims of law had never been met in his case, and that he had been released only by an unjustifiable interference with established law; while every good citizen and subject would mourn and tremble at the fatal blow struck at the dearest interests involved in the maintenance of moral government. The transgressor, therefore, is not *justified*. His relations to truth and justice have not been properly adjusted, so that there can either be peace in his own soul, or peace to the subjects of that government. The ruler has impaired all confidence in his own righteous character and just administration, which, in God's case, would be the utter overthrow of His government: for the moment that His integrity is impeached, His authority is forever at an end. Human governments may do wrong, and still continue. But one act of wrong on the part of God would bury His throne and the universe in ruins. When His character is gone, all is gone. We assert, therefore, that the justification of sinners under the moral government of God, without some provision through an expiatory offering for answering the ends of justice and making peace, is an impossibility. The question, then, in regard to the teachings of the Bible on this subject, is not merely whether the doctrine of atonement is revealed there, but whether there is any doctrine of *justification*. Does the Bible teach that sinners are justified? If so, then there must be an atonement.

It is apparent, again, *that it is a rejection of the whole gospel, to deny the sinner's release from the penalty of the law.*

There is a system claiming for itself the authority of the Bible, which insists that the penalty of the law never can be set aside, God himself having no means of doing it, and that the sinner must meet the punishment due to his iniquities, either in this or the future world. It is claimed that, by this process of punishment, men are to be purified, and all ultimately prepared for heaven, the entire race being thus finally saved. This scheme betrays an ignorance of the first principles of government, and is accordant neither with grace nor law. Turning penalty into a mere disciplinary process for the good of the transgressor, it overthrows law as effectually as it does grace, breaking down all government. But it does one thing most thoroughly: it denies all possibility of justification to a sinner—denies that God himself can do it; thus setting aside the whole gospel from beginning to end. We claim that the Bible is simply a revelation of God's plan for justifying the ungodly. But if this cannot be done, then the book containing such a revelation is a stupendous fraud—a disgrace to all law, to all truth, to all government—a disgrace to the whole character of God; for it pretends to be His revelation, containing His plan for honorably justifying the wicked, and proclaiming His righteousness therein. That great doctrine now is pronounced a lie by the system of which we speak. It denies and scoffs at an atonement for sin, whereby the transgressor is released from the just penalty of the law. It denies the justification of the sinner—denies his salvation, and asserts that the righteous only can hope for the favor of God, there being no forgiveness of sins. It is consequently an utter rejection of Christ and His gospel.

It is apparent, again, *what is meant by the righteousness of faith.*

It is the system of justification by faith, and that righteousness which faith in Jesus Christ secures to a sinner. Why does God pardon and justify a transgressor? Because He is innocent, and can justly demand it as His right? Not at all: for by the very supposition he is a transgressor, and therefore worthy of condemnation and death. If he appear before God, his confession, and his only confession must be of sin—sin multiplied and great beyond all that he can estimate. How, then, shall God contradict these facts by justifying him? He does it through Jesus Christ as his propitiation. What, then, is demanded of the sinner? *Faith in Jesus Christ.* He must accept Christ as his righteousness, relying solely upon His obedience and sufferings as the only ground of his forgiveness and acceptance with God—the only basis of his release from deserved condemnation and death. In other words, it is the acceptance of God's plan of justifying the ungodly. This is the righteousness of faith—the righteousness which a sinner gets by faith upon the renunciation of his own. It accepts Jesus as a propitiation for sin.

If this, then, is "the righteousness of God without the law," being witnessed by the law and the prophets, and this the only name given under heaven among men whereby they must be saved, we may see what prospect they have for being saved who are aiming to lead decent lives—who have formed respectable characters, being pure, honest, upright men. There are multitudes who are building all their hopes of favor from God on this ground. They have no other conception of the gospel than such an effort to build up a good character. Some preach this as the very gospel of Christ, and know none beside. It is, however, nothing short of an absolute denial and rejection of the entire gospel. God's plan is to justify sinners—justify those who have no character of their own but what merits damnation; and therefore the righteousness of Christ is provided and freely offered to those who will accept it, and thank God for it. The man, now, who is cherishing the fond delusion that he is no sinner deserving of death—that he has never been enlisted in the great rebellion against heaven, but clings to the idea of a fair character and standing in the sight of God, that man utterly denies Christ, and puts dishonor upon His entire mission to earth. That man will not consent to be justified and saved *as a sinner*. His whole soul rebels against it. That doctrine of justification by faith condemns him as a transgressor. It would strip him in a moment of all his boasted righteousness and meritorious excellence of character. It would show that all his virtues were but the delusion of a self-deceived, wicked heart, and leave his naked soul, covered all over with defilement, exposed without a shelter to the threatenings of a violated law.

The sinner, now, in the pride of his heart and the delusions of his self-righteousness, may reject and cast indignantly from him this Heaven-contrived plan for justifying the ungodly and saving the lost; but God will never put upon it the seal of His condemnation; Christ will not disown it; The Holy Ghost will not. When those Pharisees, who are so pure, and have lived so well and faithfully, come to knock at heaven's gate, "Saying, Lord, Lord, open unto us," they shall hear the answering voice from within, "I know you not whence ye are. Depart from me, all *ye workers of iniquity*. There shall be weeping and gnashing of teeth." This was terribly searching truth in Christ's day, uttered in the ears of those boasting Pharisees. It is searching doctrine still to the Pharisees of this generation. The world may rage and gnash their teeth against it; but the words of Jesus stand in spite of all the opposition of the rulers. They may be deeply offended at these sayings; but "every plant which my heavenly Father hath not planted, shall be rooted up. Let them alone: they be blind leaders of the blind: and if the blind lead the blind, both shall fall into the ditch." The everlasting truth still abides, that Jesus came to seek and to save them that were lost—to call not the righteous, but sinners to repentance.

Ho, then, ye *sinners!* You, who have no righteousness—who have not kept the commandments of God, and have no purity of heart or life—ye wanderers from God, who have prodigally wasted all your substance among harlots, and reduced yourselves to beggary, so that you would fain feed with the very swine—ye wretched and lost, who feel that you are brought to the doors of hell, there are glad tidings for you! This gospel is for you. It was contrived for you, and such only as you. God has a plan for justifying the ungodly. Here is the amazing wonder of His work. And if you will receive it, this salvation shall be yours. This Christ shall be yours, and you shall sing of redemption forever and ever. You shall enter to the marriage supper of the Lamb, to sit down with all who have humbly believed even as you, uniting with one heart and voice in that new and everlasting song, "Unto him that loved us, and washed us from our sins in his own blood, and hath made us kings and priests unto God and his Father: to him be glory and dominion forever and ever, Amen."

We see, again, *that salvation by the atonement of Christ is in perfect consistency with all the facts connected with sin, and the Divine government.*

In saving a sinner, God never falsifies any truth. No lie is anywhere wrought into the framework of the Divine plan of redemption. In the gospel, every truth and fact relating to the moral government of God and the sinner are brought clearly to light. First, God's eternal law is admitted to be holy in every requirement. The sinner is not pardoned at the expense of that law, because it is too strict and severe. Its very precept is fully vindicated, for Christ himself obeyed it to the utmost letter, being spared no temptation.

There is, then, the penalty. The sinner is not suffered to escape because it was too severe, and Divine justice shrinks from inflicting it. Its eternal righteousness is vindicated by the curse being laid upon God's own Son, He suffering, the just for the unjust. Thirdly, there is the sinner himself. He is not pardoned because his sins are few and small—because he is not deeply implicated in the rebellion, or among the chief offenders. His sins are confessed in all their number and magnitude. Not one is excused, denied, or concealed. He stands forth a criminal by his own confession, and deserving of death. Neither is there any pretence that he has done any thing, or can do any thing, to change these facts, or mitigate his guilt, or give any reason why he should not suffer the full penalty which the law metes out for his crimes. He makes no offer to satisfy the claims of justice, but confesses his just desert of punishment. Yet, in face of all these facts, he asks and hopes for pardon. And why? Because he believes in Jesus—because Christ pleads for him by His own precious blood—because Christ, by His obedience and sufferings, has answered the demands of justice, and God can now save without any compromise of His character or the interests of His holy universe. He consents to go to heaven as a sinner, ransomed from hell, whose everlasting song shall be of redeeming mercy and love.

Other schemes of salvation, however, do always deny one or more great truths connected with this subject. A lie is found in them somewhere. Some would go to heaven at the expense of the Divine precepts, charging that the law of God is too strict, and that it cannot be expected or demanded of them that they should keep it. They insinuate that God is a hard master, and hope to escape in this direction. Others make their attack upon the death penalty of the law, seeking to blot it out from Heaven's statute-book, and maintaining that it cannot be inflicted by a God of love. Others, again, deny the facts of their transgression, frittering sin down to a few little faults and errors, which can be easily overlooked—which, in fact, it would be cruel to punish with severity; while they boast themselves of no little good, for which they are not slow to claim even the reward of heaven. Others, still, deny Christ as a Mediator, and cast away His blood of atonement as a worthless thing; yea, more than worthless —as an insult to the Divine character and government. These are the falsehoods which are incorporated with all human schemes of salvation; and with these men are going up to the judgment, there certainly, if not before, to be undeceived, and to have the deception exposed to their own eternal shame and undoing.

God, however, can never falsify any truth to get a sinner to heaven. He will never dishonor himself, His law, or His gospel. He has provided a way by which *sinners* may be saved—a way infinitely honorable to himself, and safe to His universe. It is the only possible way in which a sinner can be saved. Here is a wide and open door, by which the vilest may enter in and obtain eternal redemption. But, in the nature of the case, God can never dishonor and deny His own system. Sinners, in their unbelief and wickedness, may do it to their own undoing; but God never can. If He would not suffer His law to be dishonored, but made an infinite sacrifice to maintain it, there is no possible hope for any who trample upon that blood of atonement, and reject so great salvation.

We see, in the atonement, the unspeakable gift of God. God's goodness is everywhere manifest, exceeding all our thought. But the gift of Christ is spoken of in the Bible with peculiar and strange emphasis, as something far exceeding all—something that God himself regards as wonderful, and expresssing His love in a very unusual manner, not to be looked for even from Him, and which, therefore, could not have been anticipated from Him by those who knew Him best. It was the "unspeakable gift." We may understand this, if we accept the fact that Christ was made an expiation for sin. This was something not to have been looked for. Some still assert that it is not to be believed. None, certainly, could have conceived beforehand that God would have gone to this extent of self-sacrifice. Nothing in His law or government would have demanded or indicated it. That law was a perfect embodiment of Divine goodness. But it made no provision for the expiation of sin, or the forgiveness and justification of a sinner. That gift of God's only Son as a propitiation for sin was something above law, and entirely out of its range, though still in harmony with it. "God so loved the world, that he gave his only-begotten Son, that whosoever believeth in him should not perish, but have everlasting life." The Bible designs here to convey the idea, that this was an exhibition of love out of the ordinary track of the Divine goodness, into which the very angels desire to look. It is this love that is to constitute the theme of that new and everlasting song of the redeemed on Mount Zion—the sweetest song of the universe, and which shall be to the highest honor of our God and Redeemer.

It is no wonder, therefore, that hell is opposed to this doctrine of atonement and expiation for sin, and contends against it in every possible form. It is the doctrine which shakes the gates of hell, and is destined to overthrow the powers of darkness. On this rock the Church is built, to abide for evermore.

CHAPTER XXXI.

THE LIVING CHRIST.

HAVING reached that point in the history of redemption where the work of obedience and expiation was finished, in the first mission to earth of the woman's seed, it is proper here to inquire whether the promised results of the same are sustained by human experience; or rather, whether this life of Christ does, as a fact, enter into the life of our humanity, to change the current of its history and destiny. We want to know whether Christ is a living power in the earth; whether there is any peculiar link between Him and the sons of men, which demonstrates that His work and life were a reality. We do not design to discuss the general results of Christianity in evidence of its divinity. We intend to pursue a more special train of thought in demonstrating

THAT JESUS, IN VERY DEED, IS A LIVING CHRIST.

Mark, then, that humble *man* of Nazareth (for man He truly was as any other), who, eighteen centuries ago, appeared under a claimed commission from heaven, gathered a few disciples as the Messiah of Israel, and was then delivered to death under the deepest ignominy. His cross, however, did not prove the mill-stone it was designed to be by the rulers. Rising triumphant from the grave, He proved himself the conqueror of death, and carried our humanity in His own person through and beyond those gloomy realms, to its redeemed and resurrection state. This man laid the foundation of a peculiar empire or cause on earth, which has continued to this hour, and against which no power has been able to prevail. For this success He has owed nothing to the world. The rulers would not own Him. The learned Scribes cavilled and sneered. The Pharisees denounced Him as a Samaritan and devil. The courts and councils condemned Him. The schools of philosophy, in their haughty pride, asked, "How knoweth this man letters, having never learned?" and passed by in derision. The world in all its departments disowned Him, and disdainfully shook their garments, clearing themselves from all responsibility respecting Him. The cry from every quarter was, "We will not have this man to reign over us." The eventful crisis of His destiny came, too, when these powers were seemingly to triumph over Him; and though forsaken by His own despairing disciples, yet meekly, but in sublime faith, He lifted His prayer to heaven and said, "Father, the hour is come," and without a murmuring word or show of resistance, He put himself in the hands of His rejoicing enemies.

Thus did Jesus alone, and in the greatest seeming weakness, lay the foundation of His kingdom. Through the ignominy of the cross and the grave, He passed to reach His crown; for from hence was His kingdom to arise. From this point of His deepest humiliation and overthrow, did all His power go forth to establish His name in the earth. His friends have never denied or concealed the fact that their Master was crucified between two thieves, after having been adjudged to death by His own nation. Not one has ever sought to hide that part of His history, as if ashamed of it. On the contrary, they have themselves made this the most prominent of all the events of His life. They have lifted His cross as their waving banner, and borne it in the van of their host, preaching it, glorying in it, and pointing the world triumphantly to it as their joy and crown, and the secret of all their strength. It was a strange path to glory, confounding all the wisdom of the world. This doctrine of Jesus and the cross was a stumbling-block to Jew, and foolishness to philosophic Greek. Yet Jesus, the crucified, is a living power in the earth. Though rejected, denied, and crucified, He has never wanted those who loved Him, and adhered to Him, notwithstanding that fidelity has cost them all they held dear on earth. Not floods nor flames, prisons nor tortures, nor death have been sufficient to separate the followers of Jesus from their adored Master. They have been bound to Him by a tie stronger than death itself, and for Him they have freely forsaken father and mother, wife and children, taking joyfully the spoiling of their goods, and counting not their lives dear unto them, so that they might win Christ, and be found in Him. These are facts to which the historic pages of eighteen centuries bear their concurrent testimony.

Let it be observed, also, that this interest which is felt in that crucified Nazarene, is a *personal* interest, such as brings Him into living contact with each one of His followers, they becoming united to Him by a vital force, which is represented by Christ himself as a union of the branch with the vine. In fact, the union between this man and His followers is more close, more intimate and tender, more complete and controlling, more vital and enduring, than any other union known on earth. It has a power and compass which no other relation has experience of. Christ himself claimed it as paramount to all others, and said, "If any man come to me, and hate not his father, and mother, and wife, and children, yea, and his own life also, he cannot be my disciple. And whosoever taketh not his cross and followeth after me, cannot be my disciple." This is extraordinary language to come from human lips, and passingly wonderful must be the facts to justify it.

There is nothing new in these facts now brought to notice. They are all familiar, lying upon the very surface of the gospel. As such we refer to them. And because they are thus unquestionable, we design to employ them as the basis of an argument in reference to the person and character of that man of Nazareth, *showing that He stands forever apart from all others of the race, in very deed a living Christ and Saviour.*

An examination of a few facts will show what the peculiarity of this relation of Jesus is to our humanity.

There have, then, been marked names in the history of the world—men who have stood at the fountain head of a mighty current of influence and power, which has rolled over centuries—men, whose names and memory have been cherished, whose doctrines have been taught and received, and to whom the proudest monuments have been erected, of which earth could boast. Take any of these names, it matters not which, and tell us by what tie they are bound to their friends or followers. By what link can one human being unite himself to his race, or any portion of it, after passing out of the circle of his own kindred? What is the nature of that union which has subsisted between certain men, who have had a controlling influence in the world, and those in the existing or future generations, who have been moulded thereby?

The name and memory of George Washington are sacred. His counsels and heroic deeds this people will ever cherish. But there is no present personal tie between him and us, so that we can love him as a friend or brother, or claim connection with him. There is ground for esteem, honor, reverence; and these we pay to his memory. But Washington sustains no personal relations of friendship to us. It would be presumption in any to make such claim.

Lord Bacon's system of inductive philosophy has

revolutionized the science of the world. He is justly honored of all, and we receive that philosophy which he inaugurated. But who loves Bacon? To whom is he now bound by any personal, living tie?

Aristotle! There is not another to be mentioned that has exerted a greater influence over the empire of mind. His name and philosophy for centuries ruled the world. Yet, beyond his own generation, what personal tie ever bound Aristotle to his followers? They received his teachings. They bowed to the authority of his name. They honored his memory. But this is all.

Mohammed was a prophet, in the estimation of his followers, greater than Jesus Christ; and, as such, revered as none other can be. But who among his followers loves Mohammed as a living person, with a living affection? How is he bound to them, beyond that they receive his teachings, and acknowledge him as a prophet from heaven?

In the same way we receive the prophets and Apostles as our inspired teachers, whom we hold in the deepest veneration. Yet they are related to us by no tie, such as binds us to the circle of friends about us. We are bound to parents, to children, to husband, to wife, to brothers, sisters, and friends; and hence spring those affections which so sweeten life and soften its cares. But these ties extend not beyond this circle. Much less do they reach beyond our own generation. There is no link of this kind that can connect us with those of a generation past. No man can thus personally unite himself to those of a coming age. His influence may live after him. His name, his doctrine, his example, his deeds may go down to coming times. But this is all.

With these obvious facts before us, turn now to Him of Bethlehem and Nazareth—that man so strangely allied to our humanity, and who trod the weary way of life on earth, under the burden of its sorrows and its sins. He was indeed our teacher, who spake to us from heaven. Yet after Him we needed such men as John and Paul to expound His system, and unfold, in all their fulness, the harmonies of Divine truth. As a simple teacher, it is perhaps but little, if any, aside from the truth to say, that Paul occupies as conspicuous a place as Jesus. Instruction was but a part, and a subordinate part of Christ's work. So far as the mere revelation of truth was concerned, God could have perfectly accomplished that object by such instruments as Moses, John, Paul, and others. Through the inspiration of the Holy Ghost, they could have been fully qualified for this work. Through them God could have revealed all the truth that He desired to communicate to man, with perfect clearness, and with all the binding authority of heaven.

Christ, moreover, was our example, in so far as we sustain the same relations to God and man that He did—a perfect example. But He was more than a teacher and an example. It was not for this primarily that He lived and died. He had a mission beside this, even a priesthood to fulfil, being appointed the one only Mediator between God and man, to make reconciliation, and bring in everlasting righteousness. This mediatorship was His great office, in which He was both the priest and the victim for sacrifice; for He offered himself, and by His own blood entered once into the holy place, having obtained eternal redemption for us. His own obedience and sufferings thus constituted a righteousness, on the basis of which He might mediate in behalf of the guilty, and obtain for the believing a gracious pardon. Here was Christ's great and peculiar work, in which He stands forever alone, with none to share it with Him, none to follow it up. With His expiring breath He cried, "*It is finished.*" As a teacher and example, He was followed by others, imperfectly, it may be. But as priest and Mediator, He stands alone, the work forever His own, transmitted in no sense to any other. The Bible does not say, one teacher, one example. But it does say, "One Mediator" forever between God and men.

Here, now, is laid the foundation for that peculiar, personal relation which Jesus Christ sustains to every believer. Such relation He does sustain, and in this is distinguished from every other individual of the race. He has not merely transmitted His name and memory, His teachings and deeds to other times and distant ages, but He has been able to link himself by personal ties, and those of the strongest nature known on earth, to men of every generation. Here is a fact, familiar to every true believer—a fact unlike any thing else in the history of the world—which science cannot ignore, and which demands explanation from those who claim to be philosophers, and to have investigated the laws of the human mind.

Jesus was a Divine teacher. But this affords no solution of the amazing fact of which we speak. Moses was a teacher, and Paul; and as teachers they were little, if any, inferior to Jesus, their teachings being equally reliable and valuable. We receive them with the same unqalified assurance as those of Jesus himself. But the teachings of Moses and Paul bring them into no personal relations to us. Neither would the teachings of Christ any more in themselves. And those who regard Him solely or chiefly in this light, have failed to comprehend the true mission of Jesus, or to discern the secret of His religion.

The essence of Christianity (and it is a peculiarity which belongs to this religion alone, of all others), lies in the fact of this living, personal union between Christ and the believer. It is not enough that men should acknowledge the validity and authority of His teachings, as one divinely commissioned. It is not enough that they should understand and believe the great system of truth which He taught. Many do this, and are not Christians—do not profess to be. Nor can they ever become such, until they know, by personal experience, what that relation to Christ is, which is effected by faith in Him as a Mediator. Aside from this, He is no more a Saviour to them than Moses, or John, or Paul. But there are those, and have been in every generation, to whom Jesus has been more than a teacher and example. They have been one with Him by a bond nearer and stronger than that which binds parent to child, or husband to wife. In this personal union there is a blessed reality, to which the experience of every believer will bear testimony—a reality which it is no arrogant assumption on his part to claim, which Christ regards it no dishonor to himself to acknowledge. Should we claim such a relation to Washington, to Bacon, to Aristotle, to Moses, to Paul, to any of the dead of past ages, our sanity of mind would at once be called in question; nay, it would be regarded as clear evidence of a disordered brain. Yet every true Christian claims this of Jesus Christ, who laid this down as the grand characteristic of His religion. He declared himself one with each and all of His followers, they being members of Him, and bound by closest personal ties to Him. If I am a true believer, I do not stretch across the track of eighteen centuries to reach my Saviour. He is not removed from me by that distance of time and space. He is a present, living friend, whom I know—who knows me; whom I love—who loves me; in whom I rejoice and trust, with whom I hold communion, and who has pledged himself, by solemn covenant, to be mine forever. I do not regard Him merely as one who lived many centuries ago, and blessed the world with

His instruction and example, but has passed away forever. He is now a present, living friend, to whom I am united by ties more near and sacred than those which bind me to any human being. "Whom not having seen, ye love: in whom, though now ye see him not, yet believing, ye rejoice with joy unspeakable and full of glory."

What is the extent of this devotion of the believer to Jesus, and what the reach of those claims which Christ has upon him?

What is the place which Christ may occupy in the heart of the Christian? How far may the believer go in loving, trusting, and serving this Saviour, Jesus? Can he go too far? Is there a point of devotion to Christ which could be reached by the believer in the strength of his love and faith, where he would overstep the bounds of honor due to God, and where Jesus would arrest his too ardent affection and worship, saying, as the angel to John, when he fell prostrate at his feet, "See that thou do it not." May I love Jesus *with all my heart, soul, mind, and strength?* May I devote to Him my whole being, for time and eternity? May I serve Him with all the powers which God has given me—lay myself a willing sacrifice at His feet, to be His—His alone, His forever? And will He accept such a sacrifice? Will He be mine forever? Is that the import of the covenant between Christ and the believing soul? And does Christ refuse to strike hands with the sinner, or admit him to the secret covenant which He makes with His chosen, until that sinner is brought to this point of entire, everlasting consecration to Him? Is this religion? This Christianity?

If so, who then is that wondrous One, in the form of our humanity, who thus throws himself across the track of the ages, and brings himself into a living union with the sons of men by a tie which overrides all the most sacred relationships of earth? Who is that "Wonderful," to whom our universal humanity may become personally allied by the most hallowed bonds, so that the humblest and most abject sons of want may know Him as a Friend, a Brother, a Mediator, a Redeemer, a complete Portion—the very Alpha and Omega of their being? Who, moreover, is it that thus comes to men, to solicit this love and confidence of their whole hearts, this service of all their powers, this homage and devotion of their whole being forever? Who dares demand this, than which God himself can ask no more? Surely One, who thinks it no robbery to be equal with God. And as we gaze upon that "Wonderful," thus taking our nature into alliance with His own, and making himself one with those of every clime, and kindred, and generation, who will humbly accept Him as their Redeemer, are we not compelled, involuntarily yet adoringly, to exclaim with Thomas, as the glories of a risen Saviour flashed fully upon his mind, "My Lord and my God"? Yes, verily, when we give to Christ the place in our hearts—when we repose in Him the faith, and render the service which He asks, and which is His due, we have nothing beyond that we can give to God. Christ has secured all. And with the elders around the throne, the number of whom is ten thousand times ten thousand, and thousands of thousands; and with every creature which is in heaven, and on earth, and under the earth, and in the sea, would we join the universal chorus, saying, Blessing, and honor, and glory, and power, be unto him that sitteth on the throne, and *unto the Lamb, forever and ever;* Rev. v. 13.

Thus have we travelled back until we have reached again that central doctrine of Christianity, the divinity of our Redeemer: and by what process? By taking the plainest, most practical, and undeniable facts which enter into the essence of all true religion, aside from which there is no Christianity, and following them out to their legitimate conclusions. These facts force us to this result. We must admit the supreme divinity of Jesus Christ, giving Him the place in the system which He claims, or we must deny the vital essence of Christianity, and empty it of all its truth, and glory, and power. Make Jesus Christ a mere man, and how can He be more than a simple teacher and example—of extraordinary character, it may be—who lived eighteen centuries ago, and whose doctrines are now received? Make Him a mere man, and by what known process can you bring in that first, paramount, essential truth of all Christianity, that He is bound by a personal, living tie to every humble believer, so that they become one, and members of one body? How can the personal relations of Jesus, as a mere man, spread themselves through all ages, through all climes, and among all classes of men? There is a problem for human philosophy to answer, and we press it for a solution.

This argument is confirmed also by the fact that those who regard Christ as a man simply, do ignore, and that, as a necessary consequence, this vital element of religion, as consisting in the living union of the believer with Christ, his Head. They know nothing about it. It is one of the most simple, obvious truths, and the most precious to every humble, renewed soul, that has been made to know by experience what religion is. But it is hidden from the worldly wise, who can discern naught but the glories of humanity in Jesus Christ. For no acknowledgment or reception of Him as a mere teacher can ever constitute any personal relation between Him and me, so that I shall be His, and He mine; and I may know Him as a Friend, Brother, and Mediator.

Let Christ also be made any thing less than God, and

by what process can He be thrust in between my soul and the eternal One himself, to rob Him of that supreme love, reverence, and service, which forever belong to God alone? Has He surrendered to one of His creatures the right to the supreme love and whole-hearted service of this entire race? Has God thus denied himself and given His glory to another? Yet we are logically compelled to this conclusion, or the equally fatal one of withholding our whole hearts from Jesus Christ, and refusing Him that love and obedience which He demands, and without which He does not consent to save any sinner. There is no escape from this dilemma; and either horn is fatal to the Christian system.

Thus do the facts show, incontestibly, that our humanity has a living Head, through whom its redemption will yet be effected.

The man has come, who has proved His capacity to take the leadership of our race, and constitute in and around His own person a body, which shall form a redeemed humanity. The universal lapse of our race in Adam proves that He was its first Head. The fact that Jesus Christ can, through His mediatorship, bring himself into living union with that same humanity through all its generations, with a redeeming power, is demonstration that He is the appointed second Adam—the promised seed. And what a fact is here! It has been esteemed an honor to be lineally descended from earth's nobility—to bear their names, and to have enjoyed their intimate friendship. Such distinction is courted by men. Christianity embodies this fact in its most sublime form. Christianity presents to us *the man*—the only one who is worthy the name of *man*—the only begotten and well beloved of heaven. Before the blessed name of Jesus, all others sink into insignificance. It has been exalted, not only above all the names of earth, but of heaven, too, so that to Him every knee shall yet bow. The possession of all power is to come into His hands, the principalities in heaven itself being made subject to Him. The earth is His. He has purchased it—has made himself worthy of it, and shall have it as His inheritance forever. "He shall see of the travail of his soul, and shall be satisfied." The time, too, shall come when the kingdoms of this world shall become the kingdoms of our Lord and of His Christ, and He shall reign forever and ever. That man, once crucified and rejected, shall yet be adored by the sons of men. This earth shall do Him justice. Every valley and mountain-top shall ring with His praises. Kings shall come bending at His feet, and all nations shall own Him Lord.

Christianity now offers freely to the sons of men the high honor of a personal relationship of the nearest and most endeared character to this man. We are not lineally descended from Him. Jesus Christ left no natural descendants. It was of design that He should not. He did not intend to perpetuate His honors in His own family connections. He understood the higher, nobler relation which He sustained to our universal humanity. He identified himself with the race—gave himself for the race, that it might be redeemed and exalted to its destined supremacy. He was to be constituted its glorious and everlasting Head. Who is my mother? and who are my brethren? And he stretched forth his hand toward his disciples, and said, Behold my mother and my brethren! For whosoever shall do the will of my Father which is heaven, the same is my brother, and sister, and mother; Matt. xii. 48. May I, then, be closely related to that man? Will He own relationship to me, to acknowledge me among His nearest kindred? May I claim such relationship, even the most intimate friendship? May I tell the world *that I know Jesus Christ?*

May I love Him as a brother, and be assured that He loves me—that He thinks upon me, cares for me with the tenderest solicitude—will love me to the end, and then constitute me a joint heir to share His own everlasting honor, ransoming me from the grave, putting death and corruption beneath my feet, and robing this body in the vestments of immortality, so that I shall see His face, and dwell forever in His blissful presence? Is it possible for me to be a partaker of such honor and blessedness as this? Yes, verily. I may experience a new and second birth, as to my moral nature, by which I shall become related to Jesus Christ, and enter the mysteries of a sacred union with Him, becoming a member of that body of our redeemed humanity, of which He is the Head. I may know Him, love Him, have fellowship with Him, be admitted to His secret counsels, as if no time had elapsed between His age and mine. Jesus Christ belongs to every age—is a brother to every believer. It is not nature that constitutes that sacred brotherhood. It comes not from blood, or birth, or lineal descent. None are born naturally the kindred of Jesus. No; thanks to God. This richest blessing of heaven does not flow in such a narrow channel. It may come to every wretched child of sorrow, to every weary wanderer from God, and from happiness. This new, this spiritual, this second birth by the Holy Ghost may be experienced by each and every sinner who knows how to prize its inestimable worth, and would sell all to obtain it. Born thus of God, and made new creatures in Christ, we shall know the blessedness of that noblest relationship of our humanity to its glorified Head—relationship to that second Adam—who triumphed over all our enemies, achieved for us the victory, and ascended to the right hand of power. What a prize! What a portion for our guilty, lost race! How are our souls overwhelmed with the burden of the mighty thought! Well might that anthem have been raised upon Bethlehem's plains over Bethlehem's wondrous babe, "Glory to God in the highest, peace on earth, and good-will to men." Glad tidings, indeed, of great joy are here. And well might the ascending Redeemer give His last commission to His disciples, "Go ye into all the world, and preach the gospel to every creature."

O man! do you belong to the kindred of Jesus? You may, peradventure, be poor, and have only poor relations among men. Yet to you may be the honor of being nearly related to Him to whom kings shall bow, and the principalities of heaven own subjection. Have you accepted the magnanimous proffer? Or have you been slumbering over the amazing subject? Have you been trifling with it? Have you turned your back upon Jesus, and been ashamed to bear His name, because this wicked and adulterous generation knows not how to appreciate Him? Oh, to me let the high honor remain of that second birth by repentance and faith, through which I shall enter the sacred brotherhood of our redeemed humanity, where Jesus shall be my Mediator and Priest before the throne; and united to Him, I shall share all the benefits of His obedience and sufferings; and redeemed at last from the power of the grave, enter that resurrection state, where death or sin shall nevermore be known, and where I shall behold Him face to face.

We may hence learn how Christ ought to be studied and preached.

There are three points of view from which He may be presented, and with very different effect.

The first is that of His simple humanity. He may be regarded as a man—a wonderful, and possibly a perfect man, though not always entirely free from mistakes—but nothing more than a man. This is the point from which infidelity is now aiming to develop and explain the phenomena of Christianity. Skepticism no more denies the existence of Jesus Christ, or the general history of His life. It admits these—admits that He was a very extraordinary character, who had a deep insight into Divine things, and unfolded a system of morality and truth of wonderful purity and power, such as the world needed, and which is exciting an amazing influence in the regeneration of the race. Jesus, therefore, is a man to be deeply venerated and regarded as one of the world's noblest heroes and benefactors. While all this, however, is freely conceded, it is as vehemently denied that there was any thing miraculous or supernatural in His career. His alleged miracles are converted into myths and fables, and the exaggerations of admiring friends and followers, whose weakness and folly exalted Him into something more than mortal. But the wisdom of this day is stripping off those delusions of a superstitious age, and reducing Jesus to His proper position and proportions, to whom the world is ready now to do ample justice as a man of the most extraordinary inspiration and genius. This is the system of naturalism.

The second point of view from which Christ may be regarded is that of His divinity—not, indeed, that His humanity is denied or questioned, but that it is regarded as a thing of the past—belonging to a history long since fulfilled, and to which His words and declarations can now practically have little reference. This is the position from which Christ is ordinarily presented in our pulpits and Christian literature. His words are now read by us, yet not conceived of as uttered by *a man* on earth, such as He was once known to be when tabernacling here, but by a Divine being seated on the throne. We hear those words not as falling from the lips of the Galilean and Nazarene, but from one at the right hand of power. His divinity is made to absorb the whole field of vision.

Sinners are invited to Him, not as when He appeared on earth, to listen to the words which then fell from His lips, but as uttered by a very different being, and from a widely different sphere. Christ's words have almost ceased to be the words of a man in the lowliest walks of life. We have transferred them to another character, and thus do we practically ignore the humanity of Christ, regarding it no more as a thing of the present, but only of the past. Perhaps our minds have been helped to this result by the fact that we have been called to contend so strenuously for His divinity against opposers; and, as is so often the case, we have been pushed too far, losing sight of His humanity, and failing to understand its true relations.

The third point of view from which to consider Christ is to begin where He himself began to unfold His own character and claims—that is, from His humanity—and let them speak for themselves.

Why should we not study Christ's words and life from the very point from which He presented them? Why seek to change, as it were, the whole base of Christianity, and regard what He uttered eighteen hundred years ago as a man, as now spoken by a Divine being from the eternal throne? Did not Jesus mean to be understood just as He spake? Did He not appear in His own true character? Did He not fairly represent himself? And what He spake centuries ago as a human being, is not every word of it true to-day, as it was then, and to be taken with the same meaning? Did not Jesus speak for all time, for all generations? Did He not intend that His words should continue to stand as the words of the Nazarene, so that coming ages might hear and study them as uttered by himself? Why, then, should we seek now to change the whole structure of His work, by transferring all His words from human lips to those of one who is divine and infinite alone, thus losing the benefits of His humanity?

Jesus Christ was a man—a complete man. As such He was known. Such He claimed to be, styling himself emphatically the Son of man, as if He would have this at least understood. This humanity He never denied—never ignored by word or deed. It was a wonderful problem now to solve how Jesus from this point could stand up before the world, and assert His divinity. How should He maintain and establish that supernatural character? Should He go about, declaring publicly, and in the face of His enemies, who were thirsting for His blood, that He was God? It would have been to no purpose. It would have accomplished nothing, and only insured His destruction. What, then, should He do? He must be true to himself. He must in some way advocate His claims, and not ignore His own superhuman relations, while at the same time, also, He acts in perfect consistency with His true manhood, and subjection to law. Mark, then, with what consummate wisdom the end is accomplished. Jesus does not assert His divinity directly, except on rare occasions. But He does what is equivalent thereto, and is demonstrative of the same. He holds himself up as the Alpha and Omega of all human wants—the sum of all desire, in whom every hope and necessity of the soul of man can find its complete fulfilment. He says what it would be sheer folly and madness for any mere man to say—what would blast the reputation of any mortal in a moment. This Jesus sublimely does everywhere, and on all occasions, in the face of His bitterest foes, without faltering or doubt; and those statements have stood the test of eighteen centuries. Listen to some of them, and mark their wonderful character: I am the light of the world: he that followeth me shall not walk in darkness, but shall have the light of life; John viii. 12. I am the door: by me if any man enter in, he shall be saved; chap. x. 9. I am the good shepherd; chap. x. 11. I am the way, the truth, and the life: no man cometh unto the Father, but by me; chap. xiv. 6. I am the bread of life: he that cometh to me shall never hunger; and he that believeth on me shall never thirst; chap. vi. 35. I am the living bread which came down from heaven: if any man eat of this bread, he shall live forever; chap. vi. 51. I am the resurrection, and the life: he that believeth in me, though he were dead, yet shall he live: and he that liveth and believeth in me shall never die; chap. xi. 25. I am the vine, ye are the branches. . . . If a man abide not in me, he is cast forth as a branch, and is withered; chap. xv. 5. Marvel not at this: for the hour is coming, in the which all that are in the graves shall hear his voice, and shall come forth; they that have done good, unto the resurrection of life; and they that have done evil, unto the resurrection of damnation; chap. v. 28. All that the Father giveth me shall come to me; and him that cometh to me I will in no wise cast out; chap. vi. 37. Verily, verily, I say unto you, If any man keep my saying, he shall never see death; chap. viii. 51. My sheep hear my voice, and I know them, and they follow me: and I give unto them eternal life; and they shall never perish, neither shall any pluck them out of my hand; chap. x. 27. Come unto me, all ye that labor and are heavy laden and I will give you rest; Matt. xi. 28. Whosoever therefore shall be ashamed of me and of my words, of him shall the Son of man be ashamed when he cometh in the glory of his Father with his holy angels; Mark viii. 38.

What does it mean for a human being to utter such language as this? Put any one of these statements into the mouth of a mere mortal man, and how soon would he prove his fitness for a lunatic asylum? No human being could sustain himself for a moment under such declarations. He would be deemed a fool or a lunatic who should make the attempt. Yet we suffer them from Jesus Christ. Infidelity itself will strangely listen to these most wondrous declarations from the man of Nazareth and see nothing egotistical—nothing absurd in them —nothing that indicates a disordered brain. Let any man assert that he was "the light of the world," and see if it would require eighteen centuries to brand it as a lie. Take that invitation of Jesus to the weary and heavy laden. Study it and see what it means—what the length and breadth of that promise are. Measure the wretchedness and woes of this world. Consider what resources, what unbounded wealth, what vast power would be required to relieve those necessities, and give the rest that is needed to the suffering, the weary, and down-trodden in the world. It would demand an arm of might, indeed, to protect the weak and defenceless, and strike down haughty oppression. Yet Jesus did not hesitate to hold himself up before the world as the refuge of all the poor and needy who had no protection or friends beside. "Come unto me, and I will give you rest." What did this mean? Jesus was a poor man himself, having not where to lay His head. Every body knew this. He had no political power. He could not defend His own life, but fell a victim to the rage of these same haughty despotisms, which have so long ruled and trampled on the defenceless. These facts were apparent to all. Yet still He invited a weary world to come to Him, with the promise that they should find rest to their souls. He did not see any inconsistency or absurdity in this. *The world* has not seen any; and the reason is because they secretly, in their hearts, admit His divinity, even while their infidel lips may deny it. Allow Jesus to utter these wondrous words; to make these statements concerning himself; to give these invitations and promises, and His divinity must be conceded at once. He who is the light of the world—the door to heaven—the way, the truth, the life—the resurrection and the life—the living bread upon which a perishing world may feed and live—the friend to whom every burdened, sorrowing soul may come—whose voice the dead shall hear and live—He must be the Alpha and Omega—the beginning and the ending—the sum of all desire and hope.

Why, then, should we not study Christ from this point of view? Why not preach Him from the very position from which He proclaimed himself, and pressed the claims of His own divinity? Can we improve upon the arguments and representations which He employed in commending himself to the world? Have we not lost much of the power of Christianity by practically ignoring this very humanity of our Redeemer, and holding Him up so exclusively from the point of His divinity? Have we not lost thereby the most conclusive demonstration of that divinity; and handed over His humanity, as it were, to the possession of His enemies, that they might claim it for their own?

Our Redeemer is *Immanuel, God with us.* "The Word was made flesh and dwelt among us (and we beheld His glory, the glory as of the only-begotten of the Father), full of grace and truth." "Great is the mystery of godliness. God was manifest in the flesh." If we would see this glory and feel its power, we must behold it through this same medium of the flesh. We must see God revealed in the face of Jesus Christ. We must retain that perfect humanity as it was, and study all the words of Christ without change from the very point whence they were spoken. They were the utterances of a man. There is the wonder of them. The deep mystery is that a man ever could have spoken them, and held himself up in such a position of unearthly grandeur before the world. And never can we see the full and overwhelming proof of the divinity of our Redeemer, until we train our minds to study it through this medium of His humanity, beholding the Word made flesh, and dwelling among us, full of grace and truth.

CHAPTER XXXI.

THE KINGDOM.

The revelations concerning the woman's seed developed thus far, and consummated in His first advent to earth, have been connected with His mediatorship and atonement. The truths herein embraced were required to be developed first, as they revealed the way of access for sinners to God, and the method of their justification. Accordingly, instruction was commenced on these points at the beginning, and the sacrifice of innocence was appointed, to show that without the shedding of blood there was no remission of sins.

We now turn back upon the line of revelation, to take up the next succeeding step in the history of redemption as connected with

THE KINGDOM OF CHRIST.

The germs of this subject are found in the constitution of Israel as a nation, and the choice of Jehovah as their sovereign. Previous to this, we have no intimation that Christ was to have *a kingdom* on earth. The time had not come for the unfolding of this idea, belonging, as it did, to a later age. A foundation must first be laid, upon which it might be developed. To this end *the kingdom of Israel was constituted*, and at this point the Divine revelations on this subject began.

It has been shown already how the Divine presence was manifested among men from the beginning in visible glory, dwelling between the cherubim, and how He declared himself to Moses by His own memorial name, Yahveh, the coming One, the Deliverer. He it was who dwelt in the pillar of cloud going before the host, and who spake from Sinai, proclaiming himself their God and Saviour, before whom they were to have no other gods. The time had now come when the tribes of Israel were to enter into a national organization, and be regularly constituted into a government by their own voluntary act—a fact of sublimest interest, and without a parallel in the history of the ancient nations. The first transaction occurring after the arrival of the tribes at Sinai, was the submission to them of the question, whether they would accept Him, who had gone before and led them out of Egypt, as their lawgiver and king. The nature of this transaction is worthy of the most careful study, and essential to a clear understanding of the Hebrew commonwealth, and of the kingdom of God. The record is as follows: And Moses went up unto God, and the Lord called unto him out of the mountain, saying, Thus shalt thou say unto the house of Jacob, and tell the children of Israel; ye have seen what I did unto the Egyptians, and how I bare you on eagles' wings, and brought you unto myself. Now therefore, if ye will obey my voice indeed, and keep my covenant, then ye shall be a peculiar treasure unto me above all people: for all the earth is mine: and ye shall be unto me a kingdom of priests, and an holy nation. These are the words which thou shalt speak unto the children of Israel. And Moses came and called for the elders of the people, and laid before their faces all these words which the Lord commanded him. *And all the people answered together, and said, All that the Lord hath spoken we will do.* And Moses returned the words of the people unto the Lord; Exod. xix. 3. Here was the first adoption of a national constitution by a people —the first organization of a constitutional government in the history of the world—that constitution being embraced in a single article; *that Jehovah should be their lawgiver and king, and they His people.* In the language of those times, it is called a *covenant.* We should call it a constitution. The organic law upon which the commonwealth of Israel was founded, was that Jehovah should be the supreme ruler and legislator, the nation accepting Him in this relation, and binding themselves thereto by solemn and everlasting covenant. This, moreover, is not to be taken in a merely religious sense. It was a strictly civil transaction, Jehovah being chosen as the ruler of the nation to legislate for and govern the kingdom, like any earthly sovereign. We find, accordingly, that God proceeded at once to organize the government in all its departments, enacting a complete and perfect code of laws—the most complete and beneficent that was ever ordained for any people—and establishing all their institutions. He set in operation their entire system of government, the supreme, legislative, and executive power being vested in himself. *Israel was thus God's kingdom on earth*—literally so. It was a perfect theocracy, the civil government being administered by Jehovah. At His bidding, also, the nation erected a tabernacle or palace, where He might abide among them —be approached by His appointed ministers, and make known to them all His will. And when this edifice had been duly consecrated, Jehovah descended in visible majesty, in sight of all the congregation, from the top of the mount, and entering within, filled the place with the insufferable brightness of His glory, so that even the priests could not stand to minister there. Subsequently He retired within the inner apartment, and there took up

His permanent dwelling-place over the mercy-seat between the cherubim. These were stupendous facts in the founding of that nation, which they could not mistake, which formed the whole current of their thought, and by which they were taught, from the foundation of their national history, to regard themselves as *God's kingdom on earth.*

Passing on to a later period in their history, we come to a further development of this subject, where new light begins to be thrown on the designs of heaven.

In the time of Samuel, the nation had become dissatisfied with their anomalous condition in not having a human king, like the surrounding nations, who might go out to war with them and head their armies; and they demanded of the prophet that such a one should be set over them. The thing displeased the Lord exceedingly, because, *in the intent of the nation*, it was a dissatisfaction with the Divine administration, and a *violation of the constitution* in rejecting Jehovah as their king. The people demanded a king "like all the nations"—that is, a king with unlimited authority to make laws and establish institutions. Such were the only kings known in those days; and that this was the inevitable tendency of those times, the attempted usurpations of Saul plainly show. This was the aspect of the affair that made it so displeasing to the Lord, for which He severely rebuked the nation, and *in respect to which He denied their request.* It was for the very attempt made in this direction by Saul to override the constitution, that he was set aside from the kingdom, and another chosen who would administer the government within the prescribed limits of that sacred instrument; or, in Scripture phraseology, "a man after God's own heart." To this extent there was no impropriety in the desire and request of the people for a king, and to this extent God yielded to them in the matter. Thus far it fell in with His own purposes, and accomplished His own designs, as we shall see in unfolding the coming kingdom of Christ. God, therefore, did grant the request of the nation in giving a king *with subordinate authority, and bound by the constitution ;* that is, a king who should administer the government under His direction, subject to His appointment, removable at His pleasure, and obedient in all things to His will. Thus he was styled *the Lord's Anointed.* This explains what seems so strange at first that God should have apparently granted a request with which He was so greatly displeased, and which He so severely rebuked. The appointment of a king with subordinate authority, to act as the Lord's Anointed, was in accordance with His will, and was designed to constitute the next step in unfolding the system of redemption. It corresponds very closely with the plan of the Divine revelations concerning the priesthood, sacrifices being appointed and made familiar from the beginning, while it was not until the age of Noah or Shem, that a special class was set apart to the sacred office, to represent Christ as our ever living Mediator. So the kingdom of God existed in Israel from the foundation of the nation, Jehovah being their sovereign lawgiver. But the Divine plan was for that kingdom to come into the possession of one born of woman. Jehovah, in His Divine nature, had occupied the throne of that kingdom, dwelling between the cherubim. The same was to belong to Jehovah, also, in His humanity ; and to prepare the way for this, a line of kings was introduced in the time of Samuel. So soon, too, as a man was found, like David, to fulfil all the Lord's pleasure, he was designated to stand a representative of Christ in His kingly office—even as Melchizedec shadowed Him forth in his priesthood—and the promise was made that the coming One of earth should be of his seed, and heir to his throne.

From this point the prophecies concerning the kingdom are abundant, while earth's coming Deliverer appears now as the Lord's Anointed, established as king in Zion forever, whose kingdom was to be an everlasting kingdom, and of whose dominion there was to be no end. The prophets are never weary with this sublime theme, and delight to paint, in the most glowing colors, the glory, the blessedness, and enduring continuance of Christ's reign on earth; how under His righteous sceptre, peace and joy should again return to earth, the curse be removed, every enemy subdued, and death itself finally swallowed up in victory. Prophecy also points out and describes the opposing worldly dynasties which were to arise and succeed one another, until they should all at last be broken, and made like the chaff of the summer threshing floor, when the kingdom, and the greatness of the kingdom under the whole heaven, should come into the possession of the heir of David, and He should reign forever and ever. This event was surely to be brought about, in spite of all the rage and wrath of the rulers, and their wicked counsels. The decree was established immovably that Christ must have this earth, even the uttermost parts thereof, for His inheritance.

In the course of time, this kingdom of the Messiah came to be spoken of as "the kingdom of heaven," because it was to possess so many of the elements of heaven. It was not to be one of the selfish, ambitious, grasping empires of the world, treading down the poor and needy. It was to be a kingdom of righteousness, truth, and peace, which should bring heaven down to earth, and cause God again to take up His tabernacle among men. That kingdom, however, thus described, was plainly an event to be realized in the future history of earth. It belonged to that time of restitution of all things, foretold from the beginning. These also were the glowing prophecies, which fixed the attention of the Jewish nation, and fixed their hopes, as they could be made easily to fall in with their national sympathies and ambition. They gloried in David, their great monarch, under whom their country had reached the proudest preëminence; and they looked forward with fondest anticipation to the coming of David's greater Son, when far more glorious things were to be realized, and all the promises which God had made from the beginning were to be fulfilled. Neither is it wonderful that the nation, to a large extent, had their attention so much absorbed with these prophecies respecting the kingdom, that they overlooked, and finally lost sight of that other class which told of His humiliation, His sufferings, and rejection, of His bearing our sins, and being delivered for our offences. It was difficult, no doubt, to reconcile the two—difficult to understand how He should thus triumph and be exalted, so that every knee should bow to Him and every tongue confess Him Lord; and yet that He should be a root out of dry ground, without form or comeliness, a man of sorrows and acquainted with grief, His countenance marred more than any man, and His form more than the sons of men, so that they should hide their faces from Him. They did not then see, what is now made so apparent to us, that two separate comings of Christ were here represented—one, when He should appear to place himself under law and the curse, to be made a sin-offering, and so accomplish the work of His priesthood; the other, when He should appear in His power and kingdom to remove the curse, prevail against every enemy, and bring in the long-promised, long-delayed day of earth's redemption. They did not understand His priestly character, and, above all, His relation as a victim appointed for sacrifice. It is not wonderful that they failed to discover the glory of a kingdom there, and a throne, when there was only a servant ministering to our race, and humbling himself to wash its very feet.

These distinctions are not clearly apprehended now, though we mistake in the other direction. We have seen such wonders connected with that first coming of Christ in His humiliation and priesthood, that we have confounded with it the prophecies and facts which belong to His second advent in His kingdom and glory, no more as a sin-offering, but as a triumphing conqueror. We have been taught so to glory in the *cross* of Christ, that we have been led to feel almost as if that were enough, being satisfied with the amazing work of His priesthood. In this way, the Church has lost her interest, to a large extent, in the second coming of her Lord, and ceased to make it any special object of hope, as the fulfilment of the promises and prophecies, all of which are pressed within the compass of the first advent, which has to do simply with the priesthood of an Immanuel; and thus has confusion been introduced into all our ideas respecting the coming glory and kingdom of our Jesus. Can there be a doubt that we are living still within the limits of that period when Christ is esteemed a root out of dry ground—when He is despised and rejected of men, and the cry still is, Crucify Him, crucify Him? There is no change in the essential character of the period since Christ first came. There is the same conflict going on with the powers of darkness and evil. The world still holds the empire. Christ no more rules now than He did then. The battle everywhere rages. The flock of Christ is small, and called still to watch and wait for her Lord's appearing. Iniquity abounds, and the love of many waxes cold.

With these facts of the Old Testament history thus elucidated, *let us now turn to see how the kingdom of heaven is announced by Christ himself, and those who acted in conjunction with Him.*

The announcement made by John the Baptist, by Jesus and His disciples, was, that the kingdom of heaven was at hand, for which men must prepare themselves by repentance and a new life. In one or two instances, Christ says, "The kingdom of God is come unto you," or upon you, while He frequently describes the same under the figures of a sower, a net cast for fishes, leaven hid in meal, a mustard seed, and things of a like nature, evidently representing an existing state of facts. The kingdom of God or heaven, then, is employed in the gospels *in some sense* to describe what was then being realized; from which the conclusion has been drawn that its proper signification is the gospel dispensation. With this, very many are satisfied as the explanation of the whole matter, not deeming it necessary to look or inquire any further. But this interpretation will not sufficiently meet the facts of the case. It may accord with a partial and one-sided view, but it fails entirely to explain all the facts.

Let us notice, then, what the statements are concerning the near approach of the kingdom.

John the Baptist came, preaching in the wilderness of Judea, and saying, Repent ye; for the kingdom of heaven is at hand; Matt. iii. 2. From that time Jesus began to preach, and to say, Repent; for the kingdom of heaven is at hand; Matt. iv. 17. The disciples proclaimed the same message, when they were sent forth, preaching the glad tidings of the kingdom, and healing everywhere. We are told, now, that this can refer only to the dispensation which Jesus was then inaugurating. Turn, then, to the twenty-first chapter of Luke, where Christ, in answer to a direct inquiry from the disciples respecting the events connected with His coming and the end of the world, enters into a full explanation, so that they should not be deceived or disappointed. He tells them of the time of tribulation that was coming on the earth, and how the nations were to be convulsed to their foundations. He tells them of wars and commotions—of great earthquakes, famines, and pestilences—of sore persecutions to the people of God—of abounding errors, apostacies, and wickedness, so that few would be able to endure to the end, and the love of many should wax cold. He tells them that Jerusalem shall be compassed with armies, and laid waste, being trodden down of the Gentiles *until the times of the Gentiles should be fulfilled,* which fact necessarily carries these events to a period far beyond the destruction of that city. Passing then again to the general subject and the affairs of the world, He speaks of a period of still greater distress, the things already described being but the beginning of sorrows. He tells of the signs in the sun, and in the moon, and in the stars; and upon the earth distress of *nations* (showing that it was not the land of Judea alone, but the world that was involved) with perplexity; the sea and the waves roaring; men's hearts failing them for fear, and looking after those things which are coming on the earth: for the powers of heaven shall be shaken. And then shall they see the Son of man coming in a cloud, with power and great glory. And when these things begin to come to pass, then look up, and lift up your heads: for your redemption draweth nigh.

Here, now, is clearly a description of events intervening until the second coming of Christ, when He shall be revealed in the clouds of heaven with power and great glory, and the day of redemption shall come to the suffering saints, so that they may lift up their heads with joy. It was given for the specific purpose of informing the disciples as to the time of His coming and the end of the world, concerning which they inquired. Jesus accordingly unfolds the future, and accurately portrays the character of the coming period, with its tribulations and abounding wickedness, in the midst of which but a few would be able to endure. To enforce the facts, He spake a parable, and very much to the point. "Behold the fig-tree, and all the trees; when they now shoot forth, ye see and know of your own selves that summer is now nigh at hand. So likewise, when ye see these things come to pass, *know ye that the kingdom of God is nigh at hand.*" Here, then, after centuries of war and revolutions, of persecutions and apostacies, and in immediate prospect of the Son of man, revealed in the clouds of heaven with power and great glory, to bring the promised redemption to His suffering saints, we have the clear statement of Christ that the kingdom of heaven was near, and that the events described foretokened its approach, even as the budding of the trees the Spring. The kingdom of heaven, then, in the sense here intended, is not yet come; neither can it be the gospel dispensation which is referred to, for that has been in existence during all the period of tribulation preceding. Jesus carries the minds of His disciples forward to the close of that dispensation, and then says: "When ye see these things come to pass, know ye that the kingdom of God is nigh at hand." The words of Christ immediately following are: "Verily, I say unto you, This generation shall not pass away, till all be fulfilled." The interpretation put upon this passage has thrown obscurity over the whole discourse, confining the fulfilment to the generation then living, and forcing the reference of the whole mainly to the destruction of Jerusalem. The word generation, however, in the New Testament, has very rarely the specific meaning which we ordinarily attach to it, designating those living at a given time, and embraced within the average period of human life. Its proper and common meaning is that of race, people, descent, and it is so usually employed in the New

Testament. Thus the nation is spoken of as "this evil and adulterous generation," evidently meaning this race or people, without any reference to the term of their continuance; while of Christ it is asked, Who shall declare his generation? Acts viii. 33—that is, His posterity. It may also be observed that, whenever the word is clearly used to mark a period of time, it is put in the plural number, even though translated in our version in the singular. The meaning, then, of the passage under consideration, would be, This generation shall not pass away; they shall continue, and continue *what they are, an evil and unbelieving race*, till all be fulfilled. It must be borne in mind that Christ was describing events wholly new and unexpected to the disciples, drawing the picture of a period such as they had never anticipated in the imes of the Messiah, and, to their minds, wholly contradictory to the character and destiny of that chosen people. The idea of their being delivered up to the synagogues, to be scourged, hated, and persecuted of all men, and delivered to death for the sake of Christ, was a new view of history entirely. There was, therefore, meaning to the declaration, "Verily I say unto you, This generation shall not pass away, till all be fulfilled. Heaven and earth shall pass away: but my words shall not pass away." It was equivalent to the statement, and embodied the same idea to be found at the close of that thrilling denunciation of the rulers, and the utterance of woe against Jerusalem, which led the disciples to inquire when these things should be. Behold, your house is left unto you desolate. For I say unto you, *Ye shall not see me henceforth, till ye shall say, Blessed is he that cometh in the name of the Lord*; Matt. xxiii. 38, 39. Jesus thus closes both discourses, one to the Pharisees and Scribes, the other to the disciples, concerning these coming events, with the same thought of the continuance of that evil generation. But

He did not mean that the men then living on the earth should witness the accomplishment of all these things, for they have not yet been fulfilled. Wars and famines, pestilences and earthquakes, revolutions, apostacies, and wickedness, still continue, and the powers of heaven are being shaken as never before. This unbelieving generation has not passed away.

The question now returns upon us, What is the meaning to be attached to the kingdom of God, as used in the New Testament?

The generic idea is that of the Messiah's advent, with the events therein involved.

This was the idea prominent to the mind of the nation. They conceived that when the Messiah appeared, He would take possession of the promised throne of David, and establish that kingdom which the prophets had described in such glowing language, and which should supersede all the kingdoms of the earth. This was the only conception which the nation of Israel had of the matter, so that the advent of the Messiah and the kingdom were synonymous terms to every Jewish mind. This fact, now, will explain the use of the phrase "kingdom of heaven," in the wide sense given it, and solve all the difficulties respecting it.

The kingdom had come, so far as that great central event was concerned, that the Anointed of heaven, the woman's seed, had at length appeared, who was to be the founder and glory of that kingdom, and in whom all the promises were to be fulfilled. This will clearly explain the words of Christ to those who charged Him with casting out devils through Beelzebub: But if I with the finger of God cast out devils, no doubt the kingdom of God is come upon you; Luke xi. 20. The fact intended here to be asserted was, that the very Messiah had appeared, and was demonstrating His presence by His power over all devils, binding them at His pleasure. Well and appropriately, therefore, did He say to these cavilling objectors, in language, too, which they would understand, "No doubt, the kingdom of God is come unto you;" and this without intending to distinguish between His present mission of obedience and suffering in connection with His priesthood, and His future and glorious appearing in His kingdom and power, when He should no more be subject to, but administer, law. There was no necessity for drawing the line in this instance, when pressing the argument upon the unbelieving rulers. The whole kingdom of God, in all its relations and aspects, was involved in that mission of the Messiah. Jesus, however, did not mean to assert that the kingdom was come unto them in the sense that He had taken possession of the throne of David, to rule in equity and truth. He was only a servant, now under law himself, and, by His perfect obedience unto death, proving that He was qualified, at the appointed hour, to take the reins of government, and be exalted head over all, to whom every knee should bow, and every tongue confess.

This will explain, also, the numerous parables of the Saviour, in which He likened the kingdom of heaven to various objects. He meant to explain the character of the present dispensation under His own Messiahship, and this was virtually, in the view of all, to claim the kingdom. But He did not mean to assert that the time had now come for Him to be revealed in His power and glory. On the contrary, He intended to describe the dispensation which was connected with His first mission of obedience and suffering, and necessarily antecedent to the other, as He subsequently said to the disciples: Ought not Christ to have suffered these things, and to enter into his glory? Luke xxiv. 26. Must He not come in His humiliation first, to obey as a servant, and so become qualified or made perfect as the Captain of salvation? The aim of Jesus, then, was to turn the attention of His hearers, and the nation, to the character of this preceding dispensation, which was so different from any thing that was anticipated, and of which they were wholly ignorant. It was as difficult to make this understood, as it was to open the subject of His sufferings and death to the minds of His disciples. Therefore did Jesus dwell the more upon this, bringing it up in so many varied relations, and illustrating it by so many parables, that, if possible, it might be made plain. It was necessary, moreover, that Jesus should employ this very form of expression—the kingdom of heaven—in asserting these truths, because it was the assertion of His own claims to the Messiahship, and at the same time giving a reason why the kingdom was not now revealed in the form in which they had reason to expect it—that is, the throne and the power. Jesus did not intend to deny these as properly belonging to the kingdom, but only to declare another aspect of the subject as connected with His present mission of suffering. He knew well that the promises and prophecies of the Old Testament involved two advents of the Messiah, one preparatory to the other—one fulfilling His mediatorship, the other His throne and kingdom proper. The former was the one most needing explanation to the nation, being the farthest removed from all their thoughts, and essential to an understanding of the other. It was the one, therefore, which Jesus made most prominent in His instructions, knowing well that, if this were rightly apprehended, there would be no difficulty respecting the second.

It will be evident from this statement of facts, that the unfolding of this subject was one of extreme difficulty, which has been too little appreciated. How was Jesus to assert and maintain His own Messiahship, when there was nothing connected with His person, the character of His work, or His doctrines, which indicated any sovereignty or rule, such as belonged properly to the heir of David's throne? How, without a kingdom, or the pretense of one, was He to stand up before the nation, and claim that He was the expected, promised Prince of the house of David, into whose hands the dominion and greatness of the kingdom under the whole heaven was to come? It is necessary to have these facts before our minds, if we would follow Jesus Christ through His earthly career, and get the full meaning and force of His marvellous instructions, as He developed this whole subject to His wondering, bewildered nation.

These same facts, also, will explain the difficulties and disappointments of the disciples, as they watched the incomprehensible career of their Master.

At no time previous to His death did they imagine that He had taken possession of the kingdom. He never assured them that He had. They were expecting every day that He would be revealed in His power and glory. But instead of this, He discoursed most strangely of His approaching sufferings and death, His rejection by the rulers, and delivery into the hands of the Gentiles—matters to them of deepest mystery and terror, and of which they were afraid to ask an explanation. When, too, at last, they saw Him delivered to death, and actually yield up the ghost, they were overwhelmed with consternation and despair. But soon again they beheld their risen Lord, and their minds were opened by Him to understand the Scriptures, that He needs must have suffered before entering into His glory. All their fondest hopes they now expected certainly to see immediately realized. They waited, however, for forty days, during which He was giving repeated demonstrations of His real presence among them, when, evidently growing impatient at the delay, they finally questioned Him directly respecting the matter, saying, Lord, wilt thou at this time restore the kingdom to Israel? Acts i. 6. There is no evidence in this question, as often alleged, that their views were carnal and worldly—that they had misapprehended entirely the nature of Christ's kingdom, and were looking for something that they would never realize. If their views had been what is so often represented, Christ would not, on this occasion especially, have failed to rebuke and correct them. He never failed to make such correction, even under ordinary circumstances. Above all would He not have failed at this hour, when He was about to be separated from them until His final appearing, and commit His sacred cause to their hands. If their views were as carnal and worldly as is so often represented, He could not here have kept silence—could not have failed to correct their sad misapprehensions. But there is not the slightest intimation from Him that there was any error in the case. He does not hint that any of their expectations would be disappointed. He does not tell them that the kingdom was already restored, as so many now believe. His answer simply respected the matter of time, when the event in regard to which they inquired would be fulfilled. And He told them that it was "not for them to know the times or the seasons"—that the Father had reserved them in His own power. The work to which they were now appointed was not to enjoy the peace and blessedness of the kingdom for which they waited, but to be "witnesses unto him in Jerusalem, and in all Judea, and in Samaria, and unto the uttermost parts of the earth." Witnesses of what? Witnesses of His kingdom? Not by any means; but witnesses that He was raised from the grave—raised from His state of subjection and humiliation, where He had obeyed even unto death, and that He would come again to claim the kingdom at the appointed hour. Great injustice, therefore, has been done the disciples, in charging upon them ignorance and carnal views at this point. The Master has not seen fit to do it, and they who assume the task, unwittingly condemn themselves, demonstrating that they have failed to comprehend the Scriptures and enter into their true meaning. The carnal views have been attributed to the wrong party.

"And when he had said these things," replying to their inquiry respecting the times and seasons, "while they beheld, he was taken up; and a cloud received him out of their sight." He had left them, gone up on high, and *the kingdom was not restored to Israel.* Neither had the Master told them when it would be. They were lost in wonder. But while they looked up steadfastly into heaven, as he went up, behold, two men stood by them in white apparel; which also said, Ye men of Galilee, why stand ye gazing up into heaven? this same Jesus which is taken up from you into heaven, *shall so come in like manner as ye have seen him go into heaven;* Acts i. 9. This, then, was the solution of the deep mystery. *Jesus was to return again to restore the kingdom to Israel,* and their commission was to bear witness of His resurrection, preaching through Him the remission of sins. In this work the Church is still engaged, and must continue until her Lord's return. We therefore call this the gospel dispensation—the dispensation of good tidings concerning the kingdom. By-and-by another announcement will be made, when the shout shall go up from all the dwellers upon earth, and be echoed back from heaven. The kingdoms of this world *are become* the kingdoms of our Lord, and of his Christ; and he shall reign forever and ever; Rev. xi. 15. Well and appropriately, too, does the volume of inspiration close with the thrilling, comforting words of Christ to His suffering, tried Church. "Behold,

I come." I come—"surely I come quickly;" to which the joyful response is, "Even so, come, Lord Jesus."

Turning also to the instructions of Christ, we find that He gives this very view of the subject whenever He enters into particulars, and attempts to explain *when* the kingdom of God should appear. And as they heard these things, he added and spake a parable, because they were nigh to Jerusalem, and *because they thought that the kingdom of God should immediately appear;* Luke xix. 11. The parable, then, was spoken for the purpose of correcting the misapprehension of the multitude in regard to the immediate appearance of the kingdom of the Messiah, showing that they were mistaken on that point. It is worthy of notice, also, that this instruction was given immediately before His triumphal entry into Jerusalem, being welcomed with hosannas as the royal Son of David. Jesus allowed this extraordinary honor to be paid Him, knowing what construction the multitude and His disciples also would necessarily put upon it; therefore "he added and spake a parable, because they were nigh to Jerusalem, and because they thought the kingdom of God should immediately appear." Here, then, is the specific point in controversy. Now let Jesus decide it. "He said therefore, A certain nobleman went into a far country *to receive for himself a kingdom, and to return*," referring to the familiar fact that those who sought the government of Judea, or other provinces, were obliged to go to Rome, and receive the kingdom there with the seals of office from the emperor. "And he called his ten servants, and delivered unto them ten pounds, and said unto them, Occupy till I come. But his citizens hated him, and sent a message after him [to the emperor], saying, We will not have this man to reign over us. And it came to pass, that *when he was returned, having received the kingdom*, then he commanded these servants to be called, to whom he had given the money." Christ is the nobleman here described. He departed, in order to obtain the kingdom. He was absent a considerable period, travelling into a far country, that He might secure the same. He had no authority to administer it until His return. That absence of Christ is *now the existing fact*, represented in the parable. His enemies are asserting, with great vehemence, that they will not have Him to reign over them. His faithful servants are occupying till He come, and anxiously waiting His return. He cannot administer the kingdom until He does return, when He will have authority to reward His friends, and overthrow His determined enemies. These are the obvious facts of the parable, which cannot be controverted. They are too plain to be denied or evaded; while the parable itself was given to correct the idea in the public mind "that the kingdom of God was immediately to appear." The doctrine of Christ, then, is, that His kingdom will be set up on His return at His second coming. This is the explanation which He himself gives of the matter.

Turn, now, to another discourse of Christ on this subject, to be found in Luke xvii. 20: "When he was demanded of the Pharisees, *when* the kingdom of God should come," the very question we want answered. In studying this reply of Jesus, it is essential to note who the inquirers were, as He always adapted His answers and instructions to the characters of those to whom He spake. To these captious Pharisees, then, He said, "The kingdom of God cometh not with observation: neither shall they say, Lo here! or, Lo there! for behold, the kingdom of God is within you." You Pharisees will in vain watch for outward signs, that will cause you to run here and there to find the Messias. *You* will find Him by a radical change only of all your views and feelings.

The kingdom must be found within you, and begin there. This was just the truth they needed to hear. But, as His subsequent remarks clearly show, it was only a very partial answer to their inquiry, and did not really meet the point. It was wisely adapted to these Pharisees—as much as they could digest—more, in fact, than they could receive. And to show that He had not exhausted the subject, He turned immediately, "and said unto *the disciples* [who were in a different state of mind, and to whom other instruction was adapted for their encouragement], The days will come, when ye shall desire to see one of the days of the Son of man [that is, of His kingdom and glory; for they were now beholding the days of His humiliation and sorrow], *and ye shall not see it.* And they shall say to you, See here! or, See there! go not after them, nor follow them. For, *as the lightning that lighteneth out of the one part under heaven, shineth unto the other part under heaven; so shall also the Son of man be in his day.* But first must he suffer many things, and be rejected of this generation." Did Jesus, then, tell *the Pharisees* that the kingdom of heaven would not come to them by observation; but would be found, if found at all, within them? So likewise did He as emphatically tell *the disciples*, for their comfort and instruction, under their sore disappointment in not witnessing the promised day of hope and desire, that the kingdom would come with observation, so that they need not run hither and thither to look for it, for it would be as apparent as the flash of lightning illumining the whole heavens—that, because of trial and sore persecution, they would long for the blessed day of Christ, but would be disappointed for a season. Nevertheless, it should come. "But first must he suffer many things, and be rejected of this generation." Yes, *first*, before the kingdom shall come. Christ is still suffering many things, and rejected of that generation. The people of God are still longing to see one of the days of the Son of man, and have not seen it. Their hearts have almost fainted at the long delay, while the proud and scornful foe insultingly asks, "Where is the promise of his coming?" Thus does Christ, in answering the question put by the Pharisees, clearly unfold both aspects of the subject, telling the unbelieving class where alone they must look for and find the kingdom—that is, within them—while He comforts the disciples by the assurance that, though disappointed for a season, their grandest hopes should all be realized, and they shall behold the day, and that with observation.

In the following emphatic declarations, Christ carefully distinguishes between His different missions, and marks the character of each: Verily I say unto you, That ye which have followed me in the REGENERATION, *when the Son of man shall sit upon the throne of his glory*, ye also shall sit upon twelve thrones, judging the twelve tribes of Israel; Matt. xxix. 28. Ye are they which have continued with me *in my temptations;* and I appoint unto you a kingdom, as my Father hath appointed unto me; that ye may eat and drink *at my table in my kingdom*, and sit on thrones, judging the twelve tribes of Israel; Luke xxii. 28. Here Christ speaks of His first mission as the time of His "temptations," and refers to a future period as the "regeneration," the time of restitution of all things, when the Son of man should sit upon the throne of His glory, and His disciples should have their reward, sitting down with Him "in his kingdom."

"Be patient, therefore, brethren, unto the coming of the Lord. Behold, the husbandman waiteth for the precious fruit of the earth, and hath long patience for it, until he receive the early and the latter rain." It lies buried through the snows of winter. Yet still his faith and hope fail not. "Be ye also patient; stablish your hearts: for the coming of the Lord draweth nigh;" James v. 7, 8.

Before closing this discussion, it may be necessary to notice one passage which seems to conflict with the view here taken, and which may require explanation. Verily I say unto you, There be some standing here, which shall not taste of death, till they see the Son of man coming in his kingdom; Matt. xvi. 28. If the ordinary view of this subject is correct, which makes the kingdom of Christ to commence with His first advent, then it were not necessary to assert that there were "*some* standing there which should not taste of death" until they witnessed the same, because all were witnesses to the fact at that moment. It was then already revealed to the nation. Their eyes had looked upon the king—the Lord of hosts. They had heard His words of salvation, and seen His mighty deeds. The fact, too, should so have been stated, and would have been if the view commonly entertained of this matter had been in the mind of Jesus. He could not have avoided it.

What Christ had reference to in the above statement, was the revelation of His glory in the transfiguration scene, which followed so soon after—which the three evangelists are careful to narrate in the immediate connection—and which was given for the purpose of strengthening the faith of the disciples under the overwhelming facts which Jesus had just communicated to them, respecting His death and rejection by His nation. They were in danger of being overborne by the strange and, for the present, incomprehensible facts of such deep humiliation and apparent failure. To encourage, therefore, their desponding hearts (for this was the first time that He had broached the subject of His sufferings), Jesus took three of them up into the mount and unveiled to them His glory, thus proving to them, notwithstanding His present humiliation and approaching death, that they should, at the appointed hour, behold Him revealed in His kingdom, beyond all their expectations. Nor was there an event in the history of Jesus better calculated to demonstrate to the minds of the perplexed disciples, that their Master was now in a state of strange humiliation, contradictory to all His character, and from which they should by-and-by see the veil lifted. The Apostle Peter, in referring to this very scene, thus speaks concerning it: For we have not followed cunningly devised fables, when we made known unto you the power and coming of our Lord Jesus Christ, but were eye-witnesses of his majesty. For he received from God the Father honor and glory, when there came such a voice from the excellent glory, This is my beloved Son, in whom I am well pleased. And this voice we heard, when we were with him in the holy mount; 2 Peter i. 16. Peter then declares that he had already been an eye-witness of the majesty and power with which Christ would appear, when He should come the second time in His kingdom, for of this He was speaking; and that they had followed no cunningly devised fables in preaching this doctrine concerning Jesus—that He was to rule the world in righteousness. Christ, then, had no reference to the existing gospel dispensation, when He spake of some who should not taste of death until they saw the Son of man coming in His kingdom.

CHAPTER XXXIII.

HARMONY OF THE MOSAIC AND CHRISTIAN SYSTEMS.

WE have now reached a point in the history of redemption where we may pause to consider the harmony of the system, and the relations of the Mosaic and the Christian economies. Those relations, to the minds of many, are not clearly defined; neither do they understand where the line is to be drawn between the temporary and the permanent in that former dispensation. Some would sweep it all away, asserting that it has been entirely abolished, and that the Christian is a new system, embodying new laws and principles. Others, again, find it difficult to draw the line between that which is abolished and that which still remains. Can the principle which settles this be well and clearly defined?

Consider, then, first the essential unity of the Mosaic and Christian systems.

There is a Judaism which is in antagonism to the Gospel, and which made deadly war upon it, as there is a Christianity, so-called, which denies every doctrine of the New Testament, and rejects its whole salvation. The very Jewish rulers were the men who crucified the Lord of life. But they did not represent nor understand their own system. They were not the true descendants of the great founders of the nation, Abraham, Moses, David, and the prophets; but apostates from the faith, holding on to the names of the men and the systems whose principles they rejected, as apostates always do. The Pharisees claimed to be the children of Abraham, and to sit on Moses' seat, although they had become the children of the devil. While, therefore, there is a false Judaism which corrupts the Word of God, there is a true Judaism, also, which is in perfect harmony with Christianity, and accordant with its entire spirit. Jesus Christ founded all His instructions upon the Old Testament, appealing to those Scriptures to substantiate His life and teachings in every particular, and directing His hearers to them as His witness and authority. "Search the Scriptures; for in them ye think ye have eternal life: and *they are they which testify of me.*" "Think not that I am come to destroy the law or the prophets: I am not come to destroy, but to fulfil. For verily I say unto you, Till heaven and earth pass, one jot or one tittle shall in no wise pass from the law, till all be fulfilled." So likewise after His resurrection, "beginning at Moses, he expounded to them in all the Scriptures the things concerning himself," showing how they all bore witness to His sufferings and His rejection of the rulers, as well as the glory that should follow.

When the Apostles, also, went forth upon their mission to preach the doctrine of Jesus, their appeal was invariably to the Old Testament as the Word of God. They preached to Jews who had Moses, and the prophets, and the Psalms; and their appeal was to these authoritative writings, to prove that Jesus, the rejected, crucified, and risen One, was very Christ. Paul occupied the same ground and argued mightily from these Scriptures, thus confounding the Jews, proving that they did not understand the Word of God, but had departed from its true meaning and teachings. He showed that true Judaism would lead to an acceptance of Jesus as the Christ, who was the fulfilment of all prophecy—that in Him not one jot or tittle of the law had failed.

These are the undeniable teachings of Christ and all His apostles. They assert and prove that their doctrines were in perfect harmony with the system of Moses and in fulfilment of it, and that the whole structure of Christianity was reared upon the Word of God as contained in the Old Testament. They, therefore, who lay aside or reject those Scriptures as either false, or useless, or contradictory to the New Testament, show clearly that they are ignorant of the teachings both of Jesus Christ and His apostles on this subject.

But let us pass to a specification of some particulars, which will show more clearly the harmony of the two covenants.

The system of salvation contained in both is the same.

The doctrine of the New Testament most clearly is that of justification by faith. The Apostle Paul, however, shows that this was nothing new—that while circumcision and the law were introduced temporarily for certain ends, they were never designed to subvert the doctrine of faith—the doctrine by which Abraham himself was justified, and upon which the everlasting covenant was based. "Abraham *believed* God, and it was counted to him for righteousness." That was the teaching of Moses and the prophets—the uniform teaching of the Word of God in every age, even as early as the days of Abel. The doctrine of circumcision and the law, as the ground of justification and salvation, was a false Judaism—the doctrine of Scribes and Pharisees, not of Moses and the prophets. The doctrine of the Bible was, and ever had been, "By the deeds of the law, there shall no flesh be justified in his sight. But now the righteousness of God without the law is manifested, *being witnessed by the law and the prophets;* even the righteousness of God, which is by faith of Jesus Christ unto all, and upon all them that believe; for there is no difference: for all have sinned, and come short of the glory of God." It was true, indeed, that the doctrine of faith was made to stand out with more distinctness under the new dispensation; but this simply because Christ and His atoning work, as the *objects* of faith, were more clearly unfolded to the acceptance of men. The obedience and death of Christ were new events in the history of redemption, fulfilling the great designs of heaven. As such, too, they could be held up to the faith of mankind, with a clearness and power such as did not belong to them as mere prophecies of the future. But faith itself was always taught—taught as a first principle, an elementary truth, which could never be denied or questioned. God assumed from the beginning that He was to be believed—that every word of His was worthy of acceptation, whatever it might be. Thus Abel believed God in the things that were revealed to him. So did Enoch, Noah, Abraham, and all the saints; and on this ground they were accepted as righteous. This is the method of salvation now. Christ is the object revealed, the object of faith—Jesus Christ, the suffering, crucified Christ. We are to believe in Him and so be justified. The principle and method of salvation, therefore, underlying the whole Bible, are one and the same. Sinners are saved no differently now from what they were in Moses' day.

The doctrine of sin is the same under both systems.

The Jew, indeed, claimed an exemption—claimed that the blood of Abraham was not corrupted like that of the race generally, and that those born of him were born the children of God. But this was a false and perverted Judaism. The teachings of the Bible throughout were, that men were alike sinners, under the same condemnation, needing the same forgiveness and redemption, and to sing forever of the same grace and salvation through the righteousness of faith. The blood which daily streamed from the altar of burnt-offering before the Lord, was a witness to the great fact of a nation's sinfulness, and that only through innocent blood, freely shed, could pardon and life be found. That people might, indeed, think to separate themselves from the rest of the race, saying, in their pride, "Stand by thyself, for I am holier than thou." But true Judaism taught no such doctrine, and they who put thereon any such construction, showed that they knew nothing of the spirit and meaning of their own system—that they had misconceived its aim and end, and would fail of its grace.

The doctrine of regeneration was the same under both systems.

Jesus Christ did not teach the doctrine of the new birth as any new revelation of truth, or different from what Judaism had always contained. He assumed that Nicodemus, as a master in Israel, ought to have been familiar with this as one of the elementary truths of His system—that he should have known that descent from Abraham would not make a man holy—that that which was born of the flesh was only flesh, and that he only was a child of God and an heir of the kingdom who was born anew of the Spirit. This doctrine was as old as the apostacy, was necessarily involved in the fact of that apostacy, and lay at the foundation of the system of redemption. *The form of its statement* was new, because the nation had fallen away from the true faith, and adopted the dangerous error of the holiness of their first or natural birth from Abraham. Jesus declares that this birth leaves them still in their carnal state under the dominion of the flesh, the children of Abraham no different in this respect from other men. "Marvel not then that I said unto thee, Ye must be born again."

The doctrine of Christ and the kingdom of heaven was the same under the two systems.

It was more clearly and fully unfolded under the latter, and therefore better understood. Under the former system, the times of the Messiah were looked forward to in the future, through the glass of prophecy. Under the present dispensation, we have entered upon that promised era, having already witnessed the first advent and work of the woman's seed. The Mosaic system set forth the work which the Redeemer of the world *would* accomplish when the times should be fulfilled. The gospel gives us the *actual history* of His humiliation and suffering. It was a more difficult task to describe this work in the future, than to write of it as an existing and accomplished event; and it was done through type and symbol. The sacrifice of the bleeding lamb was instituted. Man was permitted to look upon paradise, the tree of life, and the cherubim, with the indwelling glory. Subsequently the priesthood was established, and the kingdom of God on earth, shadowing forth the glorious events of the future. These types and prophecies set forth the coming Deliverer, both in the priesthood as the mediator of His people, and in His kingly office, occupying the throne of David forever.

What, now, is the New Testament, with its facts and doctrines, but a development of this very priesthood of Christ—of the offering of His great sacrifice and His mediation within the veil before the throne of God in behalf of sinners, while we are still looking, as were the saints of old, to the future for the kingdom, when He shall occupy the throne, and reign in righteousness and truth, making His enemies His footstool. The teachings, then, of the Old and the New Testaments, concern the same facts precisely, and are perfectly harmonious, one pointing them out in the distant future, the other describing them as in part fulfilled—the days of the Messiah begun. To throw away now that first revelation, antedating the facts, would be an act of folly and wickedness hardly less than that of rejecting the new revelation under the gospel. They are both the revelations of Christ, one as truly as the other, and one not to be clearly understood without the other.

The covenants and promises are the same under both dispensations.

The covenant of Christ under the Gospel is the same that was made with Abraham, the same that was made with Adam at the expulsion from Eden. The covenant has never been changed. It is the same to-day that it was three thousand years ago. It underlies both the Mosaic and Christian systems. The same is true of the promises. "The promise" made to Abraham, that in him and his seed all the families of the earth should be blessed, "is to you, and to your children, and *to all that are afar off*, even as many as the Lord our God shall call." We are the heirs of that blessed promise, even all who are the children of Abraham by faith, belonging to the true circumcision. The ancient worthies "died in faith, not having received the promises, but having seen them afar off, and embraced them, and confessed that they were strangers and pilgrims on the earth." They died in full assurance of the inheritance, and that they should be raised from the dead, to meet the Lord at His coming. This was their blessed hope. So also is it ours. And they, with us, shall enter into the promised rest.

There is the same manifested Godhead under the two dispensations.

The Jehovah of the Old Testament is the Christ of the New. He who was manifested in the glory and the cloud, dwelling between the cherubim over the mercy-seat and before the way of the tree of life, is the same divine and everlasting Word, who was made flesh in the person of Jesus, and dwelt among us, full of grace and truth. The two dispensations were thus instituted and controlled throughout by the same Divine personage. The same power was enthroned in both. What right, then, have we to deny or disparage one more than the other? To question the truth or inspiration of one more than the other? The child is not a man. In many respects they materially differ. Yet they are essential parts of humanity, one belonging to it as truly as the other, one displaying the wisdom and goodness of the infinite Author as much as the other, one no more to be denied or ignored than the other. So of God's work of redemption. The Mosaic is the childhood economy; the gospel the period of its youth. Its glorious manhood lies still in the future, for which we hope and wait, even as the child and youth ever looks forward to the day when he shall be a man of full stature, and do manhood's noble work. But blot out the child from existence, and what becomes of the man?

We thus see that Christianity is the truest Judaism, and that the disciples of the Lord Jesus are the true circumcision. Jesus Christ never renounced Judaism. Never. He fulfilled it, claiming to be himself a Jew in the strictest sense—that He came not to destroy the law or the prophets, but to fulfil. He denied concerning the Scribes and Pharisees that they were Jews, except in name and pretension, and asserted boldly that they should never see Abraham or the kingdom of God. The Apostle takes the same ground. "We (believers) are the circumcision, which worship God in the spirit, and rejoice in Christ Jesus, and have no confidence in the flesh." The others were "the concision," of whom he warns all to beware. "Now therefore ye are no more strangers and foreigners, but fellow-citizens with the saints, and of the household of God; and are built upon the foundation of the apostles and prophets, Jesus Christ himself being the chief corner-stone; in whom all the building fitly framed together groweth into an holy temple in the Lord." "For *he is not a Jew*, which is one outwardly; *neither is that circumcision*, which is outward in the flesh: but he is a Jew which is one inwardly; and circumcision is that of the heart, in the spirit, and not in the letter; whose praise is not of men, but of God." We, as believers, are the true Israel, who have entered into possession of all the promises, being the sons of God, the chosen, covenant people, even joint heirs with Christ; while the Jewish nation, as the mere outward Israel, are outcasts, being themselves aliens and foreigners, looking and waiting in vain for the promised Deliverer.

It may assist us still more perfectly to understand the harmony and relations of the Mosaic and Christian systems, by considering further the facts taught in both respecting the priesthood and the kingdom.

The priesthood was the commanding feature of the Mosaic dispensation. The tribe of Levi separated wholly unto the Lord, and dependent on the tithes of the land, the temple service, the altar of burnt sacrifice, and the sacred priests, alone admitted to the sanctuary of the Divine presence—these were the first things to arrest attention among that remarkable people. This priesthood was an essential part of their political system, and necessary to the integrity of the state. Without their constant services and mediation, there could be no citizenship and no administration of the government. The civil standing of the nation, and their proper relations to their sovereign, were dependent upon the intervention of the priests in their appointed offices. Israel was a holy nation—that is, separated unto the Lord from all uncleanness—and through the mediation of the consecrated priesthood alone, this clean state was preserved, so that the Lord might dwell among them, and they be His people. We speak of this not in a religious, but in a civil and political sense. The priesthood in Israel was part of the state, strictly so, upon whose services the entire nation was dependent for preserving the proper standing of its citizens. Many have failed to understand this fact, looking upon the priesthood simply as a religious body, like the Christian ministry in our day. But this falls entirely short of the facts of the case. If an Israelite became unclean, he lost his good civil standing; was liable to be cut off from the congregation of the Lord, which, under this peculiar system, was none other than the state, and the mediation of the appointed priest was required in his behalf, who made atonement for him, and removed his disabilities. The continuance of the nation and government, therefore, in their integrity, depended upon the priesthood. This was the standing and righteousness which the Scribes and Pharisees sought unto and attained, having no conception of religion beyond this. They observed all the civil statutes, even to the minutest letter, never coming in from the streets, or sitting down to eat, without purifying themselves. Their civil standing, therefore, was perfect, and as they saw nothing in their system beyond this, they had no sense of sin whatever, and rejoiced in a complete righteousness before God. With such an imperfect view, too, of their theocracy, there was no avenue through which a conviction of sin could come to their souls. There was no law which they were conscious of having violated.

We, however, understand, and the truly spiritual men among the Israelites understood, that this priesthood looked forward to a higher system which had to do, not with a civil standing in that earthly commonwealth, but with citizenship in the kingdom of God. It stood as a type or shadow of better things to come. When we turn, too, to Christianity, we are left in no doubt as to what was intended by these shadows of the old dispensation. Writing to his own Hebrew nation, Paul explains clearly and fully what was meant by that former priesthood, and how it was fulfilled in Christ, a priest after the order of Melchizedec, not according to "the law of a carnal commandment, but after the power of an endless life"—that is, He is a priest, not of the civil state, to secure that citizenship and standing which belong to an outward Judaism, represented by "the law of a carnal commandment," but a priest of the kingdom of God, "after the power of an endless life." "And they truly were many priests, because they were not suffered to continue by reason of death: but this man, because he continueth ever, hath an unchangeable priesthood. Wherefore he is able to save them unto the uttermost that come unto God by him, seeing that he ever liveth to make intercession for us. For such an high-priest became us, who is holy, harmless, undefiled, separate from sinners, and made higher than the heavens; who needeth not daily, as those high-priests, to offer sacrifice, first for his own sins, and then for the people's: for this he did once, when he offered up himself. Of the things, then, which we have spoken, this is the sum: *We have such an high-priest, who is set on the right hand of the throne of the Majesty in the heavens; a minister of the sanctuary, and of the true tabernacle, which the Lord pitched, and not man.* . . . Christ being come an high-priest of good things to come, by a greater and more perfect tabernacle, not made with hands, that is to say, not of this building; neither by the blood of goats and calves, but by his own blood, he entered in once into the holy place, having obtained eternal redemption for us. For if the blood of bulls and of goats, and the ashes of an heifer sprinkling the unclean, sanctifieth to the purifying of the flesh (making an acceptable citizen of the state): how much more shall the blood of Christ, who through the eternal Spirit offered himself without spot to God, purge your conscience from dead works to serve the living God?

And for this cause *He is the mediator of the New Testament*, that by means of death, for the redemption of the transgressions that were under the first testament, they which are called might receive the promise of the eternal inheritance. . . . For Christ is not entered into the holy places made with hands, which are the figures of the true; but into heaven itself, now to appear in the presence of God for us. . . . Having therefore, brethren, boldness to enter into the holiest by the blood of Jesus, by a new and living way, which he hath consecrated for us, through the vail, that is to say, his flesh; and having an high-priest over the house of God; let us draw near with a true heart, in full assurance of faith, having *our hearts* sprinkled from an evil conscience, and our bodies washed with pure water. Let us hold fast the profession of our faith without wavering; for he is faithful that promised."

The priesthood and sacrifice, then, are not done away. We have them more perfectly under the Christian than under the Mosaic system. The temple at Jerusalem, indeed, is gone. Its altar is broken down. The priests of Aaron and their sacrifices are no more. But have we no priesthood, no blood which cleanseth from sin, no mediator to go in before God to make intercession for transgressors, no tabernacle where God's anointed high-priest may stand to make atonement? Yea, verily. We have all these, not in the shadow, but the substance.

Here, then, as will be most manifest, we have the means required for making citizens of the kingdom of God. The mediation of earthly priests, and the blood of slain beasts, were sufficient to secure a standing in the outward Israel or the political commonwealth. But it needed more precious blood, and the mediation of a greater High-Priest, to secure that cleansing which would fit one for citizenship in the kingdom of God, and give a title to the eternal inheritance.

To be constituted such a Priest forever unto His people, was the sole end of that first mission of Christ to earth, which explains the fact that there was the absence of all the accompaniments of royalty and power. He occupied no throne, exercised no authority. He came not, as He himself declared, to judge or rule the world. His first office which He was to fulfil, and to which He was solemnly anointed, was that of the priesthood, which He is now administering.

This, then, is the plain teaching of this revelation—the doctrine of the kingdom of heaven. Jesus Christ is the anointed High-Priest of Israel's true commonwealth. Those who obtain citizenship there, must secure His mediation, and have atonement made by Him for their sin. There is no citizenship in that kingdom without such cleansing by blood and mediatorship; and they who reject Christ in this fundamental office as Priest, reject His whole salvation. They cut themselves off by necessity from all part in His kingdom, even as an Israelite was cut off from the congregation of the Lord, who rejected the office of the priesthood, and remained with his uncleanness upon him.

Thus the Mosaic and Christian systems are made perfectly harmonious, the last being only the fulfilment and completion of the first. It was, too, because the Jewish nation denied and rejected Christ in this relation, that He denied and cast them out from their inheritance.

But let us pass to consider more immediately the doctrine of the kingdom itself, as embodied in the two systems. We have shown heretofore how Jehovah was the constitutional Lawgiver and Head of Israel, entering into this anomalous covenant with them, so that He might administer their government, and take up His dwelling among them. In one sense, He was the God of the whole earth, and ruled among all the nations. But He was not their actual Lawgiver and civil Head, as He was of the people of Israel. We acknowledge God as the sovereign ruler over all. But He is not the civil Head of our government. Congress is the law-making power in our land, and the President is the supreme Executive, while Jehovah is not known in these departments. In the Jewish commonwealth, however, He was the ruling power, by whom the laws were enacted and the government administered, and to whom the supreme allegiance of every citizen was due. The organic law of the land was, that Jehovah should be the only and perpetual Head of the nation—a law that was forever made unalterable. God has never entered into such relation with any other people since the world began. Other nations may have been eminently blessed and favored of heaven—have been acquainted with Jehovah, and worshipped Him in a higher degree even than that covenant-people. They may have known more of His real character and His infinite perfections, yet, in the particulars now referred to, the Hebrew nation stands entirely alone, occupying a position and relation to which none other can pretend, to which none other can make any approach. No increase of piety or of Divine knowledge in our land, on the part of rulers or people, or both together, would bring us any nearer toward the consummation of such a relation; while, on the other hand, this peculiar relation subsisted among the Hebrews independently of their religious character, and in spite of all their gross ignorance of God, all their unbelief, all their perverseness and rebellions, which compelled God to deal with them in terrible judgment, even to the extent of giving them and their land into the possession of the heathen round about. Neither was the Hebrew nation chosen into this relation *because* of their piety and knowledge of God; for the history shows that they had very little of either. It would be more true to say that this relation was constituted, that *Jehovah might reveal himself unto them, and make known all His purposes of love.* The relation, therefore, itself can never grow out of any increase of piety or Divine knowledge under the present constitution of things. It is a relation *sui generis*, subsisting with that people alone, and which God will undertake again with no other.

What, now, was the meaning, what the end, which God sought to attain by this? No one will imagine that it was an end in itself—that is, that Jehovah entered into this extraordinary relation with that people merely for the purpose of providing for them a good civil government, and prospering them as a nation. There was necessarily a higher end involved—an end worthy of God and of His extraordinary working. It was part of that great typical system which shadowed forth the glorious future under the promised Messiah, when the times of regeneration should come, and His kingdom should be established on earth—that grand consummation toward which God has been working from the beginning, and all the lines of Providence have been converging. For this our groaning creation has been travailing in pain and waiting with earnest expectation.

To this period, now, of "restitution of all things," belongs the kingdom of God, when the kingdom, and the greatness of the kingdom under the whole heaven, shall come into the possession of our Immanuel, and He shall reign whose right it is, the legitimate Sovereign of earth.

To reveal and prepare the way for this new constitution of things, the Jewish nation was raised up, and all God's wondrous dealings had with that people. If, moreover, they were surpassingly wonderful in their character, we are to bear in mind that they must be so, fittingly to represent that coming order of events in earth's history, when old things shall have passed away, and all become new. If God had not gone entirely out of the ordinary track of His providence, how could He have made the nation a type of a regenerated order of things, or conveyed any knowledge to men of those coming events? The attempt would have been a failure.

God, then, did undertake to set forth in model the future and glorious things concerning the kingdom of God on earth. The patterns of the work and the redemption to be effected by Christ, the woman's seed, were given. And of that future government under our Immanuel, the Hebrew commonwealth, administered immediately by Jehovah himself, was the grand model, even as the priesthood of Aaron and Melchizedec, and the shedding of the blood of slain beasts were fulfilled in the offering and mediatorship of Christ.

It should also be borne in mind, that the model is always inferior in every respect to the thing which it represents, being constructed upon a greatly diminished scale. What a difference between the blood of bulls and goats, and that of Christ—between priests taken from among sinful, dying men, needing atonement for their own sins, and the eternal Son of God—between the earthly and the heavenly Canaan—between the tabernacle made of wood and gold, of linen and skins of beasts, and that spiritual temple made of souls renewed and sanctified by the Holy Ghost! Just so vast is the difference between that Jewish commonwealth, wondrous as it was, and the kingdom of God which is yet to be. And if the model was grand, even on its diminished scale, what shall the reality be, when all the Divine purposes shall be fulfilled?

There is no little difficulty in our really believing and accepting that amazing fact of the past, that God in very deed has dwelt on earth, and administered a government here among men through continuous centuries. Ask now of the days that are past, which were before thee, since the day that God created man upon the earth, and ask from the one side of heaven unto the other, *whether there hath been any such thing as this great thing is, or hath been heard like it?* Did ever people hear the voice of God speaking out of the midst of the fire, as thou hast heard it, and live? Or hath God assayed to go and take him a nation from the midst of another nation, by temptations, by signs, and by wonders, and by war, and by pestilence, and by a mighty hand, and by a stretched-out arm, and by great terrors, according to all that the Lord your God did for you in Egypt before your eyes? Deut. iv. 32. That same appeal might be made now to the nations which Moses made more than three thousand years ago to Israel, "whether there hath been any such thing as this great thing is, or hath been heard like it." Yet that nation were witnesses to "*this thing*." For long centuries the tabernacle of God was among men, and His visible presence was known on earth. This is part of the actual history of this world, which never can be blotted out—which cannot be ignored. It stands attested by the pen of inspiration, and the nation of Israel, through their marvellous history, is an unimpeachable witness to the fact.

We are not, however, to forget that the throne of that kingdom was promised by eternal covenant to the seed of the woman, even the heir of David, whom God should raise up; whose kingdom should be an everlasting kingdom, continuing so long as the moon endureth, even from generation to generation. In other words, the Messiah, the Lord's anointed, was to be the heir of David, to possess that throne. That *Word* which dwelt between the cherubim over the mercy-seat, and administered the government of Israel through succeeding centuries, was, in the fulness of time, to be "made flesh;" and having first become the High-Priest to make atonement, and thereby prepare a clean and holy people unto himself, was then, at the appointed hour, to come and take the kingdom, ascending the promised throne of David, and reigning over the house of Israel. The kingdom, then, is to be established in the hands of our Immanuel. Earth is to realize yet all that was shadowed forth in that wondrous government of Jehovah among His ancient people. The times of the Messiah are being now fulfilled. Already has the seed of the woman appeared and accomplished His first misson of suffering, that He might be constituted Priest forever over the house of God. We are in the midst of the latter days, the days of the Son of man, when prophecy is hastening to its fulfilment, and the long conflict of the ages is drawing near to its issue. We have witnessed the glory of our Immanuel's humiliation and suffering, have gathered around His cross and sepulchre, marking where His body was laid. And even the glory of His being made a *sacrifice for sin* has been so great, that we have been ready to say, It is enough, and continue lingering around Gethsemane and Calvary. But if these be glorious, what shall be His kingdom, and triumph, and reward? What shall it be, when He shall "so return in like manner as we have seen Him go into heaven," no more the denied and crucified, but a conqueror, coming up from Edom with garments rolled in blood, travelling in the greatness of His strength, mighty to save? Yes, we shall behold the glory, even as we have the humiliation and the suffering unto death. In that coming period of regeneration and restitution, all shall be fulfilled. The tabernacle of God shall again be with men, and He will dwell with them, and they shall be His people, and God himself shall be with them, and be their God. And God shall wipe away all tears from their eyes; and there shall be no more death, neither sorrow, nor crying, neither shall there be any more pain: for the former things are passed away. And he that sat upon the throne said, Behold, I make all things new. And he said unto me, Write: for these words are true and faithful. And he said unto me, It is done. I am Alpha and Omega, the beginning and ending; Rev. xxi. 3. Yes, verily, "The tabernacle of God" shall again be with men. If the visible presence and manifestation of God on earth for long centuries is an undeniable fact of the past, which cannot be set aside without overthrowing this entire revelation with our system of Christianity, who will undertake to say that it shall not be a more glorious fact still of the future, in that promised era for which we have so long waited and prayed, when Satan shall be thrust out, and Jesus, our Immanuel, shall have possession of the kingdom, reigning from sea to sea, and causing the desert to blossom as the rose? Let those who object to this view of Scripture, and deny it, first get rid of that amazing fact of the past, standing out with such prominence upon the pages of the Old Testament, and verified in the whole history of the Jewish nation. If we are compelled to accept the one, we may not deny the other. As surely as we have had the type, so surely must we witness the antitype. The latter cannot fail of fulfilment any more than God's promises and prophecies can fail.

If, now, we proceed a step further, to consider the nature of the Mosaic system as a typical one, to foreshadow the future things in the kingdom of God, we shall obtain the principle by which we may accurately draw the line between what was temporary and what was designed to be permanent therein. The previous discussion shows that the older books of revelation present a vast typical gallery, and, among other things, set forth the kingdom of Christ itself, in the government of the Hebrew nation. We have seen how Jehovah himself organized that government, and became its civil Head, the people adopting this as their organic law, or covenant, to abide as long as the nation itself should endure. In conformity with this constitution, Jehovah, as Lawgiver and King, with whom all authority resided, organized the entire system of government with the whole statute code, which was administered for fifteen centuries, and stands unequalled for excellence and wisdom in the history of the world.

It was a long period before the nation was brought to stand by their own constitution and covenant with Jehovah, the constant tendency being to depart therefrom, to go after other gods to serve them, for which they were sorely punished, and of which they were finally cured by their captivity in Babylon. This judgment humbled them to the dust, and changed the future current of their history, creating a new national sentiment of an intensely legal character, that would tolerate no infraction of the laws, and which inculcated the worship and service of Jehovah to the utmost letter. The Scribes and Pharisees were the embodiment of this sentiment and spirit, extreme sticklers for the letter of the law, and obeying the whole *statute code* to the last jot and tittle; while, at the same time, they knew nothing of the inward spiritual meaning of their system. These men accepted the Hebrew commonwealth in its civil aspect and constitution simply, discerning nothing beyond the State idea and relation. They did not understand that that State was but a shadow of some better thing—a pattern of a higher and spiritual kingdom. They were satisfied to be citizens of the civil commonwealth merely, and supposed that this entitled them to a part in the coming kingdom of the Messiah. The religion of the Pharisees, therefore, was entirely a State affair, a conformity to statute laws, having nothing to do with the heart and inner life, and a spiritual standing before God. It was a good civil standing and citizenship. And inasmuch as Jehovah was the constitutional Head of their State, it was just such a conception of religion as a carnal-minded man, without any knowledge of the spiritual and interior nature of that system, would necessarily gain. The deeper, truer meaning, however, embodied therein, was the embryo kingdom of God with its eternal laws and principles, into which the men of faith alone entered. They understood that that Hebrew civil State, with its wonderful constitution, was not made primarily for itself, but for another and higher system, of which the former was but a shadow. Jehovah never would have undertaken to administer the civil affairs of a nation simply to provide for it a good government. He had a higher ultimate end, which was, to familiarize the minds of men to the grand idea of the kingdom of God on earth—a kingdom separate and distinct from these worldly empires, to which lustful and ambitious men aspire. Through long centuries God administered this unique and wonderful government among His chosen, covenant people, dwelling among them in visible glory, though hidden behind the veil, and thus the way was being prepared for the introduction of that more glorious and heavenly kingdom which was to be set up, when God in very deed should dwell on earth again, and His law be written no more on tables of stone, but on the fleshly tables of the heart, a spiritual people being prepared for Him through the blood of Christ and the renewing of the Holy Ghost. These two aspects of the Hebrew commonwealth, then, are ever to be kept in view in studying the Scriptures: one, the actual, present, and civil State; the other, the typical and future, to be fulfilled under the promised Messiah.

With these facts clearly apprehended, it can easily be

understood what was permanent and what temporary in the Mosaic system.

The civil and ritual, as shadows, were to pass away, while that which belonged to the true kingdom of God was to abide. The Hebrew State, as a civil organization, was temporary in its own nature, being designed as a pattern, and not the very substance. All *statute* or *municipal law*, therefore, must necessarily be confined within the limits of the State. Such laws never have authority beyond the government that ordains them. They cannot be enforced anywhere else; and this is true of Hebrew law, as well as of any other, even though enacted by Jehovah himself.

The Ten Commandments, as delivered from Sinai, are not *statute* law, having no civil penalties attached to them as they there stand. They are the enunciation of the great moral principles which forever lie at the foundation of the kingdom of God, embodying its legislation and the principles which govern it. In organizing the Hebrew commonwealth, God designed to set forth the principles of both these governments, a lower and a higher—a present civil State, with all its existing relations, and a future spiritual kingdom, to be realized under the coming Deliverer. It must embrace not only the statute laws which were necessary for the government of that people, but also the great principles which lie at the foundation of the true kingdom of God on earth.

The Ten Commandments now are to be regarded as the statute law of that eternal kingdom, embodying its legislation and the principles by which it was to be governed. It was eminently appropriate, too, that they should here be announced at the outset, amid the terrific thunders of Sinai, inasmuch as Jehovah was now laying the first foundations of that kingdom, and unfolding the fact of its existence and its nature to the minds of men.

The Ten Commandments were the perpetual law of that kingdom for all people and for all time; and it was essential that they should here be promulgated, that the higher and eternal relations of that covenant of Jehovah with His nation might ever be kept in view, and that they might understand that there was something in their system beyond a mere civil government and its statute laws enforced by the magistrate, even as there was an eternal rest beyond their earthly Canaan, and richer blood to be shed for sin than that which streamed from their altar. They who saw nothing beyond the earthly Canaan, or the blood of beasts, or present citizenship in Israel, were but carnal men, whose eyes were blinded to the great spiritual truths of their own system. The men of faith saw beyond, and confessed themselves strangers and pilgrims, even while enjoying the earthly Canaan, "for they looked for a city which hath foundations, whose builder and maker is God." The idea, therefore, that the Old Testament did not reveal a future state, or the immortality of the soul, contradicts the fundamental conception of that entire revelation. It is equivalent to saying that there was nothing beyond a mere civil Judaism—a seed without a kernel. How a living Christianity could ever grow from such a mere shell, is more than we can understand. Civil Judaism was but the hull which held the kingdom of God wrapped up within; and while the hull fell away at the appointed time, the eternal principle lived to grow and to fill the earth. Paul explains these as the facts of the case, which the men of faith understood, dying in the full assurance that they should still enter into this inheritance, and see all God's promises fulfilled.

The Ten Commandments, we say, were not statute civil law, with their proper penalties, to be enforced by the magistrate, but the law of the kingdom—the law which binds our universal humanity. The command is,

"Honor thy father and thy mother." That is binding on us with the same authority precisely as upon the Hebrews. Their civil statute, enacted on this subject by Jehovah, was as follows: Every one that curseth his father or his mother, shall surely be put to death: he hath cursed his father or his mother: his blood shall be upon him; Levit. xx. 9. That is not binding on us, because we are not citizens or magistrates under that civil commonwealth.

The law of the Ten Commandments of universal obligation is, "Thou shalt not steal." Hebrew statute law was, "If a man steal an ox, or a sheep, and kill it, or sell it; he shall restore five oxen for an ox, and four sheep for a sheep. . . . And he that stealeth a man, and selleth him, or if he be found in his hand, shall surely be put to death." So, likewise, the adulterer was put to death.

The law of the Ten Commandments and the kingdom is, "Remember the Sabbath day to keep it holy." The statute law of the Hebrew State was, "Speak thou also unto the children of Israel, saying, Verily my sabbaths ye shall keep: for it is a sign between me and you throughout your generations; that ye may know that I the Lord doth sanctify you. Ye shall keep the sabbath therefore; for it is holy unto you. Every one that defileth it shall surely be put to death: for whosoever doeth any work therein, that soul shall be cut off from among his people. Six days may work be done; but in the seventh is the sabbath of rest, holy unto the Lord: whosoever doeth any work on the sabbath day, he shall surely be put to death." That law cannot be enforced by our magistrates.

When it is argued, now, that the law of the Sabbath is abolished because the Mosaic system is done away, it is as much to the point as if we were told that the law of honoring father and mother was abolished for the same reason; or the law against stealing and adultery. The law of the Sabbath is the law of the kingdom for our humanity, having no dependence upon the continuance or discontinuance of Hebrew statutes or State. Their municipal laws on all these subjects have shared the destiny of their government; but the laws of the kingdom are binding as they ever were.

So, likewise, is it with the law of the marriage institution. "Moses, because of the hardness of your hearts, suffered you to put away your wives: but from the beginning it was not so." A bill of divorcement was allowed by the municipal law of the Hebrews, to accommodate the necessities of the age, and the condition of woman; but the original law of marriage contemplated no such thing, and that is the law which binds our humanity to the end—the law of the kingdom.

The law for taking the murderer's life stands upon the same principle. That law was promulgated by God to Noah, immediately after the execution of the sentence of capital punishment against the race on a most fearful scale, because of the violence which had filled the earth, and for which there was no law or justice. God intended that, for the future, crime should be punished, and punished adequately. Accordingly, He gave authority to deal with the murderer, in the solemn requirement, "Whoso sheddeth man's blood, by man shall his blood be shed. . . . At the hand of every man's brother *will I require* the life of man." That is a law which was intended to underlie all human society, and no more belongs to the Mosaic system than to any other. It was promulgated centuries before Moses was born or the Hebrew State had an existence.

Neither did Jesus Christ introduce or teach any new principles, when He expounded the law of love and forgiveness. He understood perfectly the idea of the Hebrew State, comprehending Judaism, not alone in its outward letter, but also in its inward spirit. He knew what the spiritual meaning of that system was—that there was not merely a commonwealth, with its statute laws to be enforced by the magistrate with civil penalties, but the higher kingdom of God, of which the Ten Commandments were the embodied principle, and which laid its eternal requisitions on the heart. Jesus Christ had the clearest apprehension of all this; and it was just this spiritual law of the kingdom of God that He brought out in His sermon on the Mount. The Scribes and Pharisees had been in the habit of expounding the civil statute code, which required an eye for an eye, and a tooth for a tooth, as if this exhausted the truth of their whole system, and was all that was required to make an Israelite. Jesus discloses the deeper meaning which lay hidden there, declaring that if their righteousness exceeded not the righteousness of the Scribes and Pharisees, they should never see the kingdom of God. He then proceeds to unfold the true law of that kingdom—the law of love and forgiveness, even to enemies—the law of sorrow for sin, of brokenness of spirit, of inward purity of heart, of endurance of persecution for righteousness' sake. Conformity to such laws and principles would make an Israelite indeed, who should be an heir of the Messiah's kingdom, and an inheritor of all God's promises. In setting forth these, however, as the law of the kingdom, Jesus never intended to overthrow the statute laws of the commonwealth, nor interfere with their execution by judges and magistrates upon evil-doers.

It is not true, therefore, that Jesus Christ introduced any new law or principle of conduct into the world. All that He taught was involved in the Mosaic system, if only its true spiritual import had been apprehended. His enemies charged Him with overthrowing that system.

They came to Him again and again with the design of betraying Him, through subtle questions, into a denial of Moses. They wanted Him to assail that sacred law of the Old Testament, and sought in every way to push Him to this extremity, that thus they might destroy Him. But they labored in vain to this end. He foiled all their deepest-laid plots. A lawyer came thus tempting Him, asking what he should do to gain eternal life, hoping and expecting that He would announce some new doctrine that Moses never taught. The reply was, "*What is written in the law?* How readest thou? And he answering said, Thou shalt love the Lord thy God with all thy heart, and with all thy soul, and with all thy strength, and with all thy mind; and thy neighbor as thyself. And Jesus said unto him, *Thou hast answered right:* this do, and thou shalt live." The lawyer was foiled. Jesus had no new doctrine to offer in opposition to the law of Moses. He planted himself squarely upon that law and its Divine authority, only demanding that it should be understood according to its true intent and meaning.

The very charge, too, upon which Jesus was arraigned before the high court of the nation on trial for His life, was *that of subverting the laws and institutions of Moses.* It is confidently asserted in our day, that the Old Testament Scriptures are abolished, and this by the authority and doctrine of Jesus. This was the very crime laid to His charge by the Jewish rulers, and which they sought to substantiate by all the testimony, true or false, that they could collect. His enemies were mad against Him to establish this very fact to His destruction. And with what result? They failed—signally failed. Jesus had never uttered one syllable derogatory to the Old Testament or its institutions. He had ever honored them in the eyes of the nation, had ever appealed to them as the undoubted Word of God, of binding authority, and sustaining every doctrine that He preached. He had ever taught men to search the Scriptures, to find there the evidence to His own divine mission, asserting that Moses and all the prophets bore united witness to Him.

There is no doctrine, therefore, which Jesus would so indignantly denounce, as the one accepted to such an extent in our day, that He destroyed the Old Testament, or set it aside. It contradicts His whole life and teachings. "I came not to destroy the law or the prophets, but to fulfil: for till heaven and earth pass, one jot or one tittle shall in no wise pass from the law till all be fulfilled." That is the doctrine of Jesus and our Christianity. Every declaration of the Old Testament, as well as the New, is the word of God, to be fulfilled to the last letter. We stand by this Book as a revelation from heaven—the whole of it; and that most clearly is not the Christianity of Christ which denies and repudiates Moses and the prophets. We believe with Paul, that God, at sundry times and in divers manners, spake in times past unto the fathers by the prophets, and that He hath also, in these last days, spoken unto us by His Son. And that wherever, whenever, or to whomsoever God has spoken, there we find a true revelation from God to man, to be humbly and reverently received.

CHAPTER XXXIV.

CHRIST'S EXALTATION.

The ascension of Christ to heaven, and His exaltation to the right hand of power, have been regarded, in later times, as His assumption of the kingdom and promised throne of David, in fulfilment of the prophecies of the

Old Testament. Accordingly, it is common to speak of His kingdom as already established, and of Him as occupying the throne. He has not only entered upon His priesthood, but has "received the kingdom" also, although He has not returned. Thus having really begun the administration thereof, His people have lost their interest in that return, and do not look for it until the final day of judgment, and in connection with the closing up of all earthly things.

Do the Scriptures teach that the departure of Christ from earth, and His exaltation in heaven, are the same with the possession of the kingdom promised Him as the heir of David?

It is true that we speak of the government of Christ over this world—of His accomplishing all His purposes and performing His pleasure—of all power in heaven and earth being in His hands, so that He can defeat the machinations of His enemies. This, undoubtedly, is a fact and doctrine of revelation. But was not the same true before the ascension of Christ?—as true before as since? Has the ascension of Jesus to heaven made any difference in *such government of the world?* Has not Christ possessed this supremacy from the beginning, even before there was any throne of David known or promised on earth? Christ appears in two characters in revelation: one, as *the divine Word*, from everlasting, dwelling between the cherubim; the other, as *the woman's seed*, revealed in our nature. As the former, He made the world, and manages all its affairs. He was King in Israel from the foundation of the nation, their Creator and Redeemer, Jehovah, the coming One. Not only, too, did He reign over Israel, but the heathen nations also, though they knew Him not, nor bowed to His authority. But this sovereignty of Christ over the world most clearly is not what is intended by the kingdom promised Him, as the seed of the woman and the heir of David. That was an event far distant in the future, hoped and waited for by God's people. That was the kingdom announced by John the Baptist, and by Jesus himself, as approaching, but not yet established or experienced. It was something, therefore, widely different from that general government which Christ has always maintained over the world. It is the introduction of that blessed era, when the power shall be transferred from the Prince of darkness to Christ; when the dominion shall be taken from the ambitious, grasping rulers of the world, and put into the hands of our Immanuel, and He shall reign whose right it is, even from sea to sea, making earth to bloom again like paradise. This is the reign of David's greater Son, prophesied of and promised, when God should again make His tabernacle among men. and dwell with them, and be their God, and they His people. Has this specific event, so long prayed and waited for, come? Or is Christ still administering His general government over the world, even as He has from the beginning, acknowledged by a chosen remnant who endure with patience, dying in faith, not having received the promises, but seen them afar off, and still confessing themselves strangers and pilgrims here? Is Christ still rejected by the unbelieving nations—denied by His ancient Israel, who are wandering as exiles to the ends of the earth? Christ is reigning in His relation of the divine Word, and controlling the affairs of providence as from the beginning. But that sovereignty of earth, which was promised Him as the seed of the woman and the heir of David, is still a future event, nearer at hand, indeed, but no more realized now than three thousand years ago. Christ is still waiting "till His enemies be made His footstool," and laughing at all the impotent rage of the kings and the counsels of the rulers to break His bands asunder and cast away His cords from them.

With this statement of facts we are prepared to study *the true significance of Christ's absence from earth, and His ascension to heaven.*

That departure, both at the time and before it took place, was to the disciples an inexplicable mystery, a cause of deepest trial and sorrow; and that, because they looked upon it as contrary to the tenor of the Scriptures, and frustrating the whole mission of the Messiah. They could not comprehend how Christ could fulfil His work by departing from earth, and before the kingdom was established. The thing was dark and dreadful beyond all imagination, and involved, to their view, the abandonment of all hope that Jesus could be the Messiah they expected. Therefore "were they afraid to ask Him" of this matter.

How does Jesus meet this state of the disciples, and comfort them in this hour of their sorrow? He states two things. The first, *that it was expedient for them that He should go away for a season.* The second, *that He would return again to fulfil all their hopes, and that they must wait and watch for His appearing.*

These assurances do not sanction, neither did they convey the idea, that Christ was to depart, as a matter of course, because His presence here and continuance were not to be desired. On the contrary, the comforting assurance to His disciples was, that His absence was only for a season, and that He would come again to fulfil all their fondest hopes—come in His kingdom and glory—come to occupy the throne of David, and reign in righteousness and truth, subduing all enemies under His feet. He did not tell them that His presence here was not to be desired, and that they had carnal and worldly views to set their hearts upon such an object. He does not hint, in the remotest manner, that they had misapprehended the whole spirit of the Scriptures, and should never have thought of His continuing here, or desired it. He does say to them, in sympathizing tenderness, "Let not your heart be troubled: ye believe in God, believe also in me." Be not overwhelmed, nor let your faith in God or in me fail, though you behold the enemy triumph, and the very grave open to receive me. Let not your heart be troubled, as if all your hopes were to be blasted. "I tell you the truth. It is expedient for you that I go away."

Wherein was this expediency of Christ's departure and absence from His disciples?

It consisted in the fact that *Christ was now in the flesh—in His state of humiliation—under the law and the curse, and in this condition was not properly qualified to be a Saviour, or to occupy the throne.*

This fact the disciples did not, at the time, understand, and into its relations could not enter. They did not know that Christ was to come first to place himself under law, and be subject to the curse. Their only conception of Him was that of one administering law—that is, reigning, occupying the throne, and putting His enemies under His feet, not necessarily in a carnal sense, like a Roman Cæsar, but in such a sense as David, Isaiah, and all the prophets foretold. This, moreover, He will do. But it was not to be realized in His first advent, that being for a wholly different purpose. He could not enter into His kingdom and glory until He had first suffered and humbled himself unto death. In other words, He must accomplish the work of His priesthood before He could occupy the throne. Not only, too, was He to be made a priest; He was also the victim for sacrifice—the spotless Lamb to be slain, and taking away the sins of the world. Christ's first mission, therefore, had nothing to do with the kingdom and the glory, except to lay the foundation for them by His priesthood. It was a work exclusively of obedience, suffering, and subjection to law. "Lo, I come to do thy will, O my God. Yea, thy law is within my heart." That tells the spirit and character of His work.

Let us, then, clearly understand the relations of that amazing fact, that the eternal Word assumed our nature —that nature which was under the law and the curse, entered our prison, and took upon Him all our liabilities. He was "made under the law," subject to all its requirements—to all the trials, temptations, and sufferings which belong to our present fallen condition, of which death and the grave are an integral part. In this condition Christ was essentially and necessarily a servant, called to perform a wonderful work and ministry of love to our race. He was not a king to give law; He could not be, for He had not, by any service yet rendered, made himself worthy to reign, which is the true law of God's providence over this world, and which will finally give the empire into His hands. He will obtain the kingdom by this very right of faithful service. *Wherefore* hath God highly exalted him, and given him a name which is above every name; Phil. ii. 9. He was a servant under law. He says himself: "I came not to judge (*i. e.*, to rule) the world, but to save the world."

In this state of humiliation, under law himself, and bound to obey all its requirements, He was not qualified to be a Saviour, except by way of anticipation of the final result of His work, as had been the case from the time of Abel. His was essentially a condition of subjection, inconsistent with one of glory and triumph. Not only could He not deliver others; He must himself bear the cruel smiting, and, when reviled, meekly submit to the insult from His taunting foes. Even to death itself must He bow as part of the curse. To all this, however, there must be an end; and it was ended as with His expiring breath He cried, "It is finished." He had endured sublimely to the end—had drained the bitter cup to its last dregs.

From this state of subjection to the law and the curse it was necessary that Christ should pass to another, a redeemed and glorified one, in order that He might be qualified to be a Saviour in very deed. And not only so; *it was essential that His true character and work should be triumphantly vindicated in the sight of heaven and earth.*

Jesus had died—died as a transgressor, and death lies as a curse against a guilty race; the evidence being incontrovertible against every man that comes under this doom. "Death hath passed upon all men, for that all have sinned." That is God's judgment of the matter; so that death is His sentence against a sinful, condemned race. But more than this: Jesus died as no common transgressor, His name being loaded with the deepest reproach. He had been charged with being a blasphemer, a Samaritan, and devil. He had been put to death by the rulers *for the very purpose of proving that He was liable to death, like other sinners* of the race, and therefore could not be the Messiah, of whom it was foretold that He was to continue, and be the ever-living One—the Conqueror of death and all our foes.

From all this vile slander the name of Jesus must be powerfully and completely vindicated. It must be demonstrated that He was still the only-begotten and well-beloved of Heaven, though rejected and crucified by the rulers, and that, in subjection to death, He had been suffering for the sins of others, not His own.

The departure and absence of Christ from earth are to be explained by these facts. First, He must die and so depart, in order to complete His work of obedience, and enter His resurrection state, where alone He could save.

Secondly, He must be absent, in order to have the fact established by the testimony of the Holy Ghost, in connection with that of His disciples, that He was so exalted; that so He might be properly offered to men as their Prince and Redeemer.

How, then, were the name and character of Jesus vindicated?

I. *By His resurrection from the dead.*

It is not sufficiently understood what an argument it was against Jesus, that He died like other men. The reason, too, why we have not understood it, is because we have overlooked the fact that it was the universal, accepted faith of the nation, which no one questioned, that the Messiah *was not to come under the power of death.* "We have heard out of the law," said the people, on one occasion, "that Christ abideth forever. And how sayest thou that the Son of man must be lifted up? Who is this Son of man?" The prophecies did declare plainly that Christ was to "continue," proving himself the living One in very deed, who should prevail to conquer death. There was consequently no slight foundation for the idea that the Christ was not to come under this dread curse. When Jesus thus yielded himself to death as other men, and the tyrant asserted his power over Him, it was regarded by all as settled that *He* could not be the Son of God. The disciples themselves gave up the argument, and the despairing language of their hearts was, We trusted it had been he which should have redeemed Israel; Luke xxiv. 21. But alas, the disappointment of all our fondest hopes; for we have seen His head also bow in death! None is found yet strong enough to prevail against the great Destroyer.

From all this Jesus was gloriously vindicated by His resurrection. That was the powerful reversal of the decision of the rulers against Him—the seal of Heaven to all His claims. He was powerfully declared to be *the Son of God* by His resurrection from the dead. It cleared His character from every reproach of His enemies, and brought the overwhelming accusation of His blood upon them. Through this resurrection, also, He entered upon that incorruptible, glorified state, where He became the living One indeed, who was dead, but liveth evermore, and was now qualified in very deed to be a Prince and Saviour unto the uttermost.

We thus clearly see how it was expedient for the disciples that He should depart. It was by no means desirable that He should continue here in His *subject condition*, submitting always to the revilings of His foes, and His work of obedience incomplete. It was expedient that He should depart, and that the Holy Spirit should come to bear witness of His resurrection, convincing the world thereby of their sin in denying and counting Him for a transgressor, and proving that He was a Saviour in very deed, as it never could have been proved while Jesus continued in the flesh. For it is undoubtedly true that His claims to be the Messiah never could have been established while He remained in His subject condition as a servant under law. His miracles would have proved Him to have been a prophet sent from God. But it never could have been demonstrated that He was the holy and just One, the anointed Saviour of the world; for He was himself under the curse with the world, draining the bitter cup to its dregs, and unable to save himself. How, then, could it be proved that He could save others? No. He must pass out of this state of *servitude*, and be glorified, and then, as *the risen, exalted One*, His work of humiliation and subjection finished, the Holy Spirit could demonstrate that He was the Lord's Anointed, whom God had raised up—the living One, over whom death had no power, and who had prevailed to conquer every foe.

The words of Christ, in explanation of this matter, have been greatly misunderstood, where He says, Nevertheless, I tell you the truth: It is expedient for you that I go away: for if I go not away, the Comforter will not come unto you; but if I depart, I will send him unto you. And when he is come, he will reprove the world of sin, and of righteousness, and of judgment: of sin, because they believe not on me; of righteousness, because I go to the Father, and ye see me no more; of judgment, because the Prince of this world is judged; John xvi. 7. This has been understood to assert that the Holy Spirit's presence was more desirable in itself to the Church than that of Christ; and many so believe and teach, being perfectly reconciled to the absence of their Lord, and having little or no desire for His return. But Jesus intended to teach no such doctrine. He did assert the desirableness of the Spirit's presence, which could not be realized until His own departure. And why? Because the Spirit could not come *as a witness of His resurrection* until He did depart. He must of necessity finish His appointed work, even unto death, bearing all the shame, and then the Holy Ghost would come to testify with power to His resurrection, and so reprove the world of sin, and of righteousness, and of judgment. Of sin, *because they believe not on me.* In establishing the resurrection of Jesus, the Holy Ghost would convince the world of their fearful sin in not believing Him—in denying and crucifying Him; demonstrating that they had put their murderous hands to the very Lord of life, and thus overwhelming them with a sense of their guilt. "Of righteousness, because I go to the Father, and ye see me no more." However obscure this may seem at first view, it is plain and simple if we only place ourselves back where the disciples stood, and enter into the thoughts of those times. We have already stated that the death of Jesus was an utter condemnation of all His pretensions—an unanswerable argument against Him. His absence from earth, of course, was tantamount to His death and burial. We say of a man, when dead and buried, that is the end of him and his work. Thus the absence of Christ, and the discontinuance thereby of His work, were *prima facie* evidence against Him, and a demonstration of His being the transgressor the rulers alleged. What, now, was the Holy Ghost to do in the circumstances? He was to come and bear witness to the resurrection of Jesus, thus convincing the world of righteousness—of *His* righteousness, not the world's—demonstrating that He was all He claimed to be, the very Christ of God; and that, *notwithstanding His absence from earth*, "ye see me no more," but it is "because I go to the Father," and not to the devil, as the rulers affirm. They assert that I am dead, and gone to perdition. The Holy Ghost shall prove, in my resurrection, that I am the living One forevermore, and am gone to the Father, being accepted of Him. "Of judgment, because the Prince of this world is judged." This follows as a necessary result of the others. In demonstrating that I am raised from the dead, and approved to the Father, that will settle the question as to the judgment and empire of this world, that the very Prince of this world is judged, and His doom sealed; that I am He who has prevailed to conquer hell, and that the dominion is to come into my hands.

It was thus true, indeed, that the presence of the Holy Ghost, and His work of bearing witness to Christ's resurrection, were more desirable for the Church than the continuance of Jesus *in the flesh and under the law in His humiliation*. There can be no question on that point, and that is the fact which Christ intended to state. But His words do not imply, and were never designed to convey the idea, that the presence of the Comforter is more to be desired than that of our glorified Redeemer in His power and kingdom. On the contrary, He assured the disciples that that Spirit was sent as their *Comforter, to console them in His absence and until His return.* He himself represents the time of that absence as a period of sorrow to His disciples, when they should mourn and fast. "Why do we," said the disciples of John, "and the Pharisees, fast oft, but thy disciples fast not? And Jesus said unto them, Can the children of the bride-chamber mourn, as long as the bridegroom is with them? But the days will come *when the bridegroom shall be taken from them, and then shall they fast.*" And then would they need the Holy Ghost to be their Comforter, until the glad hour of their Lord's return.

II. Another fact in vindication of Jesus was *His visible ascension to heaven, and His exaltation there over the principalities and powers.*

It was not enough that Jesus rose from the dead. Others had been raised before Him. He must ascend visibly to heaven, there to receive His appointed honors and reward. That humanity which He had assumed, and in which He so wondrously obeyed and suffered, must be glorified, even with the same glory which He had with the Father before the world was. Accordingly, that human nature of Christ is now exalted over the principalities and powers in heavenly places, which we know only by revelation, the fact not being within the reach of our observation. His visible ascension to heaven, however, is a wonderful confirmation of our faith on that point. When we behold this Jesus, counted by the rulers as a transgressor, triumphing over death and the grave, and going up on high between the opening heavens, it requires no stretch of faith to receive His testimony, that all power in heaven and earth is committed to His hands—that God hath highly exalted Him, giving Him a name which is above every name.

The fact, also, is not to be overlooked, that this exaltation of Jesus to the supremacy of the angelic hosts is a new unfolding of truth not known to the ancient Church, and therefore distinct from the throne of David, and the dominion to be given him on earth. The latter is an event yet to be realized. Christ has not come into the possession of the throne of Israel, or the kingdom of earth, and will not until His second appearing. But His exaltation in heaven is already an accomplished event, made known to us entirely by revelation. When He ascends the throne of David, and takes the empire here for His own, we shall need no revelation to establish the fact. It will be a blessed reality, brought home to our own cognizance and experience. The very floods shall clap their hands, and all the trees of the wood shall rejoice together before the Lord. Every valley and mountain-top shall ring with the joyful shout. The kingdoms of this world are become the kingdoms of our Lord and of His Christ, and He shall reign forever and ever.

III. Observe again, that the Son of God, after having humbled himself to death and the curse, *must first be exalted and so approved to the Father, before He could properly be offered to men as their Prince and Redeemer.*

He could not be offered to men as a complete Saviour while yet in His humiliation, before His work of obedience was finished, and while the charge was lying against Him that He was a transgressor. That sentence of the rulers must be reversed, and Heaven's seal put upon Him as its only and well-beloved. This was the hinge of Peter's whole argument on the day of Pentecost. He demonstrated that that very Jesus, whom the rulers had crucified, God had raised up. "*Therefore* let all the house of Israel know assuredly that God hath made that same Jesus, whom ye crucified, both Lord and Christ." In His divine nature, Christ had possessed this sovereignty from the beginning. But it was a new event for the woman's seed to be carried up to this height of glory and honor. Yet such exaltation of the person of Jesus was necessary, in order to His being presented to the faith and acceptance of the world, that they might know in very deed that He was a Prince and Saviour, thoroughly approved unto God. This, therefore, was a fact preliminary and antecedent to the establishment of the kingdom, and *a necessary means thereto*, as truly so as His humiliation. The world was called upon to receive and welcome Him as King forever, *because* God had thus set Him at His own right hand in heaven; angels, and authorites, and powers there being made subject unto Him. Here was the ground upon which His empire on earth was to be established. Of course, that was not the empire itself. But if the nations would not bow to Him after such demonstration of His right to reign, and such service rendered to earth, He would, at the appointed hour, put them under His footstool, breaking them with a rod of iron, and dashing them in pieces like a potter's vessel. This, moreover, is the great question now to be tested. The rulers and nation had rejected Christ in His humiliation, as a servant under law. But this they did ignorantly in their unbelief, when they knew Him not, nor understood that He was to be made a sin-offering. Would they now have this man to reign over them, when God had exalted Him to the right hand of power? The people of Israel decided that to their own overthrow, a remnant being taken out and saved, while the nation was dashed and broken. That small remnant certainly was not the kingdom promised to Christ. The same momentous question was then submitted to the Gentiles, whether they would have this exalted man to reign over them;

and they are in process of deciding it after the same manner. A remnant is being taken out here also, while the rulers all combine to reject the Lord's Anointed. The kingdom is not to be found in this small Gentile remnant. Prophecy contemplated the fact that the heathen were to rage, and the rulers take counsel together against the Lord and against His Anointed; and that, when raised from the dead and set on the right hand of power, being thus powerfully declared to be Son of God. But what if the heathen and rulers do rage? "Sit thou on my right hand until I make thine enemies thy footstool." They shall be made His footstool. His enemies shall lick the dust. And when the demonstration shall be complete in respect to the Gentile nations and rulers, that they will not have this man to reign over them, even as it was in regard to the covenant people, Christ will suddenly return, having received the kingdom—that is, authority to take it—and His just sentence will go forth, "But those mine enemies who would not that I should reign over them, bring hither and slay them before me."

IV. It was necessary that Christ should be absent from earth and ascend to heaven, *that He might enter the sanctuary above, to accomplish the work of His priesthood.*

He came down to make His soul a sin-offering, and to bear the curse. After the victim was thus prepared and slain, it was necessary for Christ, as the constituted High-Priest, to take the blood and enter with it into the sanctuary to make atonement—the sanctuary not made with hands, of which He is the appointed minister. He appears before the throne in heaven. It was needful, however, to demonstrate this fundamental fact that Christ Jesus, as our High-Priest, has access to that sanctuary above, and that He is the ever-living One to intercede for us. What a glorious demonstration, too, of this we have, when we behold Him rising triumphant from the grave, and after establishing the proof of this, ascending to heaven in sight of the disciples, who gazed after Him in rapt wonder? There is nothing left wanting. A foundation is given upon which our faith may rest secure.

What, then, is the work that Christ is now accomplishing for us? Through what portion of the history of redemption is the Church now passing? The Apostle defines it very clearly. But Christ *being come an high-priest of good things to come*, by a greater and more perfect tabernacle, not made with hands, that is to say, not of this building; neither by the blood of goats and of calves, but by his own blood, *he entered in once into the holy place*, having obtained eternal redemption for us; Heb. ix. 11. For Christ is not entered into the holy places made with hands, which are the figures of the true; *but into heaven itself, now to appear in the presence of God for us;* ver. 24. He is performing the work of His priesthood, by entering within the vail, where alone atonement can be made, and there interceding for us with blood. He first descended that the spotless victim might be prepared for sacrifice, and killed. This done, He, as the High-Priest also, took the blood and entered the sanctuary above to make the needed intercession or atonement. It was essential, then, that Jesus should demonstrate the fact that He had been consecrated and anointed to this office, and had access to the very presence of God, where, and where alone He might perform this great work of His priesthood. It was necessary, therefore, that He should depart and be withdrawn from our sight behind the vail; and also that He should ascend visibly, so that we might know that God had indeed thus exalted Him, and given Him acce s to His own presence, where He might be our continual and prevalent intercessor before the throne. This view of the subject is fully sustained by

V. *The institution and intent of the Lord's Supper, in showing His death until He come.*

"Ye do show the Lord's death until he come." That death of Jesus had been, in the eyes of all, the crowning demonstration that He was a transgressor, as the rulers alleged. That death had silenced all His pretensions, and forever cut Him off from the kingdom which He claimed. He had been delivered over to the silence of the sepulchre, and His absence from earth was demonstration that the kingdom was not His, for He was not here to take it.

What, now, were the disciples commanded to do? *They were to show His death by a commemorative ordinance.* They were to stand up boldly before an unbelieving, scoffing world, and declare their abiding faith in the Nazarene and the crucified—declare that He was a living Saviour still in the highest sense, having spoiled the powers of hell, and passed to His resurrection state—that His absence from earth was no argument against Him, as He was not a tenant of the sepulchre, but had burst its bars, gone up on high to appear as Priest before the throne, whence He would return ere long to prove all His words true, and take possession of the kingdom. In evidence of their assured faith in all this, the disciples were, according to the command of their Master before His crucifixion, to break the bread and drink the cup, which should commemorate His death *until His return.* They were not to be ashamed of the absence of their Master, nor of the fact that He had died, being counted for a transgressor. They were never to deny or apologize for it. They were to glory in it—were themselves to show it forth—to inscribe it on their waving banners, and march under it to victory. They were to tell a scoffing world that this very Jesus, in the sublime faith, in the truth and triumph of His cause, even when approaching the cross and sinking under its weight, assured His friends that the kingdom was His, and that He would come again to take it; and appointed to them this memorial that they *must celebrate His death until He did come.* He might seem, indeed, long to delay, and the world might scoff at the idea of His return. But they must never despair; nor would they despair, if they held on firmly to this strange sheet-anchor of His death.

If we would learn, also, what has been the wonder-working power of this showing forth of the death of Christ—how it has been the very corner-stone of the Church's faith—we may read it in the fact that that most weighty argument ever urged against the Nazarene, and which was to be the millstone around His neck to sink His cause, has been completely and forever silenced; so silenced, that infidelity itself now hardly knows that it was ever any thing against Him. What sceptic or scoffer in this day ever thinks of alleging against Jesus that He was delivered over to death, and is found no more among the living on earth? Yet that was once an unanswerable argument, which even the disciples did not attempt to meet. They were overwhelmed with despair, having nothing to allege against that dreadful fact. But since they have looked upon His opened sepulchre, and known that He was made a sin-offering for us, they have themselves been showing His death until He come, assured now that He will come, and fulfil all that remains of prophecy to be accomplished concerning the glory and the kingdom. Oh, there is meaning in that wonderful institution by Jesus of the breaking of bread—deeper meaning than many, even of His own disciples, have understood. "I will not drink henceforth of this fruit of the vine," said Jesus, "until that day when I drink it new with you in my Father's kingdom." *They* were to drink it together, and that in the midst of much tribulation. But He would not sit down again to sup and feast with them until they should meet together in His kingdom. We are waiting for that time. And while we show His death, we declare, in the strongest terms possible, our faith in a risen, living, but absent Saviour, "until he come."

If this presentation of the facts be correct, it is plain that the Church has greatly misapprehended the meaning of her Lord's departure and absence. Believers have accepted it as a normal fact, with which they should be entirely satisfied, scarcely looking for or desiring His return. In truth, the idea of such return to earth has become painful to many Christian minds, so that they reject and resent it. They look upon Him as having already "obtained the kingdom;" consequently they see no object in His returning to earth again to fulfil the great promises and prophecies of revelation. Thus the Church has lost nearly all interest in the second coming of her Lord—has ceased to watch or wait for it. It does not enter into her preaching, except as changed into the believer's own death and departure from earth, or into a final terrific judgment scene. It does not form the subject of her prayers, nor the joyful theme of song in the house of her pilgrimage. It is not the one sublime event around which all her hopes and joys centre. The Church is content that her Lord took His departure—content to have Him remain absent. She knows little of the experience of those whose cry has gone up, "How long! how long, O Lord." Neither does she know how to enter into the thrilling words with which the book of Revelation closes, "Even so, come, Lord Jesus." Yea, come quickly. The bride has strangely become reconciled to the absence of the bridegroom, and scarcely desires His return—is no more looking and anxiously waiting for it. She has become satisfied with that first advent of her

Redeemer in His humiliation and sufferings. That work of obedience under the law and the accomplishment of His priesthood have assumed such glories to her delighted vision, that she is content to linger forever around His cross and sepulchre, looking back upon those as the scenes of His triumph, instead of His stripes and sore travail. Thus the thoughts and attention of the Church are, for the most part, turned backward upon the past. But if these scenes of our Saviour's humiliation, when He became a servant, are invested with such wonder and glory, what will it be when we shall behold Him in His kingdom and power? If such was the glory of His countenance when so marred that men turned and hid, as it were, their faces from Him, despised and rejected Him, scoffed at, and spit upon, and crucified Him, what will it be when He shall be seen coming up from Edom, a mighty conqueror, travelling in the greatness of His strength, His garments like him that treadeth in the wine-fat—when the day of vengeance shall be in His heart, and the year of His redeemed shall have come? We often wonder how the Jewish nation should so have misunderstood Jesus, and rejected all His claims; and that, when He came in His humiliation, a root out of dry ground, to be made a sin-offering. Is it not the more to be wondered at that we, with all the facts of that first mission of suffering fully explained to us—with all the light which it has shed upon the prophecies, the assurances of Christ's return, and our breaking of bread "until he come"—that with all this we should have so misapprehended Christ in the present and future, and lost well nigh all our interest in His second appearing? For that such is the fact there can hardly be a denial. In the New Testament there is no theme held up so radiant with hope and joy as this very one of His second coming. It is the event for which the Church is charged to watch and wait, to long and pray, and keep her loins girded—the one ever present as the goal of all her ambition and desire. It was to be the theme of her song in the house of her pilgrimage, inspiring her sweetest lays. The last words of the Old Testament give assurance of that coming. The last words of the New are, "I come." I come; surely, I come quickly. But who looks for that appearing? Where is it found in the preaching of the ministry? Where taught in the schools? Where in the prayers of the Church? Where in her songs? That coming of our blessed Lord, instead of being the subject radiant with all that is attractive and glorious to the soul of the believer, has been converted into an awful judgment scene, only calculated to fill the mind with trembling. This is the form in which the subject is presented from the pulpit and discussed in our theologies—the form in whch it enters into our sacred lyrics. The words in which the Church sings of her Lord's return are such as these:

"That awful day will surely come,
Th' appointed hour makes haste,
When I must stand before my Judge,
And pass the solemn test."

Or these:

"The day of wrath, that dreadful day,
When heaven and earth shall pass away,
What power shall be the sinner's stay?
How shall he meet that dreadful day?

"When shrivelling like a parched scroll,
The flaming heavens together roll;
And louder yet, and yet more dread,
Swells the high trump that wakes the dead.

"Oh! on that day, that wrathful day,
When man to judgment wakes from clay,
Be Thou, O Christ, the sinner's stay!
Though heaven and earth shall pass away."

We make no objection to such lyrics as representing the terrors of the final judgment day to sinners. But when the Church employs such songs, as she constantly does, to describe her Lord's appearing, and sings of that joyful event in such dark and doleful strains, it is as appropriate as it would be to sing a funeral hymn on a bridal festival. In such very funeral dirges has the Church been singing of her Lord's return, clothed in sackcloth, with ashes upon her head, and trembling at the thought of the terrible day of wrath. Let any one examine the collection of songs in common use, and see how many hymns he can find which tell, in joyful, inspiring strains, of that blessed hour when our Lord shall come. The absence of such lyrics tells, in unmistakable language, what the apostacy of the Church has been from the faith. Yea more; let one examine the originals of not a few of the hymns introduced into our collections, and he may be surprised to see how those stanzas have been carefully excluded which describe this very joyful coming of our Lord, and only a remnant left, so that the authors of those lyrics are misrepresented and misunderstood.

In the same strain of woe has the Church been weeping around the table of her Lord, singing,

"'Twas on that dark, that doleful night,
When powers of earth and hell arose
Against the Son of God's delight,
And friends betrayed Him to His foes:

"Before the mournful scene began,
He broke the bread, and blessed, and brake," &c.

As if she were weeping still with the sorrowing disciples around His grave, and knew not that He was now a risen, living Saviour, who had burst the bars of death. It was a sad scene, and trying indeed, when Jesus *first* broke the bread with His disciples. But we are not weeping now around that sepulchre of our Lord. "He is not here. He is risen. Come, see the place where the Lord lay." When, therefore, those disciples again broke the bread, it was not with sorrowing, burdened hearts. They had beheld their risen Lord, and with gratitude and joy did they now show His death till He come. Christ did not intend that His promised return should be an object of terror to His loved disciples, bringing an "awful day," of which they would only tremble to think. On the contrary, He designed that it should be the pole star of hope and joy to His suffering Church, bringing the glorious hour which should end the night of her long pilgrimage and sorrow, and usher in the glad day of jubilee to earth. Will not the bride rejoice to hear the cry, "Behold, the bridegroom cometh?"

"The Church has waited long,
Her absent Lord to see;
And still in loneliness she waits,
A friendless stranger she.
Age after age has gone,
Sun after sun has set,
And still, in weeds of widowhood,
She weeps, a mourner yet.
Come, then, Lord Jesus, come!

"Saint after saint on earth
Has lived, and loved, and died;
And as they left us one by one,
We laid them side by side.
We laid them down to sleep,
But not in hope forlorn;
We laid them but to ripen there,

Till the last glorious morn.
Come, then, Lord Jesus, come!

"The serpent's brood increase,
The powers of hell grow bold,
The conflict thickens, faith is low,
And love is waxing cold.
How long, O Lord our God,
Holy, and true, and good,
Wilt Thou not judge Thy suffering Church,
Her sighs, and tears, and blood?
Come, then, Lord Jesus, come!

"We long to hear Thy voice,
To see Thee face to face,
To share Thy crown and glory then,
As now we share Thy grace.
Should not the loving Bride,
The absent Bridegroom mourn?
Should she not wear the weeds of grief,
Until her Lord's return?
Come, then, Lord Jesus, come!

"The whole creation groans,
And waits to hear that voice
That shall restore her loveliness,
And make her wastes rejoice.
Come, Lord, and wipe away
The curse, the sin, the stain,
And make this blighted world of ours
Thine own fair world again.
Come, then, Lord Jesus, come!"

Even so, come, Lord Jesus. Amen.

CHAPTER XXXV.

THE FIRST RESURRECTION.

INTIMATELY connected with the coming and kingdom of Christ, is the doctrine of the RESURRECTION OF THE SAINTS; or, as termed in the Scriptures, *the first resurrection.* This might have been discussed in connection with the general subject of the resurrection; but it seemed necessary to establish first the doctrine of the coming and kingdom of Christ, in the light of which the resurrection of the saints has its chief significance, and aside from which it cannot be rightly appreciated.

It has been shown heretofore that the doctrine of the resurrection is among the elements of the Christian faith, taught from the beginning, and inwoven with the whole structure of redemption. Death was never any disappointment of the hopes of believers, because "they died in faith"—faith of the promised inheritance. They expected to rise again, and see all God's promises fulfilled, beholding that living Redeemer who should triumph over every foe, and bring the day of jubilee to earth. The doctrine preached by Enoch was, "Behold the Lord cometh with ten thousand of his saints," which was understood to mean, of necessity, that He brought them from the sepulchres, where they had been gathered. This great truth, set forth in the forms of the cherubim, became, from the earliest period, an essential part of the faith of God's people; so that when Christ appeared, He found it already thoroughly established, and rejected only by such skeptics as denied also the existence of angel and spirit. He found it a cherished doctrine, earnestly maintained and contended for as necessary to the work of redemption, promised through the seed of the woman. It was not understood how believers of the past could be made partakers of the inheritance of Christ, unless they were brought again from their graves. They were conceived of as living again only in the body. So real, too, was this to their apprehension and faith, that they expected these saints to return to the same bodies precisely, and to the same relationships of life as before, which was the ground of that weighty and, for the time being, unanswerable argument which the Sadducees urged, when they pointed to the case of the woman with seven husbands. That argument has no force with us, because we do not admit the existence of these present earthly relationships in that future state. The Pharisees did, and they could not reply to this objection of their antagonists. It fell, however, at once to the ground, when Christ announced the fact that these relations among men belonged to the present state, and were not to be known in the kingdom of God. These facts are important as showing how real the doctrine of the resurrection was in those former times, and thoroughly established in the faith of the nation, so as to bid defiance to all the sneers and arguments of the infidel Sadducees, even when their objections could not be answered. Martha expressed the faith of her nation, when she replied to Jesus' declaration respecting her brother, I know that he shall rise again in the resurrection at the last day; John xi. 24.

It was not, then, the work of Christ to reveal this doctrine, though He did throw upon it a flood of light by correcting the gross and sensual views which prevailed respecting it, and disclosing the new fact that the raised body was to possess a higher and spiritual nature, being no more subject to those relationships which grow out of the flesh as here constituted. It was to move upon a higher plane of existence, and to be endowed with greatly augmented powers. The risen saints were neither to marry, nor to be given in marriage, but to be as the angels; that is, in this particular. The simple statement of this fact obviated at once all the difficulty made by the Sadducees, and silenced their cavils. The Apostle enlarged on this point, when he showed how this corruptible must put on incorruption, this mortal must put on immortality; how that which is sown a natural body must be raised a spiritual body. Thus the teachings of Christ and the apostles have not revealed the doctrine of the resurrection as a new truth. They have only elucidated it—carried it up to a higher, grander position, and in the resurrection of our Immanuel, given us a living demonstration what it is to be.

In developing this doctrine as found in the Scriptures, we shall consider

I. *The time appointed for the Saints' resurrection.*

It is placed beyond doubt at the coming of Christ, of whom it was declared that He was to bring His saints with Him. It is apparent now to us that this did not occur at His first advent, when He appeared to place himself under law, and make His soul a sin-offering, accomplishing the work of His priesthood. He was, then, himself subjected to the curse. But having passed triumphantly through to His own resurrection state, and been approved to the Father, the way was prepared for His second appearing in His kingdom, when He would come to be glorified in His saints. That will emphatically be "the day of the Lord," His great day, when He will vindicate His own name, and the names of all His chosen, manifesting them forth as His sons beyond any more denial, even as Jesus himself was declared to be the Son of God with power by His resurrection from the dead. Having shown heretofore when this great day of the Lord is to be, it is not necessary here to repeat the argument. It is a day, however, which belongs distinctively to the saints, when they shall look up, and lift their heads; for their redemption draweth nigh. If we have proved that this day of Christ is, when He shall come to establish His kingdom in righteousness and truth, and restore all things, as the prophets have told from the beginning, the resurrection of the saints must then take place; for He brings them with Him.

But notice further *what peculiar prominence and distinction the Scriptures give to the resurrection of believers.*

Their resurrection is marked with peculiar emphasis, and distinguished from that of the wicked. It is, for instance, identified with Christ's coming; and to give it this peculiarity and distinction, that event must belong to the saints alone, just as the promises of justification to the believing necessarily imply that the unbelieving have no part in them. It is no distinction put upon the saints that they come with Christ in His great day, if the wicked dead also are then brought forth from their sepulchres. That advent of Christ is for the manifestation of the sainted dead. So Enoch prophesied of His coming with ten thousand of His saints. Paul says, 1 Cor. xv. 23: Every man in his own order: Christ the first-fruits; afterward they that are Christ's at his coming. Again, 1 Thess. iv. 13–17: But I would not have you to be ignorant, brethren, concerning them which are asleep, that ye sorrow not, even as others which have no hope. For if we believe that Jesus died and rose again, *even so them which sleep in Jesus will God bring with him.* For this we say unto you by the word of the Lord, that we which are alive and remain unto the coming of the Lord shall not prevent them which are asleep. For the Lord himself shall descend from heaven with a shout, with the voice of the archangel, and with the trump of God: and the dead in Christ shall rise first: then we which are alive and remain shall be caught up together with them in the clouds, to meet the Lord in the air: and so shall we ever be with the Lord. Nothing is here said of the resurrection of the wicked, nor intimation given that they have any part in the events described. That is the glorious reaping time when the harvest is to be gathered, of which the first-fruits have already been presented unto God.

But notice again *the peculiar manner in which the resurrection of believers is expressed.*

Theirs is not simply a resurrection *of* the dead, but *out of*, or *from among*, the dead. There are two modes in which this event is spoken of in the Scriptures. There is the resurrection, *νεκζων*, of the dead, describing simply the fact that the dead are raised from their graves; and there is the resurrection, *εκ νεκζων*, out of, or from among, the dead, describing the additional circumstance that some are taken, while others are left in their sepulchres. This is not a resurrection of the dead, nor a resurrection from death, nor from the grave, but a resurrection from or out of dead ones, which is the form of expression used when the resurrection of the saints is spoken of. This is a circumstance of so much importance, and the distinction is so marked, that we shall take some pains to establish and illustrate it.

The following passages employ the words *εκ νεκζων*, from among the dead; the most of them referring to Christ's own resurrection, which was unquestionably of this character, He being separated from the mass still left to the dominion of the sepulchre. And as they came down from the mountain, Jesus charged them, saying, Tell the vision to no man, until the Son of man be risen *from the dead;* Matt. xvii. 9. For as yet they knew not the Scripture, that he must rise again *from the dead;*

John xx. 9. And declared to be the Son of God with power, according to the spirit of holiness, by the resurrection *from the dead;* Rom. i. 4. In the following, both forms of expression are employed, and the distinction carefully drawn between them: Because he hath appointed a day, in which he will judge the world in righteousness, by that man whom he hath ordained: whereof he hath given assurance unto all men, in that he hath raised him *from the dead.* And when they heard of the resurrection *of the dead*, some mocked: and others said, We will hear thee again of this matter; Acts xvii. 31. The doctrine that Paul preached was the resurrection *from among the dead*—that is, Christ's resurrection. What the Athenians laughed to scorn, was the idea that the body was ever raised, which was simply the resurrection *of the dead.* This passage is important, as showing how carefully the Scriptures distinguish between the two ideas. The same is observed also in the following: Now if Christ be preached that he rose *from the dead*, how say some among you that there is no resurrection *of the dead?* 1 Cor. xv. 12. We will quote one passage more. And he said unto them, If they hear not Moses and the prophets, neither will they be persuaded, though one rose *from the dead;* Luke xvi. 31. These will suffice to show what language the Scriptures use, when they wish to convey the idea of one or more being taken out from the company of the dead, while the great mass are still left under the power of the grave.

We assert, now, that this is the form in which the saints' resurrection is described. Theirs is a resurrection not *of*, but *out of* the dead, in the same way that Christ's was.

This will appear from the following: But they which shall be accounted worthy to obtain that world, and the resurrection *from the dead*, neither marry, nor are given in marriage; Luke xx. 35. Christ was speaking here of the resurrection of believers; and theirs He describes as the resurrection from among the dead. Being grieved that they taught the people, and preached through Jesus the resurrection *from the dead;* Acts iv. 2. The doctrine preached by the Apostle was not simply the resurrection of the dead, for all the Jews believed that, excepting the Sadducees; but it was the saint's resurrection—the resurrection from among the dead, which they proclaimed through Jesus, thereby offending the rulers.

Turn now to the Old Testament, and see how this same idea is embodied there. And many of them that sleep in the dust of the earth shall awake, some to everlasting life, and some to shame and everlasting contempt; Dan. xii. 2. The lexicographer Gesenius testifies that the Hebrew word, translated "many of," "designates a part taken out of the whole." Prof. Bush renders this passage: "And many *from out of* the sleepers in the dust of the earth shall awake; these (shall be) to everlasting life, and those (shall be) to everlasting contempt;" and adds, "The awaking is evidently of the many, and not of the whole; consequently the "*these*" in the one case must be understood of the class that awakes, and the "*these*" in the other, of that which remains asleep." Mr. Barnes says: "The natural and obvious meaning of the word *many*, here, is that a large portion of the persons referred to would thus awake, but not all. So we should understand it if applied to other things, as in such expressions as these: 'many of the people;' 'many of the houses in a city;' 'many of the trees in a forest;' 'many of the rivers in a country.'"

Thus is this idea of a resurrection from among the dead—that is, a resurrection of the just to everlasting life—inwoven with the very structure of the language of the Bible, and taught by the inspired prophets of the Old Testament, as well as the apostles of the New.

These facts will serve to explain Paul's meaning, when he speaks of the high ambition he had of attaining unto the resurrection from among the dead. If by any means I might attain unto (εξαναστασις) the resurrection of [out of] the dead; Phil. iii. 11, the word resurrection being compounded with the preposition from, or out of, to convey the distinct idea of this separation from the mass. Paul had no ambition to attain unto the resurrection *of* the dead. He would secure this without any ambition or effort, even as all the unbelieving and wicked would. What he desired and labored for was the εξαναστασις, the resurrection *from among* the dead; that distinction which was to be put upon the followers of Jesus, when He should bring them with Him at His second appearing. The Scriptures intend to convey this idea of the separation of the believing dead; and they do convey it by the very terms they use, making the resurrection of the saints as one not *of*, but *out of* the dead.

We claim here, also, the resurrection of Christ himself as an argument to the same point. His clearly was a resurrection *out of* the dead, this preëminent honor being put upon Him; and He is "the first-fruits" of all that sleep in Him. Are not they, therefore, to be taken *out of* the dead, and manifested forth also as the sons of God?

To the same point, also, we claim the resurrection of that company of the saints who came out of their graves after His resurrection, and went into the holy city, and appeared unto many; Matt. xxvii. 53. These clearly were brought forth from among the dead, distinguished thereby as the saints, and anticipating the great day of the Lord. The grave, then, could scarcely hold his prey longer. Many prisoners did burst the bars of their sepulchres. By-and-by the shout will be raised, which all those sleeping ones shall hear, "Behold, the bridegroom cometh: go ye out to meet him."

The fact, moreover, is conceded by all, that there is a difference of time in the resurrection of the righteous and wicked, which is sought to be provided for on the hypothesis that, in the general resurrection at the last day (though there is no such expression in the Bible as a general resurrection, it being a phrase which has sprung up to represent the theology of our day on this subject, and entirely foreign to the Scriptures), the righteous will come forth first, and immediately afterward the wicked; yet all within the compass of a day, and in connection with the same events precisely. This representation bears too much the appearance of a mere expedient, hardly justifying the Scriptures in making a distinction with so little difference. The Bible gives a deeper significance and a far greater distinction to the resurrection of the saints. Christ thus emphasizes it, when He speaks of it as "the resurrection of the just," and not only so, but describes it as an event of its own, standing out apart and distinct from every thing else. But when thou makest a feast, call the poor, the maimed, the lame, the blind; and thou shalt be blessed: for they cannot recompense thee: for thou shalt be recompensed *at the resurrection of the just;* Luke xiv. 14. No one could have used this language, who believed in the modern doctrine of a general resurrection at the last day. Christ had before His mind the idea of a separate resurrection, standing apart from that of the wicked—identified with His own coming and kingdom, when He would put honor upon His chosen sons, and manifest them forth as His with great power. This was "the resurrection of the just." For the wicked another day is reserved—the day of final judgment—when they, too, shall be brought forth, but it will be to shame and everlasting contempt. It will be enough to seal the condemnation of any sinner, that he is left to have a part in those resurrection scenes, and be gathered with the company to which that day is devoted. The honor put upon Christ's chosen ones will be, that they have been taken out from among the dead at a day long previous, even as their great forerunner; and as that blessed company who came out of their graves after His resurrection, and appeared to many in the holy city. Of the resurrection of the wicked we shall speak further hereafter, when we come to consider the subject of the final judgment, and show that that day, with its events, belongs to them. It is not Christ's day, nor the day of the saints.

The next question demanding our attention is,

II. *With what body do they come?*

The Jews, as we have already stated, entertained the idea that the resurrection was to restore us to the same condition, relations, and employments of life as before, without change, except perhaps that the body was not again to be subject to death. Nor was this an unnatural view for them to take. The fact of a restoration and return to earth had been made known. But beyond this little was revealed. The forms of the cherubim, with their matchless powers, did indeed symbolize our redeemed nature. Yet there was little here to tell of the change which that nature was to undergo in passing from under the curse. We should, therefore, be careful how we judge the Jewish nation too severely in their conceptions of the resurrection state. They accepted the revealed fact in its most literal sense. But while they erred in this direction, failing to enter into the higher conditions of this state, we have gone as far to the other extreme, and so etherialized that spiritual body which is to be, that to all intents we have nullified the doctrine of the resurrection, and destroyed its power over our minds. It has become such a shadow, so destitute of substance and reality, that we have lost our interest in it, and almost our faith. There are not a few professing to believe the Scriptures, who deny that the body is raised. They claim, it may be, to believe a doctrine of the resurrection, but it is not the resurrection of this body that is deposited in the grave; and this is the tendency of the faith of this age. The Jews went to one extreme, and believed, but too literally. We have gone to the other, and our faith is lost in shadowy spiritualizations, without form or power.

Are there any means of arriving at the truth on this subject, or so approximating to it, that our faith may have some solid ground to rest upon? Has Divine revelation put this matter within our reach; for we may assume that nothing short of this can give us light here? The doctrine of the resurrection is one purely of revelation; and to the Word of God must we humbly go for instruction. If we do not find it there, we shall not find it anywhere. It is said of Christ that He hath abolished death, and hath brought life and immortality to light through the gospel; 2 Tim. i. 10. The word translated "immortality," is not synonymous with "life," as more commonly understood, but is the word used elsewhere to express the incorruption of the body, as when the Apostle says, This corruptible must put on *incorruption;* 1 Cor. xv. 53. Christ, then, hath abolished death, death in every form, and brought to light the life of the soul, and the incorruption of the body, or full redemption for soul and body. That is the doctrine of the gospel of Christ. The power of death is broken over the entire man, and his whole being is redeemed, body as well as soul. What, then, is that resurrection or incorruptible state to which believers are destined, and with what body do they come?

Passing the discussion of this subject by Paul in his First Epistle to the Corinthians, we shall turn directly to

Christ—to His own living, personal resurrection. There is the reality itself, which we can see and handle, as it were, and which was given us as the first-fruits of that glorious harvest of earth; for we are to be raised in His likeness, even with the same almighty power. There is a reality and tangibleness in this resurrection of Jesus, which brings the subject within our reach, so that our faith may grasp it. The simple and only question, therefore, for us to consider, is:

Did Christ wear His spiritual, incorruptible body after He came forth from the sepulchre?

The doubt and denial of this has been the chief source of the vagueness and infidelity on this whole subject. We have actually seen our Saviour burst the bars of the tomb, passing forever beyond its power, to die no more. He has appeared and talked with us through a period of forty days, to give the demonstration that there is such a resurrection state, and then He ascended on high until the appointed hour of His return.

What, now, was the physical condition of Christ in this His resurrection state? Many persons would not be prepared to give any answer to this question. They have never considered it—have never attached any particular importance to it, have never seen its connections and bearings—while of those who have thought on the subject, the more common opinion perhaps would be that Christ's body was unchanged, and still subject to the same laws and necessities as before.

But why should not Jesus enter His proper resurrection state *when He rose from the dead*, and especially when it is declared that we are to be raised in His likeness? Did Jesus return to His former condition of life this side the grave, as did Lazarus, the widow's son at Nain, and others, to be subject again to the curse? Or when He cried, "It is finished," and bowed His head in death, was that the end of this His mortal career; and when He appeared the other side of the grave, had He entered upon another and incorruptible state to die no more—no more to obey and suffer—to bear reproach, and scorn, and spitting—no more to toil, and be subject to the necessities of the flesh? Had He not passed through and beyond all these—through the iron gates of death to the land beyond, where He could now say triumphantly, I am he that liveth, and was dead; and behold, I am alive forevermore, Amen; and have the keys of hell and of death; Rev. i. 18.

We are here met with the fact and argument founded thereon, that Jesus ate with His disciples, and told them to handle Him and see, "for a spirit hath not flesh and bones, as ye see me have."

But this was no necessary denial of the fact that He was now clothed upon with His glorified body. Why did He eat with His disciples? Because He was hungry, and needed food to sustain His fainting nature? Who will assert this? The angels allowed Abraham to entertain them with his hospitality. They could and did eat; but their natures did not require food. Christ ate also, but *simply to demonstrate to His affrighted disciples that He was not a ghost*, as they imagined. "A spirit (an apparition) hath not flesh and bones, as ye see me have." It was of the deepest moment to demonstrate, in the most incontestible manner, that this appearance of Jesus was not a mere illusion of the senses, or an apparition; but that it was verily He himself, whom they had known and loved; that this was His own body, which they had seen delivered to death and the sepulchre. But in demonstrating this, He did not mean to prove that He had returned to His former condition in the flesh, or that this was not His now glorified body. The contrary was necessarily implied by all His intercourse with them.

He was now, beyond denial, in His resurrection state, having passed the portals of the grave—having triumphed over death and all its power. This is the very fact He was aiming to establish. There is not the slightest evidence now that Christ would have eaten, except for the especial purpose of demonstrating that He was not what the disciples imagined Him to be, a spirit; and *what the world to this hour would have continued to assert that He wás, aside from this very proof given.* His own friends thought Him to be an apparition, and were terrified. Why should not the world have so believed and asserted?

But again. *The facts of Christ's history during those forty days subsequent to His resurrection, are perfectly accordant with this view, and show that the laws of His being were different entirely from those of the natural body.*

Christ did not live constantly by miracle during this period. We have no right to suppose this, nor is there any evidence of it. He was either in the natural body, or the glorified, subject to the laws and conforming to the conditions of one or the other. We have no authority to resort to the supposition of constant miracle to relieve the case of difficulty. Was not the fact now most perfectly apparent to the disciples, that their Master was no more under the laws of the flesh, as once He was; but that He was moving and acting in a different sphere? Was not this impression made by His whole intercourse with them, and by all the facts of His history coming to their knowledge? There can be no doubt upon this point. All those facts, as well as His intercourse with them, were of the most unwonted and mysterious character. The disciples needed not to be told that He was operating in a higher sphere. That was abundantly evident.

He was not subject to hunger and weariness any more

as once He was, and therefore He did not require food or rest. It was not needful now that He should prepare for himself the necessaries of life, and labor for them under the law of toil, or that His friends should minister unto Him. He needed no habitation. No one ever conceives of Christ as subject to such necessities in His resurrection state. The thought of it is painful. Yet why not, if He was literally restored to the fleshly body, as were Lazarus, and others? Have we not a right to demand that those who advocate this view of the matter shall abide by all its necessities and consequences? We think so.

But notice *how Christ appeared only when, and where, and to whom He pleased, and to none others.*

The question has been asked, If Jesus really rose from the dead, why did He not appear publicly, and demonstrate the fact to the confusion of the rulers, and all opposers? This, of course, assumes that He rose in the natural body, and in some way kept himself concealed, which is alleged to have been an unwise policy; that He should, on the contrary, have appeared before the multitude, and demonstrated to them the fact of His resurrection. This, however, would have insured the defeat of Christianity. It would have required the return of Jesus to His normal state in the body, so that He might be subjected to public inspection. But this, so far from silencing opposition and denial, would only have added thereto. The question would have been started at once whether this was the Jesus that had been crucified, or whether death had really ensued on His crucifixion. It would have been easy to assume either of these positions. God most wisely did not thus submit the question of the resurrection of Jesus to the decision of His enemies, that they might sit as a jury on the case. The fact, also, that He was not within the reach of the multitude, and that He showed himself only to a few chosen witnesses, is proof that He did not return to the natural body. Christ was not necessarily seen because He was risen, as were Lazarus and the nobleman's daughter. They returned to their former condition of life, and might be seen by any who chose to visit them. But Jesus was not visible to any beside those to whom He "showed himself." This fact is distinctly stated. Him God raised up the third day, and showed him openly; *not to all the people*, but unto witnesses chosen before of God, even to us, who did eat and drink with him after he rose from the dead; Acts x. 40. He selected His own witnesses, as well as the time, place, and circumstances; and under such conditions as to prove that He had passed beyond this mortal state, and was no more subject to its laws. In this way He established the fact that there was a proper resurrection or redeemed state for the body, where death could have no more power, where there was no more curse, and where His bitterest and mightiest enemies might in vain rage against Him. He was beyond the reach of all their malice. It was the assurance of this fact that inspired those unlearned and heretofore trembling Galileans with such heroic courage and might, that they could stand up before all the potentates, and rulers, and Rabbis, declaring their unshaken faith in Him whom the nation, with wicked hands, had crucified and slain. They had seen their Jesus under such conditions, that they had the evidence of His being beyond all the power and rage of His combined foes. Therefore they did not hesitate to stand up as witnesses of His resurrection unto their nation.

This view of the case also allowed the Holy Ghost to come to bear His testimony, upon whom, after all, the chief burden and responsibility were to rest. We have shown heretofore that God did not intend that our faith in the resurrection of Jesus should depend upon mere human testimony, especially the testimony of the multitude. The Holy Ghost was to be the principal witness in the case. Therefore were the disciples chosen and qualified to this end, that the spirit might rest upon them and endorse all their statements.

The disciples, then, were the only persons to whom Jesus disclosed himself. Neither was He with them as of old. They only saw Him occasionally, at considerable intervals of time, and then for a brief period, and under such circumstances as clearly to demonstrate that the conditions of His existence were entirely changed. It is asserted, indeed, that Jesus labored to establish the fact to His disciples, that this was His very identical body which He had previous to His death, unchanged in all respects; to which end they adduce the circumstance of His eating with, and being handled by them. We assert, on the contrary, that, while He aimed to prove that it was verily He himself beyond all mistake or question, and not an apparition, He labored to establish the fact *that He was not with them in His former condition of body.* His whole intercourse with them went to prove this. He was revealed to them alone, in a mysterious manner, and for a brief space, being invisible to all others. They themselves could not command His presence in any way —could not visit Him. They did not know the place of His abode. He had none, and needed none. These were facts perfectly apparent, and which demonstrated absolutely that the conditions of His being, and His manifestations were entirely new. Did the watchful Roman guard see Him when He passed out of the sepulchre under their very eye? Was the stone moved, or the seal broken, to give Him exit; or did the angel come down and roll away that stone, to demonstrate to the guard that they were watching an empty tomb, and that their prisoner had already escaped? Yet to the disconsolate Mary He suddenly disclosed himself, as she stood weeping by the tomb, and inquiring with deepest anguish for the lost body of her Lord. His address to her on this occasion, containing the first words spoken by Him after His resurrection, are especially to be noted. What was the truth He would now reveal? What the explanation of the amazing facts now transpiring? Jesus saith unto her, Touch me not: for I am not yet ascended to my Father: but go to my brethren, and say unto them, I ascend unto my Father and your Father, and to my God and your God; John xx. 17. What did Jesus intend by this extraordinary prohibition to that devoted woman whom He thus honored by His first manifestation? He meant to forbid the natural demonstration of affection, which Mary was about to make in the delirium of her joy at her Lords restoration. And why? To let her understand that He had not returned to His former condition in the flesh, and those relationships, in which such expressions of friendship could be allowed. Mary's natural inference in seeing Jesus alive, was that He had come back to be among them as before. She would have no other conception of the matter. Jesus gave her to understand at once that this was not the case; and nothing could have been better calculated to show this, than the forbidding her approach, and the embrace of that sacred body which had passed the portals of death. When we remember what the love of this woman was toward Jesus, and what the circumstances under which He was now revealed, first of all to her, as alive from the dead, we cannot imagine any thing that would more clearly have demonstrated the changed condition of His whole being than the command so positively laid upon her, "Touch me not." Nor could she attach to it any other meaning. The prohibition, under the circumstances, for any other reason, would have been absolute cruelty to Mary, and would have belied the whole character of Jesus. The reason sometimes given, that such haste was required to bear the tidings to the disciples, as would not allow Mary to delay a moment to express her feelings on such an occasion, is absurd. There was no such haste.

But this was not all. He sends a message by her to His disciples, designed to embody the same idea. "I am not *yet* ascended," but tell them I am about to ascend. They must not imagine that I have come back to remain with them in the flesh as heretofore, as they might naturally suppose on hearing that I am alive again. Tell them that I do live indeed, but that I ascend speedily to my Father. The first aim of Jesus, therefore, was to correct the false impressions which His friends would all naturally have respecting His condition in returning to life. He aimed directly and at once to make them understand that that condition was wholly changed, and that He had passed to another and glorified state, in which He was soon to ascend. Upon this same idea, too, all His subsequent intercourse with His disciples and friends was based. When He met the other women unexpectedly in the way as they were hastening from the sepulchre, He did not tarry, neither did He go with them to the disciples, as would have been natural; but only gave them a message to bear. Again that same day He joined two of the disciples on their way to Emmaus, and the fact is here stated that, Their eyes were holden, that they should not know him; Luke xxiv. 16; while Mark says, "He appeared in *another form* unto two of them as they walked and went into the country," implying that His appearance was changed in some way; which we may easily account for, if He was in His resurrection state. These disciples did not recognize Him by voice, or manner, or person, until He disclosed himself in the breaking of bread [that is, with the significant words accompanying, This is my body, broken for you: this do ye in remembrance of me], and then vanished out of their sight. Yet again that same evening, while these two brethren were repeating their wondrous story to the eleven, did Jesus appear in the midst of them, the doors being shut,* as we are distinctly informed by John, "for fear of the Jews," which means that they were fastened. When men shut a door through fear, every one understands that they make it secure by bars and bolts; and thus had those trembling disciples secured the entrance to their room on this, their first gathering together after the crucifixion. No wonder, therefore, they were terrified and affrighted, and supposed they had seen a spirit; Luke xxiv. 37. They had every reason to think so that men could have. The narrative plainly shows that Jesus did not enter the room by the law of the natural body. That He quietly

* The following passages will clearly show what the meaning of the word "shut" is, as used in the New Testament. But thou, when thou prayest, enter into thy closet, and when thou hast *shut* thy door, pray unto thy Father which is in secret; Matt. vi. 6. But woe unto you, Scribes and Pharisees, hypocrites! for ye *shut up* the kingdom of heaven against men; chap. xxiii. 13. And they that were ready, went in with them to the marriage: and the door was *shut;* chap. xxv. 10. Trouble me not: for the door is now *shut*, and my children are with me in bed; Luke xi. 7. When the heaven was *shut up* three years and six months; chap. iv. 25. The prison truly found we *shut* with all safety, and the keepers standing without before the doors; Acts v. 23. And all the city was moved, and the people ran together: and they took Paul and drew him out of the temple. And forthwith the doors were *shut;* chap. xxi. 30. And cast him into the bottomless pit, and *shut* him up, and set a seal upon him; Rev. xx. 3. Also Rev. iii. 7; xi. 6; xxi. 25. In all these passages the idea is that of closing effectually, fastening. When, moreover, it is stated further in the case now under consideration, that "the doors were shut for fear of the Jews," there can be no doubt left, that it was designed to convey the specific idea that those doors were *locked.*

opened the door without their noticing the fact, is positively contradicted by the statement, that the door was "shut for fear of the Jews." The mystery of His entrance, therefore—for mystery it was—was designed to convey the impression, and teach the disciples that He was now in His risen state, and no more subject to the laws of this corruptible body.

Observe, also, more particularly, the bearing of the fact that Jesus did not continue with the disciples during these forty days of His manifestation.

It was only occasionally that He appeared, and then but for a few moments. He was seen three or four times on the first day, by different parties, and then not until the next Sabbath. Where was He during the interval? Who knew of the place of His abode? Did He hide himself in some secret corner? The suggestion of the thought is revolting to our minds. Yet such must have been the case, if He was in the body as before, and subject to the natural laws of the same. That the disciples, too, knew nothing of the presence or dwelling-place of their Master, is evident from the facts respecting Thomas, who was absent when Jesus met the disciples on the first Sabbath evening, and would not believe that they had seen Him. His argument undoubtedly was to this effect: You assert that our blessed Lord is risen from the dead, and that He is alive. Where, now, is He? Who of you can tell of His dwelling-place? If our Jesus were upon earth, would He not be with us as of old, and be found somewhere in the circle of His friends? Should we not know where He was? Would He not be among us, to comfort and instruct us as He was wont to do? No. It is an idle tale. You have been imposed upon, and have seen a ghost. I will not believe, neither can I be thus deceived. "For unless I can see in his hands the print of the nails;" nay verily, *I will not trust my own eyes in such a case*, but "put my finger into the print of the nails, and thrust my hand into his side, I will not believe." It was with such arguments and facts that Thomas was pressing his fellow-disciples during the week, which they had no power to meet. He seemingly, for the time, had the better of the argument. It was against the whole character of Jesus and the history of His life to leave His disciples alone at such a time of trial and darkness as they were now passing through. If He were alive and upon earth, He would surely be with them, and let them know that He had come back again to the body. But they knew nothing of Him during that week, nor could they take the doubting Thomas to the place of His abode to silence his unbelief.

It was not until the return of the next Sabbath evening, when the disciples were again assembled, "the doors being shut," as we are once more pointedly informed, that Jesus stood in the midst of them, and said, "Peace be unto you. Then saith he to Thomas, Reach hither thy finger, and behold my hands; and reach hither thy hand and thrust it into my side, and be not faithless, but believing." Who of the disciples had then seen the Master during the week, to tell Him of the very words he had spoken, and the evidence he would demand of the resurrection of his Lord? And yet Jesus was now repeating those words, and furnishing the very demonstration he had asked. Here was evidence of more than His resurrection—evidence that the unseen Jesus had been cognizant of all his words and thoughts—evidence of His divinity. And all that the astonished disciple could utter to express the overpowering emotions of his soul, was, "My Lord, and my God!" Oh, I am satisfied. It is enough—more than enough. My risen, glorified Redeemer! I ask no more.

So Jesus continued to manifest himself from time to

time during the period of forty days. He showed himself often enough, and under such different circumstances, as to demonstrate, beyond all doubt, the reality of His resurrection; while, at the same time, His absence from them the greater portion of the time, their entire ignorance of His dwelling-place, His want of all ordinary means of support, and His mysterious approach to, and withdrawal from them, were demonstration equally strong that He was now moving in a higher and spiritual sphere, of which their senses could take no cognizance. He was now in the resurrection body. The disciples could not mistake this, or have a doubt respecting it.

The facts of this sublime history show that that state involves powers and capacities which are unknown in this present condition of the body. They are supernatural as respects the present, but they are natural to that redeemed incorruptible state. Christ did not transcend the laws of the sphere in which He was moving at this time, any more than Moses and Elijah, when they appeared upon the mount of transfiguration, or the angel, when he entered the guarded prison for the release of Peter. This was within their sphere. Jesus likewise, under the same laws of the glorified body, entered where the disciples were assembled, "the doors being shut." Had He been in the natural body, as when He walked the stormy waves of Genesaret, it would have been a proper miracle. But Jesus was not living by constant miracle during the forty days subsequent to His resurrection. He was not living without food and habitation, when His necessities demanded them. It is derogatory to Him to suppose it; while by such a course the disciples would inevitably have been misled and deceived. The risen body is endowed with new and transcendant powers, which belong not to this present, dying, corruptible, dishonored condition, where we groan and sigh in our bondage, and travail in pain together. That "spiritual" body is visible to mortal eyes only as it reveals itself. Men did not necessarily behold Jesus, because He was risen from the dead, as they did Lazarus, and others. He disclosed His glorified presence only when, and where, and to whom He pleased, even as Moses and Elijah appeared to the three disciples upon the mount. The same fact is brought to light in connection with that company of the saints, which arose, and came out of their graves after his resurrection, and went into the holy city, and appeared unto many; Matt. xxvii. 52. Did these saints come back to the natural body, to be subject again to the curse? or were they raised in incorruption and glory? The latter, most clearly. When Jesus burst the bars of death, the sepulchre was hardly able to hold its prisoners longer. His triumph shook the whole empire of death, so that the prison doors of many were opened even then. This is confirmed by the statement, that "They went into the holy city, and *appeared* unto many." Had they been raised in the flesh, it would have been superfluous to state this. Of course, they appeared, if they were thus raised. They could not be hid. There would have been no meaning in a statement concerning Lazarus, that he appeared to many after his resurrection. He was restored to his normal condition and relations. Men saw him as they saw other men. They came from Jerusalem in great numbers to behold and converse with a man brought again from the grave. But there was significancy in asserting of these saints, who arose with Christ, that they "went into the holy city, and appeared unto many." It means that they were not necessarily to be seen, because risen. They were arrayed in their glorious, incorruptible forms, and appeared only where, and to whom they pleased. They must reveal themselves if they would be seen by mortal eyes. The law of their being was the same with that of Christ's resurrection body. "They appeared unto many," thereby demonstrating the fact that they had risen, and implying that they did not continue among men, and resume their stations in life as of old. They simply "appeared" to their friends, as Christ showed himself to His disciples, and then vanished again from their sight. Those saints could as easily make their appearance now, as did Moses and Elijah on the mount. A thin vail only separates these seen and unseen worlds. The facts show that that vail can easily, and at any moment, be taken from mortal eyes, so that we may gaze upon, and hold converse with, those risen and glorified ones, who have already attained unto their reward. They may be hovering near these mortal shores, and awaiting with intensest joy the hour when Christ shall burst the bars from the tombs of all His saints, and all that glorious company of the dead shall be gathered from their slumbers, clothed with incorruption and power. When, too, that joyful event shall take place, as ere long it will, and the glad hour of earth's long-promised redemption shall have come, that unseen world will not be hidden from our sight, as now it is in this night of her sorrow and travail. It will not be a rare thing for the risen saints then to appear, and hold converse with men in the flesh. It may become the natural and established order of things. We have seen how these glorified ones have revealed themselves to mortal eyes from time to time, even now, when Satan holds the empire—when the Church is in sackcloth, and fasting because of the bridegroom's absence. Is it, then, to be deemed incredible, that that intercourse of the risen saints should be an ordinary event in that coming, blessed day, when Satan shall be cast out with all his works of darkness, and this earth shall be given into their possession, to whom it rightfully belongs, that they may live and reign with

Christ? Have not the disclosures of the past on this subject been made for the purpose of foreshadowing the realities and glories of that coming day of our Immanuel, when He *shall be revealed* in His power and kingdom, and all His saints with Him?

We have not undertaken to show what the range of existence and power is to the resurrection body. We have no means of determining its limits. We know that it is not bound down to the laws of the present corruptible body, but can soar on lofty pinions. The universe itself may be the boundless theatre of its movements.

In thus dealing with the doctrine of the resurrection, we have indulged in no speculations. We have confined ourselves strictly to the facts of the Divine record—facts given for our instruction on this very subject—facts embodied in the resurrection of Him who is our forerunner, and presented to God already as the first-fruits of the coming harvest—and facts in the case of some who have anticipated the great day of the Lord, and whom the grave could not hold unto that eventful hour. The wonder, too, with many may be, that these obvious facts have to such an extent escaped our observation; and that the resurrection state has had such a dim and shadowy existence to our apprehension, when such truths as these lay before our eyes. With such facts, too, in our possession, we have no inclination for speculation on this theme. There is no occasion for it. We may build our faith on the clear records made concerning our living Redeemer, who hath triumphed over the foe, and will come ere long to bring us off conquerors too.

We have, in truth, been afraid to retain any thing material for the resurrection body, because we have despised this creation of God, and these bodies, as a part thereof. We have been taught to regard it as of inferior value, reserved only for the fires of the last day, and to be given up to utter destruction. We have not conceived that this earth was fit to be redeemed, or that God would deem it worthy of preservation. We have not cared whether it continued or not, our only desire being to be released from it, to dwell in some transcendant, far distant sphere; while the old heathen idea has been inculcated, that God made these bodies of the dust of earth, in order to humble us, as if the union of the soul with this inferior body was an ill-advised arrangement, and degrading to man's higher and spiritual nature. We have looked upon it as we do upon an unfortunate marriage, in which a noble woman throws herself away upon a man who is greatly her inferior. We pity her, and feel almost indignant at the unhappy connection. So has our theology taught us, though we have not dared to assert it, in so many words, that God made some sad mistake when He bound down the immortal soul to this clod of earth. Under the influence of this theology, our interest in the continuance of these bodies is, for the most part, gone, and their resurrection has lost its true hold and power upon our affections. All our ideas of heaven and happiness have been connected with the soul. For the redemption of the body we have cared comparatively very little. Such theology, however, most clearly, is not the theology of the Bible. We have been drifting out of our course by some powerful secret undercurrent of error, which has changed to us some of the most precious relations of truth in the system of redemption.

This presentation of the subject shows us *how inappropriate is the question of the possibility of recognizing friends in the future state.*

The starting of such a question is striking evidence how we have spiritualized almost to nothing the doctrine of the resurrection, and destroyed well nigh all its reality and power. We have reduced it to such a shadow, that there is hardly a substance left, and we are at a loss to know whether we shall preserve our own identity, or recognize the forms with which we have been familiar here on earth. When we learn to get back from this dim land of ghosts and shadows, to read the facts of the resurrection state as they lie upon the pages of the Bible, we shall perceive how foolish it was even to have started such an inquiry as the one now referred to, and that it never would have been suggested if we had studied these facts aright.

Again. *We do not undertake to assert what the extent of the glory is in which the resurrection body will be arrayed.*

We have collected certain facts illustrating the resurrection state, as we find them recorded upon the inspired page. That these are all, or more than the smaller part, we are not to imagine. These are but glimpses into that other world; enough, indeed, to confirm our faith, yet not to satisfy our knowledge. We have not asserted that Christ was clothed with the full glories of His resurrection state during those days of His manifestation unto His disciples. They were, in a measure, still hidden. It was apparent, indeed, that He was not what He had been, when under the curse. He had passed forever beyond that state, to die no more. But the full glories of that resurrection body were not disclosed to their sight. What the range of power belonging to those spiritual bodies is, and in what additional beauty and glory they may be clothed, we have no certain means now of knowing. Surpassing glories shone around the Saviour upon the mount of transfiguration, and when revealed to John in Patmos, in the midst of the golden candlesticks. Yet there was still the same human form in all its Divine lineaments; and that humanity is ever to be retained, however beautified and endowed with new and immortal powers. The Apostle characterizes it as a "spiritual" body, by which he does not mean to deny its materiality, or assert that it is itself spirit. But as the "natural" body is one, endowed with animal life, and adapted to the present condition of the soul, and the physical constitution of the world which it inhabits, so a "spiritual" body is one, adapted to the use of the soul in its future glorified state, and the moral and physical condition of the heavenly world—or that constitution of things when all shall be made new.

Are we to question or deny that God can thus glorify this now corruptible flesh? "Thou fool," says the Apostle, "that which thou sowest is not quickened, except it die. And that which thou sowest, thou sowest not that body which shall be, but bare [naked] grain, which God raises up in new and wonderful forms of beauty. The rough piece of charcoal presents no attractions, and we shun its defilement even. But let it be raised by Divine power from this condition, and crystallized, and with what delight do we now gaze upon the sparkling diamond, an incorruptible, we might almost say, a spiritual body!

May not God cause as great and glorious a change to pass upon the elements entering into this nobler creation of our humanity, dying and corruptible though it now be? Did He not give His own Son to die for it? And what is that resurrection body other than this mortality crystallized, and made to reflect forever the image and excellency of the infinite godhead.

May it be ours to attain to this honor—ours the high ambition to say with the Apostle, "If by any means I might attain unto the resurrection of [from among] the dead."

CHAPTER XXXVI.

THE REIGN OF CHRIST.

In tracing out the history of redemption and providence, we have reached that joyful era for which earth has so long waited—the coming of Christ in His kingdom and glory, when Satan shall be cast out and bound, and this groaning creation shall enter into the privileges of the sons of God. We have already described the judgments connected with that day of the Lord, when the haughty, persecuting powers, which have so long ruled the world, and trampled upon the righteous, shall themselves be trodden in the wine-press of Jehovah's wrath, and the cup of vengeance shall be pressed to their lips, that they may drain it to the dregs. We have also described the resurrection of the saints—another event to mark "that great and notable day of the Lord." And now has come that time of restitution of all things, of which prophets have spoken from the beginning. There shall be new heavens and a new earth, wherein dwelleth righteousness. "None shall have need to say to his brother, Know the Lord; for all shall know him from the least unto the greatest." "Thy people shall be all righteous."

This is the promised year of jubilee, when Christ shall have broken every yoke, and put all enemies beneath His feet. Satan shall be allowed to vex no more; and an hour of joy and redemption to earth indeed it will be, when that cruel Adversary shall be removed, and his malignant influence no more felt through all these realms. This, too, we conceive to be the teachings of the Scriptures on this subject; not merely that the power and machinations of Satan are confined within narrower limits, but that they cease. His work is now circumscribed during this present period, being bound with a chain; and the drawing of this chain still more tightly, so as to confine him within much narrower limits, would not produce any radical change so as to constitute a regeneration, or justify the striking symbol of the angel who laid hold on the dragon, that old serpent, which is the devil, and Satan, and bound him a thousand years, and cast him into the bottomless pit, and shut him up, and set a seal upon him, that he should deceive the nations no more, till the thousand years should be fulfilled; Rev. xx. 2. This clearly conveys the idea of Satan's banishment from earth, and the entire removal of his influence.

Neither is this accomplished by the agency of the truth. An angel coming down from heaven, having the key of the bottomless pit, and a great chain in his hand, does not symbolize the gospel, or the ministry of the Word, or the working of the Holy Ghost. It is the interposition of a new agency, sent for this very purpose of laying hold of the great Adversary himself, and placing him in confinement, so as to put an end to all his further influence and efforts on earth. No description could more perfectly represent such banishment from this world than that employed in the Revelation. It is mere assumption to make the binding of Satan, here described (and this is the only place in the Scriptures where it is spoken of), mean a simple limitation of his power; and that effected by the preaching the gospel. The language must be forced to extract any such meaning from it. The passage asserts far more than this, and we accept its obvious meaning.

Far too little account also has been made of this sublime event, and its bearings upon the destiny of our world have been too little understood. The warfare now going on with this dread foe is not to be perpetual. He has no right of possession here, any more than the beast or the false prophet. They are all usurpations. This earth belongs to Christ, and He is to have it in peace, undisturbed by the Prince of darkness, or any of his allies. For wise reasons they are tolerated for a season. But Christ is working for their overthrow. Mark it, *their overthrow*. They are not to be converted by the gospel. Judgment is to overtake them. And it is to be "the great and notable day of the Lord," when He shall arise in His wrath to execute the long-delayed work of vengeance on His foes. This binding of Satan is contemporaneous with the overthrow of the beast and the false prophet, and the kings of the earth with their armies, or immediately following thereupon, and connected with the coming of Christ. Neither is it any less decisive. The Bible uses the most terrific imagery to describe the scenes of that day of judgment. The vials of Heaven's wrath are poured out. The very wrath of *the Lamb* is kindled, and who shall be able to stand? The year of Christ's redeemed is come, and so is the hour of Satan's judgment also, when that evil spirit is to be apprehended, bound with a great chain, shut up in the bottomless pit, and a seal put upon him, "that he should deceive the nations no more, till the thousand years be fulfilled." Neither is it difficult to understand how soon and easily this world may be subjected to Christ, when this malignant Head of the great confederacy of wickedness is removed out of the way. A nation, then, in very deed, may be born in a day.

Nor is it to be esteemed any dishonor to Christ, or to His gospel, thus to remove Satan, banishing him from this entire territory, and overthrowing his allies. We are not aware that they have any constitutional rights here, or that Christ is under any obligation to suffer their continuance with all their evil machinations. As to their conversion, there is no expectation or promise of it. And as to peace on earth while they continue here, there never will be any. There never can be. They are deadly and eternal enemies to Christ, and must fight against Him until they are destroyed. And that is their predicted end. As to the honor of Christ and His gospel, there is none greater than that of maintaining His ground in the midst of this wide territory of Satan, in the very centre of his dominions and his strongholds, and with His "little flock" defying all the rage and malice of the enemy Like Gibraltar upon Spanish soil, it is an assertion and witness of British dominion. So Jesus Christ has planted His obnoxious cross in the centre of the dominions of the Prince of darkness, and there has been no power that could dislodge Him. The Church of God has been a little flock, sent forth like sheep into the midst of wolves; seemingly most weak and defenceless, and which, to all appearance, could be devoured in a moment. Yet the wild beasts of hell have raged around the fold, and besieged it with all their legions for eighteen centuries, but only to their own confusion. We claim, now, that this is the most glorious demonstration possible of the power of Christ. If the Adversary could not destroy this little flock in the midst of his own boasted territory, then he has forfeited every right to claim possession here. The glory of the victory belongs to our Immanuel. The triumph is complete and overwhelming. Jesus has proved His title to all this wide domain. And well may the appointed hour come, when He will bind the strong man, and, shutting him up in the bottomless pit, take possession here for himself. If, moreover, He could cast out His covenant nation, to make them a hissing and byword, when they raged and blasphemed against Him and the Holy Ghost, well may the hour come when the old serpent shall be cast out, that this earth may have rest, and be given into the possession of Christ and His saints.

This period of joy and blessedness to earth will be one of long continuance, which we argue from the statements of prophecy and the analogy of the whole work of God from the beginning respecting our race. The only argument of any seeming weight which can be adduced in favor of a short continuance of this period, is to be found in "the thousand years" allotted thereto in Rev. xx. 4, *and the forcing of the same to a literal interpretation.* As to "the end," "the end of all things," spoken of in the Scriptures, it has no reference whatever to the termination of earth's history and affairs, but simply to the end of this present age, to be followed, however, by others to come. This is the Bible use of the phrase. Yet many read it as if it described the closing up of all sublunary things, and the final destruction of the earth, if not the universe itself. The Bible, however, nowhere gives us any intimation concerning the final destruction of the earth, in the sense of its annihilation or dissolution. God *destroyed* the earth once with a deluge of waters, but it survived that catastrophe. He may destroy it again with fire; but it will survive that more terrible day of judgment, and there shall be new heavens and earth, wherein dwelleth righteousness, as the Scriptures expressly inform us.

The only evidence, then, that can be adduced to show the brief continuance of Christ's reign on earth, is found in "the thousand years" spoken of in Rev. xx. 4, taken in a literal sense. We answer this by the *argumentum ad hominem*, and say that the Revelation is a book of symbols, and so to be interpreted. We ask, therefore, why this is taken in a literal sense, without any reason shown, or even offered therefor, and *by the very men* who unhesitatingly give a symbolical interpretation to all other numbers, marking periods of duration in the same book. To the twelve hundred and sixty days, or forty and two months of the beast's power, and the three days and a half during which the two slain witnesses lie unburied, these same persons give a symbolical meaning. They therefore are forever estopped from offering a word of objection to the application of the same rule of interpretation to the thousand years of Christ's reign. The interpreter of the book of Revelation is not at liberty to give a literal or symbolical meaning to the same thing at his pleasure. Let him at least have the consistency of uniformly taking one or the other, and not either, as may suit his convenience.

We claim, then, as most interpreters do, that the numbers in the book of Revelation are symbolical; consequently, that "the thousand years" describe a period of three hundred and sixty-five thousand, a day standing for a year. This, then, is just as definitely the doctrine of the Bible concerning the continuance of Christ's reign, as that the forty and two months, and the thousand two hundred and threescore days, during which the holy city is trodden under the feet of the Gentiles, Rev. xi. 2; that the witnesses prophesy in sackcloth, chap. xi. 3; that the woman has a place prepared for her in the wilderness, chap. xii. 6; and that the ten-horned beast has power to make war with the saints, chap. xiii. 5, describe a period of twelve hundred and sixty years. We accept the latter, and, in doing this, have no ground upon which we can deny the former.

But again, *the long continuance of this period is in harmony with the whole plan of providence, and necessitated by it.*

The wisdom of that plan can hardly be vindicated or made clear without it. God has appropriated countless ages to the rearing of earth's material structure, giving long cycles to the dominion of its molluscs, fishes, and crawling reptiles, as the mere preparatory stage to the entrance of its great lord. Through long periods, God caused the light feebly to struggle in the midst of the darkness which rested upon the great deep, and not until the fourth revolving "day" did the sun finally appear, breaking through the mists, and revealing itself as the source of that light. Through the same slow-moving ages was the earth emerging from the wide waste of waters, and undergoing the preparation which was necessary to fit it as a dwelling-place for the animal tribes, and, last of all, for man himself. And then, when the habitation was complete, we have seen how nearly six thousand years have been allowed to the dominion of Satan and the curse upon this territory, during which the vast proportion of the race, aside from its infant population, has been going down to perdition.

When we remember, now, that this earth belongs to Christ, being created by Him and for Him, and redeemed unto Him at a cost which no arithmetic can calculate, and that it is to be made the theatre for the unfolding of all the depths of His infinite wisdom and love, and the rearing of that everlasting temple of His grace which is to stand to His eternal praise, we cannot but regard it as the most unworthy and unnatural conception that could be entertained, to suppose that Christ's possession of the earth is to continue only for the brief period of a thousand years. Even "the great whore" herself will have been allowed more than that, during which she may be drunk with the blood of the saints. More than double has been allowed to the great fourth or iron kingdom, presented to us in the book of Daniel. For nearly two thousand years has Christ called His beloved Church to testify to Him, clothed in sackcloth, and wait the coming of the bridegroom. And when the long-looked for hour of joy comes to this travailing creation, and the night of her sorrow is over—when the terrific conflict ends in triumph, the beast and the false prophet, with the kings of the earth and all their confederate hosts being overthrown, Satan himself cast into the bottomless pit, and the kingdom and dominion under the whole heaven given into the hands of our Immanuel, to whom it of right belongs, that He may ascend the promised throne of David, to reign so long as the moon endureth, even from generation to generation, shall we be told that this means only a thousand briefly fleeting years? We do not, cannot believe it. It contradicts and belies the entire course of Divine providence, as well as all the wisdom and grace of Him who is infinite in counsel and working, and whose ways are past finding out. Such working would scarcely equal our poor human counsels. When a man spends months or years in preparing the site for a building, and digging the foundations, employing a multitude of laborers, and expending thousands of dollars on work beneath the ground, we have the assurance that the superstructure will correspond in magnitude and cost, to awaken the admiring wonder of every beholder. If thousands are expended on the foundation, hundreds will scarce suffice to lay the topmost stone. Has Christ now wrought through nearly sixty centuries, to say nothing of the ages preceding man's entrance upon the eventful stage, to lay the foundations of His everlasting temple of grace, during all which He has been contending with the leagued powers of earth and hell for their overthrow, that He might gain possession here, and redeem this world unto himself; and do we as yet behold only the few first courses of stone in this magnificent structure, scarcely rising above the surface, amid heaps of rubbish and building materials in vast quantities on every side;

and are we to be told that ten centuries more will suffice to complete the whole to its topmost stone? Such a conception of the Divine plan and working is inexpressibly painful to our mind; nor do we wonder that so many ask for an explanation of these ways of Providence on earth, demanding why God suffers the world to continue through such a night of darkness and heathenism, during which the mass of the race is ripening for perdition. Neither do we wonder at the answer given, that the ways of God are inscrutable, and that the future alone can solve their deep mystery. The difficulty, however, is one of our own making. The theory that involves this dark problem is of our own devising.

God has never told us that the affairs of earth were to be wound up at the close of another thousand years. We believe that this earth is the inheritance of the *second* Adam, and that this is the uniform teaching of the Scriptures. If, therefore, six thousand years have been allowed to the first Adam, in which to pour down through the generations the overwhelming tide of sin and death, then certainly God is working upon a scale of stupendous grandeur in this economy of redemption, and designing plans which ages to come can alone fulfil. To the second Adam belongs that promised "world to come"—that "dispensation of the fulness of times," which shall gather into one all things in Christ, and when, through the generations of our humanity redeemed unto himself, He shall pour, as age after age rolls on, the overflowing streams of His ever-adorable love. Then shall it be seen what capacities this glorious humanity has, to work out the most amazing results, beyond all thought or imagination, in bringing to glory "a multitude which no man can number." Men will then no more think of "a few" being saved, nor speak of the followers of Christ as a "little flock." Such representations and language belong to the present dispensation—to the "old things" which are to pass away. "The end of all things is at hand." "The night is far spent; the day is at hand," and by-and-by these ages of darkness, this night of earth's sorrow, will have receded far into the distance, finally to dwindle to a mere speck upon the horizon, and be almost lost to sight. Hasten, Lord, Thy coming and kingdom. Yea, come, Lord Jesus, come quickly.

There are some points connected with this millennial state, upon which questions might be asked and answers desired. One is in respect to the presence of Christ. *Will He visibly dwell with men on earth?*

The only conception which many have of Christ's return to earth, is that of His dwelling here in the flesh, as He did eighteen hundred years ago, from which their minds revolt, as well they may. For He was then in His humiliation under the curse, and liable to all the ills of this mortal state. He was bound by space and time, and subject himself to law, as we are. In this form He will not, of course, return to dwell with men. But how is the thought painful or revolting, that Christ should come again in that glorified resurrection-body in which He showed himself to His disciples, and held such mysterious intercourse with them for forty days previous to His ascension? That redeemed humanity is not subject to the laws of this body of death, under which we are now held in bondage. It possesses, as we have heretofore shown, a higher and far transcendent character, with powers which we cannot measure or understand. The objection, therefore, so commonly urged against the visible presence of Christ, that He must necessarily be confined to a given locality, and seen by those there present, and none else, is without force. That argument lies only against Christ's natural body in the flesh and under the law, not against His glorified, spiritual body, and might as well be urged, for aught we can see, against His presence at the right hand of power. If the argument derived from locality has any weight, it applies to Christ's presence in heaven as much as on earth, forbidding His manifestation there, even as here. We are not able to say to what extent, or under what conditions, that presence of Christ may be manifested, or how the glory of the Lord shall be revealed, and all flesh see it together. The same difficulty might be started with Christ's visible appearance in the clouds of heaven at the final judgment scene, as those believe He will appear who make the objection now under consideration. It might be asked, how He can be seen by the inhabitants of the entire earth at the same time, and how they all can stand before His judgment-seat.

We may say, however, that we have no sympathy with that view of this subject, which represents Christ as occupying a literal throne, like an earthly monarch, and dwelling at Jerusalem as the literal capital of His kingdom. This is a sensual view, which is painful to us, as to most Christian minds, involving, as we think, the idea of His return to this body of flesh, and His former subject condition. Although "we have known Christ after the flesh, yet now henceforth know we him no more." He is the living, glorified One; and when He returns again, we shall see Him "so come in like manner as we have seen him go into heaven," the exalted man, over whom death hath no more power, and who cannot be subject to the laws and limitations which control this present natural body.

Will men continue in the flesh, and coexist with the risen saints?

They will, even as men lived on the earth and followed their ordinary avocations, when Jesus rose from the dead, and that company of the saints came out of their graves after His resurrection, and went into the Holy City, and appeared unto many. *There were risen, glorified saints in Jerusalem then*, mingling in its scenes and with its living inhabitants. This is a fact which cannot be controverted, yet nothing was disturbed thereby. Human affairs moved on in the same channel. Angels have been frequent visitors to earth. Moses and Elijah have appeared, and their conversation been heard. These are facts of the past, belonging to the written history of earth, and familiar to us all. Who, then, will undertake to say that the same may not be repeated on a larger scale?

Will men need to be converted, as now?

Undoubtedly; but the work of conversion will be comparatively an easy one. Men will be sanctified from their childhood, as occasionally they are even now. When the Adversary is removed out of the way, being shut up in the bottomless pit, it will be an easy task for the Holy Ghost to bring all hearts under the power of truth, and subject all to the sway of Christ.

Will death be abolished?

While we would not speak with positiveness here, we are disposed to think that this enemy will be put under the feet of our conquering Redeemer, along with the rest. Isaiah speaks of this victory over death, when he describes that future day of glory. *He shall swallow up death in victory;* and the Lord God shall wipe away tears from off all faces; and the rebuke of his people shall he take away from off all the earth: for the Lord hath spoken it. And it shall be said in that day, Lo, this is our God; we have waited for him, and he will save us: this is the Lord; we have waited for him, we will be glad and rejoice in his salvation; Isa. xxv. 8. This description refers unquestionably to the days of the Messiah, when He shall set up His kingdom on earth, and this victory over death is represented as part of His mighty achievements. It may possibly be confined to the resurrection of the saints, and refer to that event, as Paul does so apply it. So when this corruptible shall have put on incorruption, and this mortal shall have put on immortality, then shall be brought to pass the saying that is written, Death is swallowed up in victory; 1 Cor. xv. 54. But does this exhaust the victory? Does death still continue his ravages under the reign of Christ over the living generations of men? or is that foe conquered for them also, while they pass from a mortal to an immortal state, as did Enoch and Elijah at the end of their career; and as do the living saints who will "be changed" at the coming of Christ? "*We shall not all sleep*," as the Bible assures us, "but we shall all be changed;" and may not the instances in the past, just referred to, be given as a demonstration and foretaste of what is to be in that coming day of earth's regeneration and joy, when our Immanuel shall have possession here, and shall subdue all things unto himself? Had not these translations of the saints already occurred, we doubtless would have argued strenuously that they could not be. It would have contradicted all our theology thus to have abolished death, or to conceive that it could be. Yet there they are undeniable, sublime events, towering in their truth and majesty, and consistent with all the workings of Divine providence. Are they not also intended for the encouragement and assistance of our feeble faith, as to the glories of that promised day of restoration of all things, when all shall be made new, and this groaning creation, so unwillingly subjected to the curse, shall enter into the privileges of the sons of God? In those new heavens and new earth which are to be, when God shall again dwell among men and be their God, and when there shall be nothing to hurt or destroy in all the holy mountain of the Lord—when the Lord shall wipe away tears from off all faces, and take away the rebuke of His people from off all the earth, we can scarcely think that that most terrible rebuke of *death and the grave* will still lie against them, to prove that they are under the curse. That is the appointed time of restitution of *all* things—the year of jubilee and release, when every yoke shall be broken, and the joyful shout shall go up, "The kingdoms of this world are become the kingdom of our Lord and of his Christ, and he shall reign forever and ever."

We are not sure, also, but that we find some support for this, and that Paul intends this, when he says, For our conversation is in heaven; from whence also we look for the Saviour, the Lord Jesus Christ: who shall *change our vile body*, that it may be fashioned like unto his glorious body, *according to the working whereby he is able even to subdue all things unto himself;* Phil. iii. 20. The Apostle does not here speak of our being raised from the dead, but of our bodies being *changed*, and that with the same almighty power with which Christ brings every thing into subjection to His sway in that time of restitution and regeneration. There is nothing inconsistent with the nature of the Divine administration over this world, nor with the facts of the past, in the idea that death itself, the last enemy, should thus be put under the feet of our Redeemer, and the head of the old serpent bruised.

CHAPTER XXXVII.

THE JUDGMENT.

Prophecy reveals the fact that the reign of Christ is to be succeeded by another dispensation still—that Satan is to be "loosed for a little season," to have another opportunity of showing the desperate bitterness of his hate toward God and righteousness, which nothing can mitigate, and which will force the extremity of Divine and eternal wrath. Satan, unbound, will proceed to ravage and destroy, as in the paradise of old; and thus will the unconquerable malignity of sin have a last opportunity of developing itself under the economy of grace. The demonstration will be complete. Sin will have acted out all its infernal malignity to the utmost, under every dispensation of Divine forbearance and love—have shown, beyond all doubt, that its nature never changes—that it is an enemy of God—an enemy of truth and righteousness—an enemy of the universe; and that the only way for God to deal with it is, to doom it to His eternal curse, where it may howl and gnash its teeth, and the smoke of its torment go up forever and ever. God will be justified in thus dealing with sin—will be compelled thereto. No alternative will be left Him, if He would preserve His universe from its dread ravages. This, moreover, is just the character of wickedness, and will be so demonstrated to the intelligent universe. It compels Divine retribution. It never yields, but only grows more bold and insolent, ever exalting itself above the throne of God; and this last demonstration will seal its perdition. God will no more forbear, no more delay. The universe will wonder only that He has delayed so long. All His purposes, too, of mercy and love will then have been accomplished, and the way be open to strike the final blow at the empire of sin.

The record of the events and dispensation now referred to is as follows: And when the thousand years are expired, Satan shall be loosed out of his prison, and shall go out to deceive the nations which are in the four quarters of the earth, Gog and Magog, to gather them to battle: the number of whom is as the sand of the sea.

And they went up on the breadth of the earth, and compassed the camp of the saints about, and the beloved city: and fire came down from God out of heaven, and devoured them. And the devil that deceived them was cast into the lake of fire and brimstone, where the beast and the false prophet are, and shall be tormented day and night forever and ever. And I saw a great white throne, and him that sat on it, from whose face the earth and heaven fled away; and there was found no place for them. And I saw the dead, small and great, stand before God; and the books were opened: and another book was opened, which is the book of life: and the dead were judged out of those things which were written in the books, according to their works. And the sea gave up the dead which were in it; and death and hell delivered up the dead which were in them: and they were judged every man according to their works. And death and hell were cast into the lake of fire. This is the second death. And whosoever was not found written in the book of life was cast into the lake of fire; Rev. xx. 7.

In regard to "the little season" here spoken of as allowed to Satan, it may be observed, that all periods of time are relative. It is a little season that Satan has held the supremacy during these six thousand years, as compared with the period of Christ's reign; and if he should be allowed another six thousand, at the end it would still be a "little season." The length of the "season," however, we have no means of determining.

It will be apparent, on the most cursory examination of the above-described scene of judgment, that it differs very materially from those which are described in the Old and New Testaments in connection with Christ's second coming.

No mention is here made, or description given, of Christ's appearing.

He is not introduced into the scene. "The dead, small and great, stand before *God*." But no mention is made of Christ. This certainly is remarkable, considering that the common theology fixes this as the scene of that great event of His coming, for which the Church throughout her history has been taught to watch, and pray, and hope. If this is the time of Christ's second advent, it ought certainly here be made to appear, attracting the gaze of every eye. Yet from *this passage* it is certain no one could tell that He was present. This is a remarkable omission in the most important passage of Scripture, which is supposed to describe that second coming of our Lord.

The events or judgments of this day are of a wholly different character, and relate to different persons from those described by the prophets in connection with the second advent.

"I saw *the dead*, small and great, stand before God." No mention is made of the living—no intimation given that they have part in the transactions. The sea, death, and hell, delivered up their *dead*, and they were judged out of the books, and cast into the lake of fire, which is the second death. This contrasts strikingly with the calamities and judgments which the prophets describe as overtaking the living nations, when Christ comes to tread the wine-press of the fierceness of His wrath. No mention is then made of the dead. It is with His living enemies that He deals in the fury of His vengeance, His garments being all stained with their blood. They fly to the rocks and mountains for refuge. There is a fearful, desperate conflict, blood flowing to the horse-bridles, and all the fowls of heaven, and the beasts of the earth, being gathered to the prey of the mighty. This last judgment-scene of the Revelation, however, is wanting in all these particulars, the dead being the only actors who appear upon the stage.

This statement of facts accords also with the description given in the 24th and 25th chapters of Matthew. No reference is there made to the resurrection of the dead, nor intimation given that they have any part in the scenes described. "All nations" are gathered then for judgment—a word used more than one hundred and fifty times in the New Testament, and always translated nations, Gentiles, or heathen, being applied in no instance to the dead. It might have been rendered Gentiles or heathen in this instance, it being the word employed to designate them in the Scriptures; because all nations, outside of the Jewish people being idolators, it was to the same effect to speak of them as the nations, the Gentiles, or the heathen. The term is invariably applied to the living inhabitants of the earth, never to those of the grave. Nationality belongs to the former alone, not the latter. The dead, therefore, do not appear in the judgment-scene described by Matthew.

The coming of Christ, also, and the attendant judgments, are distinctly stated in this discourse to be "as the days of Noah were." "For as in the days that were before the flood, they were eating and drinking, marrying and giving in marriage, until the day that Noah entered into the ark, and knew not until the flood came and took them all away; so shall also the coming of the Son of man be. Then shall two be in the field; the one shall be taken and the other shall be left. Two women shall be grinding at the mill; the one shall be taken and the other left." This clearly refers to the living, and not the dead. It is also further stated, that this coming of the Son of man in the clouds of heaven, to gather His elect from the four winds, from one end of heaven unto the other, is immediately subsequent to the period of tribulation and sorrow, persecution and trial, apostacy and wickedness, with the physical and political revolutions which

Jesus points out as the characteristics of the existing dispensation, and *which were to continue without interruption until this revelation of Christ*, the troubles only multiplying as the end drew near, "men's hearts failing them for fear, and for looking after those things which are coming on the earth; for the powers of heaven shall be shaken. And then shall they see the Son of man coming in a cloud, with power and great glory. And when these things begin to come to pass, then look up, and lift up your heads: for your redemption draweth nigh." Thus these tribulations and commotions in the earth and among the nations are given as signs to mark the approach of that revelation of Christ, even as the budding of the trees foretokens the near coming of Spring. These signs, too, were given by Jesus at the request of the disciples, so that they might know when to look for that day of the Lord. Nor are there any other signs specified beside these. None of any different character are hinted at. They all bear this one feature of trouble, disaster, and abounding wickedness. These, moreover, are unquestionably the marked characteristics of the period since the words of Christ were uttered, to the present hour. No description could so accurately have portrayed this dispensation. "So likewise ye, when ye see these things come to pass, know ye that the kingdom of God is nigh at hand." Such events were indeed a strange budding of Spring; but they are the tokens which Christ gives, and we have no authority to change them.

There is no appearance in the final judgment scene of the righteous, nor is their reward spoken of.

Those described are the wicked dead, and their sentence alone is announced. We are told of those who suffer the second death, being cast into the lake of fire, even all who were not found in the book of life. But no other party appears. Nothing is said of the life prepared for the righteous.

The second coming of Christ is graphically described at a previous point in the Revelation.

This description may be found in Rev. xix. 11–21. Here Christ does appear beyond question, "clothed in a vesture dipped in blood: and his name is called THE WORD OF GOD. And the armies which were in heaven followed him upon white horses, clothed in fine linen, clean and white. And out of his mouth goeth a sharp sword, that with it he should smite the nations: and he shall rule them with a rod of iron: and he treadeth the wine-press of the fierceness and wrath of Almighty God. And he hath on his vesture and on his thigh a name written, KING OF KINGS, AND LORD OF LORDS." Then follows a description of the dread conflict and carnage, and the gathering of all the fowls of heaven to the slaughter, with the overthrow of the beast and the false prophet. Here, then, undeniably, is the person of Christ. It is none but He. Here is His advent described, and the great day of God Almighty, when judgment overtakes the proud foe; and it is the only place in the Revelation where He does appear upon the stage. We claim, now, that John, under the inspiration of the Holy Ghost, knew where to fix this great event; and that we have no right to take it out where John puts it, and insert it at another point where he says nothing about it. It is ours to receive these Divine revelations, not to make or amend them.

These, now, are facts which lie on the face of the passage before us, and which any one can verify for himself. The solution of the difficulty is, that two different days, very widely separated, have been confounded together, the events of both being crowded into this last judgment-scene. It has been assumed or believed, that this was the appointed time for Christ's coming; and it was taken for granted that He appeared upon the stage, although nothing was said to that effect. It was supposed, also, that this was the time of the saints' resurrection. They, too, were introduced into the scene, though no mention is made of them or their reward. In fact, the resurrection of believers had taken place at a date long antecedent, when Christ came to establish His kingdom. He then brought them with Him, and manifested them forth as His sons. That resurrection is described only a few verses before, in the same chapter, in connection with the reign of Christ, as follows: "And I saw thrones, and they sat upon them, and judgment was given unto them: and I saw the souls of them that were beheaded for the witness of Jesus, and for the word of God, and which had not worshipped the beast, neither had received his mark upon their foreheads, or in their hands; and they lived and reigned with Christ a thousand years. But the rest of the dead lived not again until the thousand years were finished. This is the first resurrection. Blessed is he that hath part in the first resurrection: on such the second death hath no power, but they shall be priests of God and of Christ, and shall reign with him a thousand years." We know the argument urged here, that this is a symbolical representation, and that they do strange violence to the passage and the book of Revelation, who put a literal construction upon this scene. We are willing, too, to meet the question on this ground, and, *for the sake of argument*, as well as testing the matter, concede that we are not to put a literal construction upon any thing in this book of symbols, even when the interpretation is given by the word of inspiration. "This is the first resurrection." Let it be admitted, then, that this appearance of the righteous dead has a symbolical, and not a literal meaning. Of course, those who insist on this law of interpretation as imperative in all cases, will concede that the next resurrection-scene, described only four verses after, in connection with the day of judgment, is also to be taken in a symbolical, and not a literal sense. They who lay down the law for others, must necessarily abide thereby themselves; and if it is doing violence to every principle of interpretation, as is so positively asserted, to understand the first resurrection-scene literally, there is no less violence done in putting the same literal construction on the one immediately following. And if the latter can be taken as a *bonâ fide* resurrection of the dead, we insist that there is no law to forbid such meaning to the former. Our principles of interpretation must be consistent, and not self-destructive. When, therefore, those who insist upon an exclusively spiritual sense, will carry such a system of interpretation out in its application to the last resurrection, we may admit that there is some force to their argument. But while they take one resurrection-scene in a spiritual, and another immediately following in a literal sense, we cannot but think that they sufficiently refute themselves, and that they have no fixed principles of interpretation by which to guide them. Neither does it become such to designate others as "Literalists," as if they were *par excellence Symbolists.* The truth is, there is no class of men who universally interpret the book of Revelation in a symbolical sense. All are compelled, at times, to adopt a literal meaning. There is no escape from it. And the only question is to determine when it shall be, and by what principle we shall be guided in so doing. The principle is, *when the nature of the subject forbids symbolization.* There are a few things that cannot be set in symbol, and must therefore be described literally. The sleeping saints and wicked dead—the resurrection—death and hell—Satan and Christ—belong to this class. They are accordingly so represented. They are, by their own nature, exceptions to the general features of the book, and need not be misunderstood. This principle relieves all the difficulty, and makes the way of the interpreter plain and consistent.

Beyond this, however, the author of the Revelation puts his own interpretation upon both these scenes, by the categorical statements, "This is the first resurrection," and "This is the second death." That settles the question; and it is wonderful that theologians and commentators will still go behind this authoritative, Divine interpretation, to find some other to suit their own theory. They might as well seek to find some better explanation of "the mystery of the seven stars which thou sawest in my right hand, and the seven golden candlesticks," than that which Christ himself has given. The seven stars are the angels of the seven churches: and the seven candlesticks which thou sawest are the seven churches, Rev. i. 20; or go behind the interpretation of Rev. xvii. 15: And he saith unto me, The waters which thou sawest, where the whore sitteth, are peoples, and multitudes, and nations, and tongues; or yet again, Rev. xx. 2: And he laid hold on the dragon, that old serpent, which is the Devil and Satan. So it is presumptuous in us to ignore the inspired interpretation, "This is the first resurrection." That decides what, and when, the first resurrection is. It is the resurrection of the saints at the second coming of Christ, that they may live and reign with Him the thousand years. In consistency, too, with this at the final judgment, when the rest of the dead are raised, no mention is made of the righteous, or their reward. The wicked dead alone appear as actors in that drama, and are judged out of the books, and according to the things written therein.

We may now see, from this unfolding of Divine revelation, *what God's dealings and designs toward the wicked are.*

We have gone over the history of the past, and shown how each dispensation has ended, and how broadly God has drawn the line between the righteous and the wicked, saving the one and destroying the other. He began by suspending the execution of the death-penalty against disobedience, and introduced an economy of grace, or remedial system for human recovery, announcing the way by which sinners might be justified; and pointing men forward with faith and hope to the coming One, who should achieve the promised redemption. A few believed God, and heartily accepted His methods of grace. But the unbelieving multitude, willing enough to take the assurance of salvation and claim the Divine favor, cleaved to their sins, and insisted on being saved in their own way. And here, at this point, the conflict has been waged between God and an unbelieving world. He has insisted on saving the penitent and believing, while the wicked have demanded an equal title to the kingdom. God early raised up His prophets, to whom He revealed the truth on this subject, and who preached that Christ would come to bring His saints with Him, and at the same time execute judgment on the ungodly. But when they paid no heed, He gave a more solemn and impressive lesson in the overwhelming waters of the Deluge, making this very distinction, in the most sublime manner, between the righteous and the wicked. God demonstrated that the former, though so few as to be contained in a single household, were of more account, in His sight, than a world of sinners. And for these few He provided an ark of refuge, while He swept away with a stroke the unbelieving multitude.

This lesson God repeated again and again, under circumstances calculated to make the truth still more clear. There were His own people, redeemed out of Egypt with a mighty hand, whom He carried through the sea, dry shod, and fed in the desert with bread from heaven. Surely they shall be brought into their inheritance. Yet God would show that their faith and obedience were essential, and that, if wanting, the same judgment would overtake them to their destruction. They expected and demanded the fulfilment of all God's promises in their unbelief. His decisive answer was their overthrow. They perished in the wilderness, while a remnant only entered in. So was it, again, with the nation at the coming of their Messiah. They expected the promised salvation, priding themselves on being eminently meet for the kingdom; but it was according to their own ideas of fitness, while they raged and blasphemed against the Lord's Anointed, and the Holy Ghost. Again would He teach the great lesson, and He ground that covenant nation to powder, taking out a remnant of believing ones, who would receive His testimony.

Now, also, is He testing the Gentile nations on the same point, to see whether they will receive Christ and bow to His sceptre; the end whereof, as we are abundantly assured, will be with judgment and terrible overthrow; while the people of God, who have long waited and believed, shall lift up their heads with joy, and behold the salvation for which they have looked. Then, too, shall the sleeping saints, who have died in the faith, awake from the dust; and as they come forth in their incorruptible forms, to live and reign with Christ, the demonstration will be complete that these, in very deed, are the sons of God, for whom the kingdom and reward have been prepared from the foundation of the world. The word of promise will have been fulfilled to those who have humbly believed and accepted Christ as their righteousness and salvation. But for the wicked and unbelieving is reserved that final day when the judgment shall be set; and they, too, shall be awaked, but to shame and everlasting contempt. That resurrection shall be their own, the righteous having been gathered long before, and manifested forth as the sons of God, shining as the brightness of the firmament. To be found among these ignominious dead on this last day will be evidence enough that there is no part in Christ, no inheritance in His promises. They are "judged every man according to his works. And death and hell were cast into the lake of fire. This is the second death. And whosoever was not found written in the Book of Life, was cast into the lake of fire." That closes the drama. There is no record of any dispensation of mercy beyond; and those who hope for such, have no authority for it from the Scriptures. They have the same wretched, destroying delusion, which the wicked have always entertained—for which they have been contending through all the dispensations of the past, but which God has so terribly rebuked again and again with His fiercest wrath. Yet, while wickedness and unbelief continue, we may expect that men will pervert and misinterpret these great truths, and treasure up unto themselves wrath against the day of wrath, and righteous revelation of God.

CHAPTER XXXVIII.

HEAVEN.

We have already alluded to the fact that some have questioned whether the doctrine of immortality and the future life was revealed in the Old Testament; and have shown that such doubts proved only our ignorance of the Scriptures, and of the method of instruction which God adopted for the early education of the race. Not only was the doctrine of immortality taught, but also the resurrection of the body, in the belief of which the saints died, assured of the possession of the inheritance, and that they would triumph over death to enter therein. So clear were the teachings of revelation on this point, that the doctrine of the resurrection became thoroughly established in the popular faith before the coming of Christ.

What, now, were the ideas of these ancient believers respecting the inheritance?

Their thoughts were unquestionably turned to *the future—to the times of the promised seed, and the redemption which He should effect.* Paradise was to them a type of the inheritance restored, the way of the tree of life being kept for them. They were denied now those fruits of immortality, and doomed for a period to the curse under an economy of grace. But a time was coming in the history of earth, when One should appear to triumph over the foe, even over death itself—remove the curse, and restore again the forfeited inheritance. So Enoch preached, "Behold, the Lord cometh with ten thousand of his saints;" while the Apostle testifies concerning the ancient worthies, These all died in faith, not having received the promises [the things promised], but *having seen them afar off*, and were persuaded of them, and embraced them, and confessed that they were strangers and pilgrims on the earth. For they that say such things declare plainly that they seek a country. And truly if they had been mindful of that country whence they came out, they might have had opportunity to have returned. But now they desire a better country, that is, an heavenly: wherefore God is not ashamed to be called their God: for he hath prepared for them a city; Heb. xi. 13. Here two facts, bearing on our present subject, are distinctly stated: the first, that these saints died in the full faith of the heavenly inheritance; the second, that they saw the fulfilment of these promises *afar off*, in the distant future—

that is, when Christ should come, bringing His saints with Him from their sleeping dust. The heaven of these believers thus lay in the future, and was to be attained through their resurrection. They died and slept in this hope. The inheritance, too, in their minds, was evidently identified with earth. They believed that Christ was to *come*—come to earth—and that here was to be the scene of His wonders and triumphs. There was nothing to convey the idea that they were to go and meet Him in some distant sphere. The whole line of thought and instruction was in the other direction. The promised seed was here to be raised up—here prevail against the hellish foe; and when He should achieve His work of redemption, He would bring His saints from their tombs, that they might enter into the fruition of their reward.

Whether these believers of former days knew any thing of an intervening state of happiness as disembodied spirits, is a matter of doubt, and here lies the difficulty of finding, in the Old Testament, the doctrine of immortality and a future life, for which men have searched with so little satisfaction. The modern conception of heaven is a state of glory, disconnected with earth, and immediately succeeding death—a removal to another sphere of blessedness upon release from the body, and absence from the same. Of such a world and state there certainly are but slight traces in the Old Testament. Whether ancient believers knew any thing of the disembodied spirit, as to its location or enjoyment, is uncertain. And here the controversy has been waged in regard to their knowledge of a future life. We have demanded to know whether they had *our* conceptions of the heavenly state, as connected with the immortality of the disembodied spirit. It is another question whether those men died in the faith, having seen the promises *afar off* in a future resurrection of the body, being persuaded of them, embracing them, and confessing that they were strangers and pilgrims here. It is another question wheher they looked for the future redemption of earth under the promised seed of the woman, and their resurrection from the grave at His coming. In regard to their knowledge and hope of the inheritance in this form, there is no doubt. Enoch preached this doctrine. God's own memorial name, by which He was known to His people, was Yahveh, the coming One —He, for whom they looked and waited—the Desire of all the ends of the earth.

At a later period, also, how clear were the promises, and how strong the hopes of the nation of Israel respecting the coming kingdom of the Son of David, and the blessedness of earth under His reign! Then was to come the joyful hour of earth's redemption, when the very desert was to bud and blossom as the rose—when wars should cease, and there should be nothing to hurt or destroy in all the holy mountain of the Lord.

These are facts lying upon the surface of Divine revelation, as well as inwoven with its whole structure. They are of easy apprehension, and they show clearly that the hopes of men were ever directed forward to the distant future—to a coming period in earth's history, when a triumph should be achieved over the powers of darkness and hell—when the bars of death should be broken, the curse removed, the inheritance restored, and access had again to the prohibited tree of life. When believers dwelt upon these promises, they did not think of the heavenly state as a departure from earth, and an entrance upon another sphere as soon as death should release them from the body. Their anxiety was not to get rid of earth, and be removed as far as possible from it. Their hopes were all connected with a return to the body, and the restitution of all things, so that God might dwell with men again, and make this earth the place of His abode.

This was to be the scene of triumph to the woman's promised seed. Here, where the foul Adversary had achieved his work of destruction, was the great redemption to be effected, and all the wonders of Divine love revealed.

From this presentation of the subject, also, have originated the idea and expression of *the ages*, of which the Scriptures are so full, more commonly spoken of by us as *dispensations*. God has worked by these from the dawn of creation. We are in the midst of these movements of the ages, and in their beginning, although they run back to a point beyond the reach of thought. But they run on also to the endless future. It is only a little while since man, for whom this creation was made, its crown and glory, entered upon the stage; and it is to him that all the grandest purposes of heaven relate. The ages now in progress and to come are to be filled up with the development of God's vast designs respecting him.

It was not, therefore, by accident that, in the revelation or history of God's work of redemption, the hopes and thoughts of men were turned to the future—to the development of these ages, and the coming of earth's great Deliverer. There lay the inheritance and the kingdom. God intended to turn the thoughts of men thus forward; and so were they turned through all the earlier dispensations, until the promised seed first appeared to accomplish the preparatory work of His priesthood.

Neither did that first coming of Christ, in His humiliation, alter in the least the direction of these hopes of men, or fulfil them. That first advent of our Immanuel was but the preparatory step toward their fulfilment. It but opened the way for the pardon of sinners, showing how they were to be justified—how Christ was to effect the promised work of redemption, but not bringing the redemption itself. The inheritance and kingdom were still in the future, it being now apparent, as it was not before, that there were two advents of Christ foretold, one of which He fulfilled when He made himself a sin-offering; for the other of which we are still to wait, and watch, and pray.

The instructions of Christ have shed additional light upon the intermediate state, or the condition of the soul immediately after death. While little or nothing is said on this subject in the Old Testament, the revelations of the New disclose the fact that the believer goes to be with Christ, and live in the enjoyment of His presence. Lazarus was borne by angels to Abraham's bosom. Christ assured the dying thief that he should be with Him that self-same day in paradise. Paul desired to depart, and to be with Christ, which he esteemed to be far better than to continue here in the flesh. Thus revelation, which before was silent on this point, begins to speak, and throws light upon the path of the departing spirit. Yet beyond this general fact, that the saint is happy with Christ, we know but very little. The veil is still drawn across that unseen world. We know not where it is, or what is passing there. It may be a state or condition rather than a world in the proper sense, or place of habitation. It is, however, a mistake to suppose that this intermediate state, upon which the Scriptures have thus shed some light, is properly the inheritance which the word of promise holds out as the hope of the believer. That state of the departed until the resurrection, might have been left in the New Testament where it is in the Old, and the believer have died in the faith, still seeing the promises afar off, and fully persuaded of them. The conception of heaven to the saint of old was not of passing immediately to glory, but of sleeping with his fathers, and waiting the coming of Christ, being then awaked to meet Him. And this full redemption of Christ, awaking in His likeness, and manifested forth as the sons of God by our resurrection from the grave, is what the word of promise still leads us to expect and hope for. Our redemption is not complete until we can sing the song of triumph over these dismantled sepulchres. We are not to be revealed or adopted as the sons of God, silencing forever all controversy, until Christ shall come again and bring these buried forms from the dust, arrayed in incorruption and power. When we die now, death is our conqueror. We may die in faith, as believers of old did, assured that the victory shall yet be ours. Yet we are compelled now to yield to the dread tyrant, and go down in chains to his dark dominions. The hour for raising that glad shout of victory, O death, where is thy sting? O grave, where is thy victory? is yet in the future; and the doctrine of the Scriptures is, Looking for and hasting unto the coming of that day of the Lord; 2 Peter iii. 12. Or, according to Paul, "If by any means I might attain unto the resurrection of [from among] the dead.

The work of redemption is a long and progressive one. It is begun in our justification, and the sealing power of the Holy Ghost, the pledges of Heaven to the fulfilment of the work. We are sons indeed, and have the evidence within us, even the witness of the Spirit, to that blessed truth; but we have not had any public recognition or adoption. God has not made declaration of His sons. He suffers them to be denied, and others to claim the honor to whom it does not and never will belong. He suffers those loved sons to groan and sigh under their bondage, to lie under the deep reproach of the curse still, going down to the grave, and there continuing undistinguished from the wicked, with all the power of that dread curse now witnessing against them, even as it did against Jesus himself, until the seal was broken and the stone rolled away from the door of the sepulchre. But the hour of full redemption is to come; yet not until the power of this last enemy shall be broken, and this mortal shall put on immortality. The soul of the believer may be happy with Christ when death releases him from the body, and this may be a new and advanced stage in the work of redemption, he being now put beyond the reach of sin, suffering, and trial. But *the inheritance* promised lies still in the future. The *ages* are not fulfilled. The purposes of God respecting this world and our humanity are yet far from their completion; and only in that completion lies the inheritance to which faith has ever looked forward. It was a blessed day when the light of Christ's first coming burst upon our dark world, and revealed Him as the Way, the Truth, and the Life. The nations which then sat in darkness saw a great light; and light sprang up to them which were in the very shades of death. But they beheld only the rising of the Morning Star. The Sun of Righteousness, in all His glory, is yet to be revealed. For that day the very creation groans, and waits with earnest expectation, destined, as it is, to share in this redemption of the sons of God, and be delivered from the curse so long resting upon it. Christ himself waits for that day. It is promised concerning Him, that He shall see of the travail of His soul, and be satisfied. He waits the hour when the Prince of darkness, with all his works of evil, shall be cast out—when judgment shall overtake the proud and persecuting foe, and the kingdom, and greatness of the kingdom under the whole heaven, shall be given into His possession, that He may reign in righteousness and truth.

The New Testament assures us that they are blessed who die in the Lord, because they rest from their labors, and are with Christ. Yet the burden of its amazing thought is ever in carrying the mind forward into the future to the day of Christ, and the accomplishment of the great purposes of His grace. Notice the following:

Having predestinated us unto the adoption of children by Jesus Christ unto himself, according to the good pleasure of his will, to the praise of the glory of his grace, wherein he hath made us accepted in the Beloved: in whom we have redemption through his blood, the forgiveness of sins, according to the riches of his grace; wherein he hath abounded toward us in all wisdom and prudence; having made known unto us the mystery of his will, according to his good pleasure, which he hath purposed in himself: *that in the dispensation of the fulness of times he might gather together in one all things in Christ, both which are in heaven, and which are on earth; even in him;* Eph. i. 5. Thus the end or consummation of all things, according to the Scriptures, is *the gathering together of all in Christ*, to be accomplished in what the Apostle calls "the dispensation of the fulness of times"—the last dispensation, fulfilling the ages, and all the Divine purposes. That shall be the completion of dispensations. The same idea is presented again, Eph. ii. 4: But God, who is rich in mercy, for his great love wherewith he loved us, even when we were dead in sins, hath quickened us together with Christ; (by grace ye are saved;) and hath raised us up together, and made us sit together in heavenly places, in Christ Jesus: *that in the ages to come he might show the exceeding riches of his grace in his kindness toward us, through Christ Jesus.* The Apostle does not here speak of heaven as if it were already an accomplished fact—a place prepared of old, to which the believer might be removed at once upon the event of death. His thoughts clearly work in another channel, running on to those ages to come, which are to witness the fulfilment of all God's grandest designs of love and mercy—those plans which He formed in the beginning of the ages, ere He laid the corner-stone of this earth, or called one atom into being—plans which He is carrying forward with all the resources of His infinite wisdom and love to their complete, triumphant fulfilment,—plans into which the angels desire to look, and which shall be the theme of wonder, joy, and song to the universe forever and ever. These plans involve the utter, final overthrow of all the powers of hell. The devil and his hosts have not yet met their judgment and doom, but are "reserved in chains under darkness" against that day when God shall have completed these purposes of His, and effected their everlasting discomfiture. Their punishment is a future event. They are miserable now, as all wicked beings must be, from the nature of the case. But their desperate rebellion against Heaven is not yet overthrown. They are prosecuting it still, and perhaps flatter themselves that they may even prevail. If, then, the very devils are reserved against the day of destruction, to be punished, awaiting the fulfilment of the Divine purposes, it is in perfect harmony with this, that the reward and inheritance of the righteous are held in reserve also, unto that dispensation of the fulness of times, when the great plans of God shall be complete, and all shall be gathered into one in Christ.

The conception of heaven, then, is not merely that of enjoyment, nor of holiness alone, nor of being with Christ; but it is that of a magnificent victory achieved—not a victory, either, of the individual believer, and the attainment of his own personal reward, but the final victory of Christ, when He shall have brought all His sons safely through, and discomfited every machination of hell. It is the overthrow of all rebellion and sin. The hope of heaven, as ordinarily presented, is that of our own individual happiness and reward, our own salvation being the end primarily considered and aimed at. But the view presented in the Scriptures is larger and grander far than this. It takes a wider scope, embracing the fulfilment of all God's designs of mercy, and that glorious gathering together of all in Christ in the ages to come. The difference is much the same as it would be in a soldier enlisted in the war against "the great Rebellion," who should have his thoughts narrowed down to himself or his own regiment, and the victories which they should achieve, instead of having his mind expanded to grasp the great national issue involved, and looking forward to the day when the Rebellion should be utterly overthrown, the Government established, and the majesty of law vindicated. It was to this final victory, this end of the conflict, that the true patriot soldier looked, and there lay the reward for all his sacrifices and sufferings. So is it in that grander conflict waged by Christ against the leagued powers of hell. This earth is the theatre for that conflict. Here the forces have been marshalled. Here the fight is being waged, and the victory is to be achieved. Christ is here to prevail, and wrest the empire out of the hands of the great Adversary, utterly crushing this rebellion, and redeeming this earth unto himself. This is the glorious hope held out to faith. It is not merely the salvation of each man's own soul, and his attainment of blessedness. That is a narrow conception of the subject. We are made one with Christ, our glorious Head, and are lifted up to gaze from the lofty mountain-top upon the scene of glory in the future—this triumph of our Immanuel, this gathering of all together in Him, this completion of Heaven's noblest designs, and the utter, eternal discomfiture of all the powers of hell. We are to rejoice in this—to be satisfied with nothing short of it. Here is the glory to be revealed—an eternal, exceeding weight of glory; and all flesh shall see it together.

Heaven is thus the culmination of a vast, inconceivably vast and grand movement of Divine providence, sweeping through the ages, over which the universe shall rejoice with unutterable joy—a movement in which all the deepest wonders of the Divine mind are brought to view, all the perfections of the Godhead revealed. A movement, too, which enlists all the passions and powers of the human mind, and offers the widest, grandest scope for their action. It does not present that tame and spiritless view of the future world, in which quietude seems to enter as the principal element; and the wonder is, whether we shall have any thing to do. Such low and unworthy conceptions of that inheritance have grown out of its entire disconnection from earth and all its interests—its removal to another sphere, of which we could form no idea, and where we could hardly imagine any thing to be done, but only that we were to be happy. But when the mind is directed along the stupendous pathway of the Divine purposes, to the accomplishment of all the will of Heaven in the perfection of our humanity under Christ its Head, its union in Him, and the redemption of this earth from the curse, there is no difficulty then in conceiving of the widest scope given for action to all of man's redeemed and immortal powers, and his endless employment in the high service of God.

When will this full consummation of the Divine purposes be attained, and the final state realized?

It is important here to observe, in regard to these revelations of the future as found in the Bible, that it was difficult, if not impossible, to indicate clearly the precise order of events, or the distance of time which should intervene between them. At least Divine wisdom did not see fit to make these things clear. As prophecy unfolded the glorious panorama of redemption through the coming ages, the eye of faith caught only the distant mountain elevations as they rose to view. But there were no means of telling what valleys stretched between. The eye could not measure the distance between the peaks.

They might seem in close proximity, while there was a vast territory intervening. Thus the nation of Israel was entirely at fault respecting the first coming of their Messiah, and these eighteen centuries of trial and suffering to the Church of God which have followed. Their attention had been fixed upon the events connected with His second advent, and they knew Him not when He came to make himself a sin-offering, and officiate as a Priest. The matter, too, was not made clear until Christ came in His humiliation as the man of sorrows, denied and rejected, and then took His departure, telling His disciples that He should come again in His glory and kingdom, to fulfil the other prophecies. We then are across one grand range of these mountains, so much of prophecy being accomplished, and therefore cleared up to our minds. But there are vast ranges still before us, and, as we survey them in the distance, we are liable to the same mistake with those who preceded us. We may drop out great intervals of time and series of events from the history, confounding together mountain summits which are very widely separated. The saints of old saw not these long centuries of darkness and trial through which the Church is now passing. They were hidden from view: if not hidden, believers were not able to identify them from such passages as Mal. iii. 2, in which the work of the great refiner is described.

In inquiring, therefore, when this consummation of the Divine purposes will be attained, and the final heavenly state reached, we need to bear in mind these facts, and remember that it is "in the ages to come." There are grand events yet to be fulfilled. "The dispensation of the fulness of times" will be the last dispensation completing the ages, after the resurrection of the wicked dead shall have taken place, and their judgment been passed, subsequent, also, to the millennial kingdom of Christ, and the final apostasy. That millennial kingdom will be a wonderful era for earth, when Christ's blessed sceptre shall extend from sea to sea; and when, through myriad ages, the race shall multiply under the reign of our Immanuel. He shall still carry on His redeeming work in the sanctification of these countless generations, and their preparation for the final state. A season, however, is still to succeed, in which Satan is to be let loose. The enemy is to prevail again, and make another onset upon the city of God, and then ere long comes the final stroke, which shall fall upon them to their everlasting overthrow. The devil is cast into the lake of fire with all who were not found in the Book of Life. The mediatorial work of Christ is ended, so that it is no longer necessary to plead for the pardon and justification of sinners—no longer necessary to contend with a rebellious host. Sin and hell are overthrown finally and forever. The great work which Christ undertook as our Mediator, and to accomplish which all power in heaven and earth was committed to His hands, is completed, even to its topmost stone, and henceforth God is all in all. The universe is now at rest.

As to portraying the happiness of that heavenly state, all our attempts must prove a failure, from the fact that it must become a matter of experience to be known and understood. Our natures forbid us to comprehend any state of enjoyment which transcends our experience, because the knowledge of such enjoyment comes to us only through this channel. Mere words cannot describe it. We cannot know, in this world, what a particular pain, or sorrow, or joy is, until we have felt them. All attempts, therefore, to portray the bliss of heaven must prove abortive. We know, of course, some of the elements which must enter into this joy, having already a foretaste here in the love of God, and the blessed communion of saints.

Yet it doth not appear what we shall be: but we know that, when he shall appear, we shall be like him; for we shall see him as he is; 1 John iii. 2. There is to be an exceeding and eternal weight of glory.

We here close this marvellous history of the economy of the ages, developing the facts embraced in the grandest of all sciences—the science of God. Some, in their narrow-mindedness and ignorance, may look down upon theology as not worthy of their investigation or study, and as belonging only to men of weak minds and a proscribed profession. The thought proves how little they comprehend of the true history of this world, and its grandest movements, even the march of the ages. This science, however, can well bide its time, even as geology, astronomy, mental philosophy, and all the sciences have been compelled to do. It is nothing against these that they were not understood by the generations past—nothing against them that they are not understood now. So likewise it is no dishonor to our Christianity that this apostate, ignorant, proud, and infidel world has not grasped its stupendous truths. It can wait, as did the Crucified himself in the midst of an adulterous, unbelieving generation, for the hour when it will be understood and appreciated. "I am not of the world," said Jesus, and "ye are not of the world," said He to His disciples. And this Christianity is not of the world. It must wait, too, that new order of things, and the incoming of a nobler, truer type of humanity that shall be able to study and comprehend the science of theology. That day will come. The ages are rolling on to this consummation. Meanwhile our glorious Christianity stands forever its own best and highest witness; and the revelation which contains this magnificent history bears its own everlasting credentials, the very seal of Heaven upon it. It is maintaining its ground, and fighting its way through the fiercest assaults of earth and hell ; and it will come off grandly triumphant. The generation will be found that shall have the faith and the wisdom to appreciate its grandeur. And Christ can wait the glorious day. He shall see of the travail of His soul, and be satisfied.

THE END.

www.ingramcontent.com/pod-product-compliance
Lightning Source LLC
LaVergne TN
LVHW021235110826
845150LV00002B/340

* 9 7 8 1 4 2 5 5 6 2 3 3 5 *